KT-591-454

500 ESSENTIAL CULT MOVIES

The Ultimate Guide • Jennifer Eiss

with JP Rutter and Steve White

ILEX

500 Essential Cult Movies: The Ultimate Guide

First published in the UK in 2010 by
ILEX
210 High Street
Lewes
East Sussex BN7 2NS
www.ilex-press.com

Copyright © 2010 by The Ilex Press Limited

Bedfordshire
County Council

9 39277439

Askews

791.4375

£15

Publisher: Alastair Campbell
Creative Director: Peter Bridgewater
Managing Editor: Nick Jones
Editor: Ellie Wilson
Commissioning Editor: Tim Pilcher
Art Director: Julie Weir
Senior Designer: Emily Harbison
Designer: Ginny Zeal

Images courtesy of the Kobal Collection

THE KOBAL COLLECTION

Any copy of this book issued by the publisher is sold subject to the condition that it shall not by way of trade or otherwise be lent, resold, hired out or otherwise circulated without the publisher's prior consent in any form of binding or cover other than that in which it is published and without a similar condition including these words being imposed on a subsequent purchaser.

British Library Cataloguing-in-Publication Data
A catalogue record for this book is available from the British Library.

ISBN: 978-1-905814-88-6

All rights reserved. No part of this publication may be reproduced or used in any form, or by any means – graphic, electronic or mechanical, including photocopying, recording or information storage-and-retrieval systems – without the prior permission of the publisher.

10 9 8 7 6 5 4 3 2 1

Printed in China

Colour Origination by Ivy Press Reprographics

BEDFORDSHIRE LIBRARIES BB BB BB

9 39277439

500 ESSENTI... S

The Ultimate Guide

CONTENTS

INTRODUCTION

JENNIFER EISS

Welcome to the weird and wonderful world of cult film, where strange and delightful (and often disturbing) visions await around every corner, ready to ambush you and possibly melt your brain. But in a good way.

Calling a movie "cult" can often be considered an insult, as it implies that only a select few will actually pay money to see it. But as this book will show, not all cult films are of low quality, or even for the most part unloved; in fact, more than Hollywood blockbusters or independent films lauded by established critics, cult movies tend to have that rare quality of longevity, an ability to first tap into a zeitgeist and then find a universality that transcends generational differences. On the other hand, some of them are just fun to watch over and over because they're so mind-bendingly terrible. It doesn't really matter either way—we're not here to judge the fans of these movies; rather our aim is to introduce well-loved and perhaps little-known gems, for whatever the reason, to a wider audience for appreciation. Why should only the current fans have all the fun?

If you're willing to experience a different kind of film—one that appeals to an open-minded sort of viewer, possibly more discerning (or less so) than the norm—then by all means crack the spine and dig in. But be prepared to put aside any narrow definitions of what a "good" movie should be; although you will find entertaining, artistically important, beautiful, and poignant movies in this book, you might not always find every one of those qualities in one film. Then again, depending on your tastes, you may find them all exactly where you never thought to look before.

WHAT MAKES A MOVIE CULT?

Many believe that a cult film is defined by its lack of popularity, but we've decided to use a broader definition: a cult film is one that inspires an almost unhealthy level of devotion in its fans, whether that fan base consists of just ten people or hundreds of thousands. While many of the films in this book are indeed of the bombed-at-the-box-office variety, some were immediate financial successes on their release and have continued to be so for decades. A few have even won Academy Awards. In the true spirit of cult, we've decided not to let popular opinion dictate our choices; as such, you'll find movies in this book that hail from both ends of the popularity spectrum, from ultra low-budget independents to Hollywood blockbusters.

WHAT WE PUT IN . . . AND WHAT WE LEFT OUT

As the old adage goes, you can't please everyone; it's almost a given that we'll have left out some of your favorite cult movies. Five hundred films certainly seem like a lot, but in the grand scheme of cinematic releases in the past one hundred years, it's just a drop in a vast ocean. We've had to make some difficult decisions on what to include, purely based on space restrictions. This is, after all, not an exhaustive list of cult movies, but rather a selection of what we consider to be essential viewing for those new to cult films, or for those just looking to expand their cult film knowledge base.

CAN A CULT MOVIE BE A MAINSTREAM MOVIE?

Some people won't agree with us when we say this, but we feel the answer is yes. It seems awfully restrictive to define cult films as low budget and/or independent alone, especially when a movie like *Star Wars* has inspired decades' worth of feverish devotion and countless fan conventions, and even *Shawshank Redemption*—which enjoyed a multi-million dollar budget and major studio backing but did poorly at the box office—is one of the most beloved films of the last fifteen years. So we've kept an open mind when choosing what to include in this book, and you will certainly find mainstream movies within these pages.

HOW TO USE THIS BOOK

We're well set up for a straight read-through or for use as a handy reference guide, as the book is organized by genre in nine sections, covering all the major narrative categories found in our essential cult movies. Each section begins with the top ten cult titles in the genre, followed by the best of the rest. You can browse sections or just read single reviews without losing the plot, although for the dedicated follower of film the cover-to-cover approach is probably best.

All the information you need for tracking down a film is in its entry's heading, including the DVD releasing agency, if applicable, but a small number of the films are not currently available on DVD or even VHS. Don't fret, though, because many older films find their way onto DVD every year, so if you read about a film here that you'd like to see and it's listed as unavailable, just keep checking as it may come out at some point in the future.

To make things even more clear, we've included the age ratings for each film, as well as star ratings that reflect the movie's quality (one star means it's terrible, and five stars is . . . well, stellar). Though all are considered essential viewing for one reason or another, you will find one-star ratings in the mix, mainly because some cult films are prized solely for how bad they are. Don't be put off by these; the reviews will explain the reasoning behind the low-quality to high-cult ratio, and these movies are generally of the so-bad-it's-good variety and worth a view for a laugh.

CHAPTER 1

DRAMATIC SITUATIONS

"ALL RIGHT, MR. DEMILLE, I'M READY FOR MY CLOSE-UP"

The films in this section are probably those we relate to most readily—they're overwhelmingly character-based, and as such they reflect our collective fears, our despair, our hopes, and our dreams. When we feel old or cast aside by society we might drag out our tattered copy of *Sunset Boulevard*; misfits have a host of titles from which to take their comfort, and dreamers can find a kind of solace in *Sid and Nancy*.

The emotional connection is strongest here, and while these aren't the cult movies of conventions or raucous midnight showings, they are the films of repeated home viewings, secret smiles, and cathartic tears.

And then there's Ed Wood, who fits into none of the above categories but is just too unintentionally funny and odd not to love.

TOP 10
DRAMATIC SITUATIONS

★★★★★

Director: Joseph L. Mankiewicz
Screenwriter: Joseph L. Mankiewicz
Produced by: Darryl F. Zanuck

Starring: Bette Davis, Anne Baxter, and George Sanders
Released by: Twentieth Century Fox (DVD)

ALL ABOUT EVE

1950, 138 mins.

Plot: Broadway megastar Margo Channing has nothing lasting in her life but her work, and even that lifeline is fading as she's getting too old to play the leads. Enter Eve, a naive, passionate fan, whom Margo first befriends, then employs as a personal assistant. But Eve turns out to be less innocent than she appears as she connives her way into becoming Margo's understudy and ensures that Margo won't make it to the theater on time on opening night. However, Eve doesn't just want Margo's job, she wants her whole life, and she's willing to do just about anything to get it.

Review: Winner of six Academy Awards, including Best Picture, and nominated for fourteen in total, *All About Eve* is a particularly female drama. It could be said that, at its core, the film is about ageism against females, particularly in the performance professions, but that would be like saying *Sunset Boulevard* is just about getting old. There is so much going on here under the surface, so many lines taut with subtextual meaning; if *Touch of Evil* is about the evil that men do, then this film is its foil, covering, as it does, the evil that women do and the underhanded, elegant ways in which they do it.

The film's strength here is that it is entirely neutral—there are no snap judgments, no "be kind to your fellow woman" moral lessons. Broadway stars operate in an industry where youth is prized almost above all else, but no one can stay young forever, so inevitably there will be a young predator waiting to take your place in the wings. It's partially implied that Margo could have gotten her big break in the same way as Eve, and as such the really rather nasty events of the film are portrayed to the audience more as a "cycle of life" story than a morality tale. One of the truly perfect old Hollywood films that hasn't lost relevance (and probably never will).

FURTHER VIEWING: ***The Barefoot Contessa***
SEE ALSO: ***A Star Is Born; Sunset Boulevard; The Bad and the Beautiful***

★★★★

Directors: Michael Powell and Emeric Pressburger
Screenwriters: Michael Powell and Emeric Pressburger
Produced by: Michael Powell and Emeric Pressburger
Starring: Deborah Kerr, David Farrar, and Kathleen Byron
Released by: Criterion (DVD)

12+

BLACK NARCISSUS

1947, 100 mins.

Plot: A group of missionary nuns are sent by their Mother Superior to the Himalayas to set up a school and an infirmary, and, of course, to convert the locals. They get more than they bargained for when they realize the people and terrain aren't going to be converted; in fact, it's the nuns who will have crises of faith in the face of the area's creeping sensuality. Complementing the "hostile" terrain is Sister Ruth, never the most mentally stable woman in the cloister, who suffers a full-blown breakdown and becomes violently jealous of the head sister, Clodagh, and Clodagh's (passionate) friendship with the local British agent. Hell hath no fury like a woman scorned, especially when she's a lunatic to begin with.

Review: Amidst stunning set pieces and the expected witty script, powerhouse directing/writing/producing team Powell and Pressburger brings us a mystical, exotic tale, which Powell considered the most erotic film he'd ever made. And it's true: considering the film is about a bunch of nuns on a religious mission, there's a surprising amount of sexuality simmering beneath the surface. Which isn't to say there's any actual sex in the film. No, this is 1947 and suggestion is key; it's also arguably more effective.

Based on the novel *Black Narcissus* by Rumer Gordon—an English-born woman who ran a dance school in Calcutta—the film, and the book, have an unusual story in that conquerors are never supposed to admit defeat, but here they do, and readily. Particularly in a missionary situation, where we have white against dark, Christian against heathen, European against exotic, repressed versus openly sensual, it's highly unusual to admit that the primitive impulse is stronger than civilization. So strong, in fact, that when European refinement is faced with Indian earthiness, that refinement simply crumbles like the façade it always was.

FURTHER VIEWING: *The Red Shoes; Peeping Tom*
SEE ALSO: *The Thorn Birds; The Far Pavilions*

★★★★★

Director: Richard Brooks
Screenwriter: Richard Brooks
Produced by: Pandro S. Berman

Starring: Glenn Ford, Anne Francis, Vic Morrow, and Sydney Poitier
Released by: Warner Home Video (DVD)

15+

BLACKBOARD JUNGLE

1955, 101 mins.

Plot: Richard Dadier is a war veteran and new teacher assigned to a troublesome inner-city high school. He finds the school to be overrun by punks and slackers, some of them violent and threatening towards the other teachers. At first Dadier tries to interest the kids in school, to make learning *fun*, but he soon learns that the only way to control the classroom is to confront the troublemakers head on and assert his dominance in the only way the kids understand.

Review: Forget *Rebel without a Cause*—this is *the* rock 'n' roll film, literally. Not only did it kickstart Bill Haley & the Comets' career by featuring their song "Rock Around the Clock," which subsequently became a huge hit, it's credited with starting a series of Teddy Boy riots in London and around the UK in 1956, when the Edwardian-inspired rock 'n' rollers would tear up seats and dance in theaters. So the next time your parents lecture you about films and video games causing anti-social behavior, politely inform them that it was your grandparents who started it.

But beyond its enormous influence on the popularity of that new-fangled rock 'n' roll music, *Blackboard Jungle* is the original "crusading teacher versus troublemaking students" film, and is notable for creating an entire subgenre of films pitting idealistic teachers against cynical and usually violent students uninterested in learning the three Rs. It reflected a new era in the fifties when kids were becoming more independent and less likely to honor their parents, which scared the hell out of the Depression generation. It is no less relevant today; in fact, one could call this film prescient, tapping into a zeitgeist of teenager fear that's only gotten worse in the fifty-plus years since it was made. Essential viewing for the feared and fearful alike.

FURTHER VIEWING: ***To Sir, with Love; Looking for Mr. Goodbar***
SEE ALSO: ***Lean on Me; 187; Dangerous Minds; Stand and Deliver***

★★★★★

Director: Dennis Hopper
Screenwriters: Peter Fonda, Dennis Hopper, and Terry Southern
Produced by: Peter Fonda
Starring: Peter Fonda, Dennis Hopper, and Jack Nicholson
Released by: Sony Pictures (DVD)

18+

EASY RIDER

1969, 94 mins.

Plot: Wyatt ("Captain America") and Billy score big on a drug deal and decide to take to the road—their only goal is to get to New Orleans in time for Mardi Gras before "retiring" in Florida to live off their ill-gotten gains. It's the new American dream. On the way they pick up hitchhikers, get thrown in jail, meet an alcoholic ACLU lawyer, experience a fatal clash with rednecks and a wild time in New Orleans, and then another (possibly) fatal run-in with rednecks. And just before the depressing climax comes Wyatt's equally grim realization that he and Billy "blew it."

Review: "A man went looking for America. And couldn't find it anywhere . . ." What *Blackboard Jungle* was to the fifties, *Easy Rider* was to the sixties. This film not only became the archetypal road movie for later generations, it reflected an entirely new counter-culture movement for young Americans at the time, one based on drugs, free love, and having a good time—values that completely clashed with those of previous generations.

In addition to its impact on American culture, *Easy Rider* influenced Hollywood to an almost unprecedented degree. It's often credited with beginning the New Hollywood (or American New Wave) era of filmmaking, in which a younger, hipper generation invaded the film industry and used Hollywood money to make films about gritty, realistic, and anti-establishment themes that were previously relegated to the independent stream. It wouldn't be too melodramatic to say that without Peter Fonda and Dennis Hopper, there would be no Coppola, Bogdanovich, or Scorsese.

But beyond its importance to the Hollywood establishment (ironically), this film is just a great road movie, not despite the trip's ultimate failure, but because of it. A somewhat bizarre and poignant buddy flick on LSD.

FURTHER VIEWING: ***The Last Movie; Out of the Blue***
SEE ALSO: ***Electra Glide in Blue; Two-Lane Blacktop***

★★★★★

Director: Hal Ashby
Screenwriter: Colin Higgins
Produced by: Colin Higgins and Charles B. Mulvehill
Starring: Ruth Gordon, Bud Cort, and Vivian Pickles
Released by: Paramount Home Video (DVD)

15+

HAROLD AND MAUDE

1971, 91 mins.

Plot: Nineteen-year-old Harold becomes obsessed with dying after an incident where his mother truly thinks he is dead . . . and he realizes he likes the attention. Between staging fake suicides at dinner parties and driving a hearse to a real funeral, Harold's mother nags him to grow up "properly" by joining the army and getting married. Harold may not know who he is or what he wants, but he knows it isn't that.

Enter Maude, a seventy-nine-year-old woman who's so in love with life that every day is a joy and an adventure for her. Harold goes on blind dates with girls his own age set up by his mother while his friendship with Maude deepens, eventually becoming sexual. But on Maude's eightieth birthday, Harold discovers her throwaway comment that eighty years old is a "proper age" to die wasn't idle at all.

Review: *Harold and Maude* is the ultimate unlikely relationship film, a seriously dark black comedy that also happens to be heartwarming and romantic. Having already seen life as a book and a stage production, the film did badly on its release, both financially and with critics; the idea of an eighty-year-old woman and a teenage boy engaging in a sexual relationship, no matter the philosophy behind it, proved too much for 1971 audiences to bear. But this film is a clear product of its era, documenting the clash of an older WWI and WWII survival generation with aimless, Vietnam-bred children and grandchildren.

This picture is now considered one of the funniest films of all time, and it is funny, no doubt, but it's a black comedy underscored by the poignancy of a sort of reverse coming-of-age tale. Harold needs to grow out of his morbid attention-seeking ways and grow up, but the only person who can show him how to do that is octogenarian Maude, who herself is in the process of growing down. When we see the concentration-camp tattoo on Maude's arm, we realize her lust for life came only with the knowledge that she was able to survive the worst of life; that she puts Harold on his own path to surviving life with her death is her greatest lesson and legacy. This film will stay with you.

FURTHER VIEWING: ***Being There; The Last Detail***
SEE ALSO: ***Ginger Snaps; The Graduate; Rushmore***

★ ★ ★ ★ ★

Director: Billy Wilder
Screenwriters: Charles Brackett and Billy Wilder

Produced by: Charles Brackett
Starring: Ray Milland and Jane Wyman
Released by: Universal Studios (DVD)

15+

THE LOST WEEKEND

1945, 101 mins.

Plot: Writer and alcoholic Don Birnam is packing for a weekend getaway with his brother Wick; Wick knows of Don's proclivities and keeps a close eye on him. When Don's girlfriend arrives with concert tickets, Don persuades his brother to go with her, leaving him alone with his hidden bottles of booze. But Wick isn't stupid—he's thrown out all the bottles. Unfortunately, Don isn't stupid either, and when he finds hidden cash (and stiffs the cleaning lady), he runs out to the nearest bar for "just one drink." What follows is a degrading descent into rock-bottom drunkenness, complete with DTs, broken relationships, a hospital visit, and, finally, an acceptance.

Review: "Let me have one, Nat. I'm dying. Just one." Anyone who thinks Billy Wilder is all about the funny has never seen *The Lost Weekend* (or *Sunset Boulevard*, for that matter). Directors are usually proficient in one genre, which they tend to stick to. Wilder, on the other hand, proved himself not only proficient but a master in several genres, from the cleverest laugh-out-loud comedy to the deepest, darkest, and most unpleasant drama, like this picture.

The Lost Weekend won four Oscars, all from the big five: Best Picture, Best Director, Best Writing, and a Best Actor award for Ray Milland. It also won the Grand Prix at the first Cannes Festival in 1946. All of the accolades are well deserved; this is not an easy film to watch, probably because of its gritty, relentlessly truthful portrayal of alcoholism. Through Milland's stunning performance, we are able to get directly into Don's head where all of his insecurities lay waiting to rear—and why Don is ready with a bottle to beat them down. This is harrowing and surprisingly modern film-making: brave, honest, and ugly.

FURTHER VIEWING: ***Ace in the Hole***
SEE ALSO: ***Drunks; Leaving Las Vegas; The Morning After; Face on the Barroom Floor***

★★★★★

Director: Miloš Forman
Screenwriters: Lawrence Hauben and Bo Goldman

Produced by: Michael Douglas and Saul Zaentz
Starring: Jack Nicholson, Louise Fletcher, William Redfield, and Brad Dourif

Released by: Warner Home Video (DVD)

15+

ONE FLEW OVER THE CUCKOO'S NEST

1975, 133 mins.

Plot: Randle P. McMurphy has the brilliant idea of playing crazy to avoid hard labor in prison; the bosses take him seriously and send him to the state mental hospital for evaluation, which is exactly what he wanted, since you can't break rocks in a padded cell. But McMurphy gets far more than he bargained for in Nurse Ratched, the most terrifying medical professional this side of Dr. Jekyll and Mr. Hyde. The free spirit and the authoritarian butt heads mercilessly; McMurphy's charisma and fun-loving attitude brings the inmates to his side, but Ratched still holds the keys . . . and the paddles to the electroshock therapy machine.

Review: Even if you haven't seen *One Flew over the Cuckoo's Nest*, you've probably heard about it, and most likely you've heard of Nurse Ratched. So many aspects of this film have made indelible marks on pop culture—the aforementioned sadistic nurse and the Chief throwing a garbage can through a window at the end in particular—that it has become a beacon for cultural reference (*The Simpsons* have done so many parodies of *Cuckoo* scenes it's impossible to keep track).

As the second of only three pictures to win all of the big five Oscars—Screenplay, Picture, Actor, Actress, and Director—even the Academy knew they were on to something special. Based on the novel by counter-culture icon Ken Kesey, *Cuckoo* is inspired by Kesey's time spent working in an actual mental ward and is a damning indictment of the treatment of mental patients; in fact, it goes so far as to criticize the prescribed nature of mental illness itself, implying that such a designation is reserved for society's misfits rather than those truly chemically imbalanced. The superior acting and up-close-and-personal directing style only serve to carry this point home on the back of a heartbreaking and beautiful story.

FURTHER VIEWING: ***Taking Off; Hair***
SEE ALSO: ***The Shawshank Redemption; Shock Corridor; Girl, Interrupted; The Hospital***

★
★
★
★
★

Director: Francis Ford Coppola
Screenwriters: Kathleen Rowell and Francis Ford Coppola
Produced by: Gray Frederickson and Fred Roos
Starring: C. Thomas Howell, Matt Dillon, Ralph Macchio, Rob Lowe, Patrick Swayze, Emilio Estevez, Tom Cruise, and Diane Lane
Released by: Warner Home Video (DVD)

12+

THE OUTSIDERS

1983, 92 mins.

Plot: Tulsa, Oklahoma is a hotbed of teenage angst and strife in this adaptation of S. E. Hinton's novel. There's a clear divide between the Greasers and the Socs, a line between poor and rich, educated and ignorant, blue collar and professional, the wrong side of the tracks and the right side. Ponyboy, a thoughtful and sensitive orphan, is firmly stationed on the Greaser side of the line; one night, he and his friend Johnny-cake get into a deadly altercation with the Socs. Forced to leave their friends behind, Pony and Johnny go on the run from the cops. They manage to gain some perspective by getting out of the thick of the constant social war in their lives, but the problem with perspective is that it only changes you . . . and the Socs are still looking for revenge.

Review: It's only fitting that Hinton's cult book became a cult movie (and it certainly helped that most of the stars of the ensemble cast were future Brat Packers). The ultimate coming-of-age story for social misfits, Coppola managed to capture the confused teenage honesty of the book perfectly on-screen. This was no mean feat, as Hinton was speaking from an in-the-moment experience—her book was published when she was only seventeen.

The Outsiders covers the gamut of young adult themes: growing up too fast and not fast enough at the same time; the injustice of being judged on things you have no control over; and the seeming futility of wanting to change yourself and the world. It's the complete lack of condescension in treating these themes that has made the film so popular not only with teenagers in 1983, but today as well. The story has a timelessness about it, a universal relevance; Coppola once again showed his talent by leaving the heart of the story unchanged. And by casting a lot of pretty young men!

FURTHER VIEWING: ***Rumble Fish; That Was Then . . . This Is Now***
SEE ALSO: ***The Warriors; Bad Boys; The Wanderers***

★★★★★

Director: Frank Darabont
Screenwriter: Frank Darabont
Produced by: Niki Marvin

Starring: Tim Robbins, Morgan Freeman, and Bob Gunton
Released by: Castle Rock (DVD)

15+

THE SHAWSHANK REDEMPTION

1994, 142 mins.

Plot: Quiet banker Andy Dufresne is accused and convicted of murdering his wife and her lover based on strong circumstantial evidence, but maintains his innocence. He's sent to Shawshank Prison for two consecutive life sentences, and though he's clearly out of place in his new environs, he begins to accumulate a circle of friends. He also catches the attention of the "The Sisters" and is repeatedly raped and beaten.

An educated, white-collar inmate is a rarity, and Andy's tax knowledge becomes valuable to the prison warden, who needs to hide his dirty money. The warden takes care of Andy's problem with The Sisters, but when new evidence comes to light proving that Andy didn't kill his wife or her lover, the warden covers it up (he needs Andy, and what Andy knows about his corrupt business practices could take him down forever). But as we learn, Andy isn't the kind of guy to let himself be beaten by the establishment, no matter the consequences.

Review: Despite its lack of success at the box office, *Shawshank* was nominated for seven Oscars . . . and didn't win a single one. But its fame has grown during its life on cable television and DVD (and VHS back in the day), becoming one of the most beloved films of the past fifteen years.

As Frank Darabont's directorial debut, this is one of the more famous of Stephen King's "Dollar Deals," in which he sells the rights of his stories to young, poor filmmakers for only a dollar. Darabont also adapted the story for the screen, and his talent was clearly evident enough to attract some of the most highly respected actors working in Hollywood today. In their performances Robbins and Freeman just exude dignity and quiet intensity, as if they drank too much of it the night before filming and are sweating it out through their pores during each take. But that they shine so brightly is due to their relationship and the story as a whole being so expertly crafted—though the film could very well cross the line into melodrama or sentimentality, the two leads and their bevy of funny and tragic friends keep everything firmly in drama territory. Thomas Newman's Oscar-nominated score is pitch-perfect, underlining the action and reinforcing the visual beauty of the picture.

FURTHER VIEWING: ***The Green Mile***
SEE ALSO: ***One Flew over the Cuckoo's Nest; In the Name of the Father; Papillon; Escape from Alcatraz***

★★★★★

Director: Frank Perry
Screenwriter: Eleanor Perry
Produced by: Roger Lewis
Starring: Burt Lancaster, Janet Langard, and Janice Rule
Released by: Sony Pictures (DVD)

12+

THE SWIMMER

1968, 95 mins.

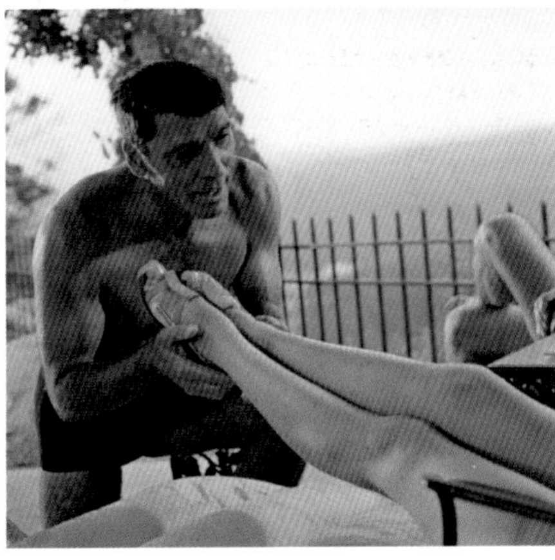

Plot: Burt Lancaster is all smiles as cheery Ned Merrill, who emerges one summer's day from the trees into the back garden of his friends' house for a dip in their pool. Having not seen him for some time, Ned's friends are warm and welcoming upon his arrival, and try their best to encourage him to join them at social events. However, Ned has a plan fixed in his mind—he intends to swim the county by traveling cross-country and taking a dip in each of the pools that make up the "Lucinda River," named after his wife. Julie Ann Hooper, a beautiful woman who used to babysit for the Merrills some time ago, joins him on his adventure. At a swinging party, most of the guests are thrilled by Ned's appearance, having also not seen him in a while. It becomes apparent that not all is what it seems, and that Ned has experienced failure and disgrace, the realization of which is his own tragic undoing.

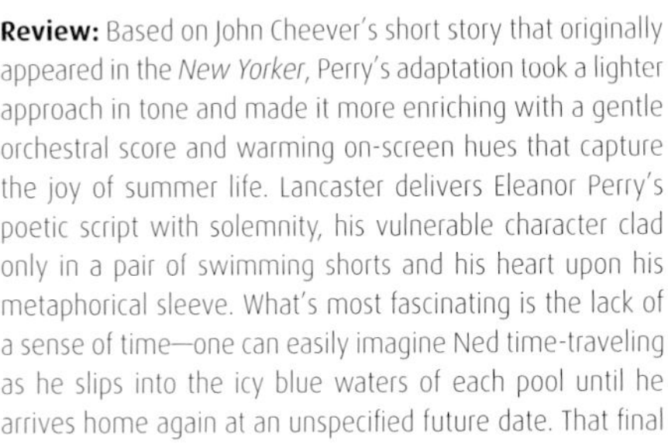

Review: Based on John Cheever's short story that originally appeared in the *New Yorker*, Perry's adaptation took a lighter approach in tone and made it more enriching with a gentle orchestral score and warming on-screen hues that capture the joy of summer life. Lancaster delivers Eleanor Perry's poetic script with solemnity, his vulnerable character clad only in a pair of swimming shorts and his heart upon his metaphorical sleeve. What's most fascinating is the lack of a sense of time—one can easily imagine Ned time-traveling as he slips into the icy blue waters of each pool until he arrives home again at an unspecified future date. That final scene is shocking and impactful, and transforms repeat viewings into an eerie and surreal experience; the film is an allegory for the fractured mind of a once great man.

FURTHER VIEWING: ***Diary of a Mad Housewife; Last Summer***
SEE ALSO: ***Death of a Salesman; The Ice Storm***

011
500

★★★

Director: Jean-Jacques Beineix
Screenwriter: Jean-Jacques Beineix
Produced by: Claudie Ossard

Starring: Béatrice Dalle, Jean-Hugues Anglade, and Gérard Darmon
Released by: Sony Pictures (DVD)

18+

37°2 LE MATIN (BETTY BLUE)

1986, 120 mins.

Plot: Happy-go-lucky workman Zorg lives day to day, painting and repairing bungalows on a beach until he meets the wild and beautiful Betty. As a part-time writer who one day hopes to become published, he allows her to type up his manuscripts to keep her out of trouble. After several incidents where Betty's rage becomes uncontrollable, Zorg must ask the question: is love enough?

Review: Still hugely popular to this day (possibly due to the amount of sex and casual nudity), Beineix's film is different in tone from the successful *Diva* down to its bright colors, warming soundtrack, and vibrant energy from its cast. The extended cut balances out the push-pull relationship between Zorg and Betty and should be the first port of call.

FURTHER VIEWING: ***Diva; Roselyne et Les Lions (Roselyne and the Lions)***
SEE ALSO: ***Fatal Attraction; Sex and Lucia***

012
500

Director: Abel Ferrara
Screenwriter: Nicholas St. John

Produced by: Preston L. Holmes, Russell Simmons, Denis Hann, and Fernando Sulichin

Starring: Lili Taylor, Christopher Walken, and Annabella Sciorra
Released by: Not Available

THE ADDICTION

1995, 82 mins.

Plot: NYU student Kathleen Conklin is attacked one night by a beautiful and seductive woman who demands that Kathleen tell her to go away. Kathleen, shaken, scared, and confused, isn't able to respond; the woman bites her, drinks her blood, and disappears. Kathleen then experiences the usual aversion to sunlight and thirst for blood that goes with being bitten by a seeming human in the night, but true to the film's title, *The Addiction* is less about the mysticism or science of vampirism, and more about the degradation Kathleen succumbs to through her blood addiction.

Review: Using vampirism as a metaphor for drug abuse, Ferrara presents an unglamorous view of these night creatures who blame everyone but themselves for their behavior as they dredge the lowest depths of their lost humanity to get the next "fix." Filmed in stark black and white, *The Addiction* features intense performances by Lili Taylor and Christopher Walken.

FURTHER VIEWING: ***King of New York; Bad Lieutenant***
SEE ALSO: ***Nadja; Habit; Near Dark***

013/500

★★★★

Director: Cameron Crowe
Screenwriter: Cameron Crowe
Produced by: Ian Bryce

Starring: Billy Crudup, Patrick Fugit, Kate Hudson, Jason Lee, and Frances McDormand

Released by: Dreamworks Video (DVD)

15+

ALMOST FAMOUS

1996, 122 mins. (original cut)/2000, 162 mins. (extended cut)

Plot: Aspiring high-school writer William Miller wants to be a rock journalist, but his overbearing mother wants him to become a lawyer. Regardless, he befriends an upcoming band called Stillwater, as well as an attractive groupie called Penny Lane, who proceed to take him through the highs—and lows—of the rock 'n' roll lifestyle.

Review: Based on Crowe's own experiences as a young music journalist for hip mags like *Creem* and *Rolling Stone*, the sights and sounds of the mid-seventies rock era are accurately blown up on the screen. Augmented by a great soundtrack and incendiary performances from Frances McDormand and Billy Crudup, the extended "bootleg" cut of the movie runs to an extra thirty-nine sweet minutes.

FURTHER VIEWING: ***Singles; Jerry Maguire***
SEE ALSO: ***High Fidelity; Detroit Rock City***

014/500

★★★

Director: Alejandro Gonzaláz Iñárritu
Screenwriter: Guillermo Arriaga
Produced by: Alejandro Gonzaláz Iñárritu

Starring: Gael García Bernal, Álvaro Guerrero, and Emilio Echevarría
Released by: Lionsgate (DVD)

AMORES PERROS

2000, 155 mins.

Plot: Three stories connected by a serious car crash in Mexico City—and cruelty to dogs—make up this powerful anthology film. In the first, Octavio wants to take his sister-in-law away from his abusive brother but can only earn the money to do so through dogfighting. In the second, a model is left in a wheelchair from the crash, which puts strain on her relationship with partner Daniel. And in the last, a hitman who also cares for dogs decides to let his estranged daughter know he's alive . . . but only after one last job.

Review: Hard to summarize in few words, this long and carefully intertwined movie is an absolute joy to watch. Gritty, well acted, and unmissable, Iñárritu has since made an impact on U.S. audiences with *Babel*.

FURTHER VIEWING: ***Babel; 21 Grams***
SEE ALSO: ***Y tu mamá también (And Your Mother Too); Traffic***

015/500

★★★

Director: Don Siegel
Screenwriters: Irene Kamp and Albery Maltz
Produced by: Don Siegel

Starring: Clint Eastwood and Geraldine Page
Released by: Universal (DVD)

15+

THE BEGUILED

1970, 100 mins.

Plot: A wounded union soldier is given shelter in a Southern girls' school. When he begins to heal, tensions mount as the girls vie for his affections and he struggles to figure out which ones won't turn him over to the enemy. Playing off one against the other, loyalties are soon strained and the sexual politics start turning ugly.

Review: For many men, this should be a dream come true. However, for Eastwood's young solider it's a gilded cage. Struggling to survive, he veers from sympathetic to vindictive and manipulative as Siegel builds the storm, creating a gripping slice of erotically charged Southern gothic.

FURTHER VIEWING: *Coogan's Bluff; Two Mules for Sister Sara; Dirty Harry; The Shootist; Escape from Alcatraz*
SEE ALSO: *Misery*

016/500

★★★

Director: Jean Negulesco
Screenwriters: Mann Rubin and Edith Sommer
Produced by: Jerry Wald

Starring: Hope Lange, Diane Baker, Suzy Parker, and Joan Crawford
Released by: Twentieth Century Fox (DVD)

A

THE BEST OF EVERYTHING

1959, 121 mins.

Plot: Three women sharing an apartment, ambitions, and careers at the same publishing company are all going through relationship hells. As they struggle to come to terms with seductions, break-ups, and pregnancies, they are lorded over by their jaded, spiteful editor as she takes her own frustrations out on her underlings.

Review: Ahead of its time in its portrayal of the Battle of the Sexes, all the great fashions in this film can't hide the ugly struggles of young, pre-PC women trying to climb the career ladder in a male-dominated office. Crawford rightfully deserves the acting plaudits but it's left to the younger actresses to prove that while romance isn't dead, in this movie it's on life support.

FURTHER VIEWING: *How to Marry a Millionaire; Three Coins in the Fountain; Woman's World; The Dark Wave; What Ever Happened to Baby Jane?*
SEE ALSO: *Valley of the Dolls; Sex in the City; Mad Men (TV)*

017/500

★ ★ ★

Director: John Milius
Screenwriter: Dennis Aaberg
Produced by: Buzz Feitshans
Starring: Jan-Michael Vincent, William Katt, and Gary Busey
Released by: Warner Home Video (DVD)

BIG WEDNESDAY

1978, 119 mins.

Plot: Set against a backdrop of good-time surfing and the threat of the Vietnam War, three young men who spend their lives at the beach under the watchful eye of surfer guru and mentor Bear must come to terms with the end of the endless summer. Two friends are shipped off to fight after failing to fool the draft board, and years later they reunite to see if they can recapture the innocence of days gone by.

Review: Featuring some great early performances by Gary Busey and Jan-Michael Vincent, it's hard to fault Milius' ode to surf. Unlike most of the stereotypical movies you'll be familiar with nowadays, the film is beautifully shot and is as feel-good as they come.

FURTHER VIEWING: *Red Dawn; Dillinger*
SEE ALSO: *American Graffiti; Point Break*

018/500

★ ★ ★

Director: William Friedkin
Screenwriter: Matt Crowley
Produced by: Matt Crowley and Kenneth Utt
Starring: Kenneth Nelson, Frederick Combs, and Cliff Gorman
Released by: Paramount (DVD)

15+

THE BOYS IN THE BAND

1970, 119 mins.

Plot: Michael is hosting a birthday party for his friend, Harold, in his New York apartment. The guests include several other gay friends, but Michael's night is thrown into confusion when his straight, old college roommate Alan unexpectedly arrives. He has something he wants to tell Michael, but as the alcohol flows, the evening doesn't go quite the way Michael planned and turns ugly.

Review: Made when gay pride was beginning to really make itself known, this film portrays a wide range of characters that deal with many of the issues surrounding the homosexual community at the time, no matter how painful or unpleasant. But in the end it proves that, no matter your sexual preferences, relationships are pretty much all the same.

FURTHER VIEWING: *The French Connection; The Exorcist; Cruising; To Live and Die in L.A.; Jade; The Hunted*
SEE ALSO: *American Beauty; The Big Chill; Milk*

019/500

★★

Director: Joel Silberg
Screenwriters: Allen DeBevoise, Charles Parker, and Gerald Scaife

Produced by: Allen DeBevoise, David Zito, Menahem Golan, and Yoram Globus

Starring: Lucinda Dickey, Adolfo Quinones, and Michael Chambers
Released by: MGM (DVD)

A

BREAKIN'

1984, 90 mins.

Plot: Jazz dancer Kelly falls in with the wrong crowd—in this case a couple of breakdancers who are in the middle of a bitter dancin' rivalry with another gang. Kelly becomes a street dancing sensation while struggling to get her classical dance teacher to accept her hybrid style, and she and her friends fight for respect through popping and locking.

Review: Like skater movies after it and disco films before it, *Breakin'* came into existence to capitalize on a pop-culture phenomenon. As such, its story is flimsy at best (a dance-off for respect—really?), the dialog is leaden, and the performances . . . well, you get the picture. But the fantastic breakdancing sequences and electro-hip-hop soundtrack are unforgettable, making the overall viewing experience a real pleasure. Also notable for featuring Ice-T in his first film role.

FURTHER VIEWING: ***Breakin' 2: Electric Boogaloo***
SEE ALSO: ***Saturday Night Fever; Fame; Gleaming the Cube***

020/500

★★★★

Director: David Lean
Screenwriters: Anthony Havelock-Allan, David Lean, and Ronald Neame (all uncredited)

Produced by: Noel Coward
Starring: Celia Johnson and Trevor Howard
Released by: Criterion (DVD)

12+

BRIEF ENCOUNTER

1945, 86 mins.

Plot: A piece of grit from a passing train changes the dull lives of two strangers forever when debonair, handsome Dr. Alec Harvey comes to the rescue of conventional, bored housewife Laura. Torn between doing the right thing and their rapidly blossoming love, they know they're doomed, but it makes the end no less devastating.

Review: As tales of unrequited love go, you'd have a hard time finding one better. David Lean's use of light and shadow captures a landscape that reflects lives like the weather—dull and dreary—and stifled by cold, heartless social conventions. This makes the struggles of the two lovers even more powerful, the stages of their romance like stages of grief: denial, anger, depression . . .

FURTHER VIEWING: ***In Which We Serve; Blithe Spirit; Doctor Zhivago; Ryan's Daughter***
SEE ALSO: ***The End of the Affair***

21
30

★★★

Director: Sam Peckinpah
Screenwriters: Gordon T. Dawson and Sam Peckinpah
Produced by: Martin Baum
Starring: Warren Oates, Isela Vega, and Robert Webber
Released by: MGM (DVD)

8+

BRING ME THE HEAD OF ALFREDO GARCIA

1974, 108 mins.

Plot: A rich Mexican landowner offers a million dollars for the man who left his daughter pregnant then fled. A low-life bartender, hoping to make a better life for himself and his girl, takes on the task. But he's not the only one after the bounty and he is soon dogged by murder, violence, and tragedy.

Review: Peckinpah cleverly starts this as a "classic" western, but then there are limos and jets, and you realize this is the present day. However, the film retains a timeless quality; the drink, women, and life are just as cheap. Oates wears his craggy, hangdog melancholy like a hangover, adding dark pathos to a small man driven to extremes and courting death with every step.

FURTHER VIEWING: ***Major Dundee; The Wild Bunch; Straw Dogs; The Getaway; The Killer Elite; Cross of Iron***
SEE ALSO: ***Dead Man; El Mariachi; Man on Fire; Once Upon a Time in Mexico***

22
30

★★★

Director: Sergei M. Eisenstein
Screenwriter: Nina Agadzhanova
Produced by: Jacob Bliokh
Starring: Aleksandr Antonov, Vladimir Barsky, and Grigori Aleksandrov
Released by: Image Entertainment (DVD)

2+

BRONENOSETS POTYOMKIN

(BATTLESHIP POTEMKIN)

1925, 70 mins.

Plot: The story of the events surrounding a mutiny by the crew of a Russian warship, sparking an uprising by the population of the *Potemkin*'s home port, Odessa. The subsequent massacre by Tsarist forces of unarmed civilians added fuel to the growing Leninist revolution.

Review: Made in Soviet Russia in 1925, this is an obviously one-sided take on the actual uprising. Played in broad black-and-white strokes—the downtrodden lower decks treated as little more than slaves, the higher ranks disdainful and contemptuous—there's little room for gray areas. Heaving with revolutionary zeal, the massacre on the stairs of Odessa is now a part of cinematic history and is referenced in numerous movies.

FURTHER VIEWING: ***Oktyabr (October); Staroye I novoye (The General Line); Ivan Groznyy I & II (Ivan the Terrible, Parts I & 2)***
SEE ALSO: ***Dr. Zhivago; The Godfather; Reds; The Untouchables***

023
500

★★★

Director: Robert Kaylor
Screenwriters: Phoebe Kaylor, Robert Kaylor, Robbie Robertson, and Thomas Baum
Produced by: Robbie Robertson
Starring: Gary Busey, Jodie Foster, and Robbie Robertson
Released by: Not Available

18+

CARNY

1980, 107 mins.

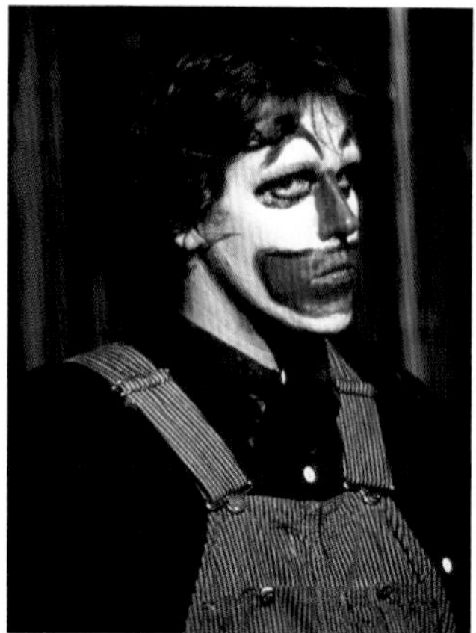

Plot: Frankie and Patch are long-time partners in a traveling carnival's dunk-the-clown game; this is back when fixing games was still legal and all carnival-goers were considered suckers with deep pockets. While on the road in the South, dissatisfied teenager Donna joins the show and must prove herself to her comrades before she's accepted as a true carny.

Review: *Carny* gives a very atmospheric view of carnival culture before it was sanitized, as well as the people who choose it as a lifestyle (never just a job). Jodie Foster as Donna is an obvious standout, but Gary Busey almost steals the show as the foul-mouthed, nutty clown.

FURTHER VIEWING: ***Derby; Nobody's Perfect***
SEE ALSO: ***Tilt; Variety Lights; Something Wicked this Way Comes***

024
500

★★★

Director: Bill L. Norton
Screenwriter: Bill L. Norton
Produced by: Gerald Ayres
Starring: Kris Kristofferson, Karen Black, and Gene Hackman
Released by: Sony Pictures (DVD)

18+

CISCO PIKE

1972, 94 mins.

Plot: Cisco Pike (Kris Kristofferson) is fresh out of jail, down on his luck, and looking for his next buck. In steps Sgt. Holland (Gene Hackman), a cop Cisco's had various run-ins with over the years, with an offer he can't refuse: move stolen grass and make $10,000 or he's going back to the clink. With only three days to raise the cash, Cisco's got his work cut out for him.

Review: You can imagine that The Dude (*The Big Lebowski*) is an older incarnation of Cisco with his similar looks, dry humor, and monumental interest in grass. Kristofferson is cool as hell as he drifts from recording studio to parties, hanging out with the weird and the wonderful. The dialog has dated, as have the haircuts, but it's still a killer movie.

FURTHER VIEWING: ***Outlaw Blues; More American Graffiti***
SEE ALSO: ***The Big Lebowski; Up in Smoke***

025
500

★★★

Director: Monte Hellman
Screenwriter: Charles Willeford
Produced by: Roger Corman
Starring: Warren Oates, Richard B. Shull, and Harry Dean Stanton
Released by: Synergy Entertainment (DVD)

18+

COCKFIGHTER

1974, 83 mins.

Plot: Warren Oates plays existential hero and championship cockfighter Frank Mansfield on the trail of the ultimate prize—The Cockfighter of the Year Award. After losing a casual cockfight in a motel room, he vows never to speak again, even if it means ruining his relationship, losing his possessions, and doing anything it takes to win that medal.

Review: Tarantino is a huge admirer of Hellman as a director for his uncompromising brutality and his artistic filmmaking. *Cockfighter* remains banned in the UK for its violent scenes of animal cruelty (just as cockfighting is illegal in the continental U.S.), making it an exploitation movie with a twist. Harry Dean Stanton appears in a supporting role.

FURTHER VIEWING: ***Two-Lane Blacktop; Back Door to Hell***
SEE ALSO: ***Fighting Mad; Hired Hand***

026
500

★★★★★

Director: Oliver Hirschbiegel
Screenwriters: Don Bohlinger, Christoph Darnstädt, and Mario Giordano
Produced by: Marc Conrad and Norbert Preuss
Starring: Moritz Bleibtreu, Christian Berkel, and Oliver Stokowski
Released by: Sony Pictures (DVD)

18+

DAS EXPERIMENT (THE EXPERIMENT)

2001, 119 mins.

Plot: Twenty men taking part in a psychological experiment are split into guards and prisoners in a simulated prison. However, the role-playing is increasingly realistic as the unconstrained guards become ever more authoritarian, excessive, and finally brutal, the experiment collapsing towards a violent, bloody result.

Review: With its allegorical reminders of concentration camps, Abu Ghraib, and Guantanamo Bay, this film, like the experiment it portrays, is constructed to bring out the best and worst in its actors. The result is an utterly gripping, thought-provoking insight into alpha-male machismo and the psychology of power. Inevitably, you're also left wondering just how far *you'd* go before cracking under pressure—or doing something terrible.

FURTHER VIEWING: ***Downfall; The Invasion; Five Minutes of Heaven***
SEE ALSO: ***Cube; Bridge on the River Kwai; Scum***

027/500

★★★★

Director: Edmund Goulding
Screenwriters: Seton I. Miller and Dan Totheroh

Produced by: Jack Warner, Hal B. Wallis, and Robert Lord

Starring: Errol Flynn, Basil Rathbone, and David Niven
Released by: Warner Home Video (DVD)

A

THE DAWN PATROL

1938, 103 mins.

Plot: France, 1915: Major Brand is the most hated man in the Royal Flying Corps' 59th Squadron—he's the one who orders pilots on the dawn patrols, which are basically suicide missions for the constant stream of replacement recruits who have little training and no experience. When the squadron is taunted by fearsome fighter pilot Von Richter, friends Courtney and Scott defy Brand's orders not to retaliate and do major damage to the German forces. Brand is promoted out of the 59th for their successful "misson," and Courtney takes his place. Under the burden of sending pilots to their deaths, he becomes everything he hated about Brand.

Review: This is a remake of the 1930 film of the same name directed by Howard Hawks, but this version is far slicker, more comfortable using sound, and has an all-star cast. But the 1930 version hasn't been completely relegated to obscurity; all of the aerial shots are recycled from Hawks' film.

FURTHER VIEWING: *Hell's Angels; Forever and a Day*
SEE ALSO: *Catch-22; Aces High; Top Gun*

028/500

★★★

Director: Terrence Malick
Screenwriter: Terrence Malick

Produced by: Bert Schneider and Harold Schneider
Starring: Richard Gere and Brooke Adams
Released by: Paramount (DVD)

12+

DAYS OF HEAVEN

1978, 95 mins.

Plot: After killing his boss, Bill flees Chicago with his girlfriend Abby and her sister in tow. Pretending to be siblings, they end up working for a wealthy but dying farmer in Texas. When he falls for Abby, Bill sees an opportunity to inherit the farmer's wealth and persuades Abby to marry him. Once he's dead, they can clean up. But when the farmer remains steadfastly healthy, the plan begins to violently unravel.

Review: Dreamy, poetic, languid, this is a unique filmmaker going about his craft as though he were a landscape painter, using celluloid as canvas and shot almost like a natural history documentary. And while the movie is a thing of beauty, it's easy to forget the romantic triangle at its heart, with some fine, poignant acting to underpin the epic cinematography.

FURTHER VIEWING: *Badlands; The Thin Red Line; The New World*
SEE ALSO: *Giant; The Misfits; There Will Be Blood*

129/500

★★★

Director: Ken Russell
Screenwriter: Ken Russell

Produced by: Ken Russell and Robert H. Solo
Starring: Vanessa Redgrave and Oliver Reed
Released by: Warner Brothers (VHS only)

8+

THE DEVILS

1971, 111 mins.

Plot: In seventeenth-century France, the town of Loudon holds out against the Catholic authorities, led by enlightened, fornicating priest Urbain Grandier. He has also aroused a firestorm of lust amongst the repressed local nuns, and with so many women scorned he is accused of witchcraft. A victim of politics, jealousy, and vengeance, his martyrdom is long and painful.

Review: Discordant, chaotic, apocalyptic, this is a sprawling canvas of sex and death. Full of wild, nightmarish imagery in puritanical black and whites, Russell creates a Hieronymus Bosch painting on celluloid, providing the perfect battleground for religious frenzy's champion, Vanessa Redrgave's twisted Sister Jeanne, and the model of enlightenment: the philosophical, world-weary priest brilliantly portrayed by Oliver Reed.

FURTHER VIEWING: ***Women in Love; Tommy; Altered States; Gothic; The Rainbow***
SEE ALSO: ***The Name of the Rose; Witchfinder General; Black Narcissus; Dark Habits; The Crucible***

130/500

★★★★

Director: Nicolas Roeg
Screenwriters: Alan Scott and Chris Bryant

Produced by: Anthony B. Unger, Frederick Muller, and Peter Katz

Starring: Julie Christie, Donald Sutherland, and Hilary Mason
Released by: Paramount (DVD)

15+

DON'T LOOK NOW

1974, 100 mins.

Plot: Based on a short story by Daphne du Maurier. After his daughter drowns in a freak accident at home, John Baxter is asked to restore a church in Venice, and he and his wife Laura take the opportunity to get away from the scene of the tragedy and repair their strained marriage. But leaving the country only seems to bring them closer to their daughter's death, as John begins to see apparitions of his daughter, and Laura falls in with an alleged psychic who claims to be in contact with her as well.

Review: *Don't Look Now* is built on a solid platform of psychological terror and mystery, but at the time of its release it was most famous for its graphic nude love scene between the two leads, played by Donald Sutherland and Julie Christie. These days the film's intensely creepy imagery of the little girl in the red coat is most often paid homage. An excellent ghost story.

FURTHER VIEWING: ***Performance; Walkabout***
SEE ALSO: ***Rosemary's Baby; The Changeling; Full Circle (The Haunting of Julia)***

031
500

★★★★

Director: Ridley Scott
Screenwriter: Gerald Vaughan-Hughes
Produced by: David Puttnam and Ivor Powell
Starring: Keith Carradine and Harvey Keitel
Released by: Paramount (DVD)

12+

THE DUELLISTS

1977, 100 mins.

Plot: Armand d'Hubert and Gabriel Féraud are French Hussars in the time of the Napoleonic Wars. Due to a minor misunderstanding Féraud begins to pursue d'Hubert and demand the two duel, a quest for satisfaction that lasts decades and becomes increasingly bitter and obsessive on Féraud's part. They fight several duels during this time, each wounding the other but never fatally. Finally, at a time when neither even remembers what started the feud, they meet at dawn for the last time

Review: *The Duellists* is based on a supposedly true short story by Joseph Conrad ("The Duel") and is Ridley Scott's feature-film debut as a director. With beautiful cinematography and an almost anal devotion to historical accuracy in costume and military convention, this will please history buffs and film fans alike.

FURTHER VIEWING: ***1492: Conquest of Paradise; Gladiator***
SEE ALSO: ***Barry Lyndon; The Adventures of Gerard***

032
500

★★★

Director: Todd Haynes
Screenwriter: Todd Haynes
Produced by: Jody Patton
Starring: Julianne Moore, Dennis Quaid, and Dennis Haysbert
Released by: Universal Studios (DVD)

FAR FROM HEAVEN

2002, 107 mins.

Plot: Set in the 1950s, the underbelly of society is exposed for its racist and homophobic tendencies when suburban housewife Cathy Whitaker (Julianne Moore) discovers that her husband is homosexual. She seeks solace in the arms of her gardener's son, a black man known as Raymond, much to the disgust of her neighbors.

Review: Haynes based the film's hauntingly accurate style on the 1950s melodramas of Douglas Sirk, whose films, while not popularly received in their own era, have since become widely recognized as classics for their cutting irony. Building on this, the concerns of prudish small-town America are discussed in a sensitive and modernistic manner that hasn't been attempted before on film.

FURTHER VIEWING: ***Safe; I'm Not There***
SEE ALSO: ***To Kill a Mockingbird; My Own Private Idaho***

★★★★

Director: Bob Rafelson
Screenwriters: Bob Rafelson and Carole Eastman

Produced by: Bob Rafelson, Bert Schneider, Harold Schneider, and Richard Wechsler

Starring: Jack Nicholson and Karen Black
Released by: Sony Pictures (DVD)

15+

FIVE EASY PIECES

1970, 98 mins.

Plot: Bobby Dupea was once a child prodigy from a family of classical musicians who now works on an oil rig. He leads an unremarkable life, drinking, gambling, and cheating on his not-very-bright waitress girlfriend, who becomes pregnant. When Bobby hears that his father is gravely ill, he makes the trip to the family compound to reconcile with his family.

Review: Before Jack Nicholson became a cultural icon and content to just play himself (or his persona) in films, he gave this incredibly subtle, nuanced performance as Bobby, hinting at a deep-seated vulnerability and almost defying the audience not to empathize with this thoroughly unlikable character. While *Five Easy Pieces* is most famous for its "chicken salad" scene, it's the quieter moments—deftly handled by Rafelson—that form the heart and soul of this picture.

FURTHER VIEWING: ***The Postman Always Rings Twice; The King of Marvin Gardens***
SEE ALSO: ***King of the Road; Fingers; The Drifter***

034
500

★★★

Director: Michael Haneke
Screenwriter: Michael Haneke
Produced by: Veit Heiduschka
Starring: Susanne Lothar, Ulrich Mühe, Arno Frisch, and Frank Giering
Released by: Kino Video (DVD)

18+

FUNNY GAMES

1998, 108 mins.

Plot: A middle-class German family arrive at their Austrian lake house and are introduced to amicable young men Peter and Paul. What starts out as an innocent family holiday and a new friendship quickly descends into nightmare when Peter and Paul take the family hostage and force them to play torturous games in order to stay alive.

Review: *Funny Games* isn't as graphically violent as most horror films, but it's certainly one of the most disturbing ever made. Visceral in its execution, this is not a film for the faint of heart, as it forces the viewer to become complicit with the violence on-screen; Haneke deftly manipulates you while he demonstrates how film violence in general is manipulative. And that isn't very funny at all, but it is a game of sorts, and it can be a rewarding one.

FURTHER VIEWING: ***Funny Games (U.S. remake); Benny's Video; Time of the Wolf***
SEE ALSO: ***A Clockwork Orange; Henry: Portrait of a Serial Killer; The Strangers***

035
500

★★★★

Director: Joseph L. Mankiewicz
Screenwriter: Philip Dunne
Produced by: Fred Kohlmar
Starring: Gene Tierney and Rex Harrison
Released by: Twentieth Century Fox (DVD)

A

THE GHOST AND MRS. MUIR

1947, 104 mins.

Plot: England, 1900: young widow Lucy Muir rents a seaside cottage despite rumors that it's haunted, and moves in with her daughter and maid. But the former owner, Daniel Gregg, hasn't left yet, despite having departed the mortal coil. He warms to the ladies and when Lucy's income dries up, he dictates his memoirs to her. They fall in love during the process; when the book becomes a bestseller she's able to stay in the house, but their hopeless situation presents a difficult decision.

Review: It's near impossible to describe how beautiful Gene Tierney is, and more so not to fall in love with her. The chemistry between Tierney and Rex Harrison's gruff sea captain builds perfectly as they both discover what they want might not be what they need. Though this is a funny and deceptively light film, it's also an intense story of unlikely but everlasting love.

FURTHER VIEWING: ***Dragonwyck; The Barefoot Contessa; The Honey Pot***
SEE ALSO: ***The Bishop's Wife; Blithe Spirit; Heaven Can Wait***

036
500

★ ★ ★

Director: John Hillcoat
Screenwriter: Nick Cave
Produced by: Evan English

Starring: David Field, Nick Cave, Dave Mason, and Vincent Gil

Released by: Umbrella Entertainment/ Street Smart Films (Region 4 DVD only)

18+

GHOSTS . . . OF THE CIVIL DEAD

1988, 93 mins.

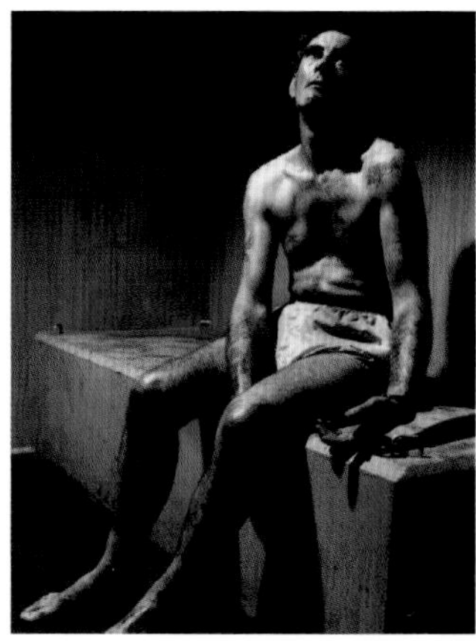

Plot: Set in an Australian outback prison in perpetual lockdown, the corrupt guards allow the inmates a long leash until a series of increasingly violent incidents force them to react. Without drugs, television, and time outside their cells to stretch their legs, tensions escalate to unbearable levels between the inmates. Musician Nick Cave gives a memorable and disturbing performance as Maynard, one of the triggers for the prison's unrest.

Review: Possibly one of the most ominous movies about isolation of the past twenty years, the minimalist sets, blood-spattered walls, and grizzled actors add to the near-constant feeling of impending doom. Cave and two of his Bad Seeds' unsettling drones underpin the slow-building madness on-screen. Chilling, but hard to tear your eyes away from.

FURTHER VIEWING: ***The Proposition; To Have and to Hold***
SEE ALSO: ***Chopper; Natural Born Killers***

037
500

★ ★ ★ ★

Director: Terry Zwigoff
Screenwriters: Terry Zwigoff and Daniel Clowes

Produced by: Barbara A. Hall, Janette Day, John Malkovich, Jonathan Weisgal, and Lianne Halfon

Starring: Thora Birch and Scarlett Johansson
Released by: MGM (DVD)

15+

GHOST WORLD

2001, 111 mins.

Plot: Best friends and high-school outcasts Enid and Rebecca finally graduate, but have no plans for their lives. Initially keeping to their comfortable roles as outsiders tormenting other outsiders, they soon grow apart when Rebecca chooses the path of a normal life. Enid, on the other hand, pursues a budding romance with awkward loner Seymour and learns that her anti-social behavior has an unpleasant knock-on effect.

Review: Nominated for an Academy Award for Best Adapted Screenplay (from Daniel Clowes' comic of the same name), *Ghost World* is a quirky, quiet drama about the trials and tribulations of non-conformity. Thora Birch won a well-deserved Golden Globe for her portrayal of the lost Enid; this is also the film that launched Scarlett Johansson's career.

FURTHER VIEWING: ***Crumb; Art School Confidential***
SEE ALSO: ***Welcome to the Dollhouse; Heathers***

038
500

★★

Director: Jack Cardiff
Screenwriters: Jack Cardiff, Ronald Duncan, and Gillian Freeman
Produced by: William Sassoon
Starring: Marianne Faithfull, Alain Delon, and Roger Mutton
Released by: Anchor Bay (DVD)

15+

GIRL ON A MOTORCYCLE

1968, 91 mins.

Plot: Newly married Rebecca decides to leave her French husband and take a roadtrip across France and Germany on her beloved motorcycle. Rebecca's destination is her lover in Germany, but out on the road, she ponders her relationship with the two men.

Review: While there's not much plot to speak of, this is actually more of a trip, metaphysically and chemically, through Rebecca's mind as, through freaked-out flashbacks, she deconstructs her life—particularly her sex life. And while there's a fetishist fascination with Faithfull's Rebecca, her catsuit, and the gorgeous Harley Super Glide she covets as much as the filmmakers covet her, this is more about encapsulating the sixties spirit of free love, free spirit, and the freedom of the road.

FURTHER VIEWING: ***Sons and Lovers; My Geisha; Penny Gold***
SEE ALSO: ***Easy Rider; The Wild Angels***

039
500

★

Director: Edward D. Wood, Jr.
Screenwriter: Edward D. Wood Jr.
Produced by: George Weiss
Starring: Bela Lugosi, Lyle Talbot, and Timothy Farrell
Released by: Image Entertainment (DVD)

15+

GLEN OR GLENDA

1953, 65 mins.

Plot: Inspector Warren finds the corpse of a transvestite and, wanting to know more about this aberrant behavior, speaks to Dr. Alton. Dr. Alton tells him the story of Glen/Glenda, a man who loved girls' sports and clothing as a boy; when he grew older he married, but his relationship suffered because of his secret transvestism. He then narrates the story of Alan/Anne, a transsexual.

Review: *Glen or Glenda* is in direct competition with *Plan 9 from Outer Space* for the Worst Film Ever Made award. It's a complete failure technically and doesn't have much to offer in the way of artistic merit, either. So why watch it? Because it's funny. It's not meant to be, but it is truly laugh-out-loud hilarious, with its stilted dialog, terrible sound, excremental acting, and incompetent direction.

FURTHER VIEWING: ***Plan 9 from Outer Space; Ed Wood; "Necromania": A Tale of Weird Love!; Ed Wood: Look Back in Angora***
SEE ALSO: ***The Christine Jorgensen Story; Let Me Die a Woman***

040
500

★★

Director: David Mamet
Screenwriter: David Mamet
Produced by: Michael Hausman
Starring: Lindsay Crouse and Joe Mantegna
Released by: MGM (DVD)

15+

HOUSE OF GAMES

1987, 102 mins.

Plot: Psychologist Margaret Ford (Lindsay Crouse), high off the success of her bestselling self-help book, is told by a patient that he owes $25,000 to a bookie and he'll be killed if he doesn't pay. Margaret confronts the bookie; he turns out to be a con man, and Margaret decides to use him and his activities as the subject of her next book. She finds herself drawn into an underworld of deception, thinking she can find the truth only to become the willing victim of lies.

Review: Though watching Lindsay Crouse act is often like witnessing a shoebox with eye holes attempt a range of human emotion, David Mamet's directorial debut provides enough plot twists as the story, and Margaret, unravel to keep you interested.

FURTHER VIEWING: ***Homicide; The Spanish Prisoner***
SEE ALSO: ***The Grifters***

041
500

★★★★★

Director: Robert Aldrich
Screenwriters: Henry Farrell and Lukas Heller
Produced by: Robert Aldrich
Starring: Bette Davis and Olivia de Havilland
Released by: Twentieth Century Fox (DVD)

15+

HUSH . . . HUSH, SWEET CHARLOTTE

1964, 132 mins.

Plot: In 1927, Charlotte's married lover is found decapitated, and though the murderer's identity is never revealed, Charlotte appears with her dress soaked in blood. Fast forward to 1964, and Charlotte is an "eccentric," wealthy old recluse fighting the government as they try to bulldoze her home for a highway. She invites her poor cousin Miriam to stay and aid the fight, but Miriam has an agenda: drive Charlotte insane and take her money.

Review: They just don't make roles like this for older actresses anymore. Though a bit of an overwrought Southern Gothic at times, this film benefits from some real star power giving exceptional performances: Bette Davis as Charlotte, Olivia de Havilland as Miriam, and Agnes Moorhead, nominated for an Oscar and a Golden Globe, as Charlotte's long-suffering but loyal maid.

FURTHER VIEWING: ***What Ever Happened to Baby Jane?; The Killing of Sister George***
SEE ALSO: ***All About Eve; Dead Ringer; What Ever Happened to Aunt Alice?***

042
500

★★★★★

Director: Elem Klimov
Screenwriter: Ales Adamovich
Produced by: Not Available

Starring: Aleksei Kravchenko, Olga Mironova, and Liubomiras Lauciavicius
Released by: Kino Video (DVD)

15+

IDI I SMOTRI (COME AND SEE)

1985, 146 mins.

Plot: Floyra discovers a rifle near his home and soon enrolls in Russia's bitter war against Nazi Germany. Left behind at a troop gathering, he meets up with the beautiful but damaged Glasha. After a sudden bomb attack where Floyra is left deaf, they decide to return to his nearby village. The reality of war begins to sink in, and Florya becomes a witness of, rather than a participant in, the atrocities of human nature.

Review: Filmed with Steadicam, the viewer is tugged gently against their will into a child's nightmare. The final thirty minutes are possibly the most harrowing war scenes committed to celluloid, where SS officers storm a village, lock the childless locals inside a barn, and burn it to the ground. An atmospheric masterpiece of tension and horror.

FURTHER VIEWING: ***Larisa; Agoniya (Agony)***
SEE ALSO: ***Ivan's Childhood; Cross of Iron***

043
500

★★★★

Director: Neil LaBute
Screenwriter: Neil LaBute
Produced by: Mark Archer and Stephen Pevner

Starring: Aaron Eckhart, Stacy Edwards, and Matt Malloy
Released by: Columbia Tristar Home Video (DVD)

18+

IN THE COMPANY OF MEN

1997, 97 mins.

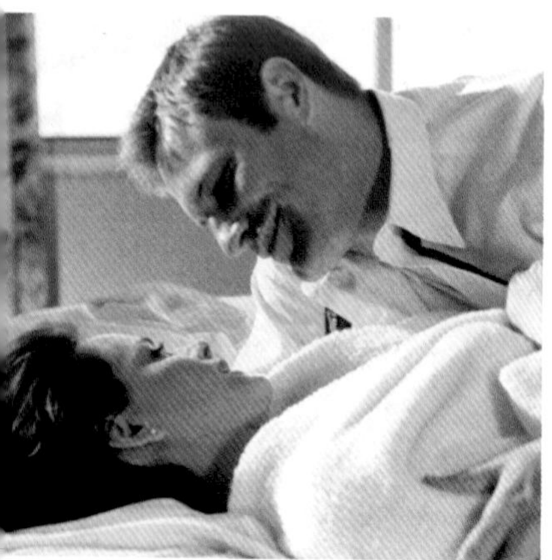

Plot: Two executives, bitter victims of woman trouble, decide to take revenge. They plan to simultaneously court the same girl then, once hooked, both dump her at the same time, leaving her emotionally shattered. They choose a self-conscious deaf secretary and the plan works swimmingly until one of the men falls for her.

Review: This is *not* a date movie. It's a treatise on misogyny in office politics, exemplified by the two leads: Eckhart's Chad, all charming veneer over vile innards, and Mally's Howard, gutless and dithering. What makes it worse is they're so utterly believable, making for depressing viewing despite the excellence of the acting and script. At its black heart this is a comedy, but the laughs are of the horrified, ironic kind.

FURTHER VIEWING: ***Nurse Betty; Your Friends and Neighbors; Possession; The Wicker Man (2006)***
SEE ALSO: ***American Psycho; Dangerous Liaisons; How to Lose a Man in 10 Days***

044/500

★★★★

Director: Larry Clark
Screenwriter: Harmony Korine
Produced by: Cary Woods
Starring: Leo Fitzpatrick, Justin Pierce, and Chloë Sevigny
Released by: Vidmark/Trimark (DVD)

KIDS

1995, 91 mins.

Plot: Too young to vote, but old enough to have unprotected sex and take drugs, a pack of teenage skater boyz roam the streets of New York, untroubled by parents, teachers, or any other form of authority. At their head is Telly, an HIV-positive specialist virgin deflowerer now on the hunt for his latest prepubescent victim.

Review: Flavored almost like a brilliant wildlife documentary on a feral mob of sexual predators, there's something squirmingly uncomfortable about watching their exploits being displayed so uncompromisingly. The boys are unpleasant braggarts, loud mouthed, sexually ruthless—typical teenagers really. The girls are generally more conscientious and, at the end, take a subtle, ironic vengeance on the main offenders.

FURTHER VIEWING: ***Another Day in Paradise; Bully; Ken Park***
SEE ALSO: ***Welcome to the Dollhouse; Flirting; The Warriors; Storytelling***

045/500

★★★

Director: Robert Aldrich
Screenwriter: Lukas Heller
Produced by: Robert Aldrich
Starring: Beryl Reid and Susannah York
Released by: Anchor Bay (DVD)

THE KILLING OF SISTER GEORGE

1968, 138 mins.

Plot: June Buckridge leads a schizophrenic life; her career is voicing charming Sister George in a soap opera, but in reality she is a bluff alcoholic and abusive to Alice, the innocent, dim girl she lives with. June discovers Sister George is to be "killed off" and begins to spiral out of control, not helped by the arrival in her life of aggressive TV producer, Mercy.

Review: Not exactly a subtle discussion on lesbianism, which it was never meant to be, it is however a wonderfully histrionic drawing-room comedy. It's aided and abetted by Beryl Reid's June, brilliantly tearing up the place as she tries to hide her inadequacies with scorching cynicism and booze. The result is an amusingly gothic melodrama that descends from pithy to sad to tragically moving.

FURTHER VIEWING: ***Flight of the Phoenix; The Dirty Dozen; Kiss Me Deadly; What Ever Happened to Baby Jane?***
SEE ALSO: ***The Haunting***

046
500

★★★★

Director: Preston Sturges
Screenwriters: Preston Sturges and Monckton Hoffe

Produced by: Albert Lewin, Buddy G. DeSylva, and Paul Jones

Starring: Barbara Stanwyck, Henry Fonda, and Charles Coburn
Released by: Criterion (DVD)

A

THE LADY EVE

1941, 94 mins.

Plot: Beautiful con artist Jean Harrington and her equally lawless father set their sights on robbing shy millionaire Charles Pike of his money. But Jean breaks the cardinal rule of conning and falls for the mark. She tries to keep Charles away from her scheming father, but when Charles finds out her true identity, he dumps her. Not one to back away, Jean poses as an English heiress and forces her way back into Charles' life, intent on having him for her own.

Review: Barbara Stanwyck was the perfect choice to play Jean Harrington in this screwball comedy; she has a genius for comedic timing, and she is undeniably alluring, but she also has a strong enough personality to be entirely convincing in a film featuring gender reversal (especially one made in the forties). Henry Fonda is her perfect foil as the hapless, naive Charles, and their outrageous love story makes fun and fanciful viewing.

FURTHER VIEWING: ***Sullivan's Travels; The Great McGinty; Christmas in July***
SEE ALSO: ***Bringing Up Baby; The Birds and the Bees***

047
500

★★★

Director: Jean-Luc Godard
Screenwriter: Jean-Luc Godard

Produced by: Georges de Beauregard, Carlo Ponti, and Joseph E. Levine

Starring: Brigitte Bardot, Michel Piccoli, and Jack Palance
Released by: Criterion (DVD)

15+

LE MÉPRIS (CONTEMPT)

1963, 103 mins.

Plot: Paul Javal is invited to commercialize a script for Homer's *Odyssey*, being made in Capri by Fritz Lang with American funding. While the money is good, Paul is having trouble balancing artistic integrity with financial security—and also having to contend with a marriage crashing onto the rocks. Marital bliss is not helped when he leaves his gorgeous wife alone with the movie's brash playboy producer.

Review: A touch semi-autobiographical and paralleling the book within the movie, Godard proved that Bridget Bardot was more than just a pretty face. It's also a scathingly cynical demystification of the movie industry, expressed perfectly by Jack Palance's flashy, vulgar producer, but a beautiful assault at that, with fine use of long takes, montages, and gorgeous cinematography.

FURTHER VIEWING: ***Alphaville; Breathless; Pierrot le fou; Week End; Amore e rabbia (Love and Anger); Passion; King Lear***
SEE ALSO: ***Bullets over Broadway; The Producers; Hearts of Darkness: A Filmmaker's Apocalypse***

048
500

★★★★

Director: Bob Fosse
Screenwriter: Julian Barry
Produced by: Marvin Worth
Starring: Dustin Hoffman and Valerie Perrine
Released by: MGM (DVD)

18+ LENNY

1974, 111 mins.

Plot: A fresh-faced Dustin Hoffman plays acerbic comedian Lenny Bruce in a moving biopic of his life and career, which ended tragically early after he was hounded through the courts for public obscenity. Haunting and unique, it charts his rise through the small clubs in the 1950s to his eventual death by overdose in 1966, and all the foul-mouthed words in between.

Review: Intercutting between the events of Bruce's life and his stage act (all played expertly by Hoffman), Fosse's drama, shot entirely in black and white, was nominated for no fewer than six Oscars despite being nihilistic and utterly depressing. The recreations of his act are spot on, and Valerie Perrine's performance as Bruce's troubled wife is also of merit.

FURTHER VIEWING: ***Star 80; Cabaret***
SEE ALSO: ***King of Comedy; The Graduate***

049
500

★★

Director: Bertrand Blier
Screenwriters: Betrand Blier and Philippe Dumarçay
Produced by: Paul Claudon
Starring: Gérard Depardieu and Patrick Dewaere
Released by: Starz/Anchor Bay (DVD)

18+ LES VALSEUSES (GOING PLACES)

1974, 117 mins.

Plot: Driven by the most basic desires—sex and money—two lowlife, smart-mouth Casanovas bum around a miserable suburban sprawl trying to find ways to entertain themselves. The result is a series of criminal and sexual misadventures, both comic and dark.

Review: This is a simple immorality "bromance" of two young men who are still just boys at heart. The two leads shift between innocently charming and unpleasantly sleazy, especially Depardieu—the brains of the outfit on a Quixotic quest for simple pleasures. Despite their darker tendencies, the drive behind them is, however, a friendship that's sweet and touchingly realized.

FURTHER VIEWING: ***Hitler, connais pas (Hitler—Never Heard of Him); Un, deux, trios, soleil (One, Two, Three, Sun); Trop belle pour toi (Too Beautiful for You); Combien tu m'aimes? (How Much Do You Love Me?); Jean de Florette; Cyranno de Bergerac***
SEE ALSO: ***A Room for Romeo Brass; Butch Cassidy and the Sundance Kid***

050
500

★★★

Director: Paul Schrader
Screenwriter: Paul Schrader
Produced by: Linda Reisman

Starring: Willem Dafoe and Susan Sarandon
Released by: Lionsgate (DVD)

15+

LIGHT SLEEPER

1992, 103 mins.

Plot: John LeTour is an ex-addict who runs drugs to rich clients in return for a steady wage. His boss, the sultry Ann (played by Susan Sarandon), is worried about his mental health and his effectiveness as a courier—he works only at night, nerves frazzled and deeply conflicted about his role in life. Hooking up with his old lover who's still using complicates things even more.

Review: Considered by the director to be the third in a trilogy of films about the isolated man (the others being *Taxi Driver* and *American Gigolo*), Willem Dafoe gives an extraordinary performance as the sleep-deprived LeTour, a walking contradiction. The film's unpredictability makes it such a compelling hidden gem.

FURTHER VIEWING: ***American Gigolo; The Comfort of Strangers***
SEE ALSO: ***Taxi Driver; Raging Bull***

051
500

★★★★

Director: Stanley Kubrick
Screenwriter: Stanley Kubrick and Vladimir Nobokov

Produced by: Eliot Hyman and James B. Harris

Starring: James Mason, Shelley Winters, and Sue Lyon
Released by: Warner Home Video (DVD)

15+

LOLITA

1962, 152 mins.

Plot: Based on Vladimir Nabokov's controversial novel of the same name, *Lolita* follows British professor Humbert Humbert on his move to a new job in Ohio where he meets desperate widow Charlotte. Humbert isn't interested, but when Charlotte's flirtatious fourteen-year-old daughter enters the picture, he falls in love with her and courts her mother to be near her. After he and Charlotte are married, Charlotte discovers his passion for her daughter, and in a fit of rage runs into the street, is hit by a car, and dies. Humbert is now free to make Lolita his, but these kinds of obsessions never end well, do they?

Review: "How did they ever make a movie of *Lolita*?" asks the original trailer. With quite a bit of censorship, apparently. Due to this, many of the sexual aspects of Humbert and Lolita's relationship were only hinted at, and Kubrick's influence meant that Nabokov's screenplay was radically changed. As such, *Lolita* is more valuable as a character study than an adaptation.

FURTHER VIEWING: ***Eyes Wide Shut; Lolita (1997)***
SEE ALSO: ***American Beauty; Baby Doll; Pretty Baby***

★★★

Director: Tony Richardson
Screenwriter: Alan Sillitoe
Produced by: Tony Richardson
Starring: Tom Courtenay and Michael Redgrave
Released by: Warner Home Video (DVD)

12+

THE LONELINESS OF THE LONG DISTANCE RUNNER

1962, 104 mins.

Plot: Colin, a young British upstart, is sent to reform school after breaking into a bakery to steal money. The head of the school (Michael Redgrave) believes that he can channel the youth's anger into sport, particularly running, as a way of reform and positive change. Through a series of moving flashbacks, we experience Colin's life and history as he did. In an important race for the institution, he commits the ultimate act of defiance against the powers that be.

Review: Richardson's bleak look at social change in England during the 1960s is still relevant today and is one of the most significant films to emerge from the British New Wave of that period. As Anti-Hollywood as they come.

FURTHER VIEWING: ***Look Back in Anger; A Taste of Honey***
SEE ALSO: ***This Sporting Life; Scum***

053
500

★★★★

Director: John Cassavetes
Screenwriters: Ted Allan and John Cassavetes
Produced by: Mehahen Golan and Yoram Globus
Starring: Gena Rowlands, John Cassavetes and Diahnne Abbott
Released by: Not Available

15+

LOVE STREAMS

1984, 141 mins.

Plot: Robert and his sister Sarah are both deeply troubled. He is an irresponsible, womanizing writer who can't take care of himself, let alone his son. Sarah is highly strung to the point of nervous breakdown, and has driven her daughter into the arms of her ex-husband. Alone in the world; they must turn to each other for solace.

Review: A great character study by one of the leading lights in American indie cinema, Cassavetes uses all his innovative filmmaking techniques, directing, and acting skills to bring to life the two central characters in a powerfully naturalistic way. He's aided greatly by his marriage to co-star Gena Rowlands, which enables them to deliver a plausibly troubled but loving sibling relationship.

FURTHER VIEWING: ***Faces; Husbands; Minnie and Moskowitz; Opening Night; Gloria; A Woman Under the Influence***
SEE ALSO: ***Minnie and Moskowitz; Hope Floats***

054
500

★★★

Director: Alfred Hitchcock
Screenwriter: Jay Presson Allen
Produced by: Alfred Hitchcock
Starring: Tippi Hedren, Sean Connery, and Diane Baker
Released by: Universal Studios (DVD)

15+

MARNIE

1964, 130 mins.

Plot: Kleptomaniac, inveterate liar, and psychologically unstable, Marnie is a nomadic schizoid thief, robbing unsuspecting men blind. But when she steals from handsome Mark Rutland, he becomes fixated on her and she becomes his bride. As he struggles to uncover her deeply troubled past, a grim secret is slowly brought to light.

Review: Another of Hitchcock's cold, troubled beauties. Tippi Hedren's repressed neurotic quivers with hysteria and loneliness, but as a thief she is calculatingly cold. Hitchcock deftly uses clever camera work and effects, and Connery's amateur zoology, as cues to her damaged psyche. The narrative itself has a strong animal theme—the free-roaming predator trapped as much inside her own head as for her crimes.

FURTHER VIEWING: ***Psycho; Vertigo; The Birds; Frenzy***
SEE ALSO: ***The Grifters***

★
★
★
★

Director: George A. Romero
Screenwriter: George A. Romero
Produced by: Richard P. Rubenstein

Starring: John Amplas, Lincoln Maazel, and Christine Forrest
Released by: Lionsgate (DVD)

8+

MARTIN

1977, 95 mins.

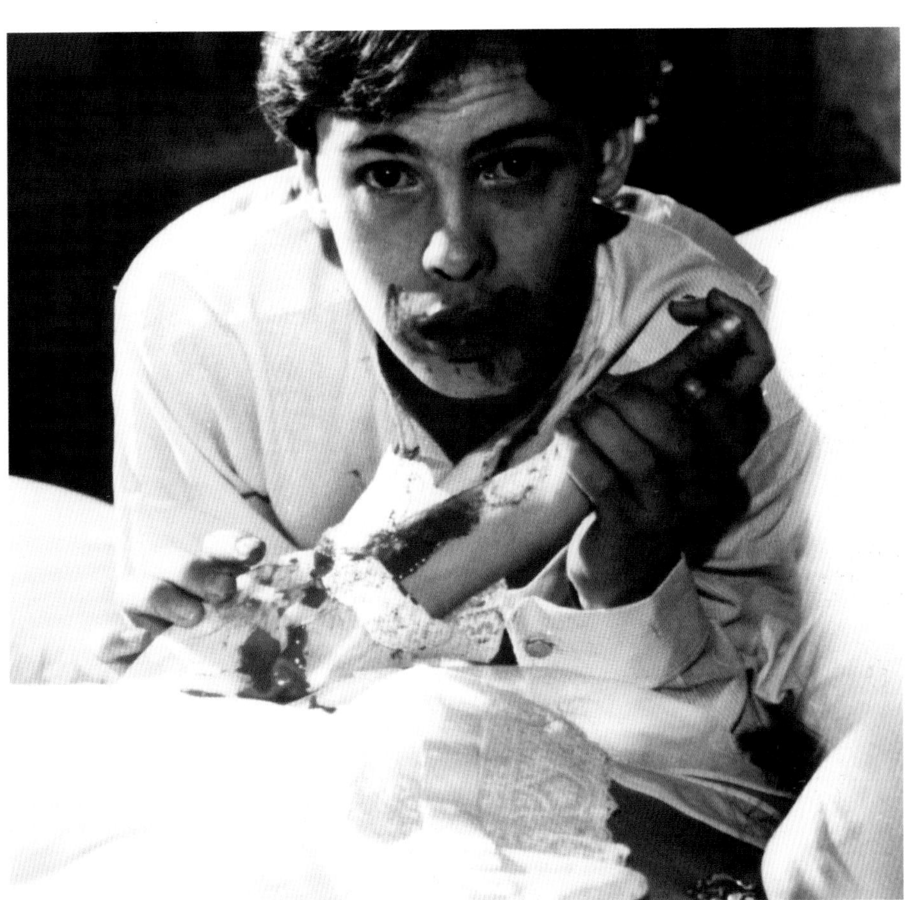

Plot: Seventeen-year-old Martin is not your average teenager: he kills people and drinks their blood. But then he's not your average vampire either: he has no problem tanning, he loves garlic, and he doesn't have fangs; instead, he slashes his victims' wrists.

Review: Romero's original take on the vampire myth poses interesting questions to the viewer: is Martin really an eighty-four-year-old vampire, or is he just a serial killer with a sick mind? But does the distinction matter, since he's a murderer in either case? Or would we look more kindly on Martin if he had the usual romantic vampire aura? This is a thoughtful, unique rendering of one of the twentieth century's most enduring myths. Watch out for Romero's cameo as a local priest.

FURTHER VIEWING: ***Night of the Living Dead; Dawn of the Dead***
SEE ALSO: ***The Hunger; Near Dark; The Addiction***

★★★★

Director: John Schlesinger
Screenwriter: Waldo Salt
Produced by: Jerome Hellman

Starring: Dustin Hoffman, Jon Voight, and Sylvia Miles
Released by: MGM (DVD)

18+

MIDNIGHT COWBOY

1969, 113 mins.

Plot: Naive Texan Joe Buck moves to New York to become a gigolo but has trouble attracting women with his bumpkin ways. He's conned out of some money by small-timer Ratso; after living on the streets for a couple of days, dead broke, Joe finds Ratso again, and Ratso offers to let Joe stay in his squat.

They begin by helping each other earn money through petty crime, but their relationship soon deepens into something more intense and intangible as these two damaged people realize that in this cold and lonely world, at least they have each other.

Review: "I'm walking here!" Winner of an Oscar for Best Picture (the only X-rated film ever to do so) as well as Best Director and Best Adapted Screenplay, *Midnight Cowboy* is, at heart, a love story between social outcasts, and it is more touching and ultimately heartrending than the controversial subject matter would lead you to believe. Essential viewing.

FURTHER VIEWING: ***Far from the Madding Crowd; A Kind of Loving***
SEE ALSO: ***Brokeback Mountain; American Gigolo; The Fisher King***

157/500

★★★

Director: Frank Perry
Screenwriters: Frank Perry, Frank Yablans, Robert Getchell, and Tracy Hotchner

Produced by: David Koontz and Frank Yablans

Starring: Faye Dunaway and Diana Scarwid
Released by: Paramount (DVD)

15+

MOMMIE DEAREST

1981, 129 mins.

Plot: Based on the memoir of Christina Crawford, Joan Crawford's adopted daughter. *Mommie Dearest* chronicles the severe emotional and physical abuse Crawford subjected her daughter to, as well as her increasingly bizarre behavior and floundering career, over an almost forty-year period.

Review: "No wire hangers!" Commercially successful but a critical failure, *Mommie Dearest* is one of those films that was reviled at the time—and mostly still is—but has earned a place as a genuine pop-culture phenomenon. Faye Dunaway received a Razzie for her OTT performance and credits the film for ruining her career, but she looks so like Crawford and is so terrifying as the OCD maniac of Christina's memoir that there is a sort of twisted brilliance lurking beneath the film's "camp classic" status.

FURTHER VIEWING: ***Diary of a Mad Housewife; Play It as It Lays***
SEE ALSO: ***Postcards from the Edge; The Sign of the Ram***

158/500

★★

Director: Russ Meyer
Screenwriter: W. E. Sprague

Produced by: George Costello and Russ Meyer

Starring: John Furlong, Antoinette Cristiani, and Hal Hopper
Released by: Arrow Films (DVD)

18+

MUDHONEY

1965, 92 mins.

Plot: At the height of the Depression, Calif McKinney arrives in the town of Spooner, Missouri. Looking for work, he's hired by local Lute Wade. McKinney is drawn to Wade's beautiful daughter, Hannah. She, however, is married to brutish womanizer Sidney, who is just after her father's money. When Calif becomes a threat to that legacy, he begins plotting against the newcomer.

Review: Though full of Meyer's signature ribald humor and bevy of busty beauties, the director tries for a more subtle path with this movie, edging towards a grittier, more dramatic, less explicit feel. That said, while satirical and with a darker message, this is still great trash cinema, packed with inbred, moonshine-swigging redneck mania.

FURTHER VIEWING: ***Heavenly Bodies!; Faster, Pussycat! Kill! . . . Kill!; Motor Psycho; Supervixens; Up!; Beneath the Valley of the Ultra-Vixens***
SEE ALSO: ***Pink Flamingos; Hairspray***

★★★

Director: Gus Van Sant
Screenwriter: Gus Van Sant
Produced by: Laurie Parker

Starring: River Phoenix and Keanu Reeves
Released by: Criterion (DVD)

15+

MY OWN PRIVATE IDAHO

1991, 104 mins.

Plot: Young hustler Mike Waters has been cruising for a long time, and longs to be reunited with his mother. In his frequent narcoleptic dreams she appears to him, and so with the help of his best friend Scott, who is in line to inherit a fortune from his father, they decide to break out of their current way of life and the gray-skied surroundings by heading to Italy.

Review: Not to be overshadowed by River Phoenix's untimely death two years later, the beautifully shot *Idaho* is a credit to his talent as a young actor. Loosely based on Shakespeare's *Henry IV: Part 1*, it also features some bizarre but creative scenes, such as a bitch session on a newsstand that you'll need to see to understand.

FURTHER VIEWING: ***Drugstore Cowboy; Even Cowgirls Get the Blues***
SEE ALSO: ***Running on Empty; Midnight Cowboy***

060
500

★ **Director:** Samuel Fuller
★ **Screenwriter:** Samuel Fuller
★ **Produced by:** Samuel Fuller

Starring: Constance Towers, Anthony Eisley, and Michael Dante
Released by: Criterion (DVD)

18+

THE NAKED KISS

1964, 91 mins.

Plot: The beginning of the film opens with prostitute Kelly beating her pimp with a handbag and grabbing the money owed to her, then escaping the city on a bus to start a new life. Arriving in a perfect small town called Grantville, she takes a job as a nurse looking after disabled children, and soon falls in love with Korean war veteran Grant, who is concealing a sinister compulsion. Pursued by a cop who knows of her dark past, Kelly's idyllic lifestyle must come to a bitter, violent end.

Review: A trashy psycho-drama with pulp overtones, the film was controversial in its time for tackling the taboo subject of child molestation, which some considered sensationalist. Absorbing, though absurd.

FURTHER VIEWING: ***Shock Corridor; House of Bamboo***
SEE ALSO: ***I Want to Live!; Belle de Jour***

061
500

★ **Director:** Leonard Schrader
★ **Screenwriter:** Leonard Schrader
★ **Produced by:** David Weisman

Starring: Mathilda May and Vincent D'Onofrio
Released by: Warner Home Video (VHS only)

NAKED TANGO

1990, 90 mins.

Plot: After witnessing a woman's suicide on an ocean liner, a woman called Alba adopts her identity to escape her failing marriage. Little does she realize that Stephanie was a mail-order bride bound for Argentina. Forced to work in a brothel, her encounter with the sophisticated gangster Cholo, an expert in the Tango dance style, begins a tempestuous and masochistic relationship that neither can forget.

Review: Schrader's moody period piece looks fabulously decadent, with amazing costume designs, sets, and choreography. The dramatic use of color emphasizes the heat between the two lovers, and Vincent D'Onofrio and Mathilda May play on this tension wonderfully. Difficult to find in any format.

FURTHER VIEWING: ***Kiss of the Spider Woman; Mishima: A Life in Four Chapters***
SEE ALSO: ***Moulin Rouge; Full Metal Jacket***

062
500

★★★★★

Director: William Peter Blatty
Screenwriter: William Peter Blatty
Produced by: William Peter Blatty

Starring: Stacy Keach, Scott Wilson, and Jason Miller
Released by: Warner Home Video (DVD)

15+

THE NINTH CONFIGURATION

1980, 118 mins.

Plot: An Army psychiatrist is sent to a highly experimental mental hospital whose inmates include a bizarre collection of soldiers supposedly suffering from battle fatigue. But while trying to ascertain if they really are ill or faking it to dodge combat in Vietnam, he exposes himself and his patients to all manner of insanity.

Review: With its brooding setting and deranged inmates, Blatty's dark musings on God, guilt, and madness swing between slapstick farce and terrifying intensity. There's also a brilliant performance by Stacy Keach as the psychiatrist whose maniacal philosophical debates with Scott Wilson's broken-down astronaut are at the film's moral center. It provides tangible proof of the old adage: you don't have to be mad to work there, but it helps.

FURTHER VIEWING: ***The Exorcist; The Exorcist III***
SEE ALSO: ***One Flew over the Cuckoo's Nest***

063
500

★★★

Director: Wim Wenders
Screenwriter: Sam Shepard
Produced by: Don Guest

Starring: Harry Dean Stanton, Dean Stockwell, and Nastassja Kinski
Released by: Twentieth Century Fox (DVD)

15+

PARIS, TEXAS

1984, 147 mins.

Plot: A grizzled drifter (Harry Dean Stanton) wanders through the Texas desert, across the broken highways and collapses, speechless, in a border town. His brother (Dean Stockwell) is called, and it transpires he's been missing for four years. His wife is lost to him, and the relationship with his son is non-existent. Resolute, he kidnaps the boy and drives to L.A. to make amends with his estranged wife.

Review: A slow-moving and epic tale of love lost and found, Wenders broke into the mainstream with this art-house flick, with striking cinematography by his longtime collaborator Robby Müller. The final scene where Stanton delivers a heartfelt monologue of what went wrong in his life, expressing his undying love for the mother of his child, is incredible.

FURTHER VIEWING: ***Der Himmel über Berlin (Wings of Desire); The State of Things***
SEE ALSO: ***Five Easy Pieces; Fool for Love***

★★★★

Director: Nicholas Ray
Screenwriters: Nicholas Ray, Irving Shulman, and Stewart Stern
Produced by: David Weisbart
Starring: James Dean and Natalie Wood
Released by: Warner Bros. Pictures (DVD)

A

REBEL WITHOUT A CAUSE

1955, 111 mins.

Plot: After moving to Los Angeles with his parents, Jim Stark enrolls in a new high school and immediately has trouble fitting in. Jim tries to stay out of trouble, but it doesn't help much that his parents are constantly fighting with him caught in the middle. When school tough-guy Buzz challenges Jim to a "Chicken Race," Jim accepts, and Buzz dies due to a wardrobe malfunction. But it takes more than one teen death to effect Jim's reconciliation with his parents.

Review: This is *the* teen rebellion film—all others fade in comparison. Released a month after James Dean's death, *Rebel without a Cause* swiftly became the fight song for kids with parents who just don't understand, man. Nicholas Ray had a marked influence on the French New Wave film-makers, and his expressionistic palette is on full display here, making this film highly watchable despite its sometimes exaggerated parable.

FURTHER VIEWING: ***Johnny Guitar; On Dangerous Ground; Lightning over Water***
SEE ALSO: ***Blackboard Jungle; Cruel Story of Youth; The Delinquents; The Legend of Billie Jean***

065
500

★★★

Director: Louis J. Gasnier
Screenwriters: Arthur Hoerl, Lawrence Meade, and Paul Franklin

Produced by: Dwain Esper, George A. Hirliman, and Samuel Diege

Starring: Dorothy Short, Kenneth Craig, and Lillian Miles
Released by: Motion Picture Ventures (DVD)

12+

REEFER MADNESS

1936, 66 mins.

Plot: Kids smoke pot, become hardcore "addicts," and start killing, raping, having premarital sex, and going insane.

Review: Smoking cigarettes is fine, but smoking "marijuana" cigarettes will turn you into a tweaking murdering rapist addict (which is hilarious considering cocaine was only outlawed in the U.S. twenty years prior to the film). Though it started out as "just say no" propaganda, *Reefer Madness* was quickly discovered by exploitation film producers, and it has since become a camp classic of the era. Like *High School Confidential!*, this morality tale is far too outrageous (and out of touch) to be effective as anything other than pure entertainment. The colorized version especially is a sight to behold with its psychedelic color scheme and Wonderland Caterpillar smoke.

FURTHER VIEWING: ***Reefer Madness: The Movie Musical***
SEE ALSO: ***High School Confidential!; Up in Smoke***

066
500

★★★

Director: Wes Anderson
Screenwriters: Wes Anderson and Owen Wilson

Produced by: Barry Mendel and Paul Shiff
Starring: Jason Schwartzman, Bill Murray, and Olivia Williams

Released by: Criterion (DVD)

15+

RUSHMORE

1998, 89 mins.

Plot: Max Fischer is one of Rushmore Academy's most industrious students; his extracurricular activities are second-to-none, but his academic skills are awful and he's threatened with expulsion. He's also fallen in love with a teacher and befriended a steel-mill owner, but Max's complex world becomes even more complicated when the teacher falls for his friend.

Review: Fischer, superbly portrayed by Jason Schwartzman, is a curious fish. You're torn between cheering on his wild plans and wanting to flush his head down the nearest toilet, even if you can't help but admire his zeal. Schwartzman is given outstanding support by Bill Murray's downtrodden steel tycoon and Olivia Williams' ethereal, melancholic teacher, plus some well-crafted storytelling, alive with quirks, charm, and clever humor.

FURTHER VIEWING: ***Bottle Rocket; The Life Aquatic with Steve Zissou; The Royal Tenenbaums; The Darjeeling Limited***
SEE ALSO: ***Dead Poet's Society; Lost in Translation***

067
500

★★★★

Director: Oliver Stone
Screenwriters: Rick Boyle and Oliver Stone
Produced by: Gerald Green and Oliver Stone
Starring: James Woods, James Belushi, and Michael Murphy
Released by: MGM/UA Video (DVD)

18+

SALVADOR

1986, 123 mins.

Plot: Bedraggled war journalist Richard Boyle tries to restore his kudos and career by heading back to El Salvador as civil war prepares to blow the country apart. He discovers, however, that there's no such thing as an impartial observer as he uncovers the horrors of the death squads and the "disappeared."

Review: In this visceral panorama of natural beauty and human misery, director Stone's Vietnam experiences bleed into his brilliant portrayal of El Salvador: same "Red" threat, same corrupt puppet governments—just different continent. Ultimately he, via Wood's career high as the edgy, neurotic journalist whore with a heart of gold, proves that if a reporter cannot be unbiased then neither can a director.

FURTHER VIEWING: ***Platoon; Born on the Fourth of July; JFK; Heaven and Earth; Nixon***
SEE ALSO: ***Welcome to Sarajevo; Videodrome***

068
500

★★★

Director: Joseph Losey
Screenwriter: Harold Pinter
Produced by: Norman Priggen
Starring: Dirk Bogarde, James Fox, and Sarah Miles
Released by: Starz/Anchor Bay (DVD)

15+

THE SERVANT

1963, 112 mins.

Plot: Rich Londoner Tony (James Fox) feels the need for a manservant, so hires Hugo Barrett (Dirk Bogarde) to look after him in his plush house. The amiable Hugo does his best to fulfill his duties to his new master and seems to enjoy his new job until Tony invites girlfriend Susan into the home. Relations become strained, and the addition of a new maid Vera (the sexy and coy Sarah Miles) brings about a role-reversal of class and power—the master becomes the servant.

Review: This class-conscious British drama, shot in black and white, was written by acclaimed playwright Harold Pinter. The slow seduction of Tony by Susan tips the scales and brings about the master's damnation. A fascinating study of ambition and power play.

FURTHER VIEWING: ***The Damned; Accident***
SEE ALSO: ***Performance; The Go-Between***

069
500

★

Director: Paul Verhoeven
Screenwriter: Joe Eszterhas

Produced by: Alan Marshall, Ben Myron, Charles Evans, Lynn Ehrensperger, and Mario Kassar

Starring: Elizabeth Berkley, Kyle MacLachlan, and Gina Gershon
Released by: MGM (DVD)

18+

SHOWGIRLS

1995, 131 mins.

Plot: Sexy Nomi hitchhikes to Vegas and becomes a stripper, then graduates to showgirl and finds out the superficial world of Vegas glamour is . . . well, superficial.

Review: There are bad films of the Ed Wood variety—doomed before the start—and then there's *Showgirls*, a film with high production values and an excellent director that just went horribly, hilariously wrong at a point that can't quite be determined. Was it the casting of Elizabeth Berkley, or could no actress save such an idiotic nonentity of a character? Was it the inclusion of truly terrifying sex scenes (the infamous pool scene, for example), or the decision to feature soft-core porn as a major plot point to begin with? A terrible film, but it can be entertaining if taken with a bucket of salt.

FURTHER VIEWING: ***Basic Instinct***
SEE ALSO: ***I Think I Do; Bound***

070
500

Director: Alex Cox
Screenwriters: Alex Cox and Abbe Wool

Produced by: Eric Fellner
Starring: Gary Oldman and Chloe Webb
Released by: Criterion (DVD)

15+

SID AND NANCY

1986, 112 mins.

Plot: Not exactly a biopic, but based on the tumultuous relationship between notorious Sex Pistol Sid Vicious and groupie Nancy Spungeon.

Review: John Lydon (aka Johnny Rotten) loathes this film, calling it "all too glib, all too easy," but that shouldn't put you off. When not taken as an exact reflection of reality, *Sid and Nancy* pulls no punches in detailing the sweet despair of soulmate love amidst the degradation of drug addiction and the self-destructive nature of the seventies punk scene. Gary Oldman's performance as man-child Vicious is especially fine, and the original soundtrack by the likes of Joe Strummer, The Circle Jerks, and The Pogues is a mix of punk rebellion and sweet flights of fantasy.

FURTHER VIEWING: ***Repo Man; Straight to Hell***
SEE ALSO: ***24 Hour Party People; The Decline of Western Civilization; Drugstore Cowboy***

071/500

★★★★★

Director: Billy Wilder
Screenwriters: Charles Brackett, Billy Wilder, and D. M. Marshman Jr.
Produced by: Charles Brackett
Starring: William Holden, Gloria Swanson, and Erich von Stroheim
Released by: Paramount (DVD)

12+

SUNSET BOULEVARD

1950, 110 mins.

Plot: Joe Gillis, a down-and-out Hollywood writer on the run from the repo men, crosses paths with former silent film star Norma Desmond. Rich, vain, and wholly insane, Norma hires Joe to write her comeback script, a film she hopes will thrust her back into the spotlight and once again garner her the adoration of audiences around the world. The arrangement ends in unrequited passion, returned but denied love, and, ultimately, murder.

Review: Nominated for a host of Academy Awards including Best Picture, it's hard to fault such a well-crafted noir nightmare. Beginning with Joe Gillis' body floating in the pool of a dilapidated mansion, Billy Wilder chronicles the events leading up to that moment by taking the viewer on a journey into the lowest depths of Hollywood psychology—a gripping insight into the perils of superficial stardom that is as poignant now as it was fifty years ago.

FURTHER VIEWING: ***The Apartment; Some Like It Hot; Stalag 17; The Front Page; The Lost Weekend***
SEE ALSO: ***All About Eve; A Star Is Born; Singin' in the Rain***

072/500

★★★★

Director: Alexander Mackendrick
Screenwriters: Ernest Lehman and Clifford Odets
Produced by: James Hill
Starring: Tony Curtis and Burt Lancaster
Released by: MGM/UA (DVD)

THE SWEET SMELL OF SUCCESS

1957, 96 mins.

Plot: Smooth-talking, immoral press agent Sidney finds his career and reputation dumper-bound after incurring the wrath of a powerful gossip columnist. Trying to hustle his way out of trouble by planting smears and insinuations, Sidney begins to question just how far he'll go—or how low he'll sink—to make the big time.

Review: Set when New York was the swinging center of the universe, the city must play second fiddle to the movie's superb leads. The verbal fencing between Curtis and Lancaster sparkles with cynical wit and venom-dripping one-liners, and as they set about their business, shown at its most unsavory and disreputable, you know that no one is walking away from this one unharmed.

FURTHER VIEWING: ***Whisky Galore!; The Man in the White Suit; The Ladykillers; The Guns of Navarone***
SEE ALSO: ***Citizen Kane; Bonfire of the Vanities; The Front Page; L.A. Confidential***

★★★★★

Director: Martin Scorsese
Screenwriter: Paul Schrader
Produced by: Julia Phillips and Michael Phillips
Starring: Robert De Niro and Jodie Foster
Released by: Sony Pictures (DVD)

18+

TAXI DRIVER

1976, 113 mins.

Plot: Travis Bickle is an insomniac loner, and possible Vietnam veteran, who works as a nighttime taxi driver. He meets and attempts to woo beautiful political campaigner Betsy, but he's so socially inept he makes the mistake of taking her to a porn film on their first date. Distraught by this failed romance, Bickle turns to stalking, violence, and vigilantism as an outlet.

Review: *Taxi Driver* is a blistering portrayal of loneliness and alienation, and how an inability to communicate with or relate to one's peers can easily transmute into violence.

Playing the intense, confused Bickle, this is possibly Robert De Niro's finest hour, and Jodie Foster shows a maturity well beyond her years as twelve-year-old prostitute Iris. *Taxi Driver* also finishes with one of the most controversial endings ever filmed; critics are still speculating whether it's a cynical social commentary or pure fantasy from an unreliable narrator.

FURTHER VIEWING: *Goodfellas; Raging Bull; Cape Fear; Bringing Out the Dead*
SEE ALSO: *A Clockwork Orange; Bad Lieutenant; Falling Down*

74/00

★★

Director: Henry Jaglom
Screenwriter: Henry Jaglom
Produced by: Howard Zucker
Starring: Dennis Hopper, Taryn Power, and Dean Stockwell
Released by: Paramount (DVD)

8+

TRACKS

1976, 92 mins.

Plot: An emotionally scarred soldier has returned to the U.S. from Vietnam to escort the body of a friend back home. On a train in California, he encounters a pretty young student, but his efforts at romance are threatened with derailment by his increasingly hallucinogenic combat flashbacks.

Review: An obvious conceit is that this train is as much symbolic as it is literal—a journey to hell. It's testament also to Hopper as an actor that much of the acting and dialog was improvised. He methods his way through deepening paranoia and disturbing hallucinations until the line between reality and flashback is lost. In the end, what's left is a disturbing film on what it means to be a combat veteran.

FURTHER VIEWING: ***A Safe Place; Eating; Venice/Venice; Déjà vu; Apocalypse Now; The Blackout; The Last Detail***
SEE ALSO: ***The Deer Hunter; The Ninth Configuration***

075/500

★★★

Director: Charles Burnett
Screenwriter: Charles Burnett
Produced by: Darin Scott
Starring: Danny Glover and Paul Butler
Released by: BFI Video (DVD Region 2 only)

12+

TO SLEEP WITH ANGER

1990, 102 mins.

Plot: When Southern drifter Harry Mention (Danny Glover) turns up on the doorstep of his old friend Gideon (Paul Butler) to pay a visit, his old friend is too kind to turn him away. Gideon's already-troubled L.A. household is ignited in debate over folklore and faith as their guest claims influence over dark powers that sow the seeds of discontent among the youngsters.

Review: Without resorting to violence or standard plot devices, Harry is able to get under the skins and bring the devil out in a mild-mannered African-American family—however, this is not a horror film in the typical sense. Critically acclaimed and widely regarded as Burnett's best film out of his outstanding career, the escalating rivalry between Glover and Butler is worth the entry price alone.

FURTHER VIEWING: ***Killer of Sheep; My Brother's Wedding***
SEE ALSO: ***The Color Purple; Grand Canyon***

★★★★

Director: Krzysztof Kieślowski
Screenwriters: *(Blue)* Krzysztof Piesiewicz, Krzysztof Kieślowski, Agnieszka Holland, and Edward Zebrowski; *(White + Red)* Krzysztof Piesiewicz and Krzysztof Kieślowski
Produced by: *(Blue + White)* Marin Karmitz; *(Red)* Yvon Crenn
Starring: *(Blue)* Juliette Binoche and Benoît Régent; *(White)* Julie Delpy and Zbigniew Zamachowski; *(Red)* Irène Jacob
Released by: Miramax (DVD)

15+

TROIS COULEURS: BLEU, BLANC, ROUGE

(THREE COLORS TRILOGY)

Blue: 1993, 110 mins./*White*: 1994, 88 mins./*Red*: 1994, 99 mins.

Plot: Based on the colors of the French flag, this triumvirate of films represents the three ideals of the French Revolution: liberty, equality, and fraternity. *Blue* focuses on a young woman's struggles to find emotional liberty through anonymity after the death of her husband and child. *White* is a dark comedy about two immigrant Poles and their plots to gain equality through wealth, power, and revenge. *Red* illustrates fraternity through the increasingly close relationships between various, seemingly unconnected characters.

Review: Kieslowski's trilogy works just as well individually as a tragedy, comedy, and romance, but is best taken as a whole. Using visual cues (such as colored objects coding each film), these films are linked, sometimes in unlikely metaphysical ways. None of the films are overt in their portrayal of their assigned ideals; they are by turns ambiguous and existential, everything you'd expect from scripts as witty as they are moving and intelligent.

FURTHER VIEWING: ***The Decalogue; The Double Life of Véronique***
SEE ALSO: ***8 1/2; La dolce vita; The Unbearable Lightness of Being***

77

★★★

Director: David Lynch
Screenwriters: David Lynch and Robert Engels
Produced by: Francis Bouygues and Gregg Fienberg
Starring: Sheryl Lee, Ray Wise, and Mädchen Amick
Released by: New Line Home Video (DVD)

8+

TWIN PEAKS FIRE WALK WITH ME

1992, 134 mins.

Plot: Who killed Laura Palmer? If you watched the *Twin Peaks* series you already know (sort of), but *Fire Walk with Me* will help you sort out the events immediately preceding her death (possibly).

Review: Following the massive success (and unfortunate decline) of the *Twin Peaks* television series and released just after its cancelation, *Fire Walk with Me* uses the classic Lynch tactics that made the series such a hit: more questions are asked than answered, cryptic information is given in bizarre dream sequences, and everyone's a suspect . . . and a nutcase. Most of the series' cast reprised their roles in the film, adding a nice continuity, but it still bombed at the box office and garnered terrible reviews. Still, it's worthwhile viewing for fans of the series, but those who haven't seen at least season one will be completely lost.

FURTHER VIEWING: ***Blue Velvet; Wild at Heart; Lost Highway; Mulholland Dr.***
SEE ALSO: ***Vanilla Sky; Happy Here and Now***

78

★★★

Director: Edward Dmytryk
Screenwriter: John Fante
Produced by: Charles K. Feldman
Starring: Laurence Harvey, Cupucine, and Jane Fonda
Released by: Sony Pictures (DVD)

5+

WALK ON THE WILD SIDE

1962, 114 mins.

Plot: A scandalous piece of cinematic history from the wrong side of the Hays Code, including what is considered the first "out" woman on the screen, played by Barbara Stanwyck. Starring Laurence Harvey, Cupucine, and Jane Fonda, this racy melodrama follows a bitter love triangle between a madame and one of her employees, and the ex-boyfriend who has been searching for his lost love.

Review: Saul Bass' title sequence with a black cat slinking across the pavement to Elmer Bernstein's brassy score quite neatly sums up what this film is about: trash and territory. Some of Hollywood's biggest names give flat performances, delivering outrageous dialog and over-the-top acting to go with the wooden sets; today it's regarded as a camp classic.

FURTHER VIEWING: ***Hitler's Children; Mirage***
SEE ALSO: ***The Carpetbaggers; The Bramble Bush***

★
★
★

Director: Laslo Benedek
Screenwriter: John Paxton
Produced by: Stanley Kramer

Starring: Marlon Brando, Mary Murphy, and Lee Marvin
Released by: Sony Pictures (DVD)

12+

THE WILD ONE

1953, 79 mins.

Plot: Johnny is the surly but smart leader of a tough California motorcycle gang. Passing through a small town, he falls for a local girl, beautiful but a "square." But his hopes of wooing her are dashed when psychotic gang leader Chino blasts into town, and then the trouble really starts.

Review: The motorcycle movie was, in part, the new western, with bands of outlaws riding into town raising hell, and the leader of the pack was *The Wild One*. This movie was apparently a warning that motorcycle gangs were a threat to the soul of American Youth, but with Brando turned into an icon for a new generation, you have to wonder what actual message the filmmakers were trying to send!

FURTHER VIEWING: ***Death of a Salesman; Bengal Brigade***
SEE ALSO: ***Hell's Angels on Wheels; Mad Max; Rebel without a Cause; Stone***

080

★
★
★
★

Director: John Huston
Screenwriter: Benedict Fitzgerald
Produced by: Kathy Fitzgerald
Starring: Brad Dourif, John Huston, and Harry Dean Stanton
Released by: Criterion (DVD)

15+

WISE BLOOD

1979, 105 mins.

Plot: Discharged from the army for an undisclosed ailment, Hazel Motes returns to his hometown to find it changed for the worse. He establishes an Atheist church—The Church without Christ—and goes door to door to preach, but soon discovers that even preaching the Word of Nothing comes with a heavy price, especially when the Word of God has been established for thousands of years.

Review: Brad Dourif is electric in his second major on-screen role after Billy in *One Flew over the Cuckoo's Nest*. Eccentric, wild-eyed, and steel-jawed, his anti-religious ravings will baffle most, and this film offers up no easy answers. With a memorable supporting cast, including Harry Dean Stanton, it's a weird and wonderful piece of Southern Gothic.

FURTHER VIEWING: ***Victory; Prizzi's Honor***
SEE ALSO: ***Eyes of Laura Mars; Ragtime***

081

★
★
★
★

Director: John Cassavetes
Screenwriter: John Cassavetes
Produced by: Sam Shaw
Starring: Peter Falk and Gena Rowlands
Released by: Geneon (DVD)

15+

A WOMAN UNDER THE INFLUENCE

1974, 146 mins.

Plot: A hardworking blue-collar husband, overbearing and angry, struggles to love his deeply troubled wife as her depression finally boils over into a nervous breakdown. On her release from the hospital, they begin the arduous process of reassembling their fractured marriage—but it's no easy homecoming.

Review: In this single movie, Cassavetes once again proves his mastery of American independent filmmaking with an epic, for want of a better description, kitchen-sink drama. Gena Rowlands' performance as the imploding, high-strung wife is nothing short of incredible, perfectly capturing housewife alienation and mental meltdown in long, unbroken scenes that are exhausting in their intensity. Peter Falk, meanwhile, gives a best-in-career turn as her hard-pressed, bewildered husband trying to keep his family intact.

FURTHER VIEWING: ***Faces; Husbands; Minnie and Moskowitz; The Killing of a Chinese Bookie; Opening Night; Gloria; Love Streams***
SEE ALSO: ***When a Man Loves a Woman***

CHAPTER 2
GRIPPING TALES

"WHY DO YOU GO ON THESE TRIPS WITH ME, ED?"

Dirty cops, unrepentant violence, unbearable tension, and edge-of-your-seat thrills—you'll find all of those here, as well as some beautifully constructed dark horses that have had enormous impact on cult audiences. Early movies from several cult directors fall into this category: both the Coen brothers' and Christopher Nolan's first feature film outings appear. We've also included some older, less-obvious movies in the genre, those that have been largely forgotten (except by their cult audiences, naturally) but have had lasting influence due to their narrative innovations or unflinching treatment of difficult subjects.

GRIPPING TALES

★★★★★

Director: Joel Coen
Screenwriters: Joel Coen and Ethan Coen
Produced by: Ethan Coen

Starring: John Getz, Frances McDormand, and Dan Hedaya
Released by: MGM (DVD)

18+

BLOOD SIMPLE

1985, 99 mins.

Plot: Bar-owner Marty suspects his wife is having an affair with one of his employees. Instead of, say, asking her about it, he skips the formalities of a confrontation and hires private detective Visser to kill both his wife and her lover. Visser gives Marty the classic "I'll take care of it" line, but Visser has his own agenda; after a double-cross and an unexpected murder, the remaining characters must deal with the downward spiral of guilt and fear while covering up evidence of their wrongdoings.

Review: This is Joel and Ethan Coen's directorial debut and a clear sign of greatness to come. Combining elements of mystery, thriller, crime, noir, black comedy, and horror, *Blood Simple* delivers a well-paced build-up to a deeply ironic twist ending that's both surprising and satisfyingly logical.

Before this film, Joel Coen worked as an assistant editor on Sam Raimi's *Evil Dead*; Raimi and the Coen brothers have collaborated frequently since then, writing *Crimewave* (directed by Raimi) and *The Hudsucker Proxy* (directed by Joel Coen) together. This is also Barry Sonnenfeld's first studio film, as cinematographer, and his innovative camera work was almost universally praised by critics. The movie itself received glowing reviews, as well as the Grand Jury Prize at Sundance and nominations for Best Film and Best Cinematography at the Independent Spirit Awards. As one would expect from the Coens, *Blood Simple* is an excellent debut, confident and well constructed.

FURTHER VIEWING: *Fargo; The Man Who Wasn't There*
SEE ALSO: *Double Indemnity; Red Rock West; After Dark, My Sweet*

★★★★★

Director: J. Lee Thompson
Screenwriter: James R. Webb
Produced by: Sy Bartlett

Starring: Gregory Peck, Robert Mitchum, and Polly Bergen
Released by: Universal Studios (DVD)

15+

CAPE FEAR

1962, 105 mins.

Plot: After eight years in prison serving time for rape and assault, Max Cady on his release makes his way straight to Sam Bowden, the prosecutor responsible for his conviction. Cady is determined to mete out his own brand of vengeful justice by raping Bowden's wife and daughter. He first embarks on a campaign of terror, always staying strictly within the law; Bowden tries to move outside the law to take care of Cady, but the tactic backfires on him. Finally, Bowden moves his family to a houseboat off Cape Fear, and when Cady inevitably shows up the resulting showdown is legendary.

Review: Forget the overly obvious 1991 Scorsese remake; the first *Cape Fear* is a nail-biting thriller that subtly explores the nature of guilt and fear, as well as the double-sided coin of good and evil.

No stranger to playing bruisers, Robert Mitchum is menacing with a hint of rough charm as the villainous Max Cady, but he also injects some vulnerability into the character when we find out society won't actually allow him to be anything other than a dumb, working-class ex-con (the scene where the woman picks him up in a bar strictly so she can slum it, and tells him so, gives extra dimension to what could be a garden-variety, one-dimensional villain). Gregory Peck, long-established as a white knight of American cinema, plays the well-to-do Sam Bowden, a socially accepted and respected lawyer, meant to be the foil to Cady's criminal, but in fact is willing to go outside the law at every opportunity in the name of protecting his family. In a sense he becomes just as much of a criminal as Cady when pushed by outside circumstances—it turns out the two have more in common than they'd like to believe.

The ending sequence, when Cady attacks Bowden's family, is one of the scariest ever filmed, despite this being neither horror nor featuring gore of any kind. Hitchcockian in its delivery and ambiguous in its message, *Cape Fear* is one of the greats.

FURTHER VIEWING: *Eye of the Devil (Thirteen); The Evil That Men Do; Death Wish 4: The Crackdown*
SEE ALSO: *The Night of the Hunter; The Stepfather; The Desperate Hours*

★★★★★

Director: John Boorman
Screenwriter: James Dickey
Produced by: John Boorman

Starring: Jon Voight, Burt Reynolds, and Ned Beatty
Released by: Warner Home Video (DVD)

18+

DELIVERANCE

1972, 109 mins.

Plot: Four businessmen from the Atlanta metropolis—"city boys"—take a trip intending to canoe down the Cahulawassee River before it's flooded by a new damn build. Lewis is an experienced outdoorsman and Ed is his less-macho companion on his adventures, but Bobby and Drew don't make a habit of traveling beyond the city limits. While on the river, the two canoes get separated; Bobby and Ed go ashore briefly, and after making a condescending remark to two rifle-wielding locals, Ed is tied up and Bobby is raped. Lewis and Drew come to their rescue (a bit late), but the consequences of their actions prove to be messy to clean, difficult to hide, and a burden to bear.

Review: "I'm gonna make you squeal like a pig!" *Deliverance* has become another one of those films that has invaded pop culture and imbedded many of its classic lines in the popular imagination as cultural reference points. From the beginning scene where Drew (Ronny Cox) plays "Dueling Banjos" with a mute, inbred hillbilly (which won a Grammy for Best Country Instrumental Performance in 1973), you just know something ain't right.

Adapted from the book by poet and novelist James Dickey, *Deliverance* is, at its heart, the story of four urban archetypes playing at being hunter-gatherers for a weekend who discover that, when faced with a real threat by lawless rural people, they have to dig deep down and release their own suppressed primal instincts to survive. This isn't for the faint-hearted, as it taps directly into the unfortunate consequences when modern civilization clashes with an older, more nature-bound way of life, and it turns out that if you rape nature . . . well, nature's going to rape you right back. And make you squeal like a pig in the process. A seminal film of the seventies that hasn't lost its edge.

FURTHER VIEWING: ***Point Blank; The General***
SEE ALSO: ***Man in the Wilderness; Southern Comfort; The River Wild***

★ ★ ★ ★ ★

Director: Don Siegel
Screenwriters: Harry Julian Fink, R. M. Fink, and Dean Riesner
Produced by: Don Siegel
Starring: Clint Eastwood, Harry Guardino, and Reni Santori
Released by: Warner Home Video (DVD)

18+

DIRTY HARRY

1971, 102 mins.

Plot: Harry Callahan is a San Francisco cop tracking a serial killer called "Scorpio." He's given a rookie partner, even though Callahan maintains he needs someone experienced because his partners have a nasty habit of getting themselves injured or killed. Scorpio demands the city pay him $100,000 to end his killing spree—after failed attempts at capture, the city finally agrees and sends Callahan to deliver the ransom. Callahan ends up torturing Scorpio to find the location of a girl he's buried alive, but Scorpio escapes, and the girl is already dead when the cops dig her up. Callahan pursues Scorpio, breaking just about every law and police procedural—and administering his own brand of justice in the process.

Review: "You've got to ask yourself one question: 'Do I feel lucky?' Well, do ya, punk?" Clint Eastwood always cuts an intimidating figure on-screen, and nowhere more so than in *Dirty Harry* as the lone-wolf, outside-the-law title character. This isn't your average renegade cop film, and Harry Callahan is more universally loved than he has a right to be. At the core, he's far-right in his political and social views, but he's also antiauthoritarian, making him a suitable (if ambivalent) anti-hero for hippies and Republicans alike. Roger Ebert may have called the film "fascist," but Callahan is probably Eastwood's most well-known role, which not only defined him as an actor but sparked the creation of an entire subgenre of crime films featuring cynical cops railing against the system. Dirty Harry the character proved so popular, in fact, the film inspired four sequels, all starring Eastwood in the title role. Unlike most film franchises, the *Dirty Harry* sequels, though not attaining the excellence of the first film, are all entertaining and well made (apart from *The Dead Pool*, which is best avoided).

FURTHER VIEWING: *Magnum Force; The Enforcer; Sudden Impact; The Dead Pool*
SEE ALSO: *Bullitt; 10 to Midnight; Walking Tall*

★★★★★

Director: Fritz Lang
Screenwriters: Fritz Lang, Thea von Harbou, Paul Falkenberg, and Adolf Jansen
Produced by: Seymour Nebenzal
Starring: Peter Lorre, Otto Wernicke, and Gustaf Gründgens
Released by: Criterion (DVD)

15+

M

1931, 110 mins.

Plot: Hans Beckert likes children a little too much. Directed to kidnap and kill children by the voices in his head, he has so far escaped detection, but now Inspector Lohmann is on the case and he's using new, cutting-edge forensic techniques such as fingerprinting and handwriting analysis. Lohmann invades the criminal underworld looking for information; this disrupts the criminals' business, so they decide to take the law into their own hands and hunt for Beckert themselves. Through an ingenious network of petty crooks and street beggars, the criminals find him first and put Beckert on trial for his crimes.

Review: *M* is an incredibly disturbing portrait of a serial killer and child predator; it is also Fritz Lang's masterpiece. Minus points, though, for turning Grieg's infectiously energetic "In the Hall of the Mountain King" into a child murderer's theme song.

M was Peter Lorre's first major film role, and it propelled him to Hollywood stardom, although he would often be typecast as the creepy villain (or villainous creep, depending on how you look at it). Allegedly based on the life of serial-killer Peter Kürten, aka the Vampire of Düsseldorf—though Lang never confirmed this—the film delves deep into the darker side of humanity, treating subjects as horrible as child rape and murder delicately but with a shadowed honesty that makes the final effect all the more awful and powerful. *M* is particularly notable for its early use of leitmotif; Lorre frequently whistles "In the Hall of the Mountain King" and the man is rarely present on-screen without the tune to accompany him. In fact, it is the tune that eventually enables the criminal vigilantes to identify him as the killer—this is an all-the-more impressive feat in light of the fact that *M* is Lang's first sound film. An extremely well-made and terrifying early thriller.

FURTHER VIEWING: ***Das Testament des Dr. Mabuse (The Last Will of Dr. Mabuse); Ministry of Fear***
SEE ALSO: ***The Night of the Hunter; The Lodger***

★
★
★
★

Director: Christopher Nolan
Screenwriter: Christopher Nolan
Produced by: Jennifer Todd and Suzanne Todd

Starring: Guy Pearce, Carrie-Anne Moss, and Joe Pantoliano
Released by: Sony Pictures (DVD)

15+

MEMENTO

2000, 113 mins.

Plot: Leonard Shelby developed anterograde amnesia (lack of short-term memory) from a head injury the night his wife was brutally raped and murdered. Leonard killed one of the attackers on the night, and he is attempting to find and avenge himself on the second attacker, despite the fact that he can't remember anything new for more than five minutes. He keeps himself (relatively) functional and focused by writing notes and taking Polaroid pictures, and getting tattoos of vital information. As the story unfolds, we find that not only can Leonard's version of past events not be trusted, but neither can the versions from his so-called friends, who have their own agendas and are willing to take advantage of Leonard's inability to remember the terrible things they do.

Review: This is Christopher Nolan's second feature film, but his first with a Hollywood-style budget (that is, millions instead of thousands). Based on a short story written by his brother, Jonathan, *Memento* utilizes a non-linear narrative technique that Nolan has become famous for. The non-linear narrative is particularly effective in this psychological thriller, as it reflects the way Leonard sees the world and gives the audience insight into his plight. Although primarily used as a narrative tool, scientists have praised *Memento* and its construction as the most realistic portrayal of anterograde amnesia and the nature of memory in general.

Memento has likewise struck a chord with critics, garnering overwhelmingly positive reviews and receiving Academy Award nominations for Best Original Screenplay and, predictably, Best Editing. A fascinating and personal look at memory and retribution.

FURTHER VIEWING: *Following; Insomnia*
SEE ALSO: *Mirage; Shattered; The Bourne Identity*

★★★★★

Director: Michael Curtiz
Screenwriters: Ranald MacDougall, William Faulkner, and Catherine Turney
Produced by: Jerry Wald
Starring: Joan Crawford, Ann Blyth, and Jack Carson
Released by: Warner Home Video (DVD)

12+

MILDRED PIERCE

1945, 111 mins.

Plot: Mildred Pierce divorces her philandering husband and finds she can't provide for her two daughters as she always has. In order to give her eldest, Veda, the luxuries she craves, Mildred takes a job as a waitress (to Veda's disapproval). When Mildred's youngest child dies, leaving her with only selfish, grasping Veda to coax love from, Mildred throws herself into work and opens a restaurant, which soon becomes a chain. Mildred and Veda are now extremely rich, but even though Veda has no problem spending her mother's money, she looks down on her background and profession. Mildred marries a penniless playboy to try to boost her standing in Veda's eyes, but when you spend your life pandering to a self-obsessed teenager, you just have to accept that things are going to go horribly wrong in the end.

Review: This film won Joan Crawford an Academy Award for Best Actress, and it's no wonder: it's difficult to think of a better-rounded or suitably challenging role for an older female in Hollywood. In fact, the female-leading cast is filled with juicy roles, and both Ann Blyth and Eve Arden were nominated for Best Supporting Actress Oscars, in addition to the film's nominations for Best Picture, Best Screenplay Writing, and Best Black-and-White Cinematography (a distinct nod to *Mildred Pierce*'s effective noir aesthetic). As Mildred, Joan Crawford is alternately sympathetic and pathetic; while we understand her desire to give her children the absolute best, her pathological need to impress her unimpressible daughter mystifies (though Crawford's inspired portrayal of Mildred means we're never give a chance to doubt the likelihood of such an unhealthy relationship—it simply is, and we react to it as an absolute). Ann Blyth as well is absolutely villainous, in many ways more terrible than any of her more obvious noir male contemporaries—there are, after all, worse things you can do to a person than just kill them. This is a wonderful film about terrible people doing even worse things to each other. Simply brilliant.

FURTHER VIEWING: ***The Breaking Point***
SEE ALSO: ***Peyton Place; Imitation of Life; The Reckless Moment; The Magnificent Ambersons***

★★★★

Director: Charles Laughton
Screenwriter: James Agee
Produced by: Paul Gregory

Starring: Robert Mitchum, Shelley Winters, and Lillian Gish
Released by: MGM/UA (DVD)

THE NIGHT OF THE HUNTER

1955, 92 mins.

Plot: Harry Powell, a charismatic preacher and serial killer, charms his way into the family of a bank robber in pursuit of the $10,000 he has secretly stashed away. However, its location is known only to the robber's children, leading to a thrilling battle of wits as Powell begins his zealous, murderous crusade to make the cash his own.

Review: Better known for his acting, this was Charles Laughton's one and only directorial effort, and judging by this particular piece, that was a great loss to filmmaking. He delivers a clever, gripping movie crawling with tension, much of it sleazing from Mitchum, who plays the twisted, misogynistic bible thumper Powell. His excellent singing voice, folksy charm, and oily charisma conflict sharply with his bile-spewing monologues, and he's starkly lit in shadow and darkness as though he were the Devil himself—he even rides a pale horse.

There's also something of the fairy tale about the movie; Powell isn't a witch, but he is a monster, a bad wolf in a dog collar, and the way he wheedles himself into Shelley Winters' desperate affections makes for a child's worst nightmare. The narrative even unfolds into a gothic, Deep South Hansel and Gretel, with the children forced to fend for themselves after they're orphaned at Powell's evil hands; that their mother is in a better place is borne out by her almost angelic appearance in death, swaying gently at the bottom of a pond in a flowing white nightgown—a tragic but strangely beautiful image.

The central hub of the movie is Powell's clashes with the astute and suspicious son played by Billy Chaplin, acting way beyond his years. However, their denouement plays very much against type; there's no climactic showdown, just a touching and poignant moment as Powell is arrested, mirroring the earlier capture of the children's father and drawing a similar reaction. His subsequent trial and execution are told almost incidentally to the children's tale finally having its happy ending.

FURTHER VIEWING: *Not available*
SEE ALSO: *Of Mice and Men; A Simple Plan; Silence of the Lambs; Cape Fear*

★★★★

Director: Sam Peckinpah
Screenwriters: David Zelag Goodman and Sam Peckinpah
Produced by: Daniel Melnick
Starring: Dustin Hoffman and Susan George
Released by: Anchor Bay Entertainment (DVD)

18+

STRAW DOGS

1971, 113 mins.

Plot: From an America in the thick of Vietnam War protesting, mathematician David Sumner escapes to his wife Amy's native village in Cornwall, England. Amy, annoyed at her husband's immersion in his work, begins to flirt with the locals doing work on her house, including her former lover. The workmen see David as condescending and Amy as a tease, and out of frustration and resentment they begin to harass the couple, going so far as to kill their cat. Amy urges David to confront the men, but he refuses and tries to make friends instead. The workmen invite him out hunting, but ditch him in order return to the house and sexually assault Amy . . . twice. Amy initially keeps the rapes a secret, but in a bizarre turn of events Amy and David run over the village idiot while driving home—they take the injured man to their house and call into town for help. It turns out the man accidentally strangled someone, so in a drunken vigilante mission the townsmen descend on the couple's house, and David finally grows a pair with disastrous consequences.

Review: This was incredibly controversial on its release, mainly due to the explicit and extended rape scene, as well as character Amy's titillated reaction to it. The film's portrayal of violence—graphic and frequent, including David Sumner's descent from pacifism into murderous rampage—added to some critics' condemnation since they considered it a glorification of violence and a condoning of vigilantism. But many critics saw the film not in favor of violence but rather a neutral exploration of the nature of violence and its relationship to man, questioning whether violent reactions are a natural state hidden only by the thin veneer of society. Regardless, the delivery is raw and disturbing. This is by no means a date movie, but it's intellectually challenging and an excellent piece of filmmaking. Not for the squeamish . . .

FURTHER VIEWING: ***The Wild Bunch; Bring Me the Head of Alfredo Garcia***
SEE ALSO: ***Deliverance; Cape Fear; Southern Comfort; Taxi Driver***

★★★★★

Director: Alfred Hitchcock
Screenwriters: Alec Coppel and Samuel L. Taylor
Produced by: Alfred Hitchcock
Starring: James Stewart, Kim Novak, and Barbara Bel Geddes
Released by: Universal Studios (DVD)

15+

VERTIGO

1958, 128 mins.

Plot: Jimmy Stewart plays James "Scottie" Ferguson, a private detective hired by a college friend to follow his wife, Madeleine, and give some insight into her odd behavior. Scottie agrees and finds that Madeleine is obsessed with her great-grandmother who committed suicide. Madeleine sometimes falls into trances and appears to speak from her great-grandmother's perspective; one day Scottie follows her to the Golden Gate Bridge where she jumps into the bay. Luckily, Scottie is in time to rescue her, and Madeline confesses that she thinks she's going crazy. They travel to a Spanish Mission Madeleine has dreamed about, where she climbs to the roof. Scottie can't follow on account of his fear of heights—he watches Madeleine plummet to her death from a window, and, having fallen in love with her, becomes overwhelmed with feelings of guilt. But the story doesn't end there—when Scottie later meets a woman who is the spitting image of Madeline, the real mystery begins.

Review: Unlike Hitchcock's previous films, *Vertigo* did not do well at the box office and received only lukewarm reviews from critics. This was partly because, as a thriller, the film clocked in at over two hours and contained minute detail that made it slow and difficult to follow. It also differed markedly from Hitchcock's earlier efforts, which were placed more firmly in the romantic-thriller category.

But *Vertigo* was taken out of circulation by Hitchcock in 1973, and when it returned ten years later critics changed their tune and decided it was one of the greatest films of all time. There is still some controversy now over whether the film deserves such accolades, but the fact remains that it has been highly influential, especially on French auteurs of the likes of François Truffaut and Jean-Luc Godard. That said, *Vertigo* is not a "love it or hate it" film; with its masterful direction, brash style, compelling score, and stunning set pieces, everyone will find something to love in it. Whether you agree that it's one of the top ten films ever made is an entirely personal decision with no right answer.

FURTHER VIEWING: *Marnie; Rear Window*
SEE ALSO: *Basic Instinct; Final Analysis; Dead Again; Laura*

092

★★

Director: Patrick Sheane Duncan
Screenwriter: Patrick Sheane Duncan
Produced by: Michael Nolin
Starring: Jonathan Emerson and Nicholas Cascone
Released by: Not Available

18+

84 CHARLIE MOPIC

1989, 95 mins.

Plot: Year, 1969. Vietnam's Central Highlands. A mopic (motion picture) team join an experienced recon team setting out on a mission. They're to make a training film but have no combat experience and are treated with scorn by the vets. Slowly, though, they build a rapport and earn respect—until, one day they come face-to-face with the realities of war.

Review: The world's first TV war gets the mockumentary treatment. Through the mopic's interviews with the team, the movie constructs a microcosm of the Vietnam experience: the boredom tinged with nerve-jangling tension, racism, politics, fraternity, and finally some cleverly executed combat scenes. There's no stirring classic music, no hordes of extras, just the terrible tedium of war.

FURTHER VIEWING: *The Pornographer; Nick of Time; Mr. Holland's Opus; Courage Under Fire*
SEE ALSO: *Dead Presidents; Hamburger Hill; Platoon*

093

★★★

Director: Billy Wilder
Screenwriters: Walter Newman, Lesser Samuels, and Billy Wilder
Produced by: Billy Wilder
Starring: Kirk Dougas, Jan Sterling, and Robert Arthur
Released by: Criterion (DVD)

A

ACE IN THE HOLE

1951, 111 mins.

Plot: An ambitious but tawdry reporter, forced to take a job in a small-town newspaper, thinks his luck has changed when a man is trapped inside a cave by a rock fall. The reporter turns the accident into a national sensation, plotting to milk the story for all it's worth. But then he goes too far and tragedy strikes.

Review: A morality play on unfettered ambition, this movie's cynical take on the manipulation of the press remains as poignant and relevant as ever. However, its central premise—that a single reporter can have so much power over the media—does stretch credibility. What saves the movie is Kirk Douglas' unstintingly honest performance that raises the questions of just how far is too far.

FURTHER VIEWING: *Double Indemnity; The Lost Weekend; Sunset Boulevard; The Seven Year Itch; Some Like It Hot; The Apartment*
SEE ALSO: *All the President's Men; Loophole; Network; Wag the Dog*

★ **Director:** Alan Parker
★ **Screenwriters:** Alan Parker and William Hjortsberg
★

Produced by: Alan Marshall, Andrew G. Vajna, Elliott Kastner, Mario Kassar, and Robert Dattila

Starring: Mickey Rourke, Robert De Niro, and Lisa Bonet
Released by: Lionsgate (DVD)

18+

ANGEL HEART

1987, 113 mins.

Plot: New York City, 1955: the mysterious but well-dressed Louis Cyphre approaches private detective Harry Angel to find Johnny Favorite, a popular singer who was wounded in World War II and treated for severe brain trauma. During his investigation Angel finds Favorite's medical records have been changed, and the people he speaks to keep turning up dead. Down in New Orleans, Angel realizes he's being framed for the murders, and Favorite is a lot closer than he thinks.

Review: Along with its famous twist ending, *Angel Heart* is a successful combination of hard-boiled crime noir and mystical horror. Like putting together a jigsaw puzzle without knowing what the picture should be, the film drops its audience obscure clues throughout its narrative so that we all join in the investigation and are just as surprised as Angel to find out where Favorite is. This film is also a chance to marvel at the former beauty of Mickey Rourke's natural face.

FURTHER VIEWING: *Midnight Express; Mississippi Burning*
SEE ALSO: *Fallen; The Skeleton Key; The Element of Crime*

095
500

★★★★

Director: Martin Donovan
Screenwriters: Martin Donovan and David Koepp
Produced by: Martin Donovan and David Koepp
Starring: Hart Bochner and Colin Firth
Released by: Anchor Bay (DVD)

15+

APARTMENT ZERO

1988, 124 mins.

Plot: In Buenos Aires, handsome, charismatic Jack moves into the apartment of disturbed, sexually confused Adrian. The two become friends, but Adrian is increasingly attracted to Jack, although suspicious of his secretive activities—could he be a serial killer haunting the city? However, his fears are unbalanced by his increasingly unhinged and obsessive desire for Jack.

Review: This is dark territory: obsession, jealousy, psychosis, and sexual repression all seeping from a textured, subtle script with a deeply disturbing climax. Hart Bochner's Jack is seductive, provocative, and dangerously attractive, while Firth gives a very nuanced performance, a battle of wills clearly raging behind his eyes of the confused, pathetic, mother-fixated loner struggling with who and what he is.

FURTHER VIEWING: ***State of Wonder; The White River; Mad at the Moon; The Substitute***
SEE ALSO: ***Bad Influence; Psycho; Repulsion***

096
500

★★★★

Director: John Carpenter
Screenwriter: John Carpenter
Produced by: J. S. Kaplan
Starring: Austin Stoker and Darwin Joston
Released by: Image Entertainment (DVD)

15+

ASSAULT ON PRECINCT 13

1976, 91 mins.

Plot: A Los Angeles gang liberates a cache of automatic weapons, so the LAPD invades their neighborhood and kills six of the gang's members. Swearing revenge, the gang orchestrates a full-on assault on Precinct 13, which is due to be closed down and only running with a skeleton crew. In order to survive until backup arrives, cop-in-temporary-charge Ethan Bishop must join forces with prisoner and convicted murderer Napoleon Wilson.

Review: Though John Carpenter is mostly known as a master of the horror genre, *Assault on Precinct 13* proves he's just as adept at constructing well-paced, suspenseful crime thrillers. But his horror roots do show, as the street gang are dehumanized and portrayed as almost supernatural beings, which only adds to the anxiety. An excellent action film.

FURTHER VIEWING: ***Escape from New York; Escape from L.A.; The Fog***
SEE ALSO: ***Dog Soldiers; The Warriors; The Nest***

197

★★★

Director: James Foley
Screenwriters: Nicholas Kazan and Elliott Lewitt
Produced by: Don Guest and Elliott Lewitt
Starring: Sean Penn, Christopher Walken, and Mary Stuart Masterson
Released by: MGM/UA Video (DVD)

15+

AT CLOSE RANGE

1986, 111 mins.

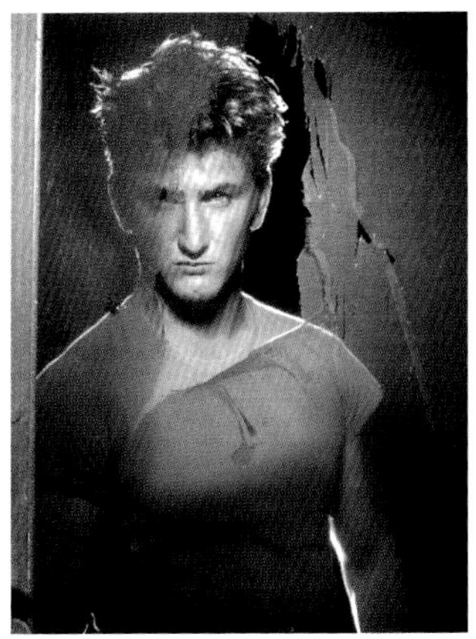

Plot: After joining the criminal organization of Brad Whitewood—local crime lord and his estranged father—Brad Jr. forms a gang of his own. Following an aborted heist, they are arrested, and his father, fearing his son may inform on him, rapes Brad Jr.'s girlfriend as a warning. But the warning goes unheeded and the son seeks revenge on his brutal father.

Review: With its backdrop of small-town angst and dysfunctional family woes, this is also paternal approval gone mad as Sean Penn's troubled son struggles to impress his crime lord father. The resulting clash between the two generations is taut, shocking, and ultimately tragic, and is pulled off superbly by Christopher Walken and Sean Penn, both of them delivering charged performances that make for a savage chemistry.

FURTHER VIEWING: *Who's That Girl; Glengarry Glen Ross; Fear; The Chamber; Confidence*
SEE ALSO: *Goodfellas; King of New York; The Onion Field; Rumble Fish*

198

★★★★

Director: Nicholas Roeg
Screenwriter: Yale Udoff
Produced by: Jeremy Thomas
Starring: Art Garfunkel, Theresa Russell, and Harvey Keitel
Released by: Criterion (DVD)

18+

BAD TIMING

1980, 117 mins.

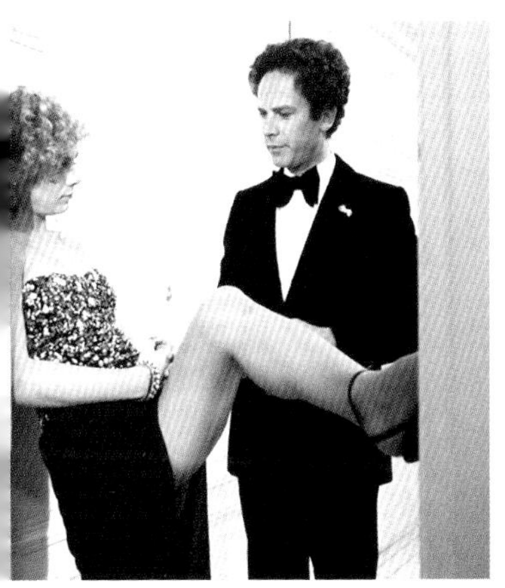

Plot: Cold War Vienna. When a young girl is rushed to the hospital after an apparent overdose, police aren't convinced it's a suicide. The focus of their suspicions is psychoanalyst Alex, who has been conducting a stormy affair with the girl. Soon, a brilliant police inspector is picking his way through the couple's troubled past to wheedle out the truth.

Review: Built around an unpredictable, non-linear structure and some beautifully clever directing, this is the raw end of the relationship spectrum. Theresa Russell has trouble written all over her; magnetic, irrepressible, tragic, it's easy to see the allure for Garfunkel's tightly wrapped, jealous analyst. With its clinical eroticism, the movie is as voyeuristic as its cruel protagonist and just as disturbed.

FURTHER VIEWING: *Performance; Walkabout; Don't Look Now; The Man Who Fell to Earth; Eureka; Insignificance; The Witches*
SEE ALSO: *9 1/2 Weeks; Last Tango in Paris; The Piano*

099/500

★★★

Director: Virginie Despentes
Screenwriters: Virginie Despentes and Coralie Trinh Thi
Produced by: Dominque Chiron
Starring: Karen Lancaume and Raffaëla Anderson
Released by: Remstar Canada (DVD)

18+

BAISE-MOI (RAPE ME)

2000, 77 mins.

Plot: After a chance meeting at a train station, two women head to Paris to escape their violent pasts. Soon, the pair realize that they share the same nihilistic outlook and embark on a campaign of twisted hedonism the likes of which the world has never seen.

Review: With Despentes casting two adult film stars in the lead roles, *Baise-Moi* cleverly blurs the line between pornography and verité filmmaking. It could be argued that the stilted acting and comical violence are contrary to the serious feminist subtext, yet all those involved in the making of this film knew it would spark such a debate. Be prepared for explicit sex, OTT violence, and little else. Not a suitable date movie, by any means.

FURTHER VIEWING: ***Not available***
SEE ALSO: ***Thelma and Louise; Deliverance; Natural Born Killers***

100/500

★★★★

Director: Michelangelo Antonioni
Screenwriters: Michelangelo Antonioni and Tonino Guerra
Produced by: Carlo Ponti
Starring: Vanessa Redgrave, Sarah Miles, and David Hemmings
Released by: Warner Home Video (DVD)

15+

BLOWUP

1966, 107 mins.

Plot: David Hemmings plays a short-tempered and arrogant London fashion photographer who craves a life more interesting than his own. While taking pictures in a local park, he follows and photographs a paranoid Jane (Vanessa Redgrave), who demands he hand over the film. Little does he realize his camera has been witness to a terrible crime.

Review: Winner of 1967's Grand Prix at Cannes, Antonioni's beautifully shot film is a cultural landmark, encapsulating the best and worst of sixties Swinging London. In an iconic performance, Hemmings' morally ambiguous Thomas spends most of the film chasing the unattainable, summarized appropriately by his participation in a mime tennis match at the film's end. An original soundtrack by Herbie Hancock adds to the hip atmosphere.

FURTHER VIEWING: ***Zabriskie Point; The Passenger***
SEE ALSO: ***Performance***

101

★ **Director:** Jennifer Chambers Lynch
Screenwriters: Jennifer Chambers Lynch and Philippe Caland
Produced by: Brigitte Caland, Carl Mazzocone, James R. Schaeffer, Larry Sugar, and Laurel Ayn Selko
Starring: Julian Sands and Sherilyn Fenn
Released by: MGM (DVD)

8+ BOXING HELENA

1993, 107 mins.

Plot: Surgeon Nick Cavanaugh (Julian Sands) becomes obsessed with the beautiful and seductive Helena. He finds her one night after she's involved in a near-fatal hit and run accident; instead of calling an ambulance like a well-adjusted person, he takes her to his mansion and treats her in secret, amputating both her legs. He needlessly amputates both her arms as well to keep her entirely dependent on him, and then she falls in love with him.

Review: It's impossible to review a Julian Sands film without mentioning how terrible an actor he is. But in his defense, this is a pretty terrible film. *Boxing Helena* is the debut feature of David Lynch's daughter, so we would expect it to be a little beyond the norm, but the characters are so maladjusted and the story so unlikely it's difficult to warm to the film. Despite (or because of) being a failure upon its release, it has since developed a cult following.

FURTHER VIEWING: *Surveillance*
SEE ALSO: *The Collector; 9 1/2 Weeks; Woman in the Dunes; Blind Beast*

102

★★★★ **Director:** Michael Haneke
Screenwriter: Michael Haneke
Produced by: Veit Heiduschka
Starring: Daniel Auteuil and Juliette Binoche
Released by: Sony Pictures (DVD)

18+ CACHÉ (HIDDEN)

2005, 117 mins.

Plot: The household of famous TV literary critic Georges Laurent falls apart when surveillance tapes of his home arrive unexpectedly in the mail. As the deliveries of tapes, and later disturbing childlike drawings, become more frequent, Georges suspects they're being sent by someone he wronged in his past.

Review: *Caché* is a tightly plotted and unique experience, shot entirely on HD and without a score. Christian Berger's cinematography deserves a mention for its sheer impact—never before has stillness been used to such unsettling effect as the viewer becomes an active participant in the voyeurism. Haneke weaves together the insecurities of the family into a tight thread before tearing them apart spectacularly with their own secrets—and for Georges, with a single act of violence. Unforgettable cinema.

FURTHER VIEWING: *Funny Games; La Pianiste (The Piano Teacher)*
SEE ALSO: *Lost Highway; Rear Window*

103/500

★★★★

Director: Francis Ford Coppola
Screenwriter: Francis Ford Coppola
Produced by: Francis Ford Coppola

Starring: Gene Hackman and John Cazale
Released by: Paramount (DVD)

15+

THE CONVERSATION

1974, 113 mins.

Plot: Here is a poignant morality tale on the dangers of surveillance: Harry Caul is a paranoid and extremely private surveillance expert working as a private contractor. Though well respected in his profession, he can't get a past job that left three people dead out of his mind, so when he's hired to record a couple's conversation that may implicate them in something illegal, he doesn't turn the tape over to the client. Harry is now on the receiving end of surveillance, and his paranoia runs out of control.

Review: Nominated for Best Picture and Best Original Screenplay Oscars (as well as, appropriately, Best Sound), *The Conversation* is a brilliant exploration of the consequences of society's shift toward an Orwellian "Big Brother" culture. However, through Harry's paranoia, it also considers the other extreme—privacy to the point of isolation—when faced with an increasingly globalized and social existence. Truly frightening stuff.

FURTHER VIEWING: ***The Godfather; The Rainmaker***
SEE ALSO: ***Blowup; Blow Out; Enemy of the State***

104/500

★★★

Directed by Ivan Passer
Screenwriter: Jeffrey Alan Fiskin
Produced by: Paul R. Gurian

Starring: Jeff Bridges and John Heard
Released by: MGM/UA Studios (DVD)

15+

CUTTER'S WAY

1981, 105 mins.

Plot: Two friends—crippled, angry Vietnam veteran Cutter and morally bankrupt playboy Bone—find themselves caught up in a murder conspiracy after Bone witnesses a young girl's body being dumped. Bone is the chief suspect, but the friends believe a local millionaire is the killer and, aided by the girl's sister, set off in pursuit of the truth.

Review: A subtle twist, perhaps, on the revenge thriller, the hunt by Heard's bitter veteran for the tycoon "fat cat" allows him to focus his blind fury on the sort of corrupt greed he believes left him crippled. Heard is brilliant; his alcohol-fueled, abusive diatribes are darkly funny because they hold a bleak truth. However, at its heart, the movie is still a superbly constructed murder mystery that builds to a grim, shattering finale.

FURTHER VIEWING: ***Law and Disorder; Ace Up My Sleeve; Haunted Summer; Pretty Hattie's Baby***
SEE ALSO: ***Blow Up; Chinatown; Disturbia; Eyes Wide Shut; Forrest Gump; Rear Window***

105

★★★★★

Director: Wolfgang Petersen
Screenwriter: Wolfgang Petersen
Produced by: Ortwin Freyemuth and Günter Rohrbach

Starring: Jürgen Prochnow and Herbert Grönemeyer
Released by: Sony Pictures (DVD)

15+

DAS BOOT

1981, 209 mins.

Plot: Autumn, 1941. As the tide turns against the Germans in the Battle of the Atlantic, a U-boat puts to sea from its pen in France to join the fray. The crew is mostly fresh-faced youngsters, but as they battle tedium and unbearable tension, as well as the British, they grow from naïve, green, excited boys into filthy, weary, damaged men.

Review: This is everyday life aboard a U-boat at war; the sub is a claustrophobic's nightmare, groaning with pressure not just from the sea outside but the fear and tension inside. Moreover, nationality is just not important. All that matters is the young men that you grow to care about. And after everything you go through with them, it just makes the ending all the more shattering.

FURTHER VIEWING: *The Perfect Storm; Troy*
SEE ALSO: *The Cruel Sea; In Which We Serve; Run Silent, Run Deep; Crimson Tide*

106

★★★

Director: John Schlesinger
Screenwriter: Waldo Salt
Produced by: Jerome Hellman

Starring: Donald Sutherland, Karen Black, and Burgess Meredith
Released by: Paramount (DVD)

18+

THE DAY OF THE LOCUST

1975, 144 mins.

Plot: In thirties Hollywood, three neighbors—melancholic, lovelorn accountant Homer Simpson; dim but gorgeous "actress" Faye; and Todd, Yale graduate and artist—are drawn deeper into the morally bankrupt, emotionally empty film industry, the whole house of cards crashing down violently at a riotous movie premier.

Review: Boldly lifting the skirt of Hollywood in the thirties, this film sets out to satirize the Technicolor taste of movie glamour. While the cast does a great job with the disparate no-hopers (especially Sutherland's neurotic, morose accountant), the movie is also visually fascinating, peppered with apparently random vignettes ranging from the bizarre to the downright grotesque. Check out, for example, the lizard-staring contest. Of course, it all pales next to the extraordinarily horrifying climax.

FURTHER VIEWING: *Billy Liar; Far From the Madding Crowd; Midnight Cowboy; Marathon Man; The Falcon and the Snowman*
SEE ALSO: *Barton Fink; The Blackout; Blazing Saddles; L.A. Confidential*

107
500

★★★★★

Director: Shane Meadows
Screenwriters: Paddy Considine and Shane Meadows
Produced by: Mark Herbert
Starring: Paddy Considine and Gary Stretch
Released by: Magnolia (DVD)

18+

DEAD MAN'S SHOES

2004, 90 mins.

Plot: When Richard leaves his home in a small, rural northern England town to join the army, his autistic younger brother is left at the tender mercies of a pack of drug dealers and wannabe gangstas. But that faux world they inhabit becomes appallingly real when Richard returns and descends upon them with furious vengeance.

Review: Meadows' brilliantly observed movie studies the lives of men fighting boredom in a bleak nowhere by masquerading as a pathetic mix of Italian mobster and West Side gangsta—and being neither. But it's Considine as the avenging brother who's the dark heart of this film: ferociously intense, tortured by guilt, his performance is an incredible portrayal of barely restrained savagery—and tragedy.

FURTHER VIEWING: ***A Room for Romeo Brass; This Is England; Somers Town***
SEE ALSO: ***Deliverance; First Blood; Straw Dogs; Taxi Driver***

108
500

★★★

Director: Rudolph Maté
Screenwriters: Russell Rouse and Clarence Greene
Produced by: Leo C. Popkin
Starring: Edmond O'Brien and Pamela Britton
Released by: Image Entertainment (DVD)

D.O.A.

1950, 83 mins.

Plot: A mild-mannered businessman, Frank Bigelow (Edmond O'Brien), decides to spend a final week of bachelordom in San Francisco before he marries his beautiful fiancée Paula. After a night on the tiles, Frank's hangover turns out to be something more sinister when he discovers he's been poisoned with a deadly luminous toxin. Doctors give him a week to live; a mere week to find who—and why—someone has killed him.

Review: Moving along at a frenetic pace, Maté's stunning noir classic still packs a solid punch, with each set piece perfectly decorated with femme fatales and hard-drinking goons delivering their dialog with suitable panache. Remade as *Color Me Dead*, and again in the eighties with Dennis Quaid, the original remains the best.

FURTHER VIEWING: ***Union Station***
SEE ALSO: ***White Heat; Out of the Past***

★ **Director:** Brian De Palma
★ **Screenwriter:** Brian De Palma
★ **Produced by:** George Litto

Starring: Michael Caine and Angie Dickinson
Released by: MGM/UA (DVD)

18+

DRESSED TO KILL

1980, 105 mins.

Plot: Successful therapist Dr. Robert Elliott is treating a beautiful but sexually frustrated woman who is then savagely murdered—using his own razor. This triggers a cascade of violence as the gender-confused killer closes in on the only witness to the killing: a gorgeous young prostitute.

Review: With its obvious homage to Hitchcock, this is a taut, erotically charged, knife-edge thriller that serves as De Palma's warning against casual sex and STDs. Balancing intelligent pacing and a gruelingly tense climax with some blood-soaked frights, it's also an interesting role for Caine as the therapist struggling with his own inner demons.

FURTHER VIEWING: *Carrie; The Fury; Blow Out; Scarface; The Untouchables; Carlito's Way; Redacted*
SEE ALSO: *Dead Ringers; Final Analysis; Psycho; Tightrope*

110
500

★★★★

Director: Steven Spielberg
Screenwriter: Richard Matheson
Produced by: George Eckstein
Starring: Dennis Weaver
Released by: Universal Studios (DVD)

DUEL

1971, 90 mins.

Plot: Dennis Mann is an unassuming businessman driving through the California desert to an appointment on a winding, mostly deserted road. Along the way he passes a rusty old truck; then the truck passes him. It happens again, and then he finds himself in a bizarre, seemingly unprovoked, and increasingly dangerous automotive contest for survival as the truck driver stalks him on the road for hours.

Review: Spielberg was wise to team with novelist and screenwriter Richard Matheson for his feature-film debut. Based on Matheson's short story, *Duel* the movie presents us with a horrifying situation: Dennis is stalked, with murderous intent, by someone he doesn't know, never hurt, and, crucially, never sees. This dehumanization of the truck driver—and showcasing of the machine as the villain—adds an almost supernatural element to the enemy without overtly suggesting it. Brilliant and terrifying storytelling.

FURTHER VIEWING: ***Poltergeist; Jaws; The Sugarland Express***
SEE ALSO: ***Maximum Overdrive; The Hitcher***

111
500

★★

Director: Richard Rush
Screenwriter: J. Wright Campbell
Produced by: Joe Solomon
Starring: Jack Nicholson and Adam Roarke
Released by: Image Entertainment (DVD)

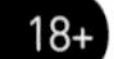

18+

HELLS ANGELS ON WHEELS

1967, 90 mins.

Plot: Brash, bold gas station attendant Poet is taken under the wing of a Hells Angels gang and, after some tight spots and violent confrontations, settles into their hedonistic lifestyle of partying and gang warfare. However, when Poet finds favor with the gang leader's girl, she forces them into a murderous confrontation.

Review: Classic exploitation fare with not much in the way of plot but all you could want from a biker movie: bar room brawls right down to chair smashing, clashes with the "pigs," sex, drugs, and knife fights. It's also an opportunity to see Jack Nicholson exercising his acting chops early in his career.

FURTHER VIEWING: ***Thunder Alley; Psych-Out; Freebie and the Bean; The Stunt Man; Easy Rider***
SEE ALSO: ***Motorpsycho; Stone; Streets of Fire; The Wild Angels; The Wild One***

112

★★★★

Director: Sidney Lumet
Screenwriter: Ray Rigby
Produced by: Kenneth Hyman
Starring: Sean Connery and Ossie Davis
Released by: Warner Home Video (DVD)

8+

THE HILL

1965, 123 mins.

Plot: Five new arrivals at a British military prison in Libya fall foul of the guards' brutal regime to break their spirits and are forced to climb "the hill," a man-made slope located in the center of the courtyard. When one of the inmates dies from the excessive drill, Joe Roberts (Sean Connery) takes it upon himself to orchestrate a rebellion to bring the Staff Sergeant responsible to justice.

Review: Sparsely shot in black and white, Lumet's testament to the limits of the human spirit still makes for powerful viewing. A fantastic ensemble cast, including Connery and Ossie Davis as two of the downtrodden inmates, provide memorable performances, and Ian Hendry is convincing as the intimidating Sgt. Williams. Unfairly overlooked in its time, this is gripping war drama.

FURTHER VIEWING: *12 Angry Men; Serpico*
SEE ALSO: *Full Metal Jacket; The Shawshank Redemption*

113

★★★★

Director: Shane Black
Screenwriters: Shane Black and Brett Halliday
Produced by: Carrie Morrow, Jessica Alan, Joel Silver, Steve Richards, and Susan Downey
Starring: Robert Downey Jr., Val Kilmer, and Michelle Monaghan
Released by: Warner Home Video (DVD)

18+

KISS KISS, BANG BANG

2005, 102 mins.

Plot: Trying to escape the police after a robbery, small-time criminal Harry Lockheart runs into a film audition and manages to get the role on offer through his "method acting." Cast as a private investigator, Harry is teamed with a real PI, "Gay" Perry van Shrike, for research purposes. The two (plus Harry's would-be girlfriend) get caught up in a real murder mystery, and the harder they try to solve it, the more abstract it becomes.

Review: As you would expect from the screenwriter of *Lethal Weapon*, this is a great, off-the-wall buddy crime/comedy. But like Glover and Gibson, Val Kilmer as Perry and Robert Downey Jr. as Harry are clearly having so much fun together that the film is elevated beyond its clever dialog and hilariously nonsensical murder mystery. A must-see for fans of more character-based action films.

FURTHER VIEWING: *Lethal Weapon; The Monster Squad; The Last Boy Scout; The Long Kiss Goodnight*
SEE ALSO: *The Big Lebowski; Get Shorty; The Hard Way*

114
500

★
★
★

Director: Jean-Pierre Melville
Screenwriter: Jean-Pierre Melville
Produced by: Raymond Borderie

Starring: Alain Delon
Released by: Artists International (DVD)

12+

LE SAMOURAÏ (THE SAMURAI)

1967, 100 mins.

Plot: Cool hitman Jef Costello carries out each of his hits in a careful and particular manner until he is seen leaving the scene of one of his killings at a jazz club by attractive pianist Valérie. Their relationship blossoms when she deliberately fails to identify him in a police lineup, and with little evidence, they release him. With officers shadowing him and his employers attempting to kill him, Costello is forced to make an honorable and ultimately redeeming sacrifice.

Review: Dialog-free for most of the duration, with the odd punctuation of smooth jazz, Melville's classic example of the French New Wave is as meticulously constructed as one of Costello's crimes, and rightly regarded as the definitive modern noir.

FURTHER VIEWING: ***Le Cercle Rouge; Le Deuxième Souffle (The Second Wind)***
SEE ALSO: ***Purple Noon; The Killer; The Driver***

115
500

★
★
★

Director: Michael Mann
Screenwriter: Michael Mann
Produced by: Dino De Laurentiis and Richard Roth

Starring: William Petersen and Brian Cox
Released by: MGM (DVD)

18+

MANHUNTER

1986, 119 mins.

Plot: Traumatized FBI profiler Will Graham is persuaded out of retirement to help capture a serial killer who specializes in slaughtering families. With time running out, he enlists the aid of the infamous Hannibal Lecter. But as the notorious cannibal begins toying with Graham, the question becomes, who exactly is helping whom?

Review: While *Silence of the Lambs* made them superstars, it was this movie that put serial killers on the map in the first place. Notable as the first cinematic outing of Hannibal Lecter, Mann's clinical, sterile approach seems more plausible, understated, and unsettling than the gothic follow-on. And with its pastel shades and monotone palette, it's a model of eighties style.

FURTHER VIEWING: ***The Keep; L.A. Takedown; The Last of the Mohicans; Heat; Collateral***
SEE ALSO: ***Red Dragon; Silence of the Lambs; Henry: Portrait of a Serial Killer; Man Bites Dog***

16

★★★★★

Director: John Frankenheimer
Screenwriters: John Frankenheimer and George Axelrod
Produced by: John Frankenheimer, George Axelrod, and Howard W. Koch
Starring: Frank Sinatra, Laurence Harvey, and Janet Leigh
Released by: MGM (DVD)

15+

THE MANCHURIAN CANDIDATE

1962, 126 mins.

Plot: Sergeant Raymond Shaw and his platoon are kidnapped during the Korean War in 1952 and taken to Manchuria. While there, they are all brainwashed to believe that Shaw has saved all their lives. For several years the men live comfortably with this lie, but then Shaw's platoon mate, Captain Marco, begins to have a nightmare in which Shaw has killed two of their friends. Distraught and suspicious, Marco investigates the meaning of his dreams, and discovers that Shaw is even less a hero than he could have imagined.

Review: Based on the novel by Richard Condon, this is a Cold War classic—which is more anti-political subterfuge than anti-communism—made in the wake of McCarthyism and the Red Scare. Brilliantly constructed, *The Manchurian Candidate* manages to be both political commentary and an entertaining mystery thriller.

FURTHER VIEWING: *The Manchurian Candidate (2004 remake); Seven Days in May*
SEE ALSO: *The Parallax View; Executive Action; Blow Out*

117

★★★★

Director: Luc Besson
Screenwriter: Luc Besson
Produced by: Patrice Ledoux
Starring: Anne Parillaud and Marc Duret
Released by: MGM (DVD)

18+

NIKITA (LA FEMME NIKITA)

1990, 115 mins.

Plot: A teenage addict is the sole survivor of a foiled drug store robbery, leaving her facing a lifelong prison sentence. Plucked from confinement, Nikita is placed into a program that will transform her into a sleeper agent for the DGSE, the French intelligence agency. Her aggressive nature makes her the perfect candidate, and after two years of training she is handed a gun in a busy restaurant and told to go to work.

Review: Besson's slick blend of Hong Kong action and Hollywood blockbuster proved a hit on both sides of the Atlantic despite generally negative reviews, and it opened the door for the director in the U.S. A shorter and more enjoyable alternative to sitting through five seasons of *Alias*.

FURTHER VIEWING: *Léon*
SEE ALSO: *The Assassin*

118/500

Director: Elia Kazan
Screenwriters: Richard Murphy, Daniel Fuchs, Edna Anhalt, and Edward Anhalt
Produced by: Sol C. Siegel
Starring: Richard Widmark and Jack Palance
Released by: Twentieth Century Fox (DVD)

12+

PANIC IN THE STREETS

1950, 96 mins.

Plot: An unidentified man is killed in a fight over a card game; during his autopsy, U.S. Public Health Service official Dr. Reed discovers the man is infected with the pneumonic plague. What follows is a race against time as Dr. Reed must find and quarantine everyone who had contact with the unknown man—including his killers—before the infection spreads out of control, and before the media report the plague infection and cause . . . *panic in the streets.*

Review: Shot completely on location in New Orleans, *Panic in the Streets* is an intense thriller that's also wonderfully evocative of New Orleans' culture and atmosphere. Additionally, it features Jack Palance (as Walter Jack Palance) in his first film role, playing the murderous gangster Blackie.

FURTHER VIEWING: ***Boomerang!; East of Eden***
SEE ALSO: ***Contagious; City of Fear; The Satan Bug***

119/500

★★★★

Director: Alan J. Pakula
Screenwriter: David Giler
Produced by: Alan J. Pakula
Starring: Warren Beatty and Paula Prentiss
Released by: Paramount (DVD)

15+

THE PARALLAX VIEW

1974, 102 mins.

Plot: Joe Frady, a drunken and irresponsible reporter with a nose for a good story, decides to investigate the assassination of a U.S. senator following the deaths of six witnesses. The trail leads to the mysterious Parallax Corporation, where through duplicity he enrolls as a member and is exposed to their rigorous initiation process. It's up to Frady to expose the organization before they conspire to kill again.

Review: Director Pakula was no stranger to conspiracy thrillers, later going on to make the Oscar-winning *All the President's Men*. From gloomy apartments to the grand architecture of the auditorium, *The Parallax View* perfectly conjures the suspicious atmosphere of Nixon's America, paving the way for the ghostly government machinations in television's *The X-Files* twenty years later.

FURTHER VIEWING: ***Klute; All the President's Men***
SEE ALSO: ***Marathon Man; The Conversation***

20

★★★

Director: Clint Eastwood
Screenwriters: Jo Heims and Dean Riesner
Produced by: Robert Daley
Starring: Clint Eastwood and Jessica Walter
Released by: Universal Studios (DVD)

8+

PLAY MISTY FOR ME

1971, 102 mins

Plot: A soulful, sexy late-night DJ receives the flattering attentions of a beautiful fan. However, what starts as casual fun soon becomes cloying infatuation and quickly accelerates into homicidal stalking.

Review: Eastwood's directorial debut is clearly a love letter to his adopted California home and his passion for jazz. However, the moment you see the edgy twitch behind the eyes of Jessica Walter's Evelyn, you realize the movie has very little to do with love. The tension doesn't let up as her giggles become tinged with hysteria, and Eastwood wears a rabbit-in-the-headlights expression of impending doom. The moral: you play with mismatches, you get psychos.

FURTHER VIEWING: *High Plains Drifter; Bird; White Hunter, Black Heart; Million Dollar Baby*
SEE ALSO: *Crush; Disclosure; Fatal Attraction*

21

★★★★

Director: Roman Polanski
Screenwriters: Gérard Brach and Roman Polanski
Produced by: Gene Gutowski
Starring: Catherine Deneuve
Released by: Criterion (DVD)

8+

REPULSION

1965, 105 mins.

Plot: A Beautiful but timid and unhinged young girl is left to her own devices in a dreary London flat. Existing in an increasingly hallucinatory state, unable to tell dream from reality, she grows steadily more unstable and, finally, murderous.

Review: Building a shadow play of darkly imaginative visual imagery, mounting paranoia, and dissolute sound, Polanski takes us deep inside the skull of the beautiful and ethereal Catherine Deneuve—then tears it down. What's left is an unnerving master class in mental terror and sexual neuroses as Deneuve's OCD depressive, surly and selfish, disintegrates.

FURTHER VIEWING: *Cul-de-sac; Rosemary's Baby; Chinatown; Frantic; La Pianiste (The Pianist)*
SEE ALSO: *Carrie; Don't Look Now; Psycho*

122
500

★★★

Director: Samuel Fuller
Screenwriter: Samuel Fuller
Produced by: Samuel Fuller
Starring: Peter Breck
Released by: Criterion (DVD)

18+ SHOCK CORRIDOR

1963, 101 mins.

Plot: Journalist Johnny Barrett desperately wants a Pulitzer. When he gets wind of an unsolved murder in a mental institution, he goes undercover as a patient to investigate. But the problem with acting crazy is that people will take you at your word, and during a riot he's given electroshock treatment. After that, it's difficult to tell whether he's still acting or whether his brain is well and truly fried.

Review: A film that's more rewarding in the journey than in the destination. Barrett's interaction with the other patients is eye-opening. What better attack on racism than to have a mentally ill black man spout vitriolic racial epithets and don a KKK mask? There are similar indictments of American life, but perhaps the most powerful is a war veteran's color-sequence flashback in this otherwise black-and-white film. Disturbing but valuable.

FURTHER VIEWING: ***The Naked Kiss***
SEE ALSO: ***One Flew over the Cuckoo's Nest; Bedlam; Behind Locked Doors***

123
500

★★★

Director: Walter Hill
Screenwriters: Walter Hill, Michael Kane, and David Giler
Produced by: David Giler and William J. Immerman
Starring: Keith Carradine, Powers Boothe, Fred Ward, and Peter Coyote
Released by: MGM (DVD)

18+ SOUTHERN COMFORT

1981, 105 mins.

Plot: A squad of Louisiana Army National Guardsmen are spending the weekend on a monthly training exercise in the swamps of Cajun country. They lose their way and decide to steal some canoes from a house on the bayou; the owners see them, and as the soldiers pull away one of them shoots blanks at the Cajuns for fun. But the Cajuns return fire, killing one of the soldiers. After the soldiers retaliate, the Cajuns put their hunting skills to work as they track the most dangerous game.

Review: Generally accepted as an allegory for the American soldier experience in Vietnam. One of these days visitors to "foreign" parts are going to learn not to taunt the swamp people (or mountain people, or forest people), but until then we get to enjoy "stranger in an inbred land" pictures like *Southern Comfort*.

FURTHER VIEWING: ***The Warriors***
SEE ALSO: ***Deliverance; Straw Dogs; Hunter's Blood***

24

★ ★ ★

Director: Lewis Milestone
Screenwriter: Robert Rossen
Produced by: Hal B. Wallis
Starring: Barbara Stanwyck, Van Heflin, and Kirk Douglas
Released by: Paramount (DVD)

2+ THE STRANGE LOVE OF MARTHA IVERS

1946, 116 mins.

Plot: After failing to escape her domineering aunt with her friend Sam, Martha accidentally kills her, the death witnessed by Walter, who blackmails Martha into marriage and her inheritance. Eighteen years later, Sam returns. Walter believes he knows the truth and plans to blackmail him and Martha, who is still in love with Sam. Soon, Walter hatches a plot to dispose of his rival.

Review: Notable for Kirk Douglas' screen debut, playing against his later machismo image as the sniveling, conniving Walter. This film has a great cast; complex, unsympathetic characters; a solid dark noir script; and a melodramatic mix of unrequited love and power-play that you know isn't going to end well.

FURTHER VIEWING: *All Quiet on the Western Front; The Front Page; Of Mice and Men; Halls of Montezuma; Ocean's Eleven*
SEE ALSO: *Double Indemnity; The Postman Always Rings Twice; Red Rock West; U-Turn*

25

★ ★ ★

Director: Bernardo Bertolucci
Screenwriter: Bernardo Bertolucci
Produced by: Giovanni Bertolucci
Starring: Giulio Brogi and Alida Valli
Released by: New Yorker Video (VHS only)

12+ STRATEGIO DEL RAGNO (THE SPIDER'S STRATAGEM)

1970, 100 mins.

Plot: A researcher returns to the small town in Italy where he was raised to find out about his father who fought, and was killed, by fascists in the 1930s. As he digs deeper into his father's murder, he becomes aware that unearthing the truth could tarnish the memory of the town's greatest hero.

Review: A complex narrative that requires attention, typical of Bertolucci who is a master of details and chronology. Deftly switching between Athos' investigation into his father's life and the past, the viewer is allowed access to the full picture of an extraordinary man's life (with father and son both played skillfully by Guilio Brogi). Beautifully photographed, it's a sin that this film isn't more widely available.

FURTHER VIEWING: *1900; Last Tango in Paris*
SEE ALSO: *Come and See; Padre Padrone (Father and Master)*

126
500

★★★★

Director: Anthony Harvey
Screenwriter: James Goldman
Produced by: John Foreman, Jennings Lang, and Paul Newman

Starring: George C. Scott and Joanne Woodward
Released by: Anchor Bay Entertainment (DVD)

A

THEY MIGHT BE GIANTS

1971, 98 mins.

Plot: After the death of his wife, grief-stricken Justin Playfair retreats into a fantasy world where he believes he is Sherlock Holmes. Institutionalized by his nefarious brother, he is befriended by psychiatrist Dr. Mildred Watson. Playfair latches onto her surname and allows her to join his Quixotic quest for his nemesis, Moriarty.

Review: The allusion to *Don Quixote* is obvious from the off in this intelligent mix of unreality and comedy. Scott's tragicomic fantasist and Woodward's sad, "adequate" psychiatrist make for a charming couple, and as she becomes drawn deeper and deeper into Playfair's fantasy, you begin to question who is the doctor and who is the patient. Uplifting and charming with a great John Barry score, and, in its own curious way, sweetly romantic.

FURTHER VIEWING: ***The Lion in Winter; The Glass Menagerie; Players; Svengali; Dr. Strangelove; Patton***
SEE ALSO: ***The Fisher King; Harvey; Without a Clue; Murder by Decree***

127
500

★★

Director: Robert Aldrich
Screenwriters: Ronald M. Cohen and Edward Huebsch
Produced by: Merv Adelson

Starring: Burt Lancaster and Roscoe Lee Brown
Released by: Not Available

15+

TWILIGHT'S LAST GLEAMING

1977, 146 mins.

Plot: After escaping from prison, a renegade U.S. Air Force general and his team seize a nuclear missile base. Armed with the launch codes, he threatens the President with atomic blackmail, saying he'll launch nine missiles unless the President makes public a file that holds the key for the real reasoning behind the Vietnam War.

Review: This high-end political thriller provides a salutary lesson on the threat not just of nuclear war but on the very presence of nuclear weapons. Burt Lancaster is the acting muscle of this taut and fascinating insight into Cold War politics; stoic and bitter, he's ably supported by a great cast and some clever direction (the use of split screens is particularly effective).

FURTHER VIEWING: ***Kiss Me Deadly; Sodom and Gomorrah; What Ever Happened to Baby Jane?; The Killing of Sister George; The Choirboys; The Dirty Dozen***
SEE ALSO: ***Dr. Strangelove; Fail Safe; Wargames; The Rock***

★★★★

Director: Robert Bresson
Screenwriter: Robert Bresson
Produced by: Alain Poiré

Starring: François Leterrier and Charles Le Clainche

Released by: Artificial Eye (DVD Region 2 only)

A

UN CONDAMNÉ À MORT S'EST ÉCHAPPÉ OU LE VENT SOUFFLE OÙ IL VEUT (A MAN ESCAPED)

1956, 99 mins.

Plot: Fontaine (François Leterrier), a member of the French Resistance, is captured by the Nazis and sent to prison. Resolute in his desire to escape, and distrusted by his fellow inmates, he begins a slow journey to freedom knowing compliancy will result in death.

Review: Despite knowing the film's outcome from the title, it's the process of how Fontaine escapes his captors that makes this film so successful. Bresson himself was a prisoner of war during WWII, and this informs Fontaine's actions so realistically on his path to escape. Don't let the simple plot underwhelm you; each scene is minimal yet suspenseful, and the revolutionary use of sound has been hugely influential on generations of filmmakers since.

FURTHER VIEWING: *Diary of a Country Priest; Pickpocket*
SEE ALSO: *Papillon; Escape from Alcatraz*

★★★

Director: Luis Buñuel
Screenwriter: Luis Buñuel
Produced by: Gustavo Alatriste
Starring: Silvia Pinal
Released by: Criterion (DVD)

15+

VIRIDIANA

1961, 90 mins.

Plot: After apparently being violated by the uncle who funded her education, a young nun is surprised to discover that, wracked with guilt, he has hanged himself and left her his wealthy estate. She plans to use his riches to help the poor but finds that her good dead won't go unpunished.

Review: A controversial story beautifully made, it's a bold movie, not morally upright, as Silvia Pinal's blindly optimistic, idealistic Viridiana is harshly stripped of her naïveté while colliding head on with grim reality. With some powerful religious symbolism (especially its portrayal of The Last Supper) and strong views on the purity of the poor, little wonder it was hated by the Vatican.

FURTHER VIEWING: ***Belle de jour; La voie lacteé (The Milky Way); Cet obscur objet du désir (The Obscure Object of Desire)***
SEE ALSO: ***Black Narcissus; Dark Habits; The Missionary***

130

★★★★

Directors: Lee H. Katzin and Bernard Girard
Screenwriter: Theodore Apstein
Produced by: Robert Aldrich
Starring: Geraldine Page and Ruth Gordon
Released by: MGM (DVD)

15+

WHAT EVER HAPPENED TO AUNT ALICE?

1969, 101 mins.

Plot: When Claire Marrable's husband dies, she discovers that he had sunk all their money into bad investments, and she's left with nothing. Remembering that she has a distant relative in the southwest, she moves to Arizona, engages a series of housekeepers, and grows pine trees in the area's hostile climate. One night, new housekeeper Alice asks about some investments she got Claire to make, and we then learn how Claire makes her garden grow.

Review: "*What Ever Happened to Aunt Alice* is more terrifying than what happened to Baby Jane." Just as good as *Baby Jane* and *Charlotte*, *Aunt Alice*'s major strength is in the interactions between its two leads, played to thrilling perfection by Geraldine Page and Ruth Gordon.

FURTHER VIEWING: *What Ever Happened to Baby Jane?; Hush . . . Hush, Sweet Charlotte*
SEE ALSO: *Sister Sister; Misery; Psycho*

131

★★★★

Director: David Lynch
Screenwriter: David Lynch
Produced by: Steve Golin
Starring: Nicholas Cage, Laura Dern, and Willem Dafoe
Released by: MGM (DVD)

18+

WILD AT HEART

1990, 124 mins.

Plot: Recently jailed Sailor and his girlfriend Lula refuse to be kept apart. Realizing that Lula's overbearing mother will never accept their relationship, they run away to California, meeting all manner of outlandish characters along the way, including some who were sent to kill them.

Review: As rebellious young lovers, Sailor and Lula's cross-country adventure mirrors that of Dorothy in *The Wizard of Oz*; Lynch acknowledges this openly with the appearance of Glinda the Good Witch, and most of the characters they encounter are similarly fantastical. Despite the bursts of extreme violence, the film's sentimental heart is never cloying, and Willem Dafoe's turn as the vile Bobby Peru is as memorable as Lynch's other grotesque creation, Frank Booth.

FURTHER VIEWING: *Blue Velvet; Twin Peaks: Fire Walk with Me*
SEE ALSO: *Badlands; True Romance*

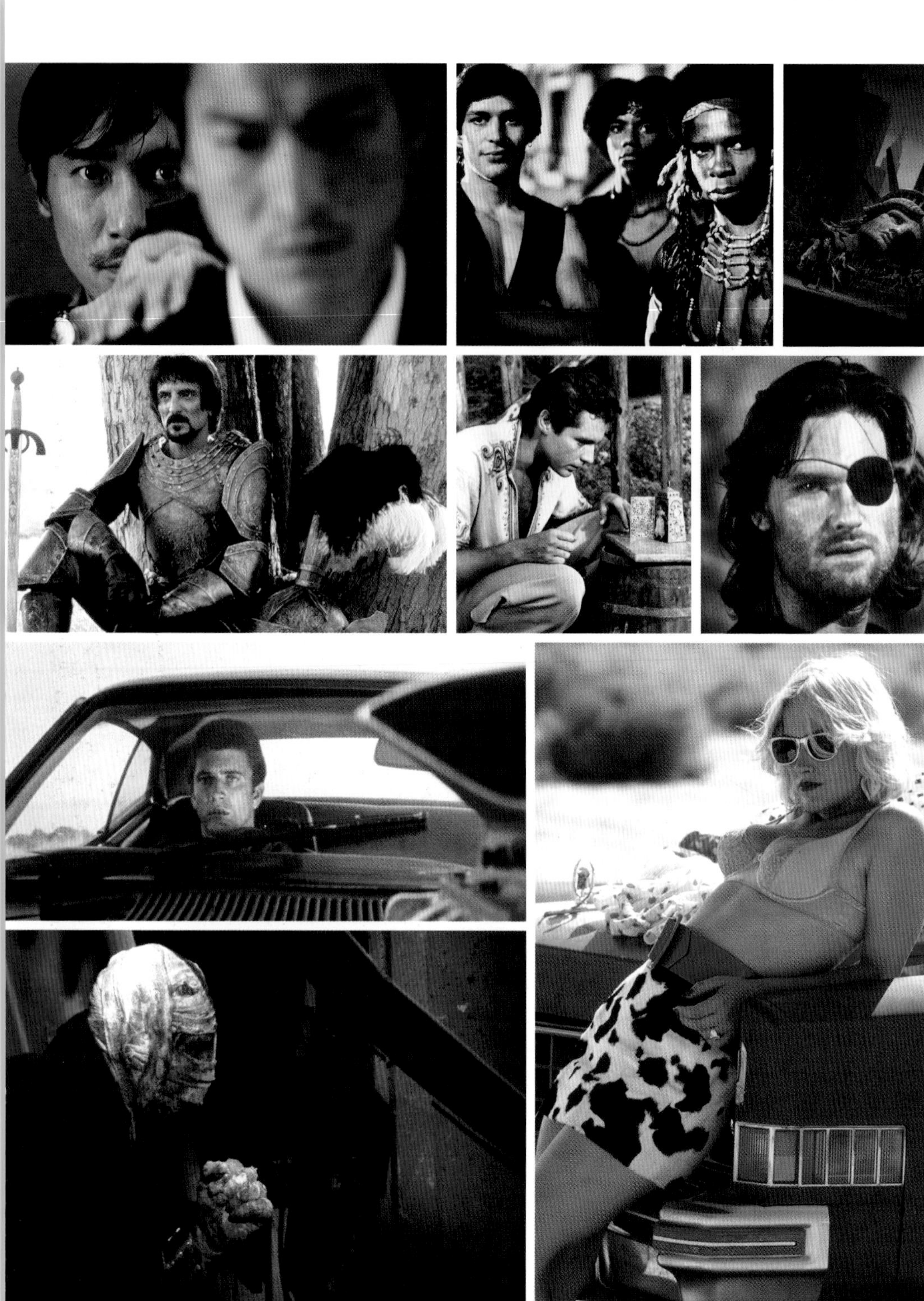

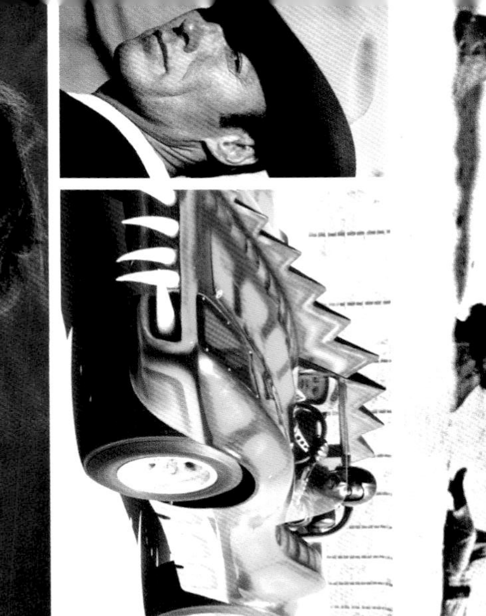

CHAPTER 3

LIGHTS, CAMERA . . . !

"DON'T PUSH IT, OR I'LL GIVE YOU A WAR YOU WON'T BELIEVE"

Let's be honest: action movies are known for their brawn more than their brains. And let's be more honest: even cult action films usually prize big bangs over character growth, and with masterfully violent revenge flicks like *Mad Max* and *Rambo* in the mix, who cares about intelligence? That's certainly a legitimate way to look at this section, but it doesn't have to be that easy (cult films rarely are), since we've also included some less categorizable movies like South Korea's breakthrough film *The Host*, which combines elements of action, horror, and family drama, as well as *Red Dawn*, which comes across as a sort of depressing Cold War social commentary . . . for teeny boppers.

TOP 10

LIGHTS, CAMERA . . . !

★
★
★
★

Director: W. D. Richter
Screenwriter: Earl Mac Rauch
Produced by: Neil Canton and W. D. Richter
Starring: Peter Weller, John Lithgow, and Ellen Barkin
Released by: MGM/UA Video (DVD)

12+

THE ADVENTURES OF BUCKAROO BANZAI ACROSS THE 8TH DIMENSION

1984, 103 mins.

Plot: Buckaroo Banzai—neurosurgeon, philosopher, musician, genius—and his trusty Hong Kong Cavaliers discover that evil Red Lectroids are planning to steal a device that will enable them to return to, and conquer, their own dimension. This may force the friendly Lectroids to destroy Earth to prevent the attack! Can Buckaroo and his cohort stop the evil aliens and prevent Armageddon?

Review: A movie that epitomizes the phrase "necessity is the mother of invention." With some cheap special effects and some great OTT performances, the filmmakers create a totally mental movie overflowing with optimism, sincerity, and love. The script is rife with some very clever humor, in-jokes, and a plethora of wonderfully bizarre and original ideas, while the cast is a confectionary box of future stars, including Peter Weller as the droll but sensitive hero/genius; Clancy Brown; Jeff Goldblum as a cowboy neurosurgeon sidekick; Christopher Lloyd; Ellen Barkin; and Jon Lithgow as the scenery-chewing, mad-haired mad scientist. All of them appear to be having a great time; the acting is deadly serious, no matter the insanity of the nonsense lines they're uttering.

And lest we forget, this is an eighties movie, complete with all the fashions, saxophone breaks, high collars, and manmade fibers from the decade style forgot. And the final scene of the team striding out to meet their future destiny is as stirring as any speech from *The Lord of the Rings*. It makes you wish you lived in a world where Buckaroo and co. were indeed the guardians of freedom, liberty, and power ballads, and with Ellen Barkin dipped in honey, what's not to love? Amazingly there are naysayers who deride the movie as confusing and cheap, having clearly missed the point while spending too much time plodding their way through *Star Trek* reruns.

FURTHER VIEWING: ***Late for Dinner***
SEE ALSO: ***Men in Black; Repo Man***

★ ★ ★ ★

Director: Paul Bartel
Screenwriters: Robert Thom and Charles Griffith

Produced by: Roger Corman and Jim Weatherill
Starring: David Carradine, Simone Griffeth, and Sylvester Stallone

Released by: Buena Vista Home Entertainment (DVD)

8+

DEATH RACE 2000

1975, 84 mins.

Plot: In 2000, the United States' infrastructure has crumbled under financial collapse, leaving it vulnerable to a military coup. The country is controlled by a fascist leader called "Mr. President," who mollifies the American people with a gladiatorial form of entertainment worse than anything the Romans could have thought up: the Transcontinental Road Race.

Frankenstein is a half-man, half-machine contestant, unbeatable in both speed and his ability to run over pedestrians (which is another way to score points in the race). When a resistance group attempts to replace Frankenstein with an agent of their own, they find he is not a willing government puppet, and Frankenstein must win his last race to get close enough to Mr. President to assassinate him.

Review: "In the year 2000, hit and run driving is no longer a felony, it's the national sport!" Here we are with yet another low-budget Roger Corman bloodfest, this time featuring a young Sylvester Stallone a year before he exploded into superstardom in *Rocky*. Though it came out in the same year as that other cult dystopian bloodsport flick, *Rollerball*, *Death Race 2000* is generally considered the better film; however, it was lambasted by critics on its release as needlessly violent and speckled with gratuitous nudity. But what more do you really need from a cult film than blood, sex, and Roger Corman?

The film's impact has been lasting—Bartel went on to direct the first film covering the Cannonball Baker Sea-to-Shining-Sea Memorial Trophy Dash (also the basis for the successful cameo-garden *The Cannonball Run*), and *Death Race 2000* was remade as the fun, but ultimately pointless, *Death Race* in 2008. This is the ultimate ultra-violent dystopian car film and the blueprint for futuristic bloodsport movies.

FURTHER VIEWING: *Death Sport; Death Race (2008 remake); Cannonball!*
SEE ALSO: *Rollerball; The Running Man; Robocop*

★★★★★

Director: John Carpenter
Screenwriters: John Carpenter and Nick Castle

Produced by: Larry J. Franco and Debra Hill

Starring: Kurt Russell, Lee Van Cleef, Ernest Borgnine, and Donald Pleasence
Released by: MGM (DVD)

15+

ESCAPE FROM NEW YORK

1981, 99 mins.

Plot: In the year 1997, at the tail-end of the Third World War, crime in the United States is out of control; predictably, the government "solves" this problem by turning the island of Manhattan into the biggest prison ever conceived. En route to a political summit, the U.S. president's plane crashes into the middle of Manhattan—he survives but is immediately taken hostage by a gang of criminals. Enter Snake Plisskin, a recently convicted criminal and ex-Special Forces soldier, to whom the government offers an exchange: save the president and receive a full pardon. To ensure his cooperation, Snake is injected with timed micro-explosives, which give him twenty-four hours to complete the mission or he'll die. Snake is dropped into a veritable war zone, and meets a bevy of colorful and dangerous characters as he races to save the president's life as well as his own.

Review: John Carpenter is most often associated with the horror genre, but he's just as involved, and astute, when it comes to action films (many of which stray into the realm of sci-fi). *Escape from New York* is one of those fast-paced films that never stops thrilling and exciting the audience; the dirty, dark, and gritty texture of future Manhattan, teeming with gangs and lit by constant fires, supports the premise and almost becomes a character in itself, a living, breathing symbol of a once-great country's moral decay.

This doesn't mark Carpenter and Russell's first collaboration (that honor goes to a made-for-TV movie about Elvis), but it does signal the turning point in Russell's career from Disney heartthrob to Hollywood leading man and, often, action hero. Snake Plisskin has become an iconic anti-hero, a (seemingly) bad man with a checkered past forced to save the world through ingenuity and eye-patched badassery alone. Snake and the film have been influential in the action and sci-fi genres across a number of platforms, from the *Metal Gear* video games to William Gibson's *Neuromancer* to J. J. Abrams' *Cloverfield*. Fun, fast, and well-deserving of its cult status.

FURTHER VIEWING: *Escape from L.A.; Assault on Precinct 13*
SEE ALSO: *Mad Max; The Road Warrior*

★
★
★
★

Director: Ted Kotcheff
Screenwriters: Michael Kozoll, William Sackheim, and Sylvester Stallone
Produced by: Buzz Fetishans
Starring: Sylvester Stallone, Richard Crenna, and Brian Dennehy
Released by: Lionsgate (DVD)

8+

FIRST BLOOD

1982, 97 mins.

Plot: John Rambo is a Vietnam veteran who wanders into the small American town of Hope after he learns that he's the last surviving member of his old unit. The sheriff doesn't take kindly to his hippie-military looks and runs him out of town, but Rambo is nothing if not stubborn. Rambo returns and is arrested; during the subsequent beatings he has flashbacks to his time as a POW. Rambo finally snaps, fights his way out of the police station, and heads to the hills, where he wages a guerilla campaign to slaughter every cop in the vicinity, Vietnam-style.

Review: Anyone who hasn't heard of Rambo has been living under a rock for the past thirty years, and that includes anyone who wasn't even born until the twenty-first century (late birth is no excuse after the family-friendly *Son of Rambow* was released in 2007). This is the film that unleashed the hyper-violent ex-Green Beret John Rambo onto an unsuspecting world in all his bullet-laden, red-headbanded glory.

Ostensibly, *First Blood* is an exploration of the psychological difficulties war veterans face when reintegrating into polite society, but actually one suspects that subplot was shoe-horned in as an excuse to kill unrepentantly and blow lots of stuff up. The film is truly mindboggling in its over-the-top violence; Rambo murders an entire county's worth of cops, guerilla-style and single-handed, because a paranoid sheriff takes exception to his long hair and veteran looks (granted, the sheriff shouldn't have physically abused a former POW with post-traumatic stress syndrome, or anyone else for that matter, but we just don't have the space for chicken-and-egg arguments here). Regardless of the subtext or military excuses, if you enter *First Blood* with the right mindset—that it's an imaginative, blood-soaked killing spree to be enjoyed for its sheer ridiculousness—then you'll join the ranks of thousands of viewers who made the film successful enough to spawn its own franchise, as well as numerous pop-culture parodies (the best of which is probably "Weird Al" Yankovic's hilarious turn as Rambo in *UHF*).

FURTHER VIEWING: *Rambo: First Blood Part 2; Rambo 3; Rambo; Uncommon Valor*
SEE ALSO: *Son of Rambow; Behind Enemy Lines; UHF*

★★★★★

Director: Bong Joon-ho
Screenwriters: Baek Chul-hyun and Bong Joon-ho
Produced by: Choi Yong-Bae

Starring: Song Kang-ho, Byeon Hee-bong, Park Hae-il, and Bae Doona

Released by: Magnolia Home Entertainment (DVD)

12+

THE HOST

2006, 120 mins.

Plot: The American military dumps toxic waste into the Han River, and several years later a giant mutant amphibian emerges. It goes on the rampage, eating people and stealing away dim-witted snack-bar worker Gang-du's little girl. The government disseminate a fake story about a virus to explain the deaths caused by the creature. Gang-du and his family are quarantined; he gets a call from his daughter, who's still alive and trapped in a sewer, and he and his family all break out of military custody to find and save her from the monster.

Review: Though made with conventional horror/sci-fi/thriller trappings—illegal waste disposal, a giant mutant monster, questionable military tactics—this low-budget Korean film is really a compelling and often humorous drama about family dynamics in a time of crisis, with a sprinkling of political commentary.

To be honest, the monster is a let-down on the special-effects front, and the sub-par CGI sticks out like a sore thumb. Normally this would be a major problem, but unlike other sci-fi films where the creature is the main draw, in *The Host* it's relegated to sub-plot status, a minor catalyst used to explore how even a dysfunctional family can overcome their differences and pull together to help one of their own. Unfettered by the normal Hollywood requirement of a happily-ever-after ending, this is a terribly sad film, heart-breaking really, but at its core beams a ray of hope so bright, self-assured, and organic that you'll come out of it feeling all will be well despite the setbacks. And that's something no manufactured Hollywood ending could ever achieve.

This is truly one of the best films of 2006 and an absolute must-see.

FURTHER VIEWING: ***The Host (2010 remake); Mother***
SEE ALSO: ***Godzilla; Dragon Wars***

Director: George Miller
Screenwriter: George Miller, Brian Hannant, and Terry Hayes
Produced by: Byron Kennedy
Starring: Mel Gibson, Steve Bisley, and Joanne Samuel
Released by: Warner Home Video (DVD)

★★★★

8+ MAD MAX

1979, 94 mins.

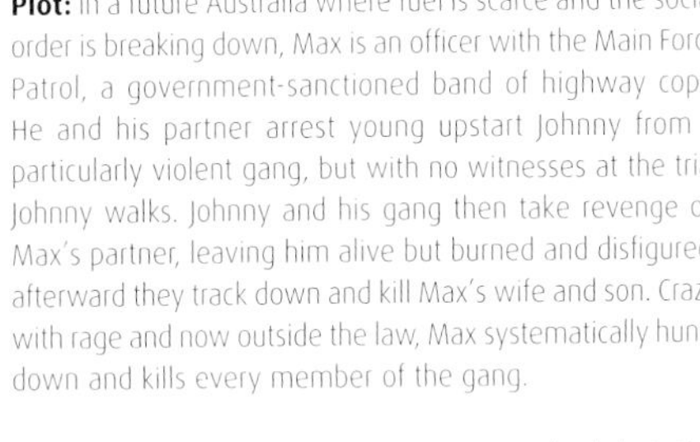

Plot: In a future Australia where fuel is scarce and the social order is breaking down, Max is an officer with the Main Force Patrol, a government-sanctioned band of highway cops. He and his partner arrest young upstart Johnny from a particularly violent gang, but with no witnesses at the trial Johnny walks. Johnny and his gang then take revenge on Max's partner, leaving him alive but burned and disfigured; afterward they track down and kill Max's wife and son. Crazy with rage and now outside the law, Max systematically hunts down and kills every member of the gang.

Review: As entertaining as it is unrepentantly violent, this low-budget Australian film detailing a crime-ridden dystopian future became a huge international hit, so much so that it introduced Mel Gibson to American audiences and spawned two popular sequels. *Mad Max* is one of the better films in a rash of bloody revenge flicks (see *First Blood*) that came out in the late seventies and early eighties. This may in part be due to director George Miller's previous career as an emergency-room doctor where he witnessed numerous catastrophic injuries, and which he later translated on-screen and in detail. In fact, the film was considered so violent and bloody that some countries initially banned it.

Though not listed in the credits, the cars are just as much characters as the actors—Max's suped-up (fictional) "Pursuit Special" is a particular favorite with fans and makes another appearance in *Mad Max 2*. In this broken future where fuel is more valuable than gold, cars represent lifelines, and people will do anything to keep them moving. In light of recent world events, *Mad Max* seems more like an eerily prescient documentary every day.

FURTHER VIEWING: *Mad Max 2: The Road Warrior; Mad Max Beyond Thunderdome*
SEE ALSO: *Death Wish; Dirty Harry*

★★★★★

Director: Jack Starett
Screenwriter: Wes Bishop
Producer: Wes Bishop

Starring: Peter Fonda, Warren Oates, and Loretta Swit
Released by: Starz/Anchor Bay (DVD)

15+

RACE WITH THE DEVIL

1975, 89 mins.

Plot: Two vacationing couples on their way to Colorado in a luxury mobile home stop off in Texas for a night to enjoy the beautiful countryside. As night falls, Frank (Warren Oates) and Roger (Fonda) spot a fire burning in the distance, and through binoculars discover it's a satanic ritual. At first convinced it's a mere orgy because of the flesh on show, their worst fears come true after one of the girls is killed in front of them. Their presence known, they barely escape with their lives after the satanists pursue them and attack the RV. The following day Frank and Roger report the attack and murder to the local sheriff, who tries to convince them that it was a bunch of hippies killing a dog. The couples are not convinced, and decide to push on to Amarillo to report the murder there. Along the way, their paranoia grows as they begin to suspect the connections to the satanists run far deeper than those involved in the ritual.

Review: For an America paralyzed by the fear of Black Sabbath, *The Exorcist*, and horror comics, *Race with the Devil* arrived at the right time to stir up anxiety about heaven's most famous fallen angel. The race is something the couples can never win—despite Frank claiming their mobile home is "self contained, baby!" and both he and Roger are expert motorcycle riders; the devil does inevitably catch up with them. The first hour is a tension-building exercise that's similar to Edward Woodward's investigation of the Pagan village in *The Wicker Man*—the everyman characters do not know who to trust. The last third by contrast is a speed-filled thrill ride as the RV comes under assault from various vehicles belonging to the cult. Leonard Rosemann's demented score adds to the creepiness.

FURTHER VIEWING: ***Cleopatra Jones; Slaughter***
SEE ALSO: ***The Hills Have Eyes; The Wicker Man***

★
★
★
★

Director: Ron Underwood
Screenwriters: Brent Maddock and S. S. Wilson

Produced by: Gale Anne Hurd, Brent Maddock, and S. S. Wilson

Starring: Kevin Bacon, Fred Ward, Finn Carter, Michael Gross, and Reba McEntire
Released by: Universal Studios (DVD)

12+

TREMORS

1990, 96 mins.

Plot: Handymen Val and Earl live in a tiny town (population fourteen) in the middle of the Nevada desert, where the only excitement for years has been the recent arrival of pretty college-student Rhonda, who's in town studying seismic activity. Val and Earl have had enough of their boring, penniless existence and leave for the nearest "big" town to seek their fortunes, but on the way they encounter the corpse of the town drunk clutching a rifle atop an electrical tower. They take the man's body back to town to the doctor (who pronounces dehydration the cause of death). The two leave town again, only to find a nearby sheepherder has been slaughtered, along with all of his flock. Val and Earl race back to town again; not long after a landslide then blocks the only road out. They soon meet the cause of the landslide: a giant worm creature that burrows through the ground, hitting enormous speeds, and attacking the town's population from below.

Review: With all the makings of an obscure but enjoyable B-movie, *Tremors* was an unlikely hit in 1990, delighting critics and viewers alike.

As an example of a 1950s B-movie homage, *Tremors* is probably one of the most successful of its class; it's modern enough to be relevant to current audiences, but reverent and knowledgeable of its influences, only adapting the best bits of those mid-century creature features. While the giant worm-monster looks decent enough not to be an eyesore, the real draw of this film is the varied and first-rate acting talent involved—Kevin Bacon and Fred Ward, in particular, have a believable and infectious on-screen buddy chemistry, rendering them highly sympathetic. The script is filled with effective situational humor, oddball characters, and enough tension to keep the story moving. *Tremors* is lighthearted sci-fi/horror viewing and tremendously enjoyable—it inspired two sequels, a prequel, and a TV series, none of which manage to replicate the magic of this first film.

FURTHER VIEWING: *Tremors 2: After Shocks; Tremors 3: Back to Perfection; Tremors 4: The Legend*
SEE ALSO: *The Blob; Critters; Them!; It Came from Outer Space*

★★★★★

Director: Akira Kurosawa
Screenwriter: Ryuzo Kikushima
Producer: Akira Kurosawa

Starring: Toshirô Mifune, Tatsuya Nakadai, Yôko Tsukasa, and Isuzu Yamada

Released by: Criterion (DVD)

12+

YOJIMBO

1961, 111 mins.

Plot: At the end of the Tokugawa Dynasty, the samurais who once served their royal masters must now serve themselves. Known as "ronin," they wander the land armed only with their swords and their wits to defend themselves. One such ronin arrives in an isolated village where Sebei and Ushitori, two gang leaders, are engaged in a bitter rivalry. At first he is treated with contempt and suspicion, and cruelly mocked by the local gang members until he makes a public display of Ushitori's gang, killing two of its members and removing the arm of another with his sword. Soon, the Sebei gang are in his thrall after he accepts a fifty ryo payment to act as their bodyguard. With expert control, he drives each of the gangs to destroy each other for his own material and honorable gain.

Review: *Yojimbo* is possibly the greatest film about manipulation ever made. Influenced primarily by the westerns of John Ford, Kurosawa ironically became more of an influence on directors in the West down to his careful directorial style, oft-comical violence, and exquisite cinematic timing. One of the earliest scenes features a dog running off with a hand in its mouth that can be seen again in David Lynch's *Wild at Heart*, for instance. With the whole town worn out from the constant battling, businesses have all but dried up, and it's questionable whether there is anything (or anyone) for the ronin to actually save. He manipulates desperate men into giving up the last of their riches in order to preserve themselves—little do they realize they've signed their own death warrants. The icy cool Toshirô Mifune plays the nameless samurai and was to appear in many of Kurosawa's films as well as many other samurai epics.

FURTHER VIEWING: *Sanjuro; Shichinin no samurai (Seven Samurai); Rashômon;*
SEE ALSO: *Zatoichi Meets Yojimbo; Rise Against the Sword; A Fistful of Dollars*

41

★★★★★

Director: Walter Hill
Screenwriters: David Shaber and Walter Hill
Produced by: Lawrence Gordon
Starring: Michael Beck, James Remar, and Deborah Van Valkenburgh
Released by: Paramount Pictures (DVD)

5+

THE WARRIORS

1979, 93 mins.

Plot: A dystopia set in a New York City ruled by roaming, violent street gangs of youths. Cyrus, head of the most powerful gang in the area, the Gramercy Riffs, calls a meeting of gang representatives in the Bronx, and The Warriors from Coney Island send their team. Cyrus wants the gangs to unite and take over the island for good (all told they outnumber the cops three to one), but rival gang The Rogues disagree with the plan and kill Cyrus, then blame The Warriors. The Warriors manage to escape the crowds and hide while still miles away from their own turf, but other gangs band together and put a bounty on The Warriors' heads. The Warriors spend the night making their way back to Coney Island while battling rival gangs and the cops, only to find The Rogues waiting when they arrive.

Review: An incredibly stylish—if often overwrought—take on youth movies, with themes of identity, conformity, and control at the fore. Interestingly, it also borrows heavily from the Greek writer Xenophon's *Anabasis*, which chronicles his experience as a mercenary without a leader deep in enemy Persian territory (while The Warriors dress with a Native American aesthetic, some of their members are named after Greek heroes and politicians).

Swapping swords and shields for guns and subways, *The Warriors* was considered controversial on its release for its frank depictions of violence and sex perpetrated by teenagers. In an echo of the London riots after the release of *Blackboard Jungle*, some overzealous *Warriors* fans engaged in vandalism, and even murder, during the film's first week of release. While this may not be the best film made about the dark side of the youth experience, it is certainly one of the most influential and visually appealing.

FURTHER VIEWING: *Streets of Fire; Southern Comfort*
SEE ALSO: *Assault on Precinct 13; Bad Boys; The Outsiders*

★★★★★

Director: Nathan H. Juran
Screenwriter: Kenneth Kolb

Produced by: Charles H. Schneer and Ray Harryhausen

Starring: Kerwin Mathews and Kathryn Grant
Released by: Sony Pictures (DVD)

A

THE 7TH VOYAGE OF SINBAD

1958, 88 mins.

Plot: On one of his adventures, Sinbad the Sailor crosses paths with the unscrupulous magician Sokurah, who shrinks Sinbad's fiancée in order to force him to recover a magic lamp. In his quest for the lamp, Sinbad fights a Cyclops, evades Sokurah's treachery, and ultimately frees a little genie from the lamp.

Review: Although the animation by the legendary Ray Harryhausen looks dated now, the skill and imagination apparent in his creations are timeless. In this interpretation of the (presumably) Persian folk tales of Sinbad the Sailor, we meet a range of fantastic mythological creatures—some scary, some alluring—and are encouraged to step into a world of magical possibility. It's mind-expanding stuff (of the legal variety) and fun for the whole family.

FURTHER VIEWING: ***Jason and the Argonauts; Clash of the Titans***
SEE ALSO: ***Labyrinth; The Dark Crystal***

43

★★★

Director: John Frankenheimer
Screenwriter: Ernest Lehman
Producer: Robert Evans
Starring: Robert Shaw and Bruce Dern
Released by: Paramount (DVD)

15+ BLACK SUNDAY

1977, 144 mins.

Plot: A deranged and suicidal 'Nam vet joins forces with Palestinian terrorist organization Black September to launch an attack on U.S. soil. Their target: the Superbowl final between Pittsburgh and Dallas. Their method of assault? A blimp armed with explosives to cause maximum damage—including the death of the President.

Review: Based on the Thomas Harris novel of the same name, *Black Sunday* has more relevance now in a post-9/11 world than it did in 1977. Don't be overly critical (as Frankenheimer himself was) of the FX during the assault on the Superbowl—the rapid editing and reaction shots keep you distracted enough to feel the sheer tension of intent. With some excellent and altogether bizarre stunt work, it's unlikely you've seen a movie end like this before.

FURTHER VIEWING: *The Manchurian Candidate; French Connection II*
SEE ALSO: *Silence of the Lambs; The Day of the Jackal*

44

★★★★

Director: John Carpenter
Screenwriters: Gary Goldman and David Z. Weinstein
Produced by: Larry J. Franco
Starring: Kurt Russell and Kim Cattrall
Released by: Twentieth Century Fox (DVD)

15+ BIG TROUBLE IN LITTLE CHINA

1986, 99 mins.

Plot: Laconic trucker Jack Burton loves nothing more than driving his rig and dishing out his homespun philosophy on the CB. But a trip to San Francisco's Chinatown finds him caught up in the theft of his best friend's green-eyed fiancée. Her captor: an ancient and totally insane sorcerer who plans to use her to help break the curse that keeps him immortal.

Review: A much-underrated Carpenter classic, this is part martial arts movie, part fantasy flick, part buddy pic, and part action-comedy, but it is never anything less than entertaining and shot through with some crackerjack lines. When the going gets weird, Russell's inept but enthusiastic Burton is totally out his depth, but how can you not love a hero whose climatic confrontation against evil is conducted while smeared in bright pink lipstick?

FURTHER VIEWING: *Assault on Precinct 13; Escape from New York; The Thing; They Live*
SEE ALSO: *Tango and Cash; Tombstone*

★★★★★

Director: Desmond David
Screenwriter: Beverly Cross
Producer: Ray Harryhausen

Starring: Laurence Olivier, Claire Bloom, Maggie Smith, and Ursula Andress
Released by: Warner Home Video (DVD)

12+

CLASH OF THE TITANS

1981, 118 mins.

Plot: Set in an era of myths and Greek legends, Perseus, the son of the god Zeus, must complete various nigh-impossible tasks to win the hand of Andromeda, the woman he loves. She's already betrothed to a hideous beast-man called Calibos, and Perseus must defeat the other suitor in combat, behead the wicked Medusa, and solve a riddle. It's not quite as simple as it sounds.

Review: *Clash of the Titans* is still revered for its pre-CGI visual trickery thanks to the inventive stop-motion techniques of Ray Harryhausen, and while some of the special effects may now seem old-fashioned, they have a charm that their digital counterparts lack. The best scene remains the fight between Perseus and Medusa that mixes animation with live actors—nostalgia buffs will get a kick out of it.

FURTHER VIEWING: ***A Nice Girl Like Me; Ordeal by Innocence***
SEE ALSO: ***The Golden Voyage of Sinbad; Jason and the Argonauts***

★ ★

Director: Don Siegel
Screenwriters: Herman Miller, Dean Reisner, and Howard Rodman

Produced by: Don Siegel
Starring: Clint Eastwood and Lee J. Cobb
Released by: Universal Studios (DVD)

15+

COOGAN'S BLUFF

1968, 93 mins.

Plot: A tough deputy sheriff heads from the rural Arizona desert to concrete-jungle Manhattan to extradite a prisoner. But when the prisoner escapes, Deputy Coogan has to track him down in wilds as dangerous as any prairie wasteland, meeting a host of freaks, weirdos, and scumbags along the way.

Review: A potent mix of Eastwood's *Dirty Harry* and Spaghetti Western movies, this could be considered an affectionate send-up of himself. His rough habits and old-fashioned manners clash with modern, liberal policing and cynical urban culture with sharply comic results. Of course, he can always resort to hitting someone with a pool cue—and does. With some success.

FURTHER VIEWING: *Madigan; Dirty Harry; The Shootist; Escape from Alcatraz*
SEE ALSO: *Hang 'Em High; High Plains Drifter; Where Eagles Dare; Brannigan*

★
★

Director: Mario Bava
Screenwriters: Mario Bava, Brian Degas, Tudor Gates, and Dino Maiuri
Produced by: Dino De Laurentiis
Starring: John Phillip Law and Marisa Mell
Released by: Paramount (DVD)

12+

DANGER DIABOLIK

1969, 100 mins.

Plot: Professional thief Diabolik steals from the government and makes a mockery of their efforts to catch him. In their hunt for the glamorous villain, the authorities clamp down on crime, provoking gang bosses to put a contract out on Diabolik. After his girlfriend is kidnapped, Diabolik rescues her, extracting bloody vengeance along the way. He now decides to take the fight to the authorities.

Review: A totally OTT camped-up, psychedelic spyfest made with élan and now fashionably kitsch. The production values and script are cheesy enough to smell the mozzarella, and the hammy acting could be fried as bacon, but to expect better is to miss the point. This is thrilling, sexy, B-movie, Bond-parody brilliance packed with European panache.

SEE ALSO: *Black Sabbath; Hercules at the Center of the Earth; Bay of Blood; Lisa and the Devil; Planet of the Vampires; Rabid Dogs*
FURTHER VIEWING: *Austin Powers: International Man of Mystery; Charlie's Angels; Our Man Flint; The Pink Panther; Hudson Hawk*

148

★★★

Director: Sam Raimi
Screenwriters: Sam Raimi, Chuck Pfarrer, Daniel Goldin, Ivan Raimi, and Joshua Goldin
Produced by: Daryl Kass and Robert G. Tapert
Starring: Liam Neeson and Frances McDormand
Released by: Universal Studios (DVD)

12+

DARKMAN

1990, 96 mins.

Plot: Peyton Westlake is developing synthetic skin to help burn victims, but he can't seem to get it to stabilize in sunlight—it degrades after ninety-nine minutes of exposure. Meanwhile, Westlake's lawyer girlfriend discovers evidence of major political corruption; when the bad guys come looking for it, they destroy the evidence by blowing up Westlake's lab with him in it. Now severely burned, Westlake uses his own invention—despite its limitation in sunlight—to avenge his near death.

Review: *Darkman* is Sam Raimi's ode to comics, made long before *Spider-Man* was even a twinkle in his eye (and mainly because he couldn't get the rights to existing comics characters). Plagued by studio conflict, there isn't much trademark Raimi about this film, but it's a fun entry into the superhero genre regardless.

FURTHER VIEWING: *Darkman 2: The Return of Durant; Darkman 3: Die, Darkman, Die; Spider-Man franchise*
SEE ALSO: *Batman franchise; Superman franchise*

149

★★★★

Director: John Woo
Screenwriter: John Woo
Producer: Hark Tsui
Starring: Chow Yun-Fat, Danny Lee, and Sally Yeh
Released by: Criterion (DVD)

18+

DIP HUET SEUNG HUNG (THE KILLER)

1989, 110 mins.

Plot: Ah Jong (Chow Yun-Fat) is a hitman about to enter retirement when he's involved in a shooting that leaves a singer from a local nightclub blinded by the gunfire. His guilt drives him to take one last job to pay for an operation that could save her sight, but not without difficulty—both the police and his employers want him out of the picture.

Review: Taking the extreme violence of Peckinpah's westerns ten steps further, Woo's tour de force of relentless bloodletting has set the agenda for the action films of the past twenty years with its stylized slow motion, endless torrents of bullets, and a final showdown where practically everyone is shot to pieces.

FURTHER VIEWING: *Lat sau san taam (Hard Boiled); Die xue jie tou (Bullet in the Head)*
SEE ALSO: *Full Contact; The Replacement Killers*

150
500

★★★★

Director: Robert Rodriguez
Screenwriter: Robert Rodriguez
Producer: Carlos Gallardo

Starring: Carlos Gallardo and Consuelo Gómez
Released by: Sony Pictures (DVD)

15+

EL MARIACHI

1992, 81 mins.

Plot: A jobless musician looking to establish himself as a mariachi guitarist in a small Mexican town ends up in over his head when his guitar case is accidently swapped with one filled with weapons. The owner of the guns, Moco, is out for the blood of his ex-partner who swindled him. Hunted and innocent, El Mariachi is suddenly caught up in the feud against his will.

Review: Allegedly made for the princely sum of $7,000 as a straight-to-VHS movie, execs at Columbia loved it so much they released it in the U.S. and made Rodriguez an overnight sensation. Full of over the top violence, tongue-in-cheek humor, and plenty of badly covered-up goofs, it's difficult to imagine the guy who made *Spy Kids* produced this.

FURTHER VIEWING: ***Desperado; Once Upon a Time in Mexico***
SEE ALSO: ***A Fistful of Dollars; From Dusk Till Dawn***

151
500

★★★★

Director: Jack Hill
Screenwriter: Jack Hill
Producer: Buzz Feitshans

Starring: Pam Grier, Antonio Fargas, Peter Brown, and Sid Haig
Released by: MGM (DVD)

18+

FOXY BROWN

1974, 94 mins.

Plot: Foxy Brown (Pam Grier) is a sassy, headstrong woman with a deadbeat brother full of criminal ambition and an undercover narc for a boyfriend. After a face-changing operation, her boyfriend is still recognizable to the wrong people and is gunned down. Foxy makes it her mission to exact revenge on the gang responsible by going undercover as a prostitute.

Review: *Foxy Brown* epitomizes the seventies stereotypes we still see today—big hair, bright clothing, a funky soundtrack, and jive dialog. It's difficult to tell where the clichés begin and the film ends, but there's honesty in how they're presented, which makes the film work so well. Pam Grier went on to make an equally strong impression in pseudo-sequel *Jackie Brown*, directed by Quentin Tarantino.

FURTHER VIEWING: ***Coffy; The Big Doll House***
SEE ALSO: ***Jackie Brown; Hit!***

52
310

★★

Director: Clint Eastwood
Screenwriters: Michael Butler and Dennis Shryack

Produced by: Robert Daley
Starring: Clint Eastwood and Sondra Locke
Released by: Warner Home Video (DVD)

8+

THE GAUNTLET

1977, 109 mins.

Plot: A drunken cop is sent to Las Vegas to bring in a witness, a sassy but terrified prostitute with damning information on high-powered criminals. A car bomb and an attack on the prostitute's house make him realize he can trust no one, least of all the cops. In the terrifying race to deliver the witness, he's now on his own.

Review: This isn't exactly the most subtle of Eastwood's movies, but it's a fun character-driven piece; even while running from a gauntlet of mob and cop gunfire, the two leads hate each other. Of course, movie etiquette demands their views soften and a romance is born. Don't expect social commentary; it's just a straight-up action—as witnessed by the spectacular, bus-destroying lead-soaked climax.

FURTHER VIEWING: *Every Which Way but Loose; Bronco Billy; Pink Cadillac; Magnum Force; Sudden Impact*
SEE ALSO: *Bullit; Cobra; Witness*

153
500

★★

Director: George A. Romero
Screenwriter: George A. Romero
Produced by: Richard P. Rubinstein

Starring: Ed Harris, Gary Lahti, and Tom Savini
Released by: Anchor Bay (DVD)

15+

KNIGHTRIDERS

1981, 145 mins.

Plot: A troupe of motorbike-riding knights travels the country performing tournaments, led by their virtuous king, Billy. He follows a just code but, in the real world, these beliefs are constantly pressured by the lure of easy money and romantic discord. Soon, the troupe begins to disintegrate and Billy, tormented by injuries and dreams, finds his beliefs tested to the limit.

Review: On paper this looks like a silly idea; what saves it is the conviction with which it's made, the cast pulling it off with humanity and pathos. There's also plenty of mock medieval action and exhilarating stunts, but the bottom line is that, in a cynical world, it's great to see someone standing up for his ideals—even if it means his downfall.

FURTHER VIEWING: ***Night of the Living Dead; Martin; Creepshow; Monkey Shines; Dawn of the Dead; Land of the Dead***
SEE ALSO: ***Excalibur; First Knight; Monty Python and the Holy Grail; The Right Stuff***

154
500

★★★

Director: Renny Harlin
Screenwriter: Shane Black
Producer: Stephanie Austin

Starring: Geena Davis and Samuel L. Jackson
Released by: New Line Home Video (DVD)

18+

THE LONG KISS GOODNIGHT

1996, 120 mins.

Plot: A housewife suffering from amnesia gradually discovers a wealth of unnatural skills that turn out to be from her past as a government-sponsored special agent. She hires a private investigator to dig into her past, and pretty soon her past is on her tail to stop her exposing a corrupt plot to detonate a bomb at Niagara Falls.

Review: *The Long Kiss Goodnight* is short on dialog and plot, long on the action and explosions. Harlin refuses to let the pace flag for a moment, and the plot is almost a mash-up of *Die Hard* and *North by Northwest*. Completely over-the-top but thoroughly enjoyable, it's also responsible for washing away the stain of the detestable *Cutthroat Island* from Geena Davis' career.

FURTHER VIEWING: ***Die Hard 2; 12 Rounds***
SEE ALSO: ***Pulp Fiction; Thelma and Louise***

★
★
★

Director: John Huston
Screenwriters: Gladys Hill and John Huston
Produced by: John Foreman
Starring: Sean Connery, Michael Caine, and Christopher Plummer
Released by: Warner Home Video (DVD)

12+

THE MAN WHO WOULD BE KING

1975, 124 mins.

Plot: Tired of bureaucratic army life, two adventurous scoundrels in Victorian India decide to seek fortune and riches. Using their vast knowledge and experience, they want to set themselves up as kings of a distant, backward region. When one of them ends up revered as a living god by locals, what looks like a bit of fun soon spins quickly out of control.

Review: John Huston brings the western to the North-West Frontier, capturing the exotic flavor of Kipling's India. However, it's Caine and Connery who dominate the sumptuous filmscape. Trading cracking, comic banter as perfect hard-living, hard-fighting soldiers of fortune, it looks like they're having a ball with the intelligent, thrilling script and the two rascals they seemed born to play.

FURTHER VIEWING: *The Maltese Falcon; The Treasure of the Sierra Madre; The Asphalt Jungle; Beat the Devil; Moby Dick; Chinatown; Annie; The Dead*
SEE ALSO: *The Four Feathers; Young Winston; Zulu*

★★★★★

Director: Wai-keung Lau
Screenwriter: Alan Mak
Producer: Wai-keung Lau

Starring: Andy Lau, Tony Leung Chiu Wai, and Anthony Wong Chau-Sang

Released by: Miramax Home Entertainment (DVD)

15+

MOU GAAN DOU (INFERNAL AFFAIRS)

2002, 101 mins.

Plot: Yan and Ming are two trainee police officers working their way up through the ranks—Yan becomes a mole in a Hong Kong criminal organization, while Ming is feeding intelligence back to the same gang to allow them to stay one step ahead of the police. When the only officer who knows of Yan's deep cover is killed, both officers are pitted in a race against the clock to discover the other's identity before their house of cards collapses.

Review: A slick and lightning-fast crime caper that led to two further sequels, *Infernal Affairs* also inspired Scorsese's *The Departed*. With such a complex plot, those who have poor attention spans may find themselves having to watch from the beginning again. Naturally, it's better than the Hollywood remake.

FURTHER VIEWING: ***Infernal Affairs 2; Infernal Affairs 3***
SEE ALSO: ***The Departed; Donnie Brasco***

★★★

Director: John Milius
Screenwriters: John Milius and Kevin Reynolds

Produced by: Sydney Beckerman and Buzz Feitshans

Starring: Patrick Swayze, C. Thomas Howell, and Lea Thompson
Released by: MGM (DVD)

RED DAWN

1984, 114 mins.

Plot: In an alternate 1984, Communism has infected most of the world outside the United States. With food shortages and social unrest, the Soviet Union—with their Central American allies—invade the U.S.; in a small town in Colorado, a group of high-school students stage an effective resistance for a high price.

Review: *Red Dawn* is a who's who of "Where are they now?" eighties teen actors—Charlie Sheen, Lea Thompson, Jennifer Grey, and C. Thomas Howell make up the ensemble cast—but this isn't your typical eighties teen film. Made during the Cold War and at the height of the Reagan administration, it highlights the constant undercurrent of fear society experiences when living in a nuclear age with only a tenuous peace keeping the superpowers at bay. It was also condemned at the time by the National Coalition on Television Violence, but then so was *Gremlins*.

FURTHER VIEWING: *Dillinger; Conan the Barbarian; Farewell to the King*
SEE ALSO: *Invasion U.S.A.; Red Nightmare; The Red Menace; Rambo: First Blood Part 2*

★★★★

Director: Geoffrey Wright
Screenwriter: Geoffrey Wright
Producer: Ian Pringle

Starring: Russell Crowe, Daniel Pollock, and Jacqueline McKenzie
Released by: Twentieth Century Fox (DVD)

18+

ROMPER STOMPER

1992, 94 mins.

Plot: Hando, a violent Australian skinhead with neo-Nazi tendencies, and his friend Davey want to keep their country pure, no matter what the cost. With other likeminded individuals in tow, they cause anarchy in their local area, assaulting anyone who isn't white. When attractive drug addict Gabe enters the picture, it creates tension between Davey and Hando that threatens to tear their group apart.

Review: Extremely controversial upon its release, it made a star out of Russell Crowe. The assault on the Vietnamese group in the underpass clearly references *A Clockwork Orange*—but rather than the futuristic setting where youth is out of control, this could be today. While overwhelming, the underlying violence-begets-violence message is clear.

FURTHER VIEWING: *Cherry Falls; Lover Boy*
SEE ALSO: *Chopper; A Clockwork Orange*

59

★★★★

Director: Gordon Parks
Screenwriters: Ernest Tidyman and John D. F. Black
Produced by: Joel Freeman
Starring: Richard Roundtree, Moses Gunn, and Charles Cioffi
Released by: Warner Home Video (DVD with *Shaft's Big Score*)

8+

SHAFT

1971, 100 mins.

Plot: Shaft is a black New York City-based private detective. When the leader of an uptown gang hires him to find his kidnapped daughter, Shaft becomes embroiled in a turf war between the black uptown gangsters and the white downtown mafia, but never loses his cool or his mojo.

Review: This is blaxploitation at its best, and not just because of the award-winning Isaac Hayes soundtrack. Based on the novel by Ernest Tidyman, who also had a hand in writing the screenplay, *Shaft* is an entertaining mix of traditional noir and modern action film presided over by the irrepressibly suave John Shaft.

FURTHER VIEWING: *Shaft's Big Score; Shaft in Africa; Shaft (2000)*
SEE ALSO: *Superfly; The Mack*

60

★★★

Director: Luc Besson
Screenwriters: Luc Besson and François Ruggieri
Produced by: Luc Besson, Louis Duchesne, and François Ruggieri
Starring: Isabelle Adjani and Christopher Lambert
Released by: UAV Entertainment (DVD)

15+

SUBWAY

1985, 104 mins.

Plot: After stealing compromising documents from a gangster, suave, chic thief Fred seeks refuge in the surreal but dangerous world of the Paris Metro. While on the run, he begins a romance with the beautiful but bored wife of the gangster—and forms his own rock band from some of the curious denizens of the subterranean depths.

Review: With its neon-lit, extreme, and existential MTV eighties style (supported by a very eighties soundtrack) this is a trip—in every sense of the word—through Luc Besson's urban desolation, with Lambert as his guide. It may be a little light on substance, but it's beautiful to look at, occasionally funny, punctuated with violence, and bristling with inventiveness and some brilliantly eccentric characters.

FURTHER VIEWING: *The Big Blue; Nikita; Taxi; Leon; The Fifth Element*
SEE ALSO: *Death Line; Creep*

161
500

★
★
★

Director: Gérard Pirès
Screenwriter: Luc Besson

Produced by: Luc Besson, Laurent Pétin, and Michèle Pétin

Starring: Samy Naceri, Frédéric Diefenthal, and Marion Cotillard
Released by: TVR Films (DVD)

15+

TAXI

1998, 86 mins.

Plot: Guilty of multiple traffic violations, Marseilles taxi driver Daniel is offered a reprieve. His license will be returned if he helps bumbling cop Émilien capture a gang of well-armed, Mercedes-driving German bank robbers. The two are soon burning rubber as the pursuit shifts into high gear.

Review: This spirited French high-speed, heist-action-comedy thriller exudes urban cool. Beautiful cars, lots of guns, gorgeous women, snappy dialog, two disparate personalities, good crook, lousy cop, epic car chases, great soundtrack—everything that you need in a great buddy flick.

FURTHER VIEWING: ***Riders; Les chevaliers du ciel (Sky Fighters)***
SEE ALSO: ***The Fast and the Furious; Point Break; Bullit; Leon***

162
500

★
★
★
★

Director: Robert Aldrich
Screenwriter: Robert Aldrich
Producer: Robert Aldrich

Starring: Michael Caine and Cliff Robertson
Released by: MGM (DVD)

15+

TOO LATE THE HERO

1970, 128 mins.

Plot: Cliff Robertson and Michael Caine star in this cynical World War II drama about a Japanese interpreter assigned to a British commando unit in the South Pacific. After witnessing combat first hand, Lieutenant Lawson begins to fear for his life when he is instructed to infiltrate Japanese territory with a small unit to destroy their radio equipment. Upon their arrival, dissent breaks out among the soldiers, and it's up to the reluctant Lawson to complete the mission.

Review: Aldrich's close attention to the relationships between the jaded companions exemplifies both the robust British spirit and the futility of war in a stark fashion. Released during the Vietnam War, it could arguably be said it pandered to the patriotic and the conscientious objectors at the time.

FURTHER VIEWING: ***The Dirty Dozen; The Flight of the Phoenix***
SEE ALSO: ***Kelly's Heroes; The Eagle Has Landed***

★★★

Director: Tony Scott
Screenwriters: Quentin Tarantino and Roger Avary

Produced by: Gary Barber, Samuel Hadida, Steve Perry, and Bill Unger

Starring: Christian Slater and Patricia Arquette
Released by: Warner Home Video (DVD)

8+ TRUE ROMANCE

1993, 121 mins.

Plot: Clarence meets Alabama at a Sonny Chiba triple feature—it's love at first sight, and they marry the next day. But Alabama is a call girl, and, sensing this will be an obstacle to their happiness, Clarence kills her pimp and steals a suitcase full of cocaine from him. In trying to sell the cocaine Clarence and Alabama attract the wrath of not only the police, but also the gangsters who claim to have originally owned the drugs.

Review: This is Tarantino's first feature-film screenplay and an indication of things to come. *True Romance* features an incredible ensemble cast, including Dennis Hopper, Val Kilmer, Gary Oldman, Brad Pitt, Christopher Walken, and Samuel L. Jackson, and is a must-see for any self-respecting Tarantino fan.

FURTHER VIEWING: *Pulp Fiction; Reservoir Dogs*
SEE ALSO: *Natural Born Killers; Badlands*

CHAPTER 4
VISIONARY UNIVERSES

"LAST NIGHT A FAIRY VISITED ME"

This is where our flights of fancy are allowed maximum wingspan as even our wildest dreams are no match for such imaginative cinematic achievements. Going slightly against the grain, we've grouped fantasy and sci-fi in the same category, but really they're just two sides of the same coin—whether you use technology or magic as the preferred method to explore the furthest reaches of your imagination, you still qualify as a visionary. In this section you'll find movies that completely reinvent reality, as well as those that merely view it from a new angle or one step to the side; these are the stories that transport us from the humdrum of the everyday to the wonders of the "other."

TOP 10 VISIONARY UNIVERSES

★★★★★

Director: Ridley Scott
Screenwriters: Hampton Fancher and David Peoples
Produced by: Michael Deeley
Starring: Harrison Ford, Rutger Hauer, and Sean Young
Released by: Warner Home Video (DVD)

15+

BLADE RUNNER

1982, 116 mins.

Plot: By 2019, technology has advanced so far that the human race has developed "replicants"—biorobotic androids used as slaves by humans. The replicants revolt "off world"; as a result, replicants are declared illegal on Earth, and "blade runners," who are trained to track, expose, and "retire" escaped replicants, find themselves with more work than they can handle. When one blade runner is killed in the line of duty, Rick Deckard is forced out of retirement to track probably the most dangerous band of replicants Earth has ever seen: possessing superhuman strength and intelligence, they've also started developing emotions.

Review: *Blade Runner* has almost as many cuts as replicants; over the years we've seen the theatrical cut, the workprint cut, the international cut, the director's cut, the final cut, the really really final cut, and the no-I-swear-this-is-it cut. But no matter—fans of this film tend to be rabid enough to buy all versions, whether they differ by two minutes or twenty, so clearly the output is justified.

Based on Philip K. Dick's novel *Do Androids Dream of Electric Sheep?*, *Blade Runner* bombed at the box office despite the fact that it starred Harrison Ford, who was still riding high on the success of *The Empire Strikes Back* and *Raiders of the Lost Ark*. But the real breakout performance in this film comes courtesy of Rutger Hauer as the deeply chilling renegade replicant leader Roy Batty. With the strength, efficiency, and intelligence of a machine, Batty wars with his developing emotions as his body deteriorates; he becomes, in effect, a "real boy" just when his pre-programmed lifespan comes to an end. The fate of Batty's character leaves us with the most questions about the nature of humanity and its relation to machines, and Hauer's portrayal of him is convincing and empathetic. An undeniably influential cult sci-fi masterpiece.

FURTHER VIEWING: ***Alien; Gladiator***
SEE ALSO: ***The Fifth Element; Minority Report; A.I.: Artificial Intelligence; Brazil; Total Recall***

★★★★★

Director: Terry Gilliam
Screenwriters: Terry Gilliam, Tom Stoppard, and Charles McKeown

Produced by: Arnon Milchan and Joseph P. Grace
Starring: Jonathan Pryce, Kim Greist, Michael Palin, and Robert De Niro

Released by: Criterion (DVD)

5+

BRAZIL

1985, 136 mins.

Plot: In a dystopian alternate reality, Sam Lowry is a low-level civil servant who daydreams about a beautiful woman to while away the time he spends at his desk. When he's assigned to correct a government screw-up involving the execution of an innocent man, he finds the man's wife's neighbor is the girl of his dreams (literally). She's wrongly suspected of terrorism, so Lowry uses his position to protect her by falsifying her records. The government finds out and attempts to torture him for information, but he's saved by a terrorist group in the nick of time . . . or so we think.

Review: Probably best known for his Monty Python work even now, Terry Gilliam isn't the kind of writer/director who makes easy films. They're beautiful, certainly, but they're also bizarre in a way that makes us feel as if we're only given glimpses into the strange and wonderful world that exists inside Gilliam's head. If *The Brothers Grimm* could be called his most accessible film, then *Brazil* is quite possibly the least.

Part of a loose trilogy of films dealing with the fine line between fantasy and reality—the others are *Time Bandits* and *The Adventures of Baron Munchausen*—*Brazil* floats on a darker undercurrent of satire than the others, as this time the fantasy is constructed within, and as an antidote to, an Orwellian nightmare of reality. The darkness in the picture, and its depressing but necessary ending, caused its Hollywood studio to shelve it for a time. But a film like this doesn't lose its relevance in a year or even twenty; we will always need imagination to combat the grim realities of day-to-day life, and if nothing else, we have someone like Gilliam and a film like *Brazil* to show us the way. Despite its rough edges, this is his finest film, and his most important.

FURTHER VIEWING: ***The Imaginarium of Doctor Parnassus; The Brothers Grimm; The Adventures of Baron Munchausen; Time Bandits; 12 Monkeys***
SEE ALSO: ***Blade Runner; Kafka; Metropolis; 1984***

★★★★★

Director: Robert Wise
Screenwriter: Edmund H. North
Produced by: Julian Blaustein

Starring: Michael Rennie, Patricia Neal, and Hugh Marlowe
Released by: Twentieth Century Fox (DVD)

A

THE DAY THE EARTH STOOD STILL

1951, 92 mins.

Plot: Alien Klaatu lands his flying saucer on Earth with a message for the humans. So the Earthlings shoot him. While recovering in an Army hospital he attempts to get an audience with the President and a host of world leaders but fails. He escapes the hospital to live among humans and experience daily life; in doing so he comes across an Einstein-like scientist who gives him a chance to speak at a meeting of scientists, and Klaatu tells him that the other planets are worried that Earth will become an intergalactic aggressor now that it has obtained nuclear power. If the people don't heed his message, "Earth will be eliminated."

Review: In the 1950s Hollywood churned out sci-fi films, and horror, like paper cups meant straight for the garbage. This was the heyday of the drive-in B-movie, after all. So when this intelligent, thoughtful, and politically aware science-fiction film was released, audiences and critics couldn't help but take notice.

As a political (and possibly religious) allegory, *The Day the Earth Stood Still* is decidedly liberal. In the midst of the Cold War, still at the height of atomic-age fear, this film championed non-partisan peace while asserting humanity was unlikely to embrace such a simple concept. Needless to say, the film wasn't well received by the establishment—it's advocating peace! It must be communist!—but it quickly became beloved by audiences for its entertaining and suspenseful story coupled with a culturally germane message. Klaatu's untranslated alien phrase "Klaatu barada nikto" has become one of the most famous and oft-quoted film lines of all time, and certainly in sci-fi—but you need look no farther than *Army of Darkness* for its use in a completely different genre (they're the magic words Ash needs to say but can't remember when retrieving the *Necronomicon*). This is sci-fi at its best, and even those who think they hate sci-fi will find something to appreciate here.

FURTHER VIEWING: *The Day the Earth Stood Still (2008 remake); The Andromeda Strain; Star Trek: The Motion Picture*
SEE ALSO: *Close Encounters of the Third Kind; The Man Who Fell to Earth*

★ ★ ★ ★

Director: Jim Henson
Screenwriters: Dennis Lee, Jim Henson, and Terry Jones
Produced by: George Lucas
Starring: Jennifer Connelly, David Bowie, and Toby Froud
Released by: Sony Pictures (DVD)

A

LABYRINTH

1986, 101 mins.

Plot: Fifteen-year-old Sarah is a lover of fairy tales and a hater of her infant half-brother Toby, whom she's forced to babysit. After making an offhand wish that goblins come and steal him away, her wish comes true. She instantly regrets it, and Jareth, the Goblin King, promises to return her brother if she solves his labyrinth in thirteen hours or less. If not, Toby will be turned into a goblin and lost forever.

Review: Puppets! M. C. Escher staircases! David Bowie in spandex! If that isn't enough to hook you, consider this: *Labyrinth* is an alluring fairy tale made frighteningly real, with all the consequences that come with finally getting your wish.

"Fear me, love me, do as I say, and I will be your slave," says Jareth to Sarah. What? That *Labyrinth* walks the line between kid film and grown-up film—especially as its fantasy puppet imagery contrasts with adult themes of control and sacrifice, domination and submission (nonsexual, one hastens to add)—probably didn't help any at the box office, where the film died a quick but excruciatingly painful death. But it does reflect in a larger sense Sarah's ascent into womanhood and the terrible confusion that comes with it, a sort of adult honesty encased in an easy-to-swallow sugared children's pill. David Bowie's soundtrack makes for a suitably odd accompaniment, all eighties and conceptual. Though clearly too offbeat for the mainstream, *Labyrinth* has become a serious cult classic in the years since its release and is now considered essential viewing for kids and parents (as well as those who are neither kids nor parents).

FURTHER VIEWING: *The Dark Crystal*
SEE ALSO: *MirrorMask; The Neverending Story; Legend*

★★★★★

Director: Guillermo del Toro
Screenwriter: Guillermo del Toro

Produced by: Guillermo del Toro, Alfonso Cuarón, Bertha Navarro, Frida Torresblanco, and Alvaro Augustin

Starring: Ivana Baquero, Doug Jones, and Sergi López
Released by: New Line Home Video (DVD)

15+

PAN'S LABYRINTH

2006, 112 mins.

Plot: In 1944, post-Civil War Spain is still in the throes of revolutionary uprising. Eleven-year-old Ofelia and Carmen, her pregnant mother, join Carmen's new husband Captain Vidal at his military outpost in the mountains. Here the narrative splits into two interlinked streams: in one, Ofelia enters the labyrinth into a fairyland where she is the lost Princess Moanna who must complete three tasks before the next full moon so she can return home to her father, the king. In the other she is the unwanted stepchild of a violent and cruel military despot, and she is caught in the fight between him and the rebels while her mother grows weaker from a difficult pregnancy.

Review: Unlike many cult films, *Pan's Labyrinth* didn't have to spend years fermenting in the public imagination before it attained critical acclaim; it became a darling of film reviewers on its initial release, prompting almost a half-hour standing ovation at its Cannes premier and universally positive (on the verge of salivating) reviews. Although it sounds too good to be true, the film deserves every accolade.

Director del Toro has a knack for combining confident, imaginative storytelling with surprising and lyrically beautiful visuals, and this film demonstrates the zenith of his achievement in that respect (so far). As an added bonus, the eleven-year-old star, Ivana Baquero, proved to be a formidable talent, anchoring the picture like a seasoned leading lady with her quiet intensity and adult vulnerability. As our window into both the horrific violence of the Spanish Civil War and the fantastic, sinister beauty of the Labyrinth world, she becomes an artful, but honest, guide and translator—the Virgil del Toro assigns to our Dante.

This is a stunning piece of filmmaking and a must-see.

FURTHER VIEWING: ***The Devil's Backbone; Hellboy; Hellboy 2: The Golden Army***
SEE ALSO: ***Labyrinth; The Spirit of the Beehive; Hope and Glory***

Director: Darren Aronofsky
Screenwriter: Darren Aronofsky
Producer: Eric Watson

Starring: Sean Gullette, Mark Margolis, and Ben Shenkman
Released by: Lionsgate (DVD)

5+

PI

1998, 84 mins.

Plot: Max Cohen (Sean Gullette) is a mathematical genius studying the significance of number patterns that he believes exist everywhere in nature. His main project is the analysis of the stock market, and if it's possible to work out the formula to predict stock rises and crashes. He is crippled by anxiety problems and paranoia, slowly killing himself with a severe diet of strong medication. As he gets closer to a breakthrough, his homemade computer Euclid produces a 216-digit number that could be the key to unlocking the Torah and the name of God. His lack of faith turns him away from this path, and he accepts a job working with a suspicious group of men claiming to be from Wall Street who want to profit from Max's theories. Slowly but surely, Max's mind begins to unravel as he starts to understand the crippling honesty of math.

Review: Aronofsky's first feature cost a mere $60,000 to produce, but was such a financial success at the box office that his next (difficult) project, *The Fountain*, was optioned by Warner Bros. Shot in high contrast black and white in New York City, *Pi*'s rapid cuts are powered by a driving drum and bass score by Clint Mansell—quite an odd choice for such a technical film. Indeed, some of the dialog can be hard to follow and apes the scientists in *Altered States* for their quickfire delivery of difficult dialog. Don't let that put you off, though, as Gullette makes for a fascinating lead, racked with obsessive compulsions and an insatiable thirst for knowledge. From all this madness, there lies only ruin. Not quite science-fiction or science-fact, it is still a stunning, award-winning debut from a great modern talent.

FURTHER VIEWING: *Requiem for a Dream; The Fountain*
SEE ALSO: *Eraserhead; Primer*

★★★★★

Director: Franklin J. Schaffner
Screenwriters: Michael Wilson and Rod Serling

Produced by: Mort Abrahams and Arthur P. Jacobs
Starring: Charlton Heston, Roddy McDowell, and Kim Hunter

Released by: Twentieth Century Fox (DVD)

12+

PLANET OF THE APES

1968, 112 mins.

Plot: A group of astronauts have been traveling through space in deep hibernation for thousands of years when they crash land on an unknown planet. In exploring they find that roles are reversed in this civilization: humans are feral and incapable of speech, and the apes, who are the more intelligent species and can speak, rule the land like humans do on Earth. Taylor (played by Heston) is captured by the apes and caged—though he gets shot in the throat and is rendered incapable of speech at first, the scientists watching over his cage soon learn he's intelligent and capable of communicating. The apes attempt to determine Taylor's origins, but even Taylor isn't sure where he comes from until he's taken out to the Forbidden Zone, the ruins of a once-great and technologically advanced human settlement. When he goes farther into the wilderness, his own origins, and those of the planet of the apes, become horribly clear.

Review: It's probably not giving anything away to mention the Statue of Liberty scene ("Damn you! Goddamn you all to hell!"); even if you haven't seen the film, you know the iconic image. This is another one of those movies that's invaded the public consciousness and reached far beyond the confines of celluloid. It would be impossible to list all the parodies and homages that have been made in the almost half a century since its release—references in *The Simpsons* alone would take up several pages.

By and large the famous "twist" ending is pretty much ruined, even for new viewers. So why bother watching it? Apart from finally understanding all those *MST3K* jokes, see it because it's a chance to watch a cracking good sci-fi yarn enhanced by visionary makeup effects (artist John Chambers was given an honorary Oscar for outstanding makeup achievement).

FURTHER VIEWING: *Planet of the Apes (2001 remake); Beneath the Planet of the Apes; Escape from the Planet of the Apes; Conquest of the Planet of the Apes; Battle for the Planet of the Apes*
SEE ALSO: *The Fantastic Planet; Omega Doom; Beyond the Time Barrier*

★
★
★
★
★

Director: Richard Linklater
Screenwriter: Richard Linklater

Produced by: Tommy Pallotta, Anne Walker-McBay, Palmer West, Jonah Smith, and Erwin Stoff

Starring: Keanu Reeves, Robert Downey Jr., Winona Ryder, and Woody Harrelson
Released by: Warner Home Video (DVD)

5+

A SCANNER DARKLY

2006, 100 mins.

Plot: Bob Arctor is an undercover agent in the future after America has failed to stem the drug epidemic, and a highly addictive, highly dangerous drug called Substance D has become almost as cheap and available as Tic Tacs. Arctor infiltrates a suspected drug ring but becomes addicted to Substance D in the process—he begins to suffer a form of brain damage in which the two hemispheres of his brain stop communicating with each other, making it impossible for him to distinguish between his roles as undercover cop and drug addict. A now-addled and identity-less Arctor is removed from duty to get "help," but the so-called rehab center reveals the true cause of his addiction and now-permanent brain damage.

Review: Philip K. Dick seems like he should be a hard writer to film, and yet, because adaptations of his work attract talented and experimental filmmakers, they tend to be some of the most interesting and beloved by fans.

A Scanner Darkly achieved its look by animating over a digital live-action recording, and the effect is realistic for an animation but detached from reality. (A bit like the mental effects Bob Arctor suffers from his addiction to Substance D.) The overall impression is rough and ready, but on closer inspection the animation is incredibly detailed down to the slightest facial nuance, so no aspect of the actors' performances is lost—it just reads ethereal. And speaking of performances, can Robert Downey Jr. do no wrong? He is absolutely hilarious as the borderline autistic, flawed genius Barris, a perfect foil to Reeves' subdued and confused Arctor. Barris may be equally confused, but at least he has conviction in it. And you have to admit, a toilet-paper-roll silencer is an idea we all wish we'd thought of, regardless of whether it works or not.

FURTHER VIEWING: *Minority Report; Total Recall; Blade Runner*
SEE ALSO: *Strange Days; The Matrix; Bringing Out the Dead*

★
★
★
★

Director: George Lucas
Screenwriter: George Lucas
Produced by: Gary Kurtz
Starring: Mark Hamill, Harrison Ford, and Carrie Fisher
Released by: Twentieth Century Fox (DVD)

A

STAR WARS A NEW HOPE

1977, 125 mins.

Plot: On a distant planet, bored farm boy Luke Skywalker discovers a hidden message and, joined by a band of miscreants, sets off to rescue a beautiful princess imprisoned by the tyrannical Empire. However, he soon finds himself caught in a desperate battle for the survival of freedom and justice across the galaxy.

Review: This is one of those rarefied movies that caused a grave tremor across the entire movie industry, changing forever the way films were marketed and packaged. But there's more to this than characters slapped on lunchboxes. It's easy to call it shallow and naïve, but this film is full of innocent heart, and that's what made it fun. Before *SW:ANH*, sci-fi had become ponderous and pretentious, but Lucas brought the fun and the thrills back into a tired genre, recapturing the heady days of *Flash Gordon* and *Buck Rogers*. Of course, the movie boasts Oscar-winning special effects that were as revolutionary in their approach as the marketing, as was the production design; gone were gleaming ships and astronauts in silver foil spacesuits, and in was the "lived-in" look. The ships, the sets, everything looked everyday, in some cases like they were held together with duct tape and bubblegum, adding a dimension of plausibility rarely seen in sci-fi before. The cast were mostly unknowns but again that just gave them an everyman feel of folk wandering through a shabby everyday existence; that they were on desert planets or space stations was incidental, and therein lay the movie's success: it could appeal to everyone.

Lest we forget it's also packed with innumerable pop-culture icons, matinee-idol fun, and crackling and quotable dialog.

FURTHER VIEWING: ***Star Wars: The Empire Strikes Back; Star Wars: Return of the Jedi; Star Wars: The Phantom Menace; THX-1138***
SEE ALSO: ***Battle Beyond the Stars; Battlestar Galactica; Family Guy: Blue Harvest; Robot Chicken: Star Wars***

★★★★★

Director: David Cronenberg
Screenwriter: David Cronenberg
Produced by: Claude Héroux

Starring: James Woods, Debbie Harry, and Sonja Smits
Released by: Criterion (DVD)

8+

VIDEODROME

1983, 89 mins.

Plot: Max Renn is the president of a softcore-porn television channel based in Toronto. Looking to boost ratings, Renn views *Videodrome* from the feed of a pirate satellite—it's a television show comprised entirely of snuff films. Renn appears on a talk show to defend his new programming direction and meets, and dates, sadomasochistic psychiatrist Nikki Brand (played by Blondie's Debbie Harry). She loves *Videodrome*, finding it sexually stimulating, and when Renn learns that the show is being broadcast from no more an exotic location than Pittsburgh, Nikki travels there to audition. But when Nikki doesn't return home, Renn is drawn into a strange web of politics and technological addiction so deep that he can never, ever escape.

Review: "First it controls your mind, then it destroys your body." *Videodrome* is as equally scary as it is disturbing in a way that only Cronenberg can pull off. Like most of his films, there's a representation of the body as something always hovering at the threshold of grotesque and disgusting—in *The Fly* it was Jeff Goldblum's body morphing into a half-man/half-fly monstrosity; here we have bodies used as video machines, and masses of techno-tumors bursting forth from desiccated flesh.

This has been called one of the scariest movies and one of the weirdest, and it is very much both. It's also Debbie Harry's feature film debut—she proves here, and later, that she has a knack for playing odd characters that exist just outside the realm of social acceptability. Essentially a morality tale on the dangers of becoming too obsessed with technology, *Videodrome* also tips its hat to urban legends surrounding said technology, particularly the early suspicion that watching television caused brain tumors, and that right-wing extremists used television to broadcast mind-controlling signals. The film certainly taps into the technology zeitgeist and all its related fears—as long as you can stomach Cronenberg's trademark grossness, this is a valuable comment on society and its difficult relationship with progress.

FURTHER VIEWING: *The Fly; Scanners; The Dead Zone*
SEE ALSO: *The Matrix; Ghost in the Machine; Brain Dead*

174/500

★★★★

Director: Stanley Kubrick
Screenwriters: Arthur C. Clarke and Stanley Kubrick
Produced by: Stanley Kubrick

Starring: Keir Dullea, Gary Lockwood, and William Sylvester
Released by: Warner Home Video (DVD)

12+

2001 A SPACE ODYSSEY

1968, 141 mins.

Plot: A mysterious monolith appears to a group of early proto-humans on the edge of extinction, galvanizing human evolution. Millions of years later, the monolith is discovered on the moon from where it sends a single transmission to Jupiter. A mission is sent to the distant planet to discover why, but the astronauts have to now contend with a homicidal computer.

Review: A film of dazzling complexity—philosophically, technically, and culturally—*2001* redefined the sci-fi genre. It wasn't just the mind-blowing subject matter; this was a movie where everything looked like it worked, aided and abetted by stunning special effects. Just don't try to understand it—simply sit back and enjoy a long, luxurious flight of fantasy.

FURTHER VIEWING: ***2010; A Clockwork Orange; The Shining; Eyes Wide Shut***
SEE ALSO: ***A.I.: Artificial Intelligence; Solaris***

175/500

★★★★

Director: Katsuhiro Ôtomo
Screenwriter: Izô Hashimoto
Producer: Haruyo Kanesaku

Starring: Mitsuo Iwata, Nozomu Sasaki, Mami Koyama
Released by: Geneon/Pioneer (DVD)

15+

AKIRA

1988, 124 mins.

Plot: Tokyo is destroyed by a nuclear blast, which is caused by a child called Akira who wields immense telekinetic powers. Years later, those who walk the neon-lit streets of Neo Tokyo live in fear of the motorcycle gangs that battle there daily. During one conflict, biker Tetsuo is injured and taken away by the military. His genetic characteristics are similar to Akira, but they are unable to control him, and Tetsuo chooses to take control of his destiny even if it means the destruction of the city once again.

Review: For those in the West, Akira is *the* anime to return to time and again. Painstakingly animated, the character designs and cityscapes are a joy to behold, setting a benchmark for future sci-fi directors that has yet to be surpassed.

FURTHER VIEWING: ***Suchîmubôi (Steamboy); Roujin Z***
SEE ALSO: ***Venus Wars; Blade Runner***

76

★ **Director:** Jean-Luc Godard
★ **Screenwriter:** Jean-Luc Godard
★ **Produced by:** André Michelin

Starring: Eddie Constantine, Anna Karina, and Akim Tamiroff
Released by: Criterion (DVD)

12+

ALPHAVILLE

1965, 99 mins.

Plot: Lemmy Caution is a secret agent on an undercover mission to destroy wheezing Orwellian computer Alpha 60, who deems all emotion and art to be illegal, and controls every aspect of daily life in Alphaville. His rebellious, emotive personality is soon at odds with Alpha 60, especially when Lemmy adds love to the equation.

Review: Mixing Mike Hammer and *Metropolis*, Godard's hugely imaginative film constantly defies expectations as the trench-coated hero—the wonderfully named Lemmy Caution—snaps between black sci-fi comedy, existential film noir, and action thriller.

The swimming pool scene alone is a Busby Berkeley nightmare, and shows categorically that sci-fi doesn't have to be the purview of spaceships and aliens, but can be a truly original, bold stroke of genius.

FURTHER VIEWING: *Breathless; Pierrot le fou; Week End; Amore e rabbia (Love and Anger); Passion; Masculin, feminine; King Lear*
SEE ALSO: *1984; Metropolis; Renaissance*

177/500

★★★

Director: Ken Russell
Screenwriter: Paddy Chayefsky
Producer: Howard Gottfried
Starring: William Hurt and Blair Brown
Released by: Warner Home Video (DVD)

18+

ALTERED STATES

1980, 102 mins.

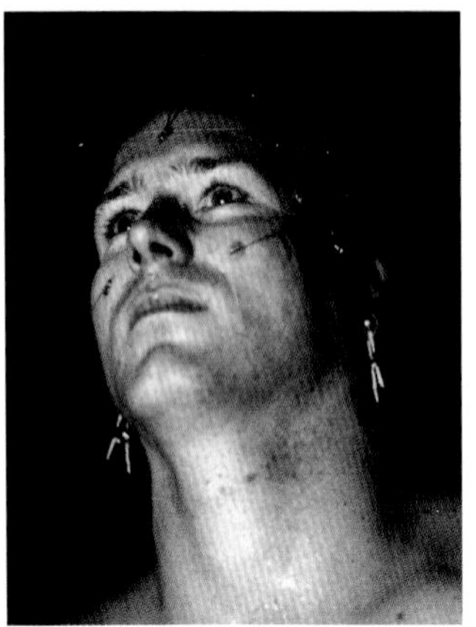

Plot: William Hurt's screen debut was as university professor Edward Jessup, who is experimenting with altered states of consciousness through sensory deprivation. At first, his visions extend to those of his late father and the existence of God, but as the experiments become more intense with the addition of strong hallucinogens, Jessup begins to regress to the earliest incarnation of man.

Review: A trippy, hugely influential movie due to its intense soundtrack and symbolic visuals, Russell's complex examination of states of consciousness is deliberately constructed to overload the senses. Characters talk a mile a minute over each other, hallucinogenic images of crucifixions pound your skull, and the conclusion will leave you breathless from its sheer boldness. Turn up the volume when you watch.

FURTHER VIEWING: ***Lisztomania; Valentino***
SEE ALSO: ***Jacob's Ladder; 2001: A Space Odyssey***

178/500

★★★

Director: Robert Wise
Screenwriter: Nelson Gidding
Produced by: Robert Wise
Starring: Arthur Hill, David Wayne, and James Olson
Released by: Universal (DVD)

THE ANDROMEDA STRAIN

1971, 131 mins.

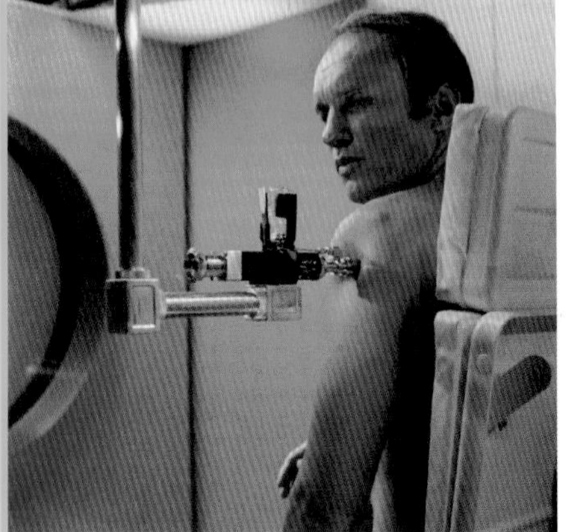

Plot: After a satellite falls to earth, the population of a small town near the crash site dies of an apparent and unexplained alien disease, leaving only two survivors: a sick old man and a baby. A crack team of scientists now race to uncover the secrets of this terrifying extraterrestrial attack.

Review: With his flair for making the horrifying entirely plausible, Michael Crichton's story delivers a great "what if" scenario. No special effects, no hysterical performances, just cutting-edge sci-fi that's loaded with tension and humanistic portrayals of scientists completely out of their depth. Director Wise pushes for complete realism in an unimaginable context and proves you don't need mutant dinosaurs for real scares; what's truly terrifying is the attack from within—a much more bitterly contested battlefield.

FURTHER VIEWING: ***The Day the Earth Stood Still; Rising Sun; Run Silent Run Deep; Coma; Westworld; Jurassic Park***
SEE ALSO: ***The Happening; Outbreak; The Quatermass Experiment; [Rec]***

★★★

Director: Roger Vadim
Screenwriter: Roger Vadim and Terry Southern
Produced by: Dino De Laurentiis
Starring: Jane Fonda, John Phillip Law, and Marcel Marceau
Released by: Paramount (DVD)

5+ BARBARELLA QUEEN OF THE GALAXY

1968, 98 mins.

Plot: Based on Jean-Claude Forest's French-published *Barbarella* comic strips. It's the fortieth century and the President of Earth has asked Barbarella to rescue some guy in a bid to save Earth. Beyond this there really is no plot, just a string of sexual romps that include the legendary "Excessive Machine," which tortures its victims by overloading them with sexual pleasure.

Review: Really just an excuse to see Jane Fonda traipsing across the galaxy in her underwear, although it's worth noting that the sex, while plentiful, is more stylized than graphic. A complete failure on its release, both critically and commercially, *Barbarella* has since become a camp classic. Mindless, so-bad-it's-good fun.

FURTHER VIEWING: *Pretty Maids All in a Row; Night Games; And God Created Woman*
SEE ALSO: *Cherry 2000; Cemetery Man; Galaxina; Battle Queen 2020*

180
500

★
★
★

Director: Hideki Takayama
Screenwriters: Shô Aikawa
Produced by: Yoshinobu Nishizaki
Starring: Bick Balse, Christopher Courage, and Rebel Joy
Released by: Central Park Media (DVD)

15+

CHÔJIN DENSETSU UROTSUKIDÔJI
(UROTSUKIDÔJI: LEGEND OF THE OVERFIEND)

1989, 108 mins.

Plot: There are three realms: human, demon, and man-beast. And a legend that every three thousand years a powerful "Overfiend" returns, uniting them all. The Overfiend exists in the body of Nagumo, a shy student, who becomes a monstrous creature, set on rebuilding the world in his own distorted vision.

Review: One of the most well known Japanese animations in the world, it became so notorious in the West for its graphic tentacle rape scenes that an entire anime genre emerged. Highly explicit and extremely violent.

FURTHER VIEWING: ***Shin chôjin densetsu Urotsukidôji: Mataiden (Urotsukidôji II: Legend of the Demon Womb); Chôjin densetsu Urotsukidôji: Mirai hen (Urotsukidôji III: Return of the Overfiend)***
SEE ALSO: ***Devil Man; Fist of the North Star***

181
500

★
★
★
★

Director: John Milius
Screenwriters: John Milius and Oliver Stone
Produced by: Raffaella De Laurentiis and Buzz Feitshans
Starring: Arnold Swarzenegger, James Earl Jones, and Max von Sydow
Released by: Twentieth Century Fox Home Entertainment (DVD)

15+

CONAN THE BARBARIAN

1982, 123 mins.

Plot: His parents slain, his people annihilated, Conan is enslaved as a small boy, but success as a gladiator forges him into a warrior and earns him his freedom. He sets off after his parents' killer, the shape-shifting demigod, Thulsa Doom. His revenge is bloody, but comes with a terrible price for Conan.

Review: When *Conan* opens with a quote from Nietzsche, you realize the script is not just blood and high adventure; there's genuine pathos, loss, and humor, but what makes this film stand out is Schwarzenegger's eponymous hero. His touching, poignant relationship with his beloved Valeria and friend and fellow thief Subotai give this movie palpable heart and soul.

FURTHER VIEWING: ***Conan the Destroyer; Big Wednesday; Red Dawn***
SEE ALSO: ***Red Sonja; Hawk the Slayer; Jaws; Apocalypse Now!***

82

★★★

Director: Andrew Fleming
Screenwriters: Andrew Fleming and Peter Filardi
Produced by: Douglas Wick, Ginny Nugent, and Lisa Tornell
Starring: Fairuza Balk, Robin Tunney, and Neve Campbell
Released by: Sony Pictures (DVD)

15+

THE CRAFT

1996, 101 mins.

Plot: Bonnie, Nancy, and Rochelle are three outcast Wiccans at a Catholic high school in Los Angeles. Their afterschool activities mainly consist of chanting in the woods and hoping for power, but it doesn't come to anything until "gifted" Sarah enrolls. Together the four develop real witchy power, and of course they use it to take revenge on their classmates. In a time-honored "be careful what you wish for" lesson, they ultimately turn on each other and only the least greedy will survive.

Review: Welcome to the dark side of the teen experience. Those of us who know Fairuza Balk as Dorothy in the delightfully strange *Return to Oz* are in for a surprise here; grown up and gothed up, she gives a stand-out performance as the desperate, power-mad Nancy.

FURTHER VIEWING: *Bad Dreams*
SEE ALSO: *Teen Witch; Ginger Snaps; Little Witches*

83

★★★

Director: Jean-Pierre Jeunet
Screenwriter: Gilles Adrien
Producer: Claudie Ossard
Starring: Pascal Benezech, Dominique Pinon, and Marie-Laure Dougnac
Released by: Lionsgate (DVD)

15+

DELICATESSEN

1991, 99 mins.

Plot: In post-apocalyptic France, out-of-work circus performer Louison takes an apartment above a delicatessen, living alongside a bunch of eccentrics and sex-mad neighbors. The shop hires people who later disappear, having been turned into meat. The daughter of the butcher befriends Louison and, realizing what's coming, must protect him from the salivating mouths of the other tenants.

Review: Jeunet's sepia-toned world brings Gilliam to mind in the first instance—filmed entirely on specially constructed sets (that are later wrecked in a spectacular flooding at the end of the film), we can appreciate the intimacies and infuriation of living in close proximity to lunatics. Despite the bleak premise, it's a surprisingly gentle film with a positive conclusion.

FURTHER VIEWING: *Amélie; The City of Lost Children*
SEE ALSO: *12 Monkeys; Brazil*

184
500

★★★

Director: Donald Cammell
Screenwriters: Roger Hirson and Robert Jaffe
Produced by: Herb Jaffe
Starring: Julie Christie and Fritz Weaver
Released by: Warner Home Video (DVD)

15+

DEMON SEED

1977, 94 mins.

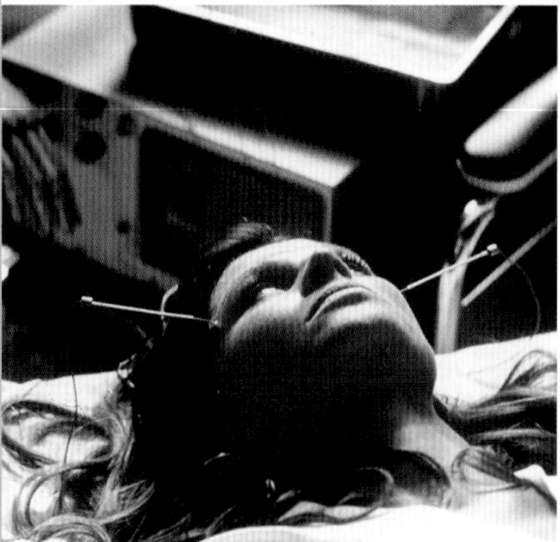

Plot: Alex Harris is a man obsessed with his work. He's in charge of the top-secret Proteus IV project, which is a partially organic system of artificial intelligence. But Proteus soon outgrows his "box," and in a bid to escape his confines he forces Alex's estranged wife, Susan, to carry and give birth to his half-man, half-machine offspring. Good thing Susan's a child psychologist—she's going to need all her expertise for this one.

Review: Based on the novel by master horror writer Dean Koontz, *Demon Seed* is an above-average sci-fi/horror film. The always lovely Julie Christie gives a convincing performance as the neglected and imprisoned Susan, while Robert Vaughn (uncredited) is an emotionless and sinister Proteus. Engagingly high concept.

FURTHER VIEWING: ***Performance; Wild Side***
SEE ALSO: ***2001: A Space Odyssey; Homewrecker; Colossus: The Forbin Project***

185
500

★★

Director: Joseph Ruben
Screenwriters: David Loughery, Joseph Ruben, and Chuck Russell
Produced by: Bruce Cohn Curtis
Starring: Dennis Quaid, Max von Sydow, and Christopher Plummer
Released by: Image Entertainment (DVD)

15+

DREAMSCAPE

1984, 99 mins.

Plot: Young psychic Alex is "recruited" against his will into a secret government program. Initially using his skills benignly, Alex uncovers a plot to use psychics as assassins by affecting the target's dreams—including those of the President who, plagued by nuclear night terrors, wants to end the arms race, a view not popular with some in his administration.

Review: Switching between political thriller and surreal phantasmagoria, this is the flip side to the *Nightmare on Elm Street* coin: less horrific and more intelligent. That said, some of the dream sequences are unsettling, especially the President's atomic horrors and the creepy "snake-man." There's also some able acting to support a sci-fi conceit that could have been plain hokey were it not so well handled.

FURTHER VIEWING: ***Gorp; The Stepfather; Sleeping with the Enemy; Return to Paradise***
SEE ALSO: ***Bloodmoon; Brainscan; Brain Storm; Inner Space; A Nightmare on Elm Street***

186

★★

Director: David Lynch
Screenwriter: David Lynch
Produced by: Dino De Laurentiis
Starring: Kyle MacLachlan and Virginia Madsen
Released by: Universal Studios (DVD)

15+

DUNE

1984, 137 mins.

Plot: Based on the Frank Herbert novel. In the distant future the universe is ruled by a single emperor, and whoever controls the supply of "spice"—a substance that extends life and allows space travel—can have dominion over the universe. The House Atreides is the emperor's only true threat; Duke Atreides' son Paul has the "sight" and is subject to prophetic visions. Because of this, Paul foretells the emperor's elaborate plot to destroy the House Atreides, and the two families engage in a fight to the death over the spice.

Review: All in all, *Dune* is a bit of a mess—sprawling and disjointed, the over-complicated story proves difficult to follow. It was a complete flop on release, and even Lynch, the director, attempted to distance himself from the film. This is just one of those movies you'll either love or hate.

FURTHER VIEWING: *Eraserhead; Twin Peaks: Fire Walk with Me; Blue Velvet*
SEE ALSO: *Blade Runner; The Empire Strikes Back; Flash Gordon; Excalibur*

187

★★★★★

Director: Tim Burton
Screenwriters: Tim Burton and Caroline Thompson
Produced by: Tim Burton, Caroline Thompson, Denise Di Novi, and Richard Hashimoto
Starring: Johnny Depp and Winona Ryder
Released by: Twentieth Century Fox (DVD)

12+

EDWARD SCISSORHANDS

1990, 105 mins.

Plot: In a crumbling mansion high atop a hill overlooking cookie-cutter suburbia, a lonely old inventor builds an artificial son but dies before finishing, leaving him with scissors for hands. The man, Edward, attempts to integrate into society, but prejudice and fear of the unknown prevail, rendering him an outcast and denying him the love for which he so fervently longs.

Review: Tim Burton's imagination is as beautiful as it is bizarre, and he creates a stunning landscape in which to explore themes of communication, social need, and otherness, as well as the fear it naturally engenders. This is also Johnny Depp's breakthrough role; it not only elevated him from teen heartthrob to serious actor, it formed the basis of a long and fruitful creative relationship with Burton.

FURTHER VIEWING: *The Corpse Bride; Vincent (short); Frankenweenie (short)*
SEE ALSO: *Frankenstein; D.A.R.Y.L.; The City of Lost Children*

188
500

★
★
★

Director: John Boorman
Screenwriter: Rospo Pallenberg
Producer: John Boorman

Starring: Nigel Terry, Helen Mirren, and Nicholas Clay
Released by: Warner Home Video (DVD)

15+

EXCALIBUR

1981, 140 mins.

Plot: *Excalibur* charts the legend of the world's most famous sword through two tumultuous eras of ancient British history: the bloody regime of Uther Pendragon and his bastard son, Arthur, all under the watchful eye of the honorable wizard Merlin. After the death of Uther, the sword is buried to the hilt in a rock, and whoever can remove it becomes King. Arthur does so, and begins his journey into the annals of modern myth.

Review: The lavishly shot (and lengthy) eighties remix of the King Arthur legend feels like an earlier version of *Lord of the Rings*, with its fierce battle scenes, expensive sets, and cheeseball dialog thrown in for good measure. Two versions exist—a longer cut features more sex and violence.

FURTHER VIEWING: ***Deliverance; Exorcist II: The Heretic***
SEE ALSO: ***King Arthur; Merlin***

189
500

★
★
★
★
★

Director: François Truffaut
Screenwriters: François Truffaut and Jean-Louis Ricard

Produced by: Lewis M. Allen
Starring: Oskar Werner and Julie Christie
Released by: Universal Studios (DVD)

12+

FAHRENHEIT 451

1966, 112 mins.

Plot: An adaptation of Ray Bradbury's titular book about a dystopian society that scorns knowledge, creativity, and individuality. Montag is a fireman of the future: a man who, instead of extinguishing fires, starts them specifically to burn books. But one day a spirited girl asks him, "Do you ever read the books you burn?" He begins to read to fill the gaps in his uninspired life, forced to hide his secret library from even his wife. When he witnesses a woman die rather than see her books burn, he finds something to fight for.

Review: Apparently a world without books is a world full of drugs and flamethrowers. But before you sign up, realize that in *Fahrenheit 451* a bookless society is also homogeneous, stifling, uncreative, and utterly boring. Beautifully directed and as poignant as its source material.

FURTHER VIEWING: ***Jules et Jim (Jules and Jim); Une belle fille comme moi (A Gorgeous Girl Like Me)***
SEE ALSO: ***THX 1138; Alphaville; 1984***

90

★★★★

Director: Kurt Neumann
Screenwriter: James Clavell
Produced by: Kurt Neumann
Starring: David Hedison, Patricia Owens, and Vincent Price
Released by: Twentieth Century Fox (DVD, as part of *The Fly Collection*)

5+

THE FLY

1958, 94 mins.

Plot: Scientist Andre Delambre has invented a teleportation device. After ironing out a few wrinkles (disintegrating the family cat in the process), Delambre uses the device on himself. Unbeknownst to him, a fly teleported with him and was genetically fused to him during the journey; Delambre is now a beast, a half-human with the head, arm, and leg of a fly. Delambre tries to reverse the process but can't (due to having the brain of a fly), so he asks his wife to kill him. But where's the other half of Delambre's body?

Review: An excellent and innovative horror film, and yet another example that no gore is required to creep out an audience. Watch this and years later you'll still remember the man-fly's plaintive cry of "Help me!" at the end, as it waits stuck in a web to be devoured by a spider and Vincent Price looks on in naked horror.

FURTHER VIEWING: *The Fly (1986 remake); The Curse of the Fly; The Return of the Fly*
SEE ALSO: *The Island of Dr. Moreau; Swamp Thing; Them!*

91

★★★

Director: Fred M. Wilcox
Screenwriter: Cyril Hume
Produced by: Nicholas Nayfack
Starring: Walter Pidgeon, Anne Francis, and Leslie Nielsen
Released by: Warner Home Video (DVD)

A

FORBIDDEN PLANET

1956, 98 mins.

Plot: A mission to investigate the sudden quiet from planet Altair IV discovers only two survivors: Dr. Morbius and his beautiful daughter. But soon after arriving, members of the mission begin dying, torn apart by some unknown monster. Desperately trying to find the killer, the crew discovers Morbius is hiding a stunning secret.

Review: This is perhaps the pinnacle of pulp from the Golden Age of sci-fi. Beautiful to look at, there's a solid and not-too-cheesy script based on *The Tempest*, plus some excellent (for the time) special effects. The monster is particularly effective, and while it's hard to take Leslie Nielsen seriously after so many deadpan comedic efforts, he's actually pretty good. All in all, it's a worthy addition to the pantheon of sci-fi giants.

FURTHER VIEWING: *Lassie Come Home; Three Daring Daughters; I Passed for White*
SEE ALSO: *Alien; Prospero's Books; 20 Million Miles to Earth; War of the Worlds; When Worlds Collide*

192
500

★★★★★

Director: Ishirō Honda
Screenwriters: Ishirō Honda and Takeo Murata

Produced by: Tomoyuki Tanaka
Starring: Akira Takarada, Momoko Kōchi, and Akihiko Hirata

Released by: Classic Media (DVD with *Godzilla: King of the Monsters*)

12+

GOJIRA (GODZILLA)

1954, 98 mins.

Plot: In a clear allegory representing the fallout of the U.S. nuclear bombings of Hiroshima and Nagasaki (and made less than ten years after), Godzilla is an enormous, radioactive-fire-breathing monster that rises from the sea and proceeds to devastate Japan, mostly by walking all over it. It turns out that Godzilla is a mutation caused by the nuclear bombings, and surviving scientists must decide whether to use an even more catastrophic bomb to destroy him.

Review: Blue Öyster Cult wrote a song about him, he had his own animated series, and his first film spawned countless sequels over the course of more than fifty years. While the anti-U.S. sentiment was toned down on the film's initial release in America, *Godzilla* is still an unsettling criticism of nuclear weapons. The special effects may be dated, but its message is not.

FURTHER VIEWING: ***Rodan; Godzilla (1998 remake); Any of the Godzilla sequels***
SEE ALSO: ***The Beast from 20,000 Fathoms; Gamera: The Guardian of the Universe; The Host***

193
500

★★

Director: Gerald Potterton
Screenwriters: Len Blum and Dan Goldberg

Produced by: Leonard Mogel and Ivan Reitman

Released by: Columbia Tristar Home Video (DVD)

15+

HEAVY METAL

1981, 90 mins.

Plot: The Loc-Nar is an evil precious stone: through a series of short stories, we see its impact across time and space; in dystopian future cities; in alternate barbarian civilizations; aboard a zombie-plagued bomber during World War II; in an America overrun with mutants; and in heroic, tribal planets led by beautiful warrior amazons.

Review: Made when comics and animation were struggling to escape their juvenile "fluffy animals and superheroes" persona, this contains generous helpings of sex and violence to help boost its appeal to adults. With a more European aesthetic—the source material is French—it features some elegant design work by several renowned comics creators and voice work by several stars-on-the-rise, including John Candy, Eugene Levy, and Harold Ramis.

FURTHER VIEWING: ***George and the Christmas Star; Ozma of Oz; The Wonderful Wizard of Oz***
SEE ALSO: ***Creepshow; Fritz the Cat; Ghostbusters; The Outer Limits; The Twilight Zone***

★★★★

Director: Jack Arnold
Screenwriter: Richard Matheson
Produced by: Albert Zugsmith

Starring: Grant Williams, Randy Stuart, and April Kent

Released by: Universal (DVD as part of *The Classic Sci-Fi Ultimate Collection*)

THE INCREDIBLE SHRINKING MAN

1957, 81 mins.

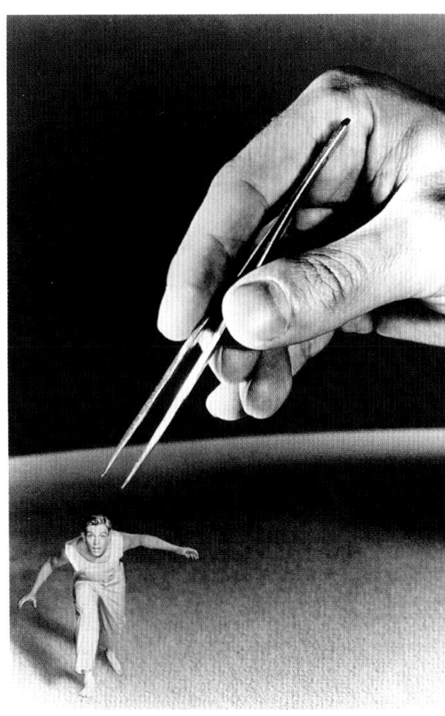

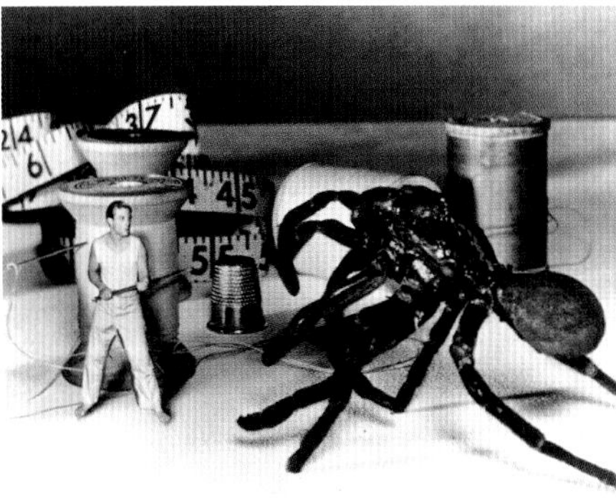

Plot: Scott Carey is just minding his own business, sunning himself on a yacht, when he's suddenly engulfed by a cloud of radioactive pesticides. Soon after he starts to shrink—first to the size of a midget, at which point he joins a circus, then even smaller, until he's threatened by a spider in his own home. But it doesn't stop there; once he's too small to be seen, Scott resigns himself to growing ever smaller and even looks forward to discovering new, albeit tiny, realms. The moral of the story? Tanning's more dangerous than you think.

Review: Adapted by the versatile Richard Matheson from his own novel, *The Incredible Shrinking Man* poses scientific and philosophical questions: is importance relative to size? Does a man lose his identity when he can no longer look other men in the eye? Does he cease to exist just because others of his kind can't see him? Is smallness infinite or does it stop somewhere, and if it does, will Scott die or just vanish into the ether? But possibly the most uncomfortable aspect of this film is Scott's deteriorating relationship with his wife, for as he shrinks, his viciousness and anger grow exponentially, and it becomes an uneasy study of a couple who (literally) grow apart.

FURTHER VIEWING: *The Incredible Shrinking Woman; Creature from the Black Lagoon*
SEE ALSO: *The Devil Doll; Honey, I Shrunk the Kids; Attack of the Puppet People*

195/500

★★★

Director: Kazuhisa Takenôchi
Screenwriter: Thomas Bangalter
Starring: Romanthony (voice)
Released by: Virgin Records US (DVD)

12+

INTERSTELLA 5555

THE STORY OF THE SECRET STAR SYSTEM

2003, 68 mins.

Plot: Inspired and irreparably tied to French electronic act Daft Punk's album *Discovery*, *Interstella 5555* is a Japanese animated movie about an alien pop group who are taken prisoner by a record executive who brainwashes them and foists them on the people of Earth. One by one, the aliens try to regain their personalities and return home to their people.

Review: Featuring the entire album as a soundtrack, no dialog, and minimal sound effects, you can appreciate *Interstella 5555* as an extended music video if you're a fan of the group, or a beautiful homage to the eighties Toei animation style backed by a retro racket. Telling a story with no dialog is no mean feat, but this seems to manage it with ease.

FURTHER VIEWING: ***Gekijô-ban—Bishôjo senshi Sêrâ Mûn R (Pretty Sailor Moon R); One Piece Movie 5***
SEE ALSO: ***The Wall; Tommy***

196/500

★★★★★

Director: Don Siegel
Screenwriters: Daniel Mainwaring, Jack Finney, and Richard Collins
Produced by: Walter Wanger
Starring: Kevin McCarthy, Dana Wynter, and Larry Gates
Released by: Republic Pictures (DVD)

12+

INVASION OF THE BODY SNATCHERS

1956, 80 mins.

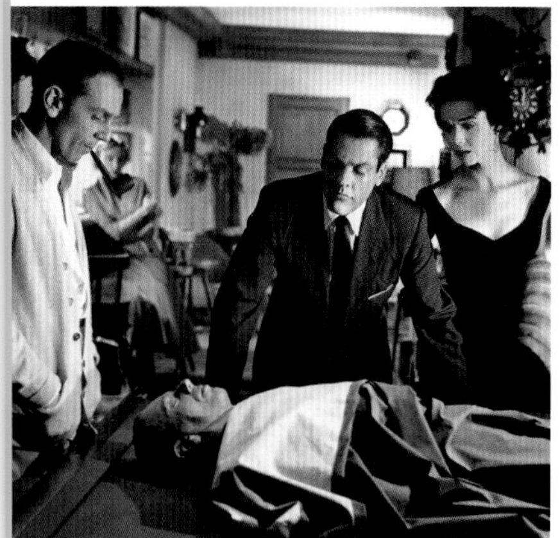

Plot: Small-town doctor Miles Bennell arrives home from vacation just in time to witness an outbreak of strange behavior among his patients. People who had been begging for appointments are suddenly fine, but their family members suspect they aren't who they claim to be, despite looking and acting exactly as they should. Bennell soon discovers the townspeople are being replaced by exact alien replicas bent on turning Earth into an emotionless utopia.

Review: Better known these days for playing idiots and crazy old men, Kevin McCarthy cuts a handsome and dashing figure as Bennell, the only man with the skills to save the town. Overall, *Invasion* is a cracking sci-fi thriller, suspenseful enough to induce nail-biting, but also thought provoking as it asks if there can be true happiness without music, art, or love.

FURTHER VIEWING: ***Invasion of the Body Snatchers (1978 remake); The Invasion***
SEE ALSO: ***Village of the Damned; The Day of the Triffids***

97

★★★★★

Director: Mamoru Oshii
Screenwriter: Kazunori Itô
Producer: Mitsuhisa Ishikawa

Starring: Atsuko Tanaka and Akio Ôtsuka
Released by: Palm Pictures (DVD)

5+

KÔKAKU KIDÔTAI (GHOST IN THE SHELL)

1995, 82 mins.

Plot: In the near-future, crime and corruption are rife, leading a government organization to create Section 9, a covert division whose cybernetic operatives are specialists in technological crime solving. One such agent, Major Motoko Kusanagi, is in pursuit of the shadowy criminal known as "The Puppet Master," who can hack into other people's personalities and manipulate them.

Review: Based on Masamune Shirow's cyberpunk manga series, the film takes a less pulpy approach to the storytelling and turns *Ghost in the Shell* into a serious scientific drama, making early use of digital computer effects that are now commonplace in both anime and feature films. The story is complicated, but worth sticking with as the intrigue builds to a fine ending.

FURTHER VIEWING: *Kôkaku Kidôtai 2: Inosensu (Ghost in the Shell 2: Innocence); Patlabor: The Movie*
SEE ALSO: *Akira; Dominion Tank Police*

98

★★★★★

Director: Carl Macek and Toyoo Ashida
Screenwriter: Hideyuki Kikuchi, Tom Wyner, and Yasushi Hirano

Produced by: Carl Macek, Hiroshi Kato, and Mitsuhisa Koeda

Starring: Michael McConnohie
Released by: Urban Vision

5+

KYÛKETSUKI HANTÂ D (VAMPIRE HUNTER D)

1985, 80 mins.

Plot: "D" is a half-human, half-vampire hunter who kills vampires for a living in the year AD 12090. He's tortured, of course, by his warring natures within and his warrior purpose without. On possibly his most dangerous mission, D must save a human girl from the clutches of a mysterious and powerful vampire only known as The Count.

Review: There is much blood and a good bit of sexuality in this (keep your eyes peeled for cartoon nipples in the extended shower scene), but that shouldn't overshadow the fact that this is an engaging story expertly told. Above all, the art is of such a high caliber and at such an exquisite level of beauty that you're guaranteed to marvel.

FURTHER VIEWING: *Banpaia hantâ D (Vampire Hunter D: Bloodlust)*
SEE ALSO: *Blade; Blood: The Last Vampire; Vampire Princess Miyu: Unearthly Kyoto*

199/500

★★★

Director: Slava Tsukerman
Screenwriter: Anne Carlisle
Producer: Slava Tsukerman
Starring: Anne Carlisle and Paula E. Sheppard
Released by: Telavista (DVD)

18+

LIQUID SKY

1983, 112 mins.

Plot: Set in the druggy world of SoHo, artists, musicians, and junkies comingle in an eighties version of Andy Warhol's *Factory*. Aliens in a flying saucer land on the room of a bisexual punk to accumulate the endorphins given off by heroin users. They soon discover that a greater high can be taken from those at the moment of orgasm, and burying themselves deep in the punk girl's brain, they have her lure men to sleep with her so they can feed.

Review: Difficult to compare to any other movie, this psychedelic sci-fi drama is like a Duran Duran video on acid, smothered with a primitive electronic soundtrack and brightly lit neon. The hammy acting doesn't affect your enjoyment—it's a surreal visual feast with no peers.

FURTHER VIEWING: ***Iona and David Elin; Stalin's Wife***
SEE ALSO: ***The Brother from Another Planet; Altered States***

200/500

★★★★

Director: Michael Anderson
Screenwriter: David Zelag Goodman
Produced by: Saul David and Hugh Benson
Starring: Michael York, Richard Jordan, and Jenny Agutter
Released by: Warner Home Video (DVD)

LOGAN'S RUN

1976, 120 mins.

Plot: In the year 2274, a domed city holds the world's last survivors of war and overpopulation; to prevent another Malthusian crisis, inhabitants of the dome are euthanized at the age of thirty unless they agree to take part in "carousels," gladiatorial battles in which those who follow the rules are promised reincarnation. Logan is a Sandman, responsible for catching Runners, people who refuse euthanasia and carousel, but when he falls for a beautiful Runner, he begins to question his purpose and his society.

Review: Future dystopian societies are often challenged by women, and *Logan's Run* is no different. While not particularly well acted, and with relatively cheap-looking special effects, the film did well enough to spawn a short-lived TV series about Logan and Jessica's adventures outside the dome.

FURTHER VIEWING: ***Logan's Run (TV series); 1984; Doc Savage: The Man of Bronze***
SEE ALSO: ***Blade Runner; Mad Max; THX 1138; Fahrenheit 451; The Running Man***

11

★★★

Director: Nicolas Roeg
Screenwriter: Paul Mayersberg
Producer: Michael Deeley
Starring: David Bowie, Rip Torn, and Candy Clark
Released by: Criterion (DVD)

3+

THE MAN WHO FELL TO EARTH

1976, 139 mins.

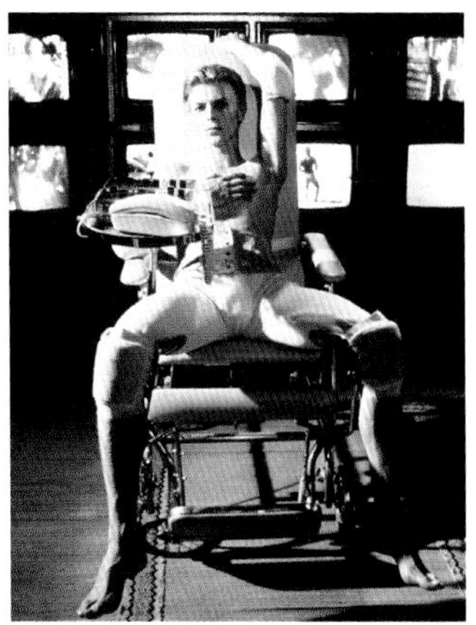

Plot: David Bowie stars as an alien who arrives on Earth to transport water back to his dying planet and save his family. To make the money required to build the ship he needs to transport the water, he patents various inventions that make him rich overnight. However, he becomes distracted by television, sex, and alcohol, which threaten to derail his good intentions.

Review: Playing on his androgynous looks and previous history as a Spider from Mars, Bowie fits effortlessly into Roeg's extraterrestrial vision and is as alien to acting as the characters perceive him themselves. It also dares to suggest that nobody is strong-willed enough to resist Earth's charms—a wonderfully arrogant presumption.

FURTHER VIEWING: *Don't Look Now; Walkabout*
SEE ALSO: *Starman; Man Facing Southeast*

12

★★★

Director: Roger Corman
Screenwriters: Robert Dillon and Ray Russell
Produced by: Roger Corman
Starring: Ray Milland and Diana Van der Vlis
Released by: MGM/UA (DVD)

8+

X THE MAN WITH THE X-RAY EYES

1963, 79 mins.

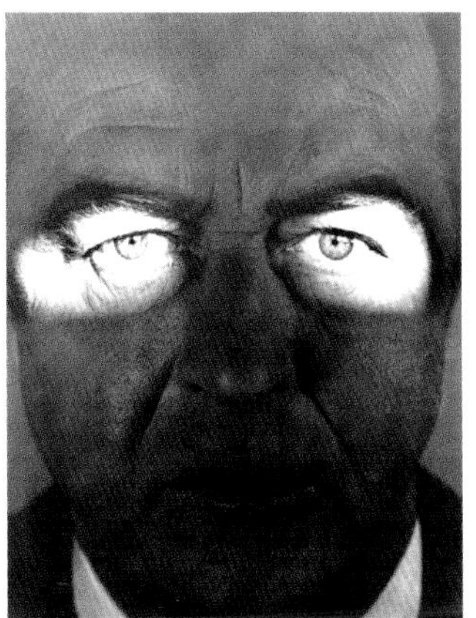

Plot: Dr. James Xavier develops a new eye drug intended to broaden human vision into the X-ray and UV ends of the spectrum. After testing the drug on himself, he realizes it is far more powerful than he expected; he can spot medical aliments, cheat at cards, and see things way beyond human comprehension. Naturally, he goes mad.

Review: A classic "revolutionary science makes mad scientist" movie, this is more subtle and philosophical fare from exploitation maestro Roger Corman. Ray Milland is great as the scientist whose mutated eyes become black holes sucking in his sanity, and what starts out as a cheap party to trick to see people in their underwear leads to a powerful and tragic demise. Superb.

FURTHER VIEWING: *Beast with a Million Eyes; Attack of the Crab Monsters; The Wasp Woman; House of Usher; The Terror; Frankenstein Unbound*
SEE ALSO: *The Fly; Invisible Man; The Hollow Man; The Incredible Shrinking Man*

★★★★

Director: Fritz Lang
Screenwriter: Thea von Harbou
Produced by: Erich Pommer

Starring: Alfred Abel, Gustav Fröhlich, and Rudolf Klein-Rogge
Released by: Paramount Pictures (DVD)

12+

METROPOLIS

1927, 153 mins.

Plot: In a future totalitarian city-state, the population is divided into an elite living in decadent skyscrapers, and workers surviving in underground destitution. When one of the ruling class falls for a beautiful minion, he is horrified by the conditions she and the workers live in. He joins their planned revolt, which sweeps through the city, bringing it to its knees.

Review: The film that wrote the book on "dystopian future" sci-fi films, its influence is as potent now as it ever was. The incredible art deco design and sets are counterpointed by existential, philosophical, and political metaphors, allegories to Soviet Russia, and foreshadowings of Nazi Germany. All this aside, it is the zero point for pretty much all sci-fi that followed.

FURTHER VIEWING: *Der müde Tod; Dr. Mabuse; M*
SEE ALSO: *Blade Runner; Logan's Run; The Matrix; THX 1138*

★★★

Director: Dave McKean
Screenwriters: Neil Gaiman and Dave McKean

Produced by: Martin G. Baker, Lisa Henson, Simon Moorhead, and Michael Polis

Starring: Stephanie Leonidas, Jason Barry, and Rob Brydon
Released by: Sony Pictures (DVD)

12+

MIRRORMASK

2005, 101 mins.

Plot: Helena's got the childhood fantasy backwards: she wants to run away from the circus where her mother and father work and join real life. But real life is not in her reach when she's mistaken for the Princess of the Land of Shadows, and she must save the City of Light from being engulfed by darkness while trying to swap her place back with the true princess.

Review: For a Neil Gaiman story, *Mirrormask*'s narrative is pretty standard and unexceptional, but the visual world McKean has created is worth the price of admission. Flexing his full mixed-media muscles, McKean creates a changeable fantasy world that's as engaging when it flips to two dimensions as it is in three—unfortunately, his focus on the visuals mean the story gets lost somewhat.

FURTHER VIEWING: *Stardust; Coraline*
SEE ALSO: *Labyrinth; The Dark Crystal; Pan's Labyrinth*

205/500

★★★★★

Director: Hayao Miyazaki
Screenwriter: Hayao Miyazaki
Produced by: Toshio Suzuki

Starring: Gillian Anderson, Billy Crudup, and Claire Danes

Released by: Buena Vista Home Entertainment (DVD)

12+

MONONOKE-HIME (PRINCESS MONONOKE)

1997, 134 mins.

Plot: In ancient Japan, where monsters and gods still haunt the forests, a young prince saves his village from demons but pays a terrible price. With a cursed injury slowly killing him, he heads to the forest for a cure, but gets caught up in a war between the spirits and encroaching, greedy humans.

Review: About as far from the formulaic, homogenized American studio animations as possible, this isn't just beautiful to look at. It has a complex story rich in pathos and philosophical conflict between industrialization and nature. Moving and endlessly creative, it demands repeat viewing just to pick up the nuances of the story—the irony of lovingly cared-for lepers making advanced weapons, for instance—and the magical artwork.

FURTHER VIEWING: ***Nausicaä of the Valley of Wind; Porco Rosso; Howl's Moving Castle; Spirited Away; Tales from Earthsea***
SEE ALSO: ***Akira; Barefoot Gen; The Lord of the Rings trilogy; Paprika***

206/500

★★★

Director: Vincent Ward
Screenwriters: Geoff Chapple, Kely Lyons, and Vincent Ward
Produced by: John Maynard

Starring: Bruce Lyons, Chris Haywood, and Hamish McFarlane
Released by: AV Channel (DVD)

12+

THE NAVIGATOR A MEDIEVAL ODYSSEY

1988, 93 mins.

Plot: As plague ravages fourteenth-century England, a small village awaits the disease's imminent arrival. They hope to save their homes using the visions of a young boy. He leads a group of adventurers into a cave, to dig for copper—they keep digging until they enter twentieth-century New Zealand!

Review: Cleverly conceived, the narrative for this curious film is seen through the wide-eyed amazement of the young boy as he emerges from the bleak monotones of the Dark Ages into Technicolor New Zealand. Free from clichés and overblown special effects, it simply endeavors to show that, whether it's the fourteenth or twentieth century, we're all still worried about war and pestilence, be it the plague or AIDS.

FURTHER VIEWING: ***Vigil; Map of the Human Heart; What Dreams May Come; Rain of the Children***
SEE ALSO: ***The Name of the Rose***

207

★★★★★

Director: Henry Selick
Screenwriters: Tim Burton and Caroline Thompson
Produced by: Tim Burton and Denise Di Novi
Starring: Danny Elfman, Chris Sarandon, and Catherine O'Hara
Released by: Walt Disney Studios Home Entertainment (DVD)

12+

THE NIGHTMARE BEFORE CHRISTMAS

1993, 76 mins.

Plot: Jack Skellington, the Pumpkin King of Halloween Town, is tired of the same old scares every year. While wandering and lost in thought, he manages to open a door to Christmas Town, and, dazzled by all the bright shiny happiness, decides to kidnap Santa and hold his own version of Christmas. But dead things don't make good Christmas presents, and when the military gets wind of a Santa imposter, they do what they do best: shoot at him.

Review: A highly entertaining stop-motion musical from master of the macabre Tim Burton, with music and lyrics (and the singing voice of the inimitable Jack) by frequent Burton collaborator Danny Elfman. *The Nightmare Before Christmas* is one of those rare children's films that manages to be fun, funny, and engaging for all ages.

FURTHER VIEWING: ***The Corpse Bride; Beetlejuice; Sleepy Hollow***
SEE ALSO: ***Coraline; The Addams Family; The Legend of Sleepy Hollow; How the Grinch Stole Christmas***

208

★★★★

Director: Timur Bekmambetov
Screenwriters: Timur Bekmambetov, Laeta Kalogridis, and Sergei Lukyanenko
Produced by: Aleksei Kublitsky, Aleksei Kulibin, Anatoly Maximov, and Arthur Gorson
Starring: Konstantin Khabenskiy, Vladimir Menshov, and Valeriy Zolotukhin
Released by: Twentieth Century Fox (DVD)

NOCHNOY DOZOR (NIGHT WATCH)

2004, 114 mins.

Plot: Anton's relationship problems aren't the only hiccup in his life—while trying to get his wife back, he discovers he's an "Other," part of a race of humans with special powers who back either the light or the dark. Anton joins the light and becomes part of the Night Watch, which fights the dark to ensure the balance between the two are maintained.

Review: A breakout Russian blockbuster horror film by yet another Roger Corman-discovered director. With a style reminiscent of *Blade* and *The Matrix*, but more daring and in-your-face than either, *Night Watch* provides an exciting, varied visual feast despite the sometimes confusing narrative. Highly recommended for those who like their vampires to be brutish and stylish.

FURTHER VIEWING: ***Dnevnoy dozor (Day Watch)***
SEE ALSO: ***Blade; Blade 2***

★★★★★

Director: Boris Sagal
Screenwriter: John William Corrington
Producer: Walter Seltzer

Starring: Charlton Heston, Anthony Zerbe, and Rosalind Cash
Released by: Warner Home Video (DVD)

12+

THE OMEGA MAN

1971, 98 mins.

Plot: A military doctor called Robert Neville (Charlton Heston) believes himself to be the last man alive after germ warfare wipes out most of the world's population. The fallout from the attack created vampiric albino creatures who cannot survive in the daytime and spend their nights trying to kill Neville. His rescue by a group of survivors he didn't know existed could be the key to restarting the human race, providing he can create a serum to protect them in time.

Review: One of Heston's "Apocalypse Trilogy" of sci-fi films, it was based on Richard Matheson's novel *I Am Legend* but given a seventies spin. The soundtrack and afros aside, *The Omega Man* is compelling for Heston's bravado alone.

FURTHER VIEWING: ***The 1,000 Plane Raid; World War III***
SEE ALSO: ***Soylent Green; I Am Legend***

★★★★

Director: Jean Cocteau
Screenwriter: Jean Cocteau
Producer: André Paulvé

Starring: Jean Marais, François Périer, and María Casares
Released by: Criterion (DVD)

12+

ORPHÉE (ORPHEUS)

1950, 95 mins.

Plot: Based on the ancient Greek myth about a musician who descends into the underworld to rescue his wife, Cocteau's film brings the story up to date by moving it to Paris in the forties and making the lead a poet. When a rival of Orpheus is gravely injured in a brawl, he travels with the Princess of Death in her car to deliver the body to the underworld. His interest in her becomes an obsession, driving a wedge between him and his loving wife.

Review: The simplistic set-up soon develops into an intricate discourse on the nature of love, obsession, and the pursuit of art. Experimental in parts, Cocteau's liberal use of innovative special effects are surprising even today.

FURTHER VIEWING: *The Blood of a Poet; Testament of Orpheus*
SEE ALSO: *The Seventh Seal; La voce del silenzio*

211
500

★★★

Director: Peter Hyams
Screenwriter: Peter Hyams
Produced by: Richard A. Roth

Starring: Sean Connery, Peter Boyle, and Frances Sternhagen
Released by: Warner Home Video (DVD)

15+

OUTLAND

1981, 109 mins.

Plot: O'Niel is a Federal Marshal assigned to a mining outpost on Jupiter's moon Io. The outpost's miners are dying in mysterious ways, usually after committing acts of heinous violence, and O'Niel traces the source to a speed-like drug that increases productivity but also causes psychosis. When O'Niel finds out that the mining company itself is importing and distributing the drug, he confronts the boss, but all that gets him is a couple of assassins riding his tail, with no one to help.

Review: As a sci-fi retelling of classic western *High Noon*, *Outland* actually does quite a good job of transferring a small-town sheriff's story to the outer reaches of space. Sean Connery is just as believable as Gary Cooper, if not more so, playing the solitary warrior for justice.

FURTHER VIEWING: ***2010; Capricorn One***
SEE ALSO: ***Silent Running; High Noon; Lifeforce; Saturn 3; Serenity***

212
500

★

Director: Edward D. Wood Jr.
Screenwriter: Edward D. Wood Jr.
Produced by: J. Edward Reynolds

Starring: Gregory Walcott, Mona McKinnon, and Duke Moore
Released by: Image Entertainment (DVD)

12+

PLAN 9 FROM OUTER SPACE

1958, 78 mins.

Plot: A flying saucer is seen on Earth, and people are scared, but all the aliens want is to communicate with humans and seek their help. The humans refuse to listen, so the aliens reanimate the dead. The humans certainly notice that, and what follows is too nonsensical to even try to explain.

Review: There is absolutely nothing commendable about this film—no aspect of it manages to claw its way out of despicably bad to attain even a below average rating. And therein lies its charm: legendary for being very possibly the Worst Film Ever Made, *Plan 9* is now regarded as a camp classic and has wormed its way into being a cornerstone of modern pop culture.

FURTHER VIEWING: ***Glen or Glenda; Bride of the Monster; Night of the Ghouls***
SEE ALSO: ***Ed Wood; Orgy of the Dead; Queen of Outer Space; Santa Claus Conquers the Martians***

★
★
★

Director: Christian Volckman
Screenwriters: Alexandre de La Patellière, Mathieu Delaporte, Michael Katims, Jean-Bernard Pouy, and Patrick Raynal

Produced by: Timothy Burrill, Aton Soumache, and Alexis Vonarb
Starring: Daniel Craig, Romola Garai, and Ian Holm

Released by: Miramax (DVD)

15+

RENAISSANCE

2006, 105 mins.

Plot: In a built-up, industrial nightmare of Paris in the year 2054, scientist and employee of the overarching Avalon corporation Ilona has been kidnapped. Cop and abduction specialist Karas gets assigned the case as a top priority, but he isn't the only one looking for Ilona, and the further he goes to find her the tighter the net of conspiracy becomes.

Review: Convential wisdom tells us black and white doesn't sell, but conventional wisdom has clearly never taken in the stark, motion-capture beauty of *Renaissance*. The level of detail and the smoothness of the action is outstanding, but the narrative does have a tendency to drag. Daniel Craig is excellent as the tight-lipped Karas.

FURTHER VIEWING: *Maaz (short)*
SEE ALSO: *eXistenZ; Alphaville; A Scanner Darkly; Metropolis*

214/500

★★★★

Director: Norman Jewison
Screenwriter: William Harrison
Produced by: Norman Jewison and Patrick J. Palmer
Starring: James Caan, John Houseman, and Maude Adams
Released by: MGM (DVD)

15+

ROLLERBALL

1975, 125 mins.

Plot: In 2018, the world is a hegemonic dystopia controlled by global corporations. These corporations created Rollerball—an incredibly violent sport on skates—to demonstrate the futility of individuality, so when star player Jonathan E.'s fame peaks, they'll do anything to force him to retire, including organizing a Rollerball bloodbath that no one is expected to survive.

Review: *Rollerball*'s visuals have dated badly, but its ideas have not. William Harrison has created a world where crime has been eradicated and normal human desires for extreme emotions can only be played out on a hyper-violent, gladiatorial stage. The corporate culture that exists today, which prizes teamwork over individual talent, has become the global social structure. The violence in this picture is not its most harrowing aspect; it's the vision of a faceless, soulless future that will give you nightmares.

FURTHER VIEWING: ***Rollerball (2002 remake); F.I.S.T.***
SEE ALSO: ***Death Race 2000; Logan's Run***

215/500

★★

Director: Nicholas Webster
Screenwriter: Glenville Mareth
Producer: Paul L. Jacobson
Starring: John Call, Leonard Hicks, and Vincent Beck
Released by: Alpha (DVD)

A

SANTA CLAUS CONQUERS THE MARTIANS

1964, 81 mins.

Plot: Two Martian parents become concerned that their two children, Bomar and Girmar, have been spending too much time in front of the video screen watching Earth shows. They're both obsessed with a larger-than-life character from their programs—Santa Claus. The parents organize the capture of Santa so he can bring joy and presents to the children of Mars.

Review: A ludicrous premise if there ever was one, children who saw this and got nothing for Christmas were probably made even more hysterical thinking St. Nick was flying about the cosmos delivering presents to alien beings instead of them. The cheap special effects and cringe-inducing acting secured it a slot in cult movie infamy, especially around the festive period.

FURTHER VIEWING: ***Gone Are the Days; Dead to the World***
SEE ALSO: ***Mars Attacks!; War of the Worlds***

16

★★★

Director: Christian Duguay
Screenwriter: Dan O'Bannon
Producer: Franco Battista

Starring: Paul Weller, Roy Dupuis, and Jennifer Rubin
Released by: Sony Pictures (DVD)

8+

SCREAMERS

1995, 108 mins.

Plot: The planet Sirius 6B is home to a new breed of cybernetic life known as "screamers." Created by man to hunt down anything with a pulse, these blade-spinning death machines are practically unstoppable and, having learned how to replicate themselves and evolve, are now impossible to eliminate. With both sides of an endless civil war now looking for peace, Alliance officers must traverse deadly territory to begin peace proceedings.

Review: Philip K. Dick's short story "Second Variety" was the inspiration for *Screamers*, one of his many high-concept ideas that have been translated to the silver screen. Peter Weller portrays the war-weary Joe Hendrickson doing his best to bring solidarity to the destroyed planet. Gritty, action-packed sci-fi.

FURTHER VIEWING: *Scanners II: The New Order; The Art of War*
SEE ALSO: *Leviathan; Starship Troopers*

17

★★★

Director: Douglas Trumbull
Screenwriters: Deric Washburn, Michael Cimino, and Steven Bochco

Produced by: Douglas Trumbull, Marty Hornstein, and Michael Gruskoff
Starring: Bruce Dern, Cliff Potts, and Ron Rifkin

Released by: Universal Studios (DVD)

A

SILENT RUNNING

1972, 89 mins.

Plot: In the future, all plant life on Earth is extinct, but six space freighters just off Saturn harbor enormous forests; it is expected that the plant and animal life within can someday be returned to Earth and used to repopulate the devastated surface. When resident botanist Lowell receives an order from Earth to destroy the freighters, he risks his own life (and the lives of others) to preserve them.

Review: *Silent Running* is special-effects master Douglas Trumbull's directorial debut, and an early example of an eco-thriller. While the narrative is often dismissed as overly simple, the film has had a wide-ranging influence on the sci-fi genre, mostly due to its sophisticated visuals.

FURTHER VIEWING: *Brainstorm*
SEE ALSO: *Android; Outland; Solaris; Sunshine*

★
★
★

Director: Andrei Tarkovsky
Screenwriter: Arkadi Strugatsky
Producer: Aleksandra Demidova

Starring: Aleksandr Kaidanovsky, Alisa Frejndlikh, and Anatoli Solonitsyn
Released by: Kino Video (DVD)

12+

STALKER

1979, 163 mins.

Plot: On the outskirts of a small Russian town is an unnatural place known as the Zone. Deep within exists the Room, where man can experience his greatest desires. Heavily guarded by the military, only Stalkers can lead others to it for personal, not intellectual, profit.

Against his wife's wishes, the Stalker takes Writer and Scientist to the Zone. Along the way they discuss their reasons for leaving their lives behind and what they hope to discover in the Room.

Review: A close-to-three-hour running time is demanding on any viewer, and complete attention is required to understand and appreciate why Tarkovsky's film is so highly regarded. This bleak metaphysical odyssey is the closest you can get to a moving work of art.

FURTHER VIEWING: ***Solyaris (Solaris), Zerkalo (The Mirror)***
SEE ALSO: ***The Wizard of Oz; 2001: A Space Odyssey***

★★★★

Director: Nicholas Meyer
Screenwriters: Nicholas Meyer and Jack B. Sowards

Produced by: Robert Sallin and Harve Bennett

Starring: William Shatner, DeForest Kelley, and Leonard Nimoy
Released by: Paramount (DVD)

2+

STAR TREK THE WRATH OF KHAN

1982, 113 mins.

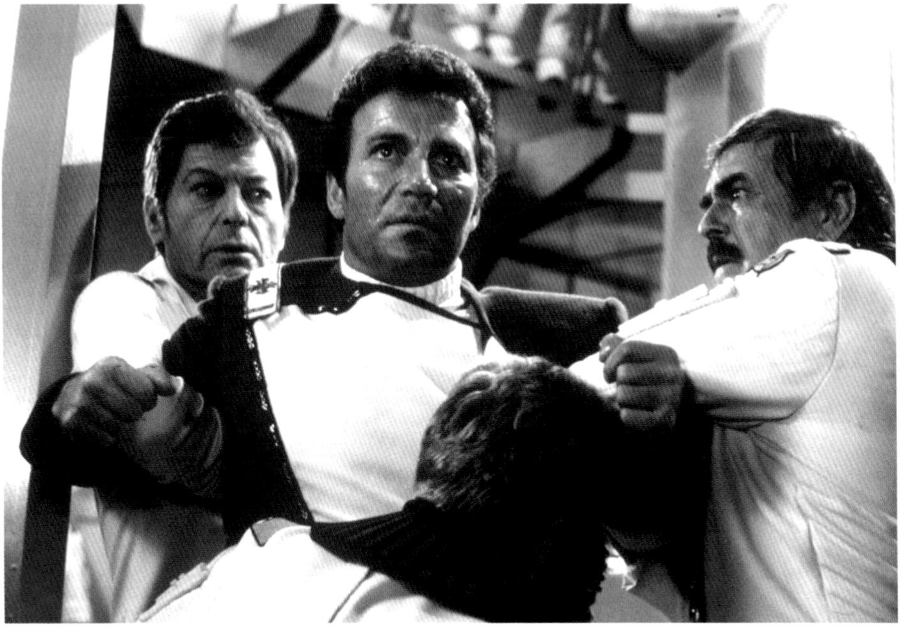

Plot: The crew of the *USS Enterprise* is back in the saddle again as one of Kirk's old enemies, the genetically engineered Khan, seeks to punish Kirk for seeing to his imprisonment on a remote planet. They fight over the Federation's top-secret Genesis machine, which is capable of transforming an entire planet into a habitable world.

Review: "KHAAAAAAAN!" Most people who haven't even seen the film know of Captain (now Admiral) Kirk's famous, furious cry of his enemy's name. A gorgeously melodramatic performance from Ricardo Montalbán as Khan (who gets extra points for shamelessly displaying his mutant pectorals), a healthy dose of humor, and fast, exciting starship dogfights made this the film that subsequently informed the franchise.

FURTHER VIEWING: *Star Trek III: The Search for Spock; Star Trek IV: The Voyage Home*
SEE ALSO: *Galaxy Quest; Star Trek Generations; Return of the Jedi*

220
500

★★★

Director: John Carpenter
Screenwriter: John Carpenter
Produced by: Andre Blay, Larry J. Franco, Sandy King, and Shep Gordon
Starring: Roddy Piper, Keith David, and Meg Foster
Released by: Universal Studios (DVD)

18+

THEY LIVE

1988, 93 mins.

Plot: Homeless construction worker George finds a pair of magic Ray-Bans that allow him to see Young Republicans for what they really are: crusty reptile alien beings who have mesmerized people with subliminal messages transmitted through television (Fox News, presumably). George is the only one who sees the truth and tries to take down the aliens by destroying the television signal that allows them to hide in plain sight.

Review: Part black comedy and part social commentary, *They Live* is so eighties it hurts, but it's also very fun no matter what the decade. Bonus: George is played by "Rowdy" Roddy Piper, an eighties World Wrestling Federation star.

FURTHER VIEWING: *The Thing; Dark Star*
SEE ALSO: *V; Alien Nation; Invasion of the Body Snatchers; Society*

221
500

★★

Director: Lee Frost
Screenwriters: Lee Frost, Wes Bishop, and James Gordon White
Produced by: Wes Bishop and Jonathan Lawrence
Starring: Rosey Grier and Ray Milland
Released by: MGM (DVD)

THE THING WITH TWO HEADS

1972, 93 mins.

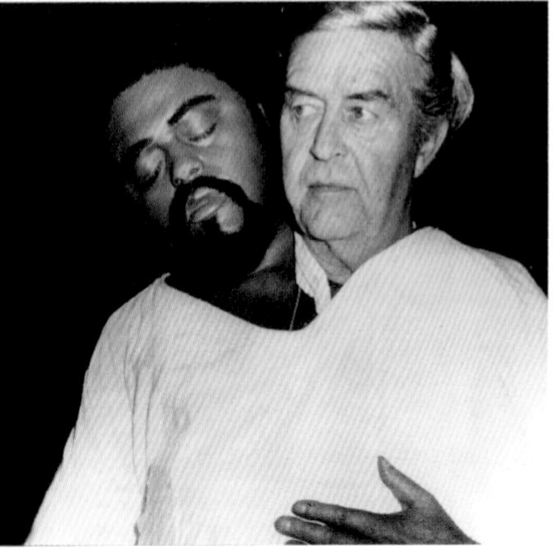

Plot: Racist white scientist Max is dying but wealthy enough to demand his head be grafted onto a healthy body. After experimenting with a gorilla, something goes wrong and he wakes up with his head sewn onto black death-row inmate Jack. The catch? Jack's head is still on the body as well.

Review: "They transplanted a white bigot's head onto a soul brother's body!" *The Thing with Two Heads* is absolutely hilarious in the worst possible way. This is bad-taste humor at its lowest point on the evolutionary scale, but it's impossible not to laugh at the absurdity of it all. Watch out for Academy Award-winning special-effects master Rick Baker's stellar performance as the gorilla.

FURTHER VIEWING: *Policewomen; Dixie Dynamite; The Scavengers*
SEE ALSO: *Dr. Black and Mr. White; Heart Condition; The Watermelon Man; The Incredible Two-Headed Transplant*

22

★★★

Director: George Lucas
Screenwriters: George Lucas, Matthew Robbins, and Walter Murch

Produced by: Edward Folger, Francis Ford Coppola, and Larry Sturhahn

Starring: Robert Duvall, Donald Pleasence, and Maggie McOmie
Released by: Warner Home Video (DVD)

5+

THX 1138

1971, 86 mins.

Plot: In a future underground dystopia where people are designated by numbers rather than names and given drugs by the government to suppress their emotions, LUH 3417 stages a private revolution by not taking her drugs. She replaces her roommate's—THX 1138—drugs with a placebo, and as they both begin to feel genuine emotion they enter into a sexual relationship. But sex, like emotion, is illegal, and they are both arrested; THX 1138 is sent to a barren limbo for punishment, but his newfound emotions push a desire to escape to the forefront of his mind.

Review: George Lucas' debut feature film proved to be a commercial bomb when it was first released and fared no better after the massive success of *Star Wars*. But *THX 1138*'s Orwellian subject matter—with shades of *Fahrenheit 451*—and excellent special effects for the time have given it a special place in the hearts of science fiction fans.

FURTHER VIEWING: *Star Wars; Electronic Labyrinth THX 1138 4EB (short)*
SEE ALSO: *Fahrenheit 451; 1984; Brazil; Logan's Run*

23

★★★★

Directors: Steven Lisberger and Robert Meyer Burnett
Screenwriters: Steven Lisberger and Bonnie MacBird

Produced by: Harrison Ellenshaw, Donald Kushner, Jeff Kurtti, and John Bernstein

Starring: Jeff Bridges, David Warner, and Bruce Boxleitner
Released by: Walt Disney Video (DVD)

2+

TRON

1982, 96 mins.

Plot: Computer genius Kevin Flynn works for ENCOM, a computer software corporation, and programs video games off the clock with a view to starting his own company. When evil programmer Ed Dillinger steals Kevin's work, Kevin attempts to break into the Master Control Program to find proof, but the MCP digitizes Kevin and traps him in the mainframe.

Review: Although it demonstrated the height of computer-based special effects in 1982, *Tron* wasn't a box-office success, and it really hasn't aged well. Nevertheless, as the first major studio picture to feature computer graphics heavily (and ironically discounted for a Special Effects Award by the Academy because computers were considered "cheating" at the time!), it represented a huge leap in film effects and had a wide-ranging influence on the industry. And, it has to be said, the light cycles are still pretty cool.

FURTHER VIEWING: *Tron Legacy; Slipstream*
SEE ALSO: *The Last Starfighter; The Lawnmower Man; eXistenZ; The Matrix*

224
500

★★★

Director: M. Night Shyamalan
Screenwriter: M. Night Shyamalan
Produced by: M. Night Shyamalan, Barry Mendel, and Sam Mercer

Starring: Bruce Willis and Samuel L. Jackson
Released by: Walt Disney Video (DVD)

12+

UNBREAKABLE

2000, 107 mins.

Plot: Security guard David Dunn is traveling home to Philadelphia from New York when he becomes a victim of one of the worst passenger train accidents ever recorded. Everyone aboard dies, but David Dunn walks away without a scratch. He is soon contacted by a man called Elijah Price, who has a rare disease that causes his bones to break easily. Elijah believes David is a superhero, immune to injury and with a sixth sense for wrongdoing. David soon finds that Elijah is right about his condition, but Elijah himself isn't quite what he seems.

Review: Though not as well received, critically or at the box office, as *The Sixth Sense*, *Unbreakable* is an adept psychological thriller with a trademark Shyamalan twist at the end that, unlike his later films, doesn't feel contrived.

FURTHER VIEWING: ***The Sixth Sense; The Village; Lady in the Water***
SEE ALSO: ***Darkman; The Dead Zone; Fearless***

225
500

★★

Director: Michael Crichton
Screenwriter: Michael Critchton
Produced by: Paul Lazarus III

Starring: Yul Brynner, Richard Benjamin, and James Brolin
Released by: MGM Home Entertainment (DVD)

15+

WESTWORLD

1973, 83 mins.

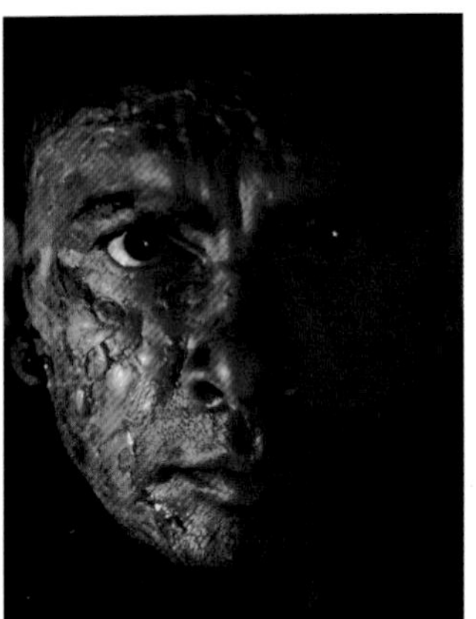

Plot: In a future Wild West amusement park populated by sophisticated robots, the very rich can indulge in all manner of violent and sexual fantasies. But when the robots malfunction and the safeties come off, one holiday-maker must pit human survival instincts against unstoppable killing machines.

Review: The computer revolution was in its infancy when Crichton tapped into the growing fear of complex machines violently escaping the control of their human masters. The sets look cheap and the robots haven't dated too well, but the film remains relevant because it presages current concerns about self-aware artificial intelligence—and because of Brynner's steely-eyed, black-clad robot Spartacus, ruthless as any Terminator.

FURTHER VIEWING: ***Coma; Looker; Runaway; Jurassic Park; Rising Sun***
SEE ALSO: ***The Andromeda Strain; Futureworld; The Terminator; The Simpsons: "Itchy & Scratchy Land"***

★★★★★

Director: Victor Fleming
Screenwriters: Noel Langley, Florence Ryerson, and Edgar Allan Woolf

Produced by: Mervyn LeRoy and Arthur Freed

Starring: Judy Garland, Frank Morgan, Ray Bolger, Bert Lahr, and Jack Haley
Released by: Warner Home Video (DVD)

A THE WIZARD OF OZ

1938, 101 mins.

Plot: Based on L. Frank Baum's novel of the same name, *The Wizard of Oz* follows Dorothy from Kansas as she dreams of a life more exciting. She gets her wish when she's caught up in a twister and lands in the magical kingdom of Oz, but spends her time there trying to get back to her family in Kansas while evading warring witches and taking long snoozes in suspiciously hallucinogenic poppy fields.

Review: *The Wizard of Oz* wasn't considered a box-office success on its initial release, although it did receive several Academy Award nominations and was partly responsible for the release of further Technicolor fantasy films in 1940. In fact, it wasn't until the film hit television that it became the cultural icon it is today. It is now one of the most famous—and one of the most watched—films in history.

FURTHER VIEWING: *Return to Oz; The Wiz; Tin Man (TV miniseries); The Patchwork Girl of Oz*
SEE ALSO: *Mary Poppins; A Wrinkle in Time; Chitty Chitty Bang Bang*

CHAPTER 5

CRIMINAL UNDERWORLDS

"I CAN'T FIGURE OUT IF YOU'RE A DETECTIVE OR A PERVERT"

Like the crime genre itself, criminal activity in cult movies runs the gamut of human experience, from the absurdist suburban nightmare of *Blue Velvet* to the stylized noir tension of *Les Diaboliques*. But whether it's the perverse kingpin of Anytown, USA or a wife drowning her husband in the swimming pool with the help of his mistress, there's something more compelling in the following movies than your average hard-boiled detective mystery: a charismatic murderer, possibly based on real life; a heist so perfectly portrayed it becomes legendary, or so badly executed that the consequences are tragic. Often, a shocking level of violence is simply enough to catapult a crime movie to cult status. This is where we plumb the depths of depravity and anti-heroism, with brief asides to action and comedy, all the while trying to figure out whether our hero is the detective, the pervert, or both.

CRIMINAL UNDERWORLDS

★★★★

Director: Terrence Malick
Screenwriter: Terrence Malick
Produced by: Terrence Malick

Starring: Martin Sheen and Sissy Spacek
Released by: Warner Home Video (DVD)

18+

BADLANDS

1973, 94 mins.

Plot: This is a fictionalized account of the Charles Starkweather and Caril Ann Fugate murder spree that saw eleven dead and terrorized in Nebraska and Wyoming in 1957. Kit, a twenty-something garbage man with a James Dean fascination, falls in with teenaged Holly, who lives alone with her father. When Holly's father tries to force Holly to stop seeing Kit, Kit shoots him and burns down the house to cover it up. The pair take off on a road trip that turns into a killing spree, becoming the most publicized couple in crime since Bonnie and Clyde.

Review: The differences between this film and its source material are many: Terrence Malick moved the action of the film to the much more scenic South Dakota Badlands, though Sheen's Kit retains Starkweather's real-life James Dean obsession. While in reality Fugate's involvement in the murders was never truly established—Starkweather first claimed he did all the killing and then changed his story to say that Fugate did shoot some of the victims, whereas Fugate maintained she was an innocent hostage during the spree—in *Badlands* the adolescent Holly is a willing companion to Starkweather throughout the spree but never participates in the murders.

Well received by critics on its release, *Badlands* is less interested in documenting true events than using this bizarre story to present a unique character study of two social outcasts divorced from reality and, thus, morality. The two rarely speak to each other; there are long stretches of silence in the film broken only by the sound of their latest vehicle's engine. Even the murders are regarded by both Kit and Holly with the same enthusiasm one might have when comparing the prices of competing brands of milk. There are no easy answers to be found here, no clear theories, but the journey is beautiful and captivating in its incongruous banality.

FURTHER VIEWING: ***Starkweather; Days of Heaven***
SEE ALSO: ***The Frighteners; Bonnie and Clyde; Natural Born Killers; The Honeymoon Killers***

★★★★★

Director: David Lynch
Screenwriter: David Lynch
Produced by: Fred C. Caruso and Richard A. Roth

Starring: Isabella Rossellini, Dennis Hopper, Kyle MacLachlan, and Laura Dern

Released by: MGM (DVD)

8+

BLUE VELVET

1986, 120 mins.

Plot: All-American college student Jeffery Beaumont returns home after his father has a stroke. He finds a severed ear in a vacant lot, but the police aren't interested; curious, Jeffrey investigates the case with Sandy, the police detective's daughter. Sandy tells Jeffrey about the suspicious nightclub singer Dorothy, and Jeffrey breaks into her apartment. She comes home early and seduces him, but then Frank arrives—he's a sadistic, sociopathic monster who has kidnapped Dorothy's husband and son in order to force her to perform bizarre and often violent sex acts. Jeffrey finds himself equally attracted to the virginal Sandy and Dorothy, who repeatedly demands that Jeffrey hit her during sex. Frank soon finds out that Jeffrey is involved with Dorothy, which causes a slight problem as Frank is just powerful enough, and sick enough, to torture and/or kill anyone who steals his toys.

Review: David Lynch is no stranger to exposing the dark underbelly of cookie-cutter American suburbia, and this is his finest effort to that effect. If we were to oversimplify *Blue Velvet*, we'd probably call it a mystery with its noir trappings of femme fatales and morally ambiguous heroes. But a film like this is, at its heart, indefinable; Lynch has a peculiar talent for avoiding categorization, which is part of the reason his films make lasting impressions on the movie community and attract such devoted followers.

With its stellar performances, haunting score by Angelo Badalamenti, and highly stylized, symbolic direction, *Blue Velvet* became a critical darling on its release and did quite well financially. It's seen its life, and influence, continue through constant video and DVD releases during the past three decades, and it's now regularly ranked as one of the greatest films ever made.

FURTHER VIEWING: *Twin Peaks: Fire Walk with Me; Wild at Heart; Lost Highway*
SEE ALSO: *Bitter Moon; The Passion of Darkly Noon; The Element of Crime*

★★★★★

Director: Michael Winner
Screenwriter: Wendell Mayes

Produced by: Michael Winner, Bobby Roberts, Dino De Laurentiis, and Hal Landers

Starring: Charles Bronson, Hope Lange, and Vincent Gardenia
Released by: Paramount (DVD)

18+

DEATH WISH

1974, 93 mins.

Plot: Architect Paul Kersey is living the American dream in New York. He and his family have just returned from a vacation in Hawaii; a group of street thugs break into Paul's apartment and brutally rape his married daughter, killing his wife in the process. The police offer no help as they protest that it's unlikely they'll be able to apprehend a group of off-the-grid criminals. With his daughter in a coma, Paul takes a business trip to Tucson, Arizona, where a client slips him a gun as a going-away present. Despite having been a conscientious objector during the Korean War, Paul begins a spree of vigilantism when he returns to New York, shooting and killing all muggers unlucky enough to cross his path. The police struggle to find the city's Batman-wannabe as the public voice is securely in Paul's favor.

Review: That *Death Wish* is graphically violent and seemingly pro-vigilantism didn't help its reception; many critics felt it glorified depictions of immoral and illegal behavior. But the film clearly struck a chord with audiences, who in early 1970s America were dealing with rising crime rates and corrupt, ineffectual law enforcement in big cities. Viewers reportedly cheered every time Paul Kersey killed a mugger, and *Death Wish* proved a financial success that was capitalized on in four sequels, all starring Charles Bronson.

Bronson was a relative unknown on the American film scene, but afterward he became a bankable leading man, which echoed his previous success in Europe. The film also features Jeff Goldblum in his first movie role as one of the rapists.

Whether or not *Death Wish* encourages anti-social behavior is a moot point—anti-heroes always seem to garner the loudest cheers, and this is valuable as possibly the first film to feature western-style revenge themes in a modern, urban setting. While this first installment in the series was thoughtful enough to provoke debate on personal justice, the sequels became popular solely as over-the-top bloodfests.

FURTHER VIEWING: ***Death Wish 2; Death Wish 3; Death Wish 4: The Crackdown; Death Wish 5: The Face of Death***
SEE ALSO: ***Vigilante; Man on Fire; Joe***

★★★★★

Director: Sidney Lumet
Screenwriter: Frank Pierson

Produced by: Martin Bregman, Martin Elfand, and Robert Greenhut

Starring: Al Pacino, John Cazale, and Charles Durning
Released by: Warner Home Video (DVD)

8+

DOG DAY AFTERNOON

1975, 125 mins.

Plot: Based on a true story. Sonny Wortzik and his friend Sal try to rob a bank in Brooklyn, New York, to pay for Sonny's wife Leon's sex reassignment surgery. If that weren't ridiculous enough, absolutely everything goes wrong during the heist. First, Sonny and Sal attempt to rob the bank just after the daily pick-up, so there's no money. Sonny tries to make up the balance with traveler's checks instead, but as he burns the register, smoke billows out the window and nearby businesses call the cops. Once the police arrive, Sonny and Sal officially take the bank employees and customers hostage, a few of whom fall ill and require medical attention. The cops bring both Sonny's wife and his mother down to the bank to try to talk him into abandoning his foolish plan, but they don't succeed, and Sonny is apprehended on his way to JFK airport, while Sal is killed.

Synopsis: This is an odd sort of crime drama; not nearly as gritty as most of the urban violence pictures coming out of the 1970s, it exudes humor and good nature, but never loses sight of the fact that Sonny and Sal are committing a crime, and there will be consequences. The inspiration for the film came from an article in *Life* magazine covering the real robbery, in which some of the hostages asserted that, far from feeling threatened by the armed robbers, they actually developed a strong liking for them. In the film this sentiment is reflected in the crowd that gathers around the bank, most of which is sympathetic to Sonny and Sal.

First and foremost, *Dog Day Afternoon* is a crime film, as its fast pace attests. But the strongest aspect of this Lumet gem is its unusual, and unusually well-rounded, characterizations, resulting in a collection of lovable and compelling oddballs you can't help but root for.

FURTHER VIEWING: *Serpico; Prince of the City*
SEE ALSO: *Black Tuesday; The Sugarland Express; Mad City*

★★★★

Director: John Woo
Screenwriters: John Woo, Barry Wong, and Gordon Chan

Produced by: Amy Chin, Linda Kuk, and Terence Chang

Starring: Chow Yun-Fat, Tony Leung Chiu Wai, Teresa Mo, Philip Chan, and Philip Kwok
Released by: Dragon Dynasty (DVD)

18+

HARD BOILED

1992, 126 mins.

Plot: In Hong Kong, Officer "Tequila" and his partner Benny bust in on a gun deal but are ambushed; the resulting firefight kills Benny and wounds several other officers. Tequila takes the disaster personally, and after his superior orders him off the case, he pursues the gang members on his own. He finds an undercover cop, Alan, who's working as an assassin for the mob, and the two team up to pursue the mob's top man. The film's climax involves a shootout in a hospital maternity ward (no joke), with Alan and Tequila killing mobsters with abandon while safely evacuating the babies from the hospital.

Review: "As a cop, he has brains, brawn, and an instinct to kill!" Thus proclaims the American poster for *Hard Boiled*, which also features Chow Yun-Fat holding a shotgun in one hand and a diapered baby in the other. Brilliant.

This is John Woo's last Hong Kong film before he became a popular director in America, and it's considered one of his best from those days, even if it is rawer and less polished than his later Hollywood offerings. Like all Woo films, *Hard Boiled* features stylized, almost balletic action sequences that in this case more than make up for a convoluted plotline, but, really, the action makes up almost the entire film so plot is rendered almost unnecessary. Which isn't to say the film is brainless; it may not be a narrative masterpiece, but Woo's action scenes are considered among the best, if not *the* best, ever committed to celluloid. Big, brash, and seriously fun.

FURTHER VIEWING: *The Killer; Face/Off; Hard Target*
SEE ALSO: *Die Hard; The Wild Bunch; Time and Tide*

★★★★

Director: Perry Henzell
Screenwriters: Perry Henzell and Trevor D. Rhone
Produced by: Perry Henzell

Starring: Jimmy Cliff, Janet Bartley, and Carl Bradshaw
Released by: Criterion (DVD)

15+

THE HARDER THEY COME

1972, 120 mins.

Plot: Ambitious country dandy Ivan Martin comes to town hoping for work and dreaming of a record deal. Finding little success, he drifts the streets until a lucky break propels him to stardom—and infamy—as he locks horns with music mafiosi, drug dealers, and corrupt cops.

Review: The film that made Jimmy Cliff reggae's first superstar, this rich slice of Jamaican life has the feel of an early martial arts and blaxplotation movie or spaghetti western. The acting and direction are a bit rough around the edges but also surprisingly innovative in places.

Cliff begins the film as something of a naïve charmer hoping simply to make records. Okay, so he's a bit of a scoundrel and leads young girls astray, much to the annoyance of the church that's taken him under its wing. But soon he gets a taste of the real world—making you wonder if this isn't all a little semi-autobiographical for Cliff—when Ivan discovers talent counts for nothing in an industry where money is king, and there is an unending pool of blithely innocent victims to be plundered and taken advantage of. From there it's a downward spiral as the film makes no bones about what drives the economical heart of Jamaica: drugs, reggae, and money, with corruption the glue that holds the whole sordid business together.

And while the movie isn't exactly an advert for the island as a vacation venue, it is a keen-eyed study of Jamaica as a struggling third-world nation. There are no sets here in the rough, tough shantytowns—this is street-life filmmaking full of cast members who look like they were pulled into shot by the crew and told to act. And if it looks a little hackneyed in places, big deal, because, after all, the real star is the awesome reggae soundtrack.

FURTHER VIEWING: *No Place Like Home*
SEE ALSO: *Babylon; The Great Rock 'n' Rock Swindle; Reggae Sunsplash; Scarface*

★
★
★
★

Director: Michael Campus
Screenwriter: Robert J. Poole
Produced by: Harvey Bernhard

Starring: Max Julien, Richard Pryor, and Carol Speed
Released by: New Line Home Video (DVD)

18+

THE MACK

1973, 110 mins.

Plot: John "Goldie" Mickens is a reformed drug dealer recently released from prison into the Bay Area. A lot has changed during the time Goldie was away—his brother has turned militant, his mother is convinced that only Jesus can save him now, and he's got two nutty white cops on his tail threatening to send him back to prison. So Goldie does what he does best, and vows to "be the meanest mack [pimp] there ever was!" Of course, this only sets him up for a fight with rival pimp Pretty Tony and for conflict with his black nationalist brother.

Review: *The Mack* is blaxploitation at its finest, released in the heyday of the genre, but that doesn't mean it's any good. The music is listenable and Richard Pryor's small appearance is as funny as you'd expect (and reflects his "Pimp on Blow" routine from his stand-up act at the time), but otherwise the film is largely an exercise in inept film-making, with its nonsensical script, wooden acting, crass stereotypes, and accidental camera work. So why watch it? And more importantly, why is it even on this list? Because it's *fun*, that's why, and its sometimes surreal dialog is eminently quotable: "They're going to talk about me the way they used to talk about Jesus," "Truth is pimples, garlic, and armpits," and, "A pimp is only as good as his product—and his product is women!"

Despite, and often because of, its (massive) shortcomings, *The Mack* is truly hilarious, and its influence can be seen throughout pop-culture even today.

FURTHER VIEWING: ***The Education of Sonny Carson***
SEE ALSO: ***Trick Baby; Superfly; Willie Dynamite***

★★★★★

Director: John Boorman
Screenwriter: Alexander Jacobs
Produced by: Judd Bernard
Starring: Lee Marvin, Angie Dickinson, and Keenan Wynn
Released by: Warner Home Video (DVD)

15+

POINT BLANK

1967, 92 mins.

Plot: Based on Richard Stark's novel *The Hunter*, Lee Marvin plays the hard-boiled Walker, who burns up the screen in the pursuit of bloody retribution. Double-crossed by his wife and friend Reese at a smash-and-grab robbery on Alcatraz, he's shot and left for dead in an empty cell. Barely alive, Walker escapes the island to reclaim the $93,000 he was assassinated for. Two years pass, during which he befriends the mysterious character Yost (Keenan Wynn) who promises to give him the location of Reese and Chris in exchange for any information he can gather on The Organization—the criminal group Reese belongs to. Walker visits his wife first, bursting into her bedroom and firing round after round into an empty bed. Reese is long gone; he's moved further up The Organization's chain and (foolishly) thinks he's out of reach. Yet for a man like Walker, no one is untouchable.

Review: Boorman's blend of film noir and flourishes of the French New Wave makes for gripping viewing. Clever use of sound and razor-sharp editing create a virtual mix-tape of a movie, speeding backwards and forwards through time in an almost dizzying manner, and constantly keeping the audience second-guessing. The meeting between Walker and his killer flips between a violent struggle on an apartment balcony and another from their past, with Reese lying on top of Walker begging him to trust him. The words are hollow; he ends up as street pizza. Fittingly, Marvin's avenging angel is bloody-minded and spiritually destitute. By the end of the film, his mission complete, instead of collecting the money he'd killed for, he dissolves into the shadows as if he'd never been there. The whole adventure could have been a dream as each character leaves the stage with nothing. Stylish and violent, it hasn't dated.

FURTHER VIEWING: ***Deliverance; Hell in the Pacific; Payback (1999 remake)***
SEE ALSO: ***The Killing***

★★★★★

Director: Joseph Sargent
Screenwriter: Peter Stone
Produced by: Edgar J. Scherick

Starring: Walter Matthau and Robert Shaw
Released by: MGM (DVD)

15+

THE TAKING OF PELHAM ONE TWO THREE

1974, 104 mins.

Plot: Transit Authority Officer Zach Garber expects that the only major disruption to his daily routine will be having to take the directors of the Tokyo subway on a tour of the New York subway command center. But while Garber wise-cracks his way through the tour, a train makes an unscheduled stop, and a man calling himself Mr. Blue demands a million dollars in an hour or he'll start killing one passenger for every minute the money is late. It turns out a team of four identically dressed men—armed with submachine guns and distinguished only by the names of colors—boarded and isolated the Pelham 123 train earlier in the day. The money makes it a bit late after a shootout with some overenthusiastic cops, and the four men ask for the tracks to be cleared for their escape to South Ferry. But Garber believes they must have left the train already and makes his way into the tunnels on foot to track the men.

Review: *The Taking of Pelham One Two Three* is such an accomplished thriller, it makes filmmaking look easy. Walter Matthau as Garber and Robert Shaw as Mr. Blue are the perfect nemeses—Garber is cynical, lazy, and none-too serious, while Mr. Blue proves to be a cold, calculating, former British mercenary. The contrast between Garber's motley team and Blue's band of ruthless killers is emphasized by their respective spaces; most of the film's action takes place in only two small rooms, namely Garber's command center and Blue's subway car. Although this discord could be a problem in a lesser film, the brilliant screenplay—based on John Godey's book of the same name—manages to seamlessly combine light-hearted humor and suspenseful thrills without seeming in the least bit schizophrenic, ultimately proving that the sum can be far greater than its parts.

FURTHER VIEWING: ***The Taking of Pelham 1 2 3 (2009 remake)***
SEE ALSO: ***The Great Train Robbery; The Incident; The Laughing Policeman***

★★★★★

Director: Orson Welles
Screenwriter: Orson Welles
Produced by: Albert Zugsmith

Starring: Charlton Heston, Janet Leigh, and Orson Welles
Released by: Universal Studios (DVD)

TOUCH OF EVIL

1958, 92 mins.

Plot: Newlywed Mexican drug cop Mike Vargas investigates a car bombing incident on American soil, which originated in Mexico. When Vargas discovers Quinlan, the local police chief, has planted evidence to frame a suspect in the bombing case, he switches the focus of his investigation to Quinlan. Bad move. To discredit Vargas, Quinlan injects Vargas' wife with drugs and frames her for murder; Vargas has no means of getting proof of this until Quinlan's partner Menzies steps forward as an ally. Menzies meets with Quinlan, and Quinlan confesses to him that he has framed suspects in the past but claims that they were all guilty and deserved what they got. Luckily, Menzies is wired and Vargas is following them with a radio to record the confession; unluckily, Quinlan discovers the ruse and shoots Menzies with Vargas' gun. Menzies stays alive long enough to shoot his former friend, and in a moral gray-area twist we find out that the framed suspect in the bombing was guilty all along.

Review: It is no surprise to find an Orson Welles film on this list, or on any "best of" list; he is a masterful filmmaker, universally considered one of the best directors who ever lived, and, more importantly, he was in *The Muppet Movie*.

Touch of Evil reads almost noir-ish in its use of shadows and light, a stark visual metaphor of the evil that men do. Welles himself plays the morally ambiguous Quinlan, who has been obsessed with his personal brand of justice ever since the murder of his wife years before. Quinlan is hardly a likeable character, but he has his reasons, and Welles plays him with enough force and determination that we simply can't explain away his actions as the desperation of a broken man. Coupled with the film's shocking end revelation, Welles invites the audience to consider their own moral standpoint: can the end ever justify the means?

FURTHER VIEWING: *The Lady from Shanghai; Othello*
SEE ALSO: *Kiss Me Deadly; Night Falls on Manhattan; L.A. Confidential*

237/500

★★★

Director: Jean-Luc Godard
Screenwriter: Jean-Luc Godard
Produced by: Georges de Beauregard

Starring: Jean-Paul Belmondo, Jean Seberg, and Daniel Boulanger
Released by: Fox Lorber (DVD)

À BOUT DE SOUFFLE (BREATHLESS)

1960, 90 mins.

Plot: After killing a policeman, smooth, ruthless murderer Jean-Paul flees to Paris to collect a debt before heading on to Rome. However, he is distracted by the desire to rekindle a romance he shared with a beautiful American student. Yet the road to true love is never smooth, and the police drive the killer and his confused lover towards inevitable tragedy.

Review: Directed with flair and oozing street smarts, this is the ultimate in European cinematic fashion. The leads are beautiful and hip, encapsulating the anti-establishment youth cultures coming to the fore in 1960. But their breed of tortured romance and the movie's effortless style never goes out of fashion.

FURTHER VIEWING: ***Charlotte et son Jules (Charlotte and Her Jules); Le mépris (Contempt); Alphaville; Week End***
SEE ALSO: ***Jules et Jim (Jules and Jim); Badlands; Bonnie and Clyde; True Romance***

238/500

★★★★

Director: Jack Sholder
Screenwriters: Jack Sholder, Robert Shaye, and Michael Harrpster

Produced by: Benni Korzen, Robert Shaye, and Sara Risher

Starring: Jack Palance, Donald Pleasence, and Martin Landau
Released by: Image Entertainment (DVD)

ALONE IN THE DARK

1982, 92 mins.

Plot: Donald Pleasence is a hippie with a license to heal; he runs an asylum for the criminally insane that has no bars, only electronic locks. When a new doctor arrives a group of patients decide he must have killed their old doctor and plot their revenge; they get their chance when the locks fail during a convenient power outage. The patients make their way to the doctor's house and terrorize him and his family.

Review: Please don't mistake this for the Uwe Boll crapfest of the same name. This is an odd sort of eighties horror film in that it neither stars nor is aimed at teenagers—most of the cast are quite advanced in years. But this proves positive as it allowed seasoned and respected actors such as Jack Palance and Martin Landau to stretch their considerable horror muscles. A brilliant and unexpected plot twist caps the excellent performances.

FURTHER VIEWING: ***Nightmare on Elm Street 2: Freddy's Revenge; The Hidden***
SEE ALSO: ***Halloween; Nightmare on Elm Street; Friday the 13th***

39

★★★★

Director: Otto Preminger
Screenwriter: Wendell Mayes
Produced by: Otto Preminger
Starring: James Stewart, Lee Remick, and Ben Gazzara
Released by: Columbia/Tristar (DVD)

2+

ANATOMY OF A MURDER

1959, 160 mins.

Plot: An astute and cunning small-town lawyer finds his declining career revived when he's offered the opportunity to defend a murderer in a high-profile case. However, what appears to be a cut-and-dry case of a soldier avenging the rape of his wife soon becomes far more entangled.

Review: A quintessential courtroom drama, this movie has it all: the thrust, block, and parry between the lawyers; the unexpected revelations; the surprise witnesses and mounting tension. The plot is fairly straightforward but is meticulously built, and the sharp, snappy dialog is loaded with humor and sass. With Stewart at his laconic and worldly best, a Saul Bass opening credit sequence, and a Duke Ellington soundtrack, this is classic filmmaking.

FURTHER VIEWING: *The Moon is Blue; The Man with the Golden Arm; Porgy & Bess; Exodus*
SEE ALSO: *Mister Smith Goes to Washington; It's a Wonderful Life; A Few Good Men; The Verdict; The Accused*

40

★★★

Director: Joseph H. Lewis
Screenwriter: Philip Yordan
Produced by: Sidney Harmon
Starring: Cornel Wilde, Richard Conte, and Brian Donlevy
Released by: Image Entertainment (DVD)

2+

THE BIG COMBO

1955, 89 mins.

Plot: Police lieutenant Leonard Diamond is on a personal mission against crime lord Mr. Brown. However, his crusade may have more to do with his infatuation with Brown's girlfriend, Susan, but when hospitalized after an attempted suicide, she hints at an unexpected clue that provides the leverage Diamond needs to topple his nemesis.

Review: Inventive not just with its storytelling (you'll never look at a hearing aid in quite the same way) but also with its pervasively dark atmosphere, director Lewis turns what could be a bog-standard crime thriller into a striking piece of filmmaking. Laden with sleaze, sadism, psychosexual and homoerotic subtexts, an emotionally crippled anti-hero, and some very twisted relationships, it can rightfully take its place at the high tide of the noir genre.

FURTHER VIEWING: *Gun Crazy; The Return of October; A Lawless Street*
SEE ALSO: *The Big Heat; Casablanca; The Killing; L.A. Confidential*

241/500

★★★

Director: Roger Corman
Screenwriter: Robert Thom

Produced by: Samuel Z. Arkoff, Roger Corman, Norman T. Herman, and James H. Nicholson

Starring: Shelley Winters, Pat Hingle, and Don Stroud
Released by: MGM (DVD, as part of the Corman Collection)

18+

BLOODY MAMA

1970, 90 mins.

Plot: "Say it with bullets!" Based on the legend of a real-life gangster mama, Ma Barker is shown to be the brains (and sometimes brawn) behind her lawless sons in the Prohibition era. Huge amounts of blood and a large pinch of sexual depravity are the driving forces behind this film.

Review: "King of the Bs" Roger Corman is probably at least indirectly responsible for every single post-1955 film on this list, whether because he just inspired low-budget filmmakers or because he discovered the likes of Jack Nicholson, Martin Scorsese, and Robert De Niro (who makes an appearance in this film) among countless others. Anything Corman touches is The Real Cult Thing, and this is one of his most tasteless and entertaining.

FURTHER VIEWING: ***Anything directed or produced by Corman***
SEE ALSO: ***The Goonies; Dillinger***

242/500

★★★★

Director: Andy Wachowski and Larry Wachowski
Screenwriters: Andy Wachowski and Larry Wachowski

Produced by: Andy Wachowski, Larry Wachowski, Andrew Lazar, and Jeffrey Sudzin

Starring: Jennifer Tilly, Gina Gershon, and Joe Pantoliano
Released by: Republic Pictures (DVD)

18+

BOUND

1996, 108 mins.

Plot: Violet is a lonely, dissatisfied mafia wife just ripe for seduction. Predictably, when attractive ex-con plumber Corky begins work in her building, the romance takes off; unpredictably, Corky is a woman (played by megasexy Gina Gershon). The two plot to get Violet away from her husband, Caesar, by stealing two million dollars of his blood money, but their plan goes awry when Violet's husband finds out, and they must find a way to keep the money and ensure Caesar can't follow them.

Review: Though the Wachowski brothers went on to make the extremely successful *Matrix* trilogy, they first cut their teeth on this odd little lesbian noir film. Strongly and unapologetically sexual, *Bound* explores the ways we restrict ourselves, specifically regarding sexuality but also pertaining to societal expectations in general. A fascinating and rewarding film.

FURTHER VIEWING: ***The Matrix trilogy***
SEE ALSO: ***Lolita; The Last Seduction; Body Heat***

43

★★★★★

Director: Rian Johnson
Screenwriter: Rian Johnson

Produced by: Ram Bergman and Mark G. Mathis

Starring: Joseph Gordon-Levitt, Nora Zehetner, and Lukas Haas
Released by: Universal Studios (DVD)

5+

BRICK

2005, 106 mins.

Plot: High schooler Brendan gets a mysterious phone call from his ex, Emily, asking for help. Emily soon turns up dead, and Brendan infiltrates an underworld of drugs, violence, and femme fatales to find out why.

Review: Sometimes films featuring teenagers in overly mature narratives just come off as creepy and distasteful, but *Brick* turns this idiosyncrasy into black-comedy gold. Though the dialog and cadence are straight out of a forties noir film, *Brick* never loses sight of its contemporary high-school context. In a particularly witty scene, Brendan and his school's vice principal step into the rogue cop and captain roles: "You got disciplinary issues with me, you write me up or suspend me. I'll see you at the parent conference." Priceless.

FURTHER VIEWING: *The Brothers Bloom*
SEE ALSO: *Heathers; Alpha Dog; The Usual Suspects*

44

★★★★★

Director: Andrew Dominik
Screenwriter: Andrew Dominik

Produced by: Al Clark, Martin Fabinyi, Michael Gudinski, Michele Bennett, and Yvonne Collins

Starring: Eric Bana, Simon Lyndon, and David Field
Released by: Image Entertainment (DVD)

8+

CHOPPER

2000, 94 mins.

Plot: Based on the life of Australian criminal Mark "Chopper" Read. In and out of jail since he was a teenager, Chopper tries to spring his friend from prison by kidnapping a judge—it doesn't quite work out and he's sentenced to the same prison for sixteen years. On his release he finds the world he left is very different, but he falls back into his old patterns and is once again sent to a cell. This time he writes a book about his criminal activities on the outside (and inside) and becomes a larger-than-life cult figure.

Review: This is Australian actor Eric Bana's (*Hulk; Munich*) breakthrough performance, and it's no wonder: he is mesmerizing as the hyperactive, unhinged, self-aggrandizing Chopper.

FURTHER VIEWING: *The Assassination of Jesse James by the Coward Robert Ford*
SEE ALSO: *Romper Stomper; Ghosts . . . of the Civil Dead; Man Bites Dog*

245
500

★★★★

Director: Wim Wenders
Screenwriter: Wim Wenders

Produced by:
Joachim von Mengershausen

Starring: Dennis Hopper,
Bruno Ganz, and Lisa Kreuzer
Released by: Anchor Bay (DVD)

12+

DER AMERIKANISCHE FREUND
(THE AMERICAN FRIEND)

1977, 125 mins.

Plot: Tom Ripley, an American who sells forged art at auction in Germany, inadvertently suggests Jonathan Zimmerman, a picture framer dying from a blood disorder, as a potential hitman to his employers. Concerned for his family's wellbeing after his death, Jonathan reluctantly accepts the offer. After his first awkward killing, a second offer inevitably follows. But Tom doesn't think he can pull it off, and decides to step in . . .

Review: While the beginning of the movie seems confusing as it jumps between New York and Hamburg, it soon becomes engrossing as it follows Jonathan's clumsy descent into a life of crime. The developing relationship between Tom (a remarkably subdued Hopper) and Jonathan is the film's beating heart, providing action and sentimentality in manageable doses.

FURTHER VIEWING: ***Paris, Texas; Kings of the Road***
SEE ALSO: ***Blue Velvet; Wings of Desire; Ripley's Game***

246
500

★★★

Director: Edgar G. Ulmer
Screenwriter: Martin Goldsmith
Produced by: Leon Fromkess

Starring: Tom Neal,
Ann Savage, and Claudia Drake
Released by: Alpha Video (DVD)

A

DETOUR

1945, 67 mins.

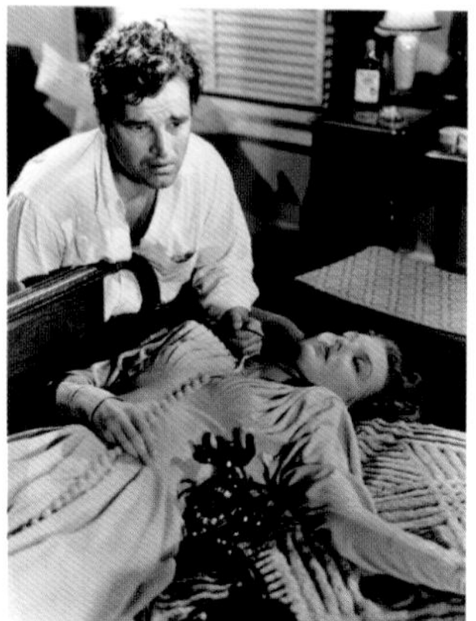

Plot: Down-on-his-luck hitchhiker Al is picked up by a man who dies during the journey. A model citizen, Al robs and then dumps the body, taking the man's flash car. He in turn picks up his own hitcher, Vera, who recognizes the car and blackmails him for his money. Greed inevitably turns into murder.

Review: There's a reason there are so many noir films, old and new, on this list—they capture the imagination with sex, style, death, and daring. Roger Ebert writes of *Detour*, "This movie [is] filled with technical errors and ham-handed narrative, [and] should have faded from sight soon after it was released in 1945. And yet it lives on, haunting and creepy, an embodiment of the guilty soul of film noir." It's the soul of noir and not its body that enthrals us; nowhere better is this exemplified than in *Detour*.

FURTHER VIEWING: ***The Strange Woman; Murder Is My Beat***
SEE ALSO: ***The Postman Always Rings Twice; Out of the Past; The Strange Love of Marta Ivers***

247

★★★

Director: John Milius
Screenwriter: John Milius
Produced by: Buzz Feitshans
Starring: Warren Oates, Ben Johnson, and Michelle Phillips
Released by: MGM (DVD)

8+ DILLINGER

1973, 108 mins.

Plot: Indiana, 1933. John Dillinger becomes the most wanted criminal in FBI history after he and his gang murder five agents while escaping from a botched robbery. With most of his crew dead, Dillinger's complicity gets him captured by the G-men and thrown into jail. But in the words of Dillinger himself, "No jail can hold me . . . it's an exercise in futility!" He escapes, but not without a dogged FBI agent hot on his heels.

Review: This uncompromisingly violent drama apes Peckinpah's best westerns, and despite its low-budget appearance features some excellent casting in the form of Warren Oates as Dillinger and Ben Johnson as Agent Purvis. Perhaps too sentimental at times, Milius' hard-boiled dialog still makes this a gangster film unlike any other.

FURTHER VIEWING: *The Wild and the Lion; Red Dawn*
SEE ALSO: *Bonnie and Clyde; The Wild Bunch*

248

★★★

Director: Walter Hill
Screenwriter: Walter Hill
Produced by: Lawrence Gordon
Starring: Ryan O'Neal, Bruce Dern, and Isabelle Adjani
Released by: Twentieth Century Fox (DVD)

15+ THE DRIVER

1978, 89 mins.

Plot: Ryan O'Neal plays a getaway driver for anyone willing to pay the right price. Known only to the police (and the viewer) as "The Cowboy," he's ruthlessly pursued by a cop who is determined to bring him down. For a man as elusive as The Cowboy, getting caught is not an option. That's when the cop comes up with the ultimate sting to haul in his bad guy: organizing a bank job where The Cowboy's the driver.

Review: Hill's crime drama is notorious for its jaw-dropping car chase scenes that make up the majority of the movie, but also for the lack of dialog that Ryan O'Neal's character speaks. A no-frills, fast-paced, and straight to the point classic.

FURTHER VIEWING: *The Warriors; Hard Times*
SEE ALSO: *Vanishing Point; Mad Max*

249/500

★★★★

Director: Gus Van Sant
Screenwriters: Gus Van Sant, Daniel Yost, and William S. Burroughs
Produced by: Cary Brokaw, Karen Murphy, and Nick Weschler
Starring: Matt Dillon, Kelly Lynch, and James LeGros
Released by: Lionsgate (DVD)

18+

DRUGSTORE COWBOY

1989, 102 mins.

Plot: Junkie Bob Hughes and his drug-addicted companions travel across the Pacific Northwest in the 1970s, robbing drugstores to support their habits. After one of the merry band of junkies dies from an overdose, Bob decides to kick his addiction, but finds out that when drugs are a lifestyle, it's the life and not just the substances that need to be left behind.

Review: Based on James Fogle's novel of the same name, *Drugstore Cowboy* won Best Screenplay awards from several well-respected bodies, including the Independent Spirit Awards and the New York Film Critics Circle. Sometimes funny, sometimes trippy, the film's overriding message seems to be that it's good while it lasts, but nothing lasts forever. Watch out for William S. Burroughs' appearance as a recovering addict/disgraced priest.

FURTHER VIEWING: ***My Own Private Idaho; Mala Noche***
SEE ALSO: ***The Man with the Golden Arm; Leaving Las Vegas; Jesus' Son***

250/500

★★★

Director: Russ Meyer
Screenwriter: Russ Meyer
Produced by: Russ Meyer
Starring: Tura Satana, Haji, and Lori Williams
Released by: RM International (DVD)

18+

FASTER PUSSYCAT! KILL! . . . KILL!

1965, 83 mins.

Plot: Three go-go dancers (you can see where this is going already) are drag racing in the desert when they come across a young couple. They kill the man and kidnap the girl. The ladies soon hear of an old hermit who's alleged to have scads of money on his property; they devise a plan to trick him out of his cash, but the old man more than matches their lust for mayhem and blood.

Review: The quintessential cult exploitation film, but if you're looking for full frontal, go elsewhere. This movie has violence in spades, but, interestingly, no nudity (unlike the vast majority of Russ Meyer's films). A sexy, stylish, and eminently watchable film from a genre that most often isn't.

FURTHER VIEWING: ***Mondo Topless; Supervixens; Mudhoney***
SEE ALSO: ***Big Doll House; The Switchblade Sisters***

★★★★★

Director: Martin Scorsese
Screenwriters: Martin Scorsese and Nicholas Pileggi

Produced by: Barbara Di Fina, Bruce S. Pustin, and Irwin Winkler

Starring: Robert De Niro, Ray Liotta, Joe Pesci, and Lorraine Bracco
Released by: Warner Home Video (DVD)

8+

GOODFELLAS

1990, 146 mins.

Plot: Irish-Italian Henry Hill has always wanted to be a gangster. He marries a nice Jewish girl and starts a family, but his mob activities eventually land him in prison where he sells drugs to keep his family solvent. Once out of the joint, a severely addicted Henry defies his mafia brethren and gets heavily involved in the drug trade; caught between the mob and the police, he turns state's evidence and enters the witness protection program to be just another nobody on the street.

Review: Ranging from the fifties to the eighties, *Goodfellas* follows the ups, downs, hilarity, and darkness of being a mafia foot soldier. There is not one weak performance in the entire film, and Ray Liotta simply shines in the lead role. This is storytelling at its best from master director Scorsese.

FURTHER VIEWING: *Mean Streets; Casino*
SEE ALSO: *The Godfather; Donnie Brasco; Men of Respect*

★★★★

Director: Stephen Frears
Screenwriter: Donald E. Westlake

Produced by: Barbara De Fina, Jim Painter, Martin Scorsese, Peggy Rajski, and Robert A. Harris

Starring: Anjelica Huston, John Cusack, and Annette Bening
Released by: Miramax Home Entertainment (DVD)

18+

THE GRIFTERS

1991, 110 mins.

Plot: Con artist-in-training Roy Dillon is caught between his mother and his girlfriend in this noir coming-of-age tale. Roy is beaten almost to death after a con goes wrong, prompting his mother to rethink bringing him into the grifter lifestyle. Roy's girlfriend—an older, small-time scam artist—tries to include him on a big job; when he refuses she sees his mother as the cause and vows to kill her. But his mother has problems of her own and will do anything to get enough money to escape the dangerous bookie she works for.

Review: With a casting trifecta that includes John Cusack, the incomparable Anjelica Huston, and Annette Bening, this understated noir fable is a real attention-grabber. Though it can be a bit flashback-y and relentlessly depressing, if you like watching selfish people do horrible things, this film's for you.

FURTHER VIEWING: ***Dangerous Liaisons; The Hit***
SEE ALSO: ***Hard Eight; Criminal; House of Games***

253

★
★

Director: Robert Aldrich
Screenwriter: Leon Griffiths
Produced by: Robert Aldrich

Starring: Kim Darby, Scott Wilson, and Tony Musante
Released by: MGM (Video & DVD)

15+

THE GRISSOM GANG

1971, 128 mins.

Plot: A gang of thieves accidentally kidnap an heiress after a robbery turns fatal, but the villainous Grissom family kill the robbers and steal the heiress. They demand a million dollars from her family, even though they have every intention of killing her anyway. Problems arise, however, when one of the Grissom boys falls in love with the heiress.

Review: Tough Depression-era crime thriller or macabre family drama with a lot of blood and bullets? Could be either, as the tension mounts and things turn nasty and hysterical, and what began as the worst kind of family dysfunction, under the auspices of the Medusa-like mother, becomes a curiously unexpected romance.

FURTHER VIEWING: *Kiss Me Deadly; The Flight of the Phoenix; The Dirty Dozen; Ulzana's Raid; The Killing of Sister George*
SEE ALSO: *Bloody Mama; Bonnie and Clyde; O Brother, Where Art Thou?*

254

★
★
★

Director: Jack Arnold
Screenwriters: Robert Blees and Lewis Meltzer
Produced by: Albert Zugsmith

Starring: Russ Tamblyn, Jan Sterling, and John Drew Barrymore
Released by: Republic Pictures (DVD)

12+

HIGH SCHOOL CONFIDENTIAL!

1958, 85 mins.

Plot: Drugs and rock 'n' roll go hand-in-hand at this all American high school, but the cops have them made, sending in a too-cool-for-school narc to bring down the school dope ring and kill everyone's buzz.

Review: Drugs are bad! Crime will follow! Dope is everywhere, hide hide hide! This is the fifties equivalent of an hysterical after-school special, but much more entertaining due to its over-the-top marijuana exploits and the fact that it inadvertently makes fifties dope smokers look really cool. Being a teen B-movie, there are some surprising young actor/musician appearances—look out for Jerry Lee Lewis (honestly, you can't miss him), John Barrymore, and Charlie Chaplin's kid. Put on your best black leather, slick your hair back, and enjoy the rocky Caddy ride.

FURTHER VIEWING: *Outside the Law*
SEE ALSO: *Reefer Madness; The Narcotics Story; Teenage Devil Dolls*

★★★

Director: Leonard Kastle and Donald Volkman
Screenwriter: Leonard Kastle
Produced by: Warren Steibel
Starring: Shirley Stoler, Tony Lo Bianco, and Mary Jane Higby
Released by: Criterion (DVD)

18+

THE HONEYMOON KILLERS

1970, 107 mins.

Plot: Overweight, lonely nurse Martha writes to a matchmaking service, and New Yorker Ray replies. They begin a passionate letter liaison, but Ray abruptly ends it. Martha threatens to kill herself, and Ray asks her to visit New York, where she discovers that Ray is a conman who seduces lonely women then robs them blind. Martha joins him in his con by posing as his sister, but her jealousy gets the better of her and they start leaving bodies in their wake.

Review: Loosely based on the true story of Martha Beck and Ray Fernandez, dubbed the "Lonely Hearts Killers" in the forties. Yes, there's blood; yes, there's betrayal; and yes, the low budget makes the whole thing look like an unsigned garage band's first music video. But at the heart of this film is a passionate love story that is just sweet enough to be unmissable.

FURTHER VIEWING: *Not available*
SEE ALSO: *Breathless; Badlands; Sid and Nancy*

256

★★★

Director: Liliana Cavani
Screenwriter: Liliana Cavani
Produced by: Esa De Simone
Starring: Dirk Bogarde, Charlotte Rampling, and Philippe Leroy
Released by: Criterion (DVD)

8+

IL PORTIERE DI NOTTE

(THE NIGHT PORTER)

1974, 108 mins.

Plot: Ex-SS officer Maximilian Theo Aldorfer (Dirk Bogarde) works as a night porter for a classy hotel in Vienna. In true contradictory fashion, he dotes on his guests while hiding a history of torturing and degrading Jews during the Holocaust. When Lucia, one of his victims from the war, arrives at his hotel, it reinvigorates a dark obsession that they had both long thought buried.

Review: Still shocking today, Cavani's complex study of sadomasochism remains controversial for daring to discuss sexuality during the Holocaust. Its most famous scene features a semi-clad Charlotte Rampling miming a Marlene Dietrich song in a Nazi uniform; Aldorfer's gift to her is the head of one of her tormentors. Not easy viewing, but fascinating nevertheless.

FURTHER VIEWING: *Beyond Obsession; Berlin Affair*
SEE ALSO: *The Damned; Last Tango in Paris*

257

★★★★

Director: Abel Ferrera
Screenwriter: Nicholas St. John
Produced by: Augusto Caminito and Mary Kane
Starring: Christopher Walken, David Caruso, and Laurence Fishburne
Released by: Lionsgate (DVD)

8+

KING OF NEW YORK

1990, 106 mins.

Plot: On drug lord Frank White's release from prison, his first act is to regain his dominance in the New York underworld by having his boys crack a few heads. Then he decides to save a poor hospital in the South Bronx. But in serving his heart of gold and attempting to use dirty money to fund the hospital, Frank makes a lot of enemies, including the police.

Review: As a gangster with a dream, you can't help but believe Frank White when he declares, "I never killed anyone who didn't deserve it"; that Christopher Walken can sell the line and the image is testament to his immense character-acting skills. As this modern-day Robin Hood and his band of Merry Murderers tear through the streets of New York robbing the criminal rich to give to the poor, your moral compass will undoubtedly be tested and come away the better for it.

FURTHER VIEWING: *Bad Lieutenant; The Hold Up*
SEE ALSO: *Scarface; Dillinger; L.A. Takedown*

★★★

Director: Mathieu Kassovitz
Screenwriter: Mathieu Kassovitz
Produced by: Christophe Rossignon

Starring: Vincent Cassel, Hubert Koundé, and Saïd Taghmaoui
Released by: Criterion (DVD)

15+

LA HAINE

1995, 96 mins.

Plot: The brutal beating of an Arabic teenager in Paris sparks violent clashes between the police and youths in the projects. Saïd, Vinz, and Hubert, friends from different ethnic backgrounds united in their frustrations, spend a day drifting into inflammatory situations, encountering police, television cameras, and other gangs. Tension between them escalates when the hot-tempered Vinz threatens to kill a cop.

Review: Shot in stark black-and-white, Kassovitz's well-paced and humane film drags the viewer into uneasy situations where violence threatens to bubble over at any moment, and often does. *The Wire* couldn't have existed without this.

FURTHER VIEWING: *Les Rivières Pourpres (The Crimson Rivers); Assassin(s)*
SEE ALSO: *Menace II Society; Boyz N the Hood*

59

★★★

Director: John Dahl
Screenwriter: Steve Barancik

Produced by: Alysse Bezahler, Jonathan Shestack, and Nancy Rae Stone

Starring: Linda Fiorentino, Bill Pullman, and Michael Raysses
Released by: Lionsgate (DVD)

8+ THE LAST SEDUCTION

1994, 110 mins.

Plot: Femme fatale Bridget steals close to a million dollars from her husband, Clay, and stops in a small town on her way to Chicago. She meets bored nice-guy Mike and tricks him into agreeing to kill Clay, whom she knows is after her, but Mike discovers what Bridget has done and joins forces with Clay. But even two men against this irresistible ice queen are not nearly enough.

Review: If the prospect of seeing Linda Fiorentino in a reverse cowboy film shouting "I'm a bitch!" doesn't tempt you to see this, stop reading. She's brilliant as the cold, sociopathic, man-eating Bridget, and Bill Pullman is a pleasant surprise as her husband and emotional equivalent. A real downer, this, but nice to see a woman in a stereotypical man's role, for once.

FURTHER VIEWING: *The Last Seduction 2; Rounders*
SEE ALSO: *Malice; Femme Fatale; Body Heat*

60

★★★

Director: Jean-Pierre Melville
Screenwriter: Jean-Pierre Melville

Produced by: Georges de Beauregard and Carlo Ponti

Starring: Jean-Paul Belmondo, Serge Reggiani, and Jean Desailly
Released by: Criterion (DVD)

12+ LE DOULOS

1962, 108 mins.

Plot: No sooner is burglar Maurice released from prison than he murders his supposed friend Gilbert. He then sets about a robbery only to be chased and wounded by the police. Maurice is starting to think that an associate, Silien, might actually be a police informer and sets out to uncover the complicated truth—which proves far tougher than anticipated.

Review: A very French take on American hard-boiled thrillers, this has a plot as complicated as anything written by Chandler. Focused around the notion of honor among thieves, the film is as two-faced as its characters, veering from one narrative thread to another, but aided by a judicious use of flashbacks, never losing its logic. And if it all gets too much just lie back and enjoy Melville's beautiful black and white underworld.

FURTHER VIEWING: *Les enfants terribles (The Strange Ones); Bob le Flambeur (Bob The Gambler); Le Samurai; Le circle rouge (The Red Circle); Breathless*
SEE ALSO: *The Asphalt Jungle; The Big Heat; The Killing*

261
500

★★★★★

Director: Luc Besson
Screenwriter: Luc Besson

Produced by: Luc Besson, Bernard Grenet, Claude Besson, John Garland, and Patrice Ledoux

Starring: Jean Reno, Gary Oldman, and Natalie Portman
Released by: Sony Pictures (DVD)

18+

LÉON (THE PROFESSIONAL)

1994, 110 mins.

Plot: Léon is a lonely hitman, divorced from society, who is "adopted" by an abused, precocious twelve-year-old girl who lives down the hall. When Mathilda's family is murdered by corrupt cops, she takes refuge with Léon, asking him to train her in the ways of assassination so she can avenge her little brother's death. Initially reluctant, Léon warms to Mathilda and makes the ultimate sacrifice to ensure her well being.

Review: Luc Besson's American directorial debut is an unlikely but heart-warming film about a professional killer and the neglected young outcast who befriends him. As the coke-snorting dirty cop, Gary Oldman is just a bit too evil, a bit too Al Pacino-esque to fit comfortably with the film's quietude, but Jean Reno and Natalie Portman's camaraderie more than make up for it. This is Portman's first starring role and her finest.

FURTHER VIEWING: ***Nikita***
SEE ALSO: ***Grosse Point Blank; The Killer; Gloria; Training Day***

262
500

★★★★★

Director: Henri-Georges Clouzot
Screenwriter: Henri-George Clouzot
Produced by: Henri-Georges Clouzot

Starring: Simone Signoret, Véra Clouzot, and Paul Meurisse
Released by: Criterion (DVD)

15+

LES DIABOLIQUES (THE DEVILS)

1955, 116 mins.

Plot: Michel Delasalle is the headmaster of a girl's boarding school; he's also a complete bastard. Openly flaunting his relationship with his mistress, Nicole, he mistreats his wife and, in an unusual twist, wife and mistress join forces to rid the world of Michel. They succeed in their clandestine murder, dumping his body in the swimming pool. Then the body disappears . . .

Review: This film could easily be classed as horror, but it almost defies categorization as it's a singular kind of intelligent, female-defined fear that drives the picture, one that isn't treated at all condescendingly. No less a master of psychological thrills than Hitchcock, Clouzot drags you into Christina and Nicole's claustrophobic hell and will not let you go until he's finished with you. Deliciously cruel filmmaking.

FURTHER VIEWING: ***La vérité (The Truth)***
SEE ALSO: ***The Hand that Rocks the Cradle; Vertigo; Rear Window***

53

★★★★

Director: Steven Soderbergh
Screenwriter: Lem Dobbs
Produced by: John Hardy and Scott Kramer
Starring: Terence Stamp, Lesley Ann Warren, Luis Guzmán, and Peter Fonda
Released by: Lionsgate (DVD)

8+ THE LIMEY

1999, 89 mins.

Plot: Career criminal Wilson (Stamp), newly released from jail in the UK, flies to Los Angeles to investigate the death of his daughter. Assisted by her friends Ed (Guzmán) and Elaine (Warren), he explores the murky affairs of her boyfriend (Fonda) with bloody results.

Review: The plot is, as the summary suggests, straightforward, but Soderbergh forges a complicated study of memory and time from the simple revenge drama. It's a masterpiece of editing and structure, with flashbacks and flashforwards giving us a sophisticated idea of Wilson's perceptions, some very funny dialog, luminous cinematography, and pitch-perfect performances from the cast—especially Stamp, Fonda, and the terrific Guzmán. Modern noir at its most rewarding, and more complicated than many of Soderbergh's better-known movies.

FURTHER VIEWING: *Traffic; Schizopolis; Erin Brockovich*
SEE ALSO: *The Third Man; Point Break; L'Annee Derniere a Marienbad (Last Year at Marienbad)*

54

★★★

Director: Robert Altman
Screenwriter: Leigh Brackett
Produced by: Jerry Bick
Starring: Elliott Gould, Nina Van Pallandt, and Sterling Hayden
Released by: MGM (DVD)

8+ THE LONG GOODBYE

1973, 111 mins.

Plot: After dropping a friend at the Mexican border, sleuth Philip Marlowe is arrested as an accomplice in the murder of his friend's wife. On being freed, he discovers his friend is now dead; he's also hired by a beautiful woman to find her abusive husband, then discovers that the mob thinks he owes them $350,000. Marlowe begins to realize that these seemingly unrelated cases are indeed tightly interwoven.

Review: Anyone expecting hard-nosed, ice-cool Humphrey Bogart will be in for a surprise; Elliot Gould's incarnation of Chandler's P.I. is an anti-social, maudlin loser but still manages to have integrity as he bumbles through the complex plot. Punctuated with flashes of brutal violence but beautifully made, the film does everything to throw the viewer's expectations—and succeeds.

FURTHER VIEWING: *McCabe & Mrs Miller; Thieves Like Us; M*A*S*H; The Player; Short Cuts*
SEE ALSO: *Chinatown; The Asphalt Jungle; The Big Sleep; Kiss Me Deadly; The Maltese Falcon*

265
500

★★★★★

Director: John Mackenzie
Screenwriter: Barrie Keeffe
Produced by: Barry Hanson, Chris Griffin, Denis O'Brien, and George Harrison
Starring: Paul Freeman, Leo Dolan, and Kevin McNally
Released by: Starz/Anchor Bay (DVD)

18+ THE LONG GOOD FRIDAY

1982, 114 mins.

Plot: Old-fashioned gangster Harold Shand is trying to go legit but remains the kingpin of the London underworld. His dominance is shaken, however, when a series of murders indicates someone is attempting to usurp his throne. Despite his pretension to legitimacy, Shand uses every brutal trick in the book—and then some—to discover his challenger.

Review: Bob Hoskins is mostly known to American audiences through his work on such light films as *Who Framed Roger Rabbit?* and *Hook*, but as this film shows, Hoskins is the original British gangster. It's a shame *The Long Good Friday* isn't more widely known—it more than holds its own against genre classics like *The Godfather* and *Scarface* and deserves similarly large audiences. Pay attention for a young and beautiful Pierce Brosnan's blink-and-you'll-miss-him appearance.

FURTHER VIEWING: ***The Fourth Protocol; The Last of the Finest***
SEE ALSO: ***Mona Lisa; Scarface; Get Carter; The General; The Limey***

266
500

★★★★

Director: Martin Scorsese
Screenwriter: Martin Scorsese
Produced by: Jonathan T. Taplin
Starring: Robert De Niro, Harvey Keitel, and David Proval
Released by: Warner Home Video (DVD)

18+ MEAN STREETS

1973, 112 mins.

Plot: Small-time crook Charlie is working his way through the ranks as a wiseguy in Little Italy collecting debts, but is conflicted about his Catholic devotion and the mob lifestyle. When his loud-mouthed friend Johnny finds himself in too deep with the wrong people, Charlie's loyalties are torn between protecting his friend and his own salvation.

Review: Essentially a blueprint for the greatness that was to follow, Scorsese's primary interests—Catholicism, wise guys, family, honor, and, of course, the killer soundtrack—are all here. Yet as his first fully fledged work, it's not a juvenile exercise but a carefully crafted film that launched Harvey Keitel and Robert De Niro into the American consciousness.

FURTHER VIEWING: ***Goodfellas; Taxi Driver***
SEE ALSO: ***Fingers; Laws of Gravity***

67

★★★★

Director: Richard Fleischer
Screenplay: Earl Belton
Produced by: Stanley Rubin

Starring: Charles McGraw, Marie Windsor, and Jacqueline White
Released by: Turner Home Entertainment (DVD)

THE NARROW MARGIN

1952, 71 mins.

Plot: Detective Walter Brown is reluctantly assigned to protect a mob boss's wife on her way to testify in court. Taking the train, policeman and wife do not get on at all, but Brown encounters an attractive woman, whom trailing mob killers assume to be their target. Soon, Brown is fighting to save the lives of both women.

Review: Claustrophobically tense, this is about as good as film noir gets. The terse dialog between escort and escorted shimmers with nasty wisecracks. Some original thinking (the use of reflections in the climactic shoot-out, for instance), taut writing, and clever use of the camera overcome the cheap sets, and the whole movie builds up a head of steam, rushing toward a very clever pay-off.

FURTHER VIEWING: *20,000 Leagues Under the Sea; The Vikings; The Boston Strangler; Tora! Tora! Tora!; 10 Rillington Place; Soylent Green; The Jazz Singer*
SEE ALSO: *From Russia with Love; Runaway Train*

68

★★★★

Director: Guillame Canet
Screenwriter: Guillame Canet
Produced by: Alain Attal

Starring: François Cluzet, Marie-Josée Croze, and André Dussollier
Released by: Music Box Films (DVD)

5+

NE LE DIS À PERSONNE (TELL NO ONE)

2006, 125 mins.

Plot: Eight years after the murder of Alex Beck's wife, Margot, he remains tortured with guilt over her death. To deal with the grief, he throws himself into his pediatric work. When two bodies turn up at the lake where his wife's body was found, the police decide to reopen the case—with Alex as the prime suspect. However, Alex believes his wife to still be alive, and must prove this to clear his name.

Review: Canet's stunningly realized drama became a word of mouth phenomenon in 2006 upon its release, and has already been optioned for a U.S. remake. Chiefly inspired by Hitchcock's best "Everyman" films, you'll be hard pressed to say you saw the ending coming.

FURTHER VIEWING: *Anything You Say*
SEE ALSO: *Caché; Vertigo*

269
500

★
★
★

Director: Chan-wook Park
Screenwriter: Jo-yun Hwang
Produced by: Seung-yong Lim
Starring: Min-sik Choi, Ji-tae Yu, and Hye-jeong Kang
Released by: Tartan Video (DVD)

18+

OLDBOY

2003, 120 mins.

Plot: Based on the manga of the same name, *Oldboy* charts the journey of a man called Oh Dae-Su who's kidnapped and held against his will in a room for fifteen years. With only a television and steamed dumplings to keep him company, he learns of his wife's murder and that his daughter has been placed in foster care. After many attempts to escape and commit suicide, he is released without warning and left to discover by whom—and why—he was imprisoned.

Review: The second film in Park's "Vengeance Trilogy" and winner of the 2004 Grand Prix at Cannes, *Oldboy* is a powerful story of revenge with a wicked twist in the tail. The final act is memorable for its sheer brutality.

FURTHER VIEWING: ***Sympathy for Mr. Vengeance; Sympathy for Lady Vengeance***
SEE ALSO: ***Kill Bill Volume 1; The Count of Monte Cristo***

270
500

★
★
★

Director: Phil Karlson
Screenwriter: Crane Wilbur
Produced by: Samuel Bischoff and David Diamond
Starring: John McIntire, Richard Kiley, and Kathryn Grant
Released by: Not Available

15+

THE PHENIX CITY STORY

1955, 87 mins.

Plot: At the end of the Second World War, lawyer John Patterson returns home to Phenix City, only to find it a den of vice and corruption sucking in dollars from a nearby army base. Determined to end the criminality, he campaigns to have his father voted in as attorney general. However, the crime syndicates who run the city up the ante—violently.

Review: A fictionalized semi-documentary of real events, this cleverly constructed movie was shot almost as a newscast and used some of the actual, notorious locations. Grim, tragic in places, and pretty explicit (for the time), the *veritas* feel is helped by some solid acting, and although it does play things a little too black and white in places, it's all for the greater good.

FURTHER VIEWING: ***Kid Galahad; A Time for Killing; Ben***
SEE ALSO: ***Night of the Living Dead; The Wargame***

71

★★★

Director: Bob Rafelson
Screenwriter: David Mamet
Produced by: Bob Rafelson, Andrew Braunsberg, Charles Mulvehill, and Michael Barlow
Starring: Jack Nicholson, Jessica Lange, and John Colicos
Released by: Warner Home Video (DVD)

8+ THE POSTMAN ALWAYS RINGS TWICE

1981, 122 mins.

Plot: Drifter and small-time conman Frank stops at a roadside cafe for a quick lunch, but when he lays eyes on the proprietor's beautiful wife Cora he decides to stay awhile. He gets to know her while working for her husband as a mechanic, and the two plot to kill her husband. They succeed on the second attempt, but turn on each other during the subsequent criminal investigation.

Review: The first film adaptation of the eponymous novel—made in 1946 and starring Lana Turner—is better known, but this version has the attraction of writing talent David Mamet and stars Jack Nicholson and Jessica Lange. Rafelson, a frequent Nicholson collaborator and former *Monkees* director, impeccably evokes the roadside isolation of the dusty Californian forties, and the chemistry between Nicholson and Lange is palpable.

FURTHER VIEWING: *The Postman Always Rings Twice (1946); Five Easy Pieces; Black Widow*
SEE ALSO: *Double Indemnity; Kiss Me a Killer; The Killers*

72

★★★

Director: Joseph Losey
Screenwriter: Dalton Trumbo
Produced by: Sam Spiegel
Starring: Van Heflin, Evelyn Keyes, and John Maxwell
Released by: Not Available

5+ THE PROWLER

1951, 92 mins.

Plot: Webb Garwood, a disgruntled cop investigating a peeping tom at the house of a married couple, soon becomes attracted to the lady of the house and her wealthy surroundings. Against all better judgment, they fall in love, and Garwood plots the murder of the woman's husband to collect a payout. Pregnant and alone, they escape into the country to begin a new, and ultimately doomed, life.

Review: *Black Dahlia* writer James Ellroy described *The Prowler* as his favorite film for its sheer creepiness, and it's easy to see why he identified with it. The bleak backdrop and nihilistic outcome became signatures throughout Losey's career (and indeed in Ellroy's fiction). A concise and very dark study of sexual obsession.

FURTHER VIEWING: *Time without Pity; The Criminal*
SEE ALSO: *The Postman Always Rings Twice; Double Indemnity*

★★★★★

Director: Quentin Tarantino
Screenwriters: Quentin Tarantino and Roger Avary

Produced by: Harvey Keitel, Lawrence Bender, Monte Hellman, Richard N. Gladstein, and Ronna B. Wallace

Starring: Harvey Keitel, Tim Roth, Michael Madsen, Chris Penn, and Steve Buscemi
Released by: Lionsgate (DVD)

18+

RESERVOIR DOGS

1992, 99 mins.

Plot: Gangster Joe Cabot brings together six criminals, unknown to each other, to pull off a jeweler heist. Though meant to keep them safe, their anonymity causes more problems when something goes very wrong during the robbery, indicating a set-up. Everyone knows that one of the gang's members is psychotic, but they have yet to find out that another is an undercover cop.

Review: *Reservoir Dogs* owes a huge debt to one of our Top Ten films, *The Taking of Pelham One Two Three*. But cult films inevitably breed cult, so that can be forgiven as this is also classic Tarantino: the audience is presented with a fractured story in which not even the characters are aware of the consequences of their actions, leaving us all gasping for closure until the final scene. Extra merit points for making a heist movie that never actually shows the heist.

FURTHER VIEWING: ***Pulp Fiction; Death Proof***
SEE ALSO: ***The Taking of Pelham One Two Three; The Usual Suspects; The Driver***

74

★★★★

Director: Alfred Hitchcock
Screenwriter: Arthur Laurents
Produced by: Sidney Bernstein

Starring: James Stewart, John Dall, and Farley Granger
Released by: Warner Brothers (DVD)

ROPE

1948, 80 mins.

Plot: Two highly educated college students murder a close friend to see if they can get away with it. To prove the hypothesis of their "perfect" crime, they hide the body in plain sight and invite the friends and family of the deceased over to a party. Only when guest Rupert Cadell (Jimmy Stewart) becomes suspicious, their carefully made plans begin to unravel.

Review: Based on Patrick Hamilton's play, the film version certainly feels like a stage production, relying on little trickery other than the odd quick cut and some moving furniture. The slow build to the bitter finale is almost excruciating, as is every approach by the party guests to tidy up the makeshift table that hides the body. Masterfully suspenseful.

FURTHER VIEWING: *Strangers on a Train; Rear Window*
SEE ALSO: *Compulsion; Gaslight*

75

★★★★

Director: Takeshi Kitano
Screenwriter: Takeshi Kitano

Produced by: Masayuki Mori, Hisao Nabeshima, and Takio Yoshida

Starring: Takeshi Kitano, Aya Kokumai, and Tetsu Watanabe
Released by: Buena Vista Home Video (DVD)

SONATINE

1993, 94 mins.

Plot: World-weary Yakuza boss Murakawa and his clan are sent to Okinawa to oversee a gangland peace treaty. However, things turn violent and they hole up in an isolated beach house, killing time in various interesting ways while awaiting orders. But then the bad news arrives; Murakawa's clan is to be expelled from the gang and he is has two choices: disband or fight.

Review: Takeshi's tour of Japan's seedy criminal underbelly lacks any glitz or glamour; killings having all the emotion of robots chopping carrots. Takeshi's clan only comes alive at the beach, leading to some touching, funny moments, but Takeshi's laconic anti-hero can have no happy ending, and it's sad to watch his final vengeance against his violent past.

FURTHER VIEWING: *Violent Cop; Hana-bi (Fireworks); Kikujio; Zatôichi (The Blind Swordsman: Zatoichi)*
SEE ALSO: *Gangster No.1; Sexy Beast; Black Rain; The Killer; Hard Boiled*

276/500

★★★

Director: Melvin Van Peebles
Screenwriter: Melvin Van Peebles
Produced by: Melvin Van Peebles and Jerry Gross
Starring: Simon Chuckster, Melvin Van Peebles, and Hubert Scales
Released by: Cinemation Industries (DVD)

18+

SWEET SWEETBACK'S BAADASSSSS SONG

1971, 97 mins.

Plot: Whorehouse performer Sweetback (played by Melvin Van Peebles) was raised in a brothel and has a lot to be angry about, but isn't. At least, not until he gets arrested for a crime he didn't commit. He escapes by beating the officers with his handcuffs, and spends the remainder of the film making his way to the Mexican border.

Review: The progenitor of a long line of seventies blaxploitation films, *Sweet Sweetback* has often been imitated, but never duplicated. Clearly low budget, it's roughly shot and the acting is just this side of unwatchable. But judging the production value is missing the point—this is a product of its time; the birth of a genre. It's also angry as hell and a lot of fun.

FURTHER VIEWING: ***Panther; How to Get the Man's Foot Outta Your Ass***
SEE ALSO: ***The Spook Who Sat by the Door; Soul Vengeance; Dolemite***

277/500

★★★

Director: Seijun Suzuki
Screenwriter: Kôhan Kawauchi
Produced by: Tetsuro Nakagawa
Starring: Tetsuya Watari, Chieko Matsubara, and Hideaki Nitani
Released by: Criterion (DVD)

12+

TÔKYÔ NAGAREMONO (TOKYO DRIFTER)

1966, 83 mins.

Plot: Tetsu Hondo has become a drifter following the disbandment of his Yakuza organization. The failure of a rival gang to recruit him forces him back into the open, where a dangerous hitman pursues him after his boss sells him over a real estate scam. Tetsu evades being killed until his return to Tokyo to confront the one man whom he would have died to protect.

Review: Trippy, hip, and maddeningly confusing, instead of making a regular Yakuza feature, Suzuki produced an explosive color comic book for the screen—part musical, part surrealist comedy, and wholly entertaining. Hugely influential to this day, the whistling assassin can still be seen in the likes of *Kill Bill Vol. 1* and *The Wire*.

FURTHER VIEWING: ***Branded to Kill; Youth of the Beast***
SEE ALSO: ***The Naked Kiss, Le Samourai (The Samurai)***

★★★★★

Director: Bryan Singer
Screenwriter: Christopher McQuarrie

Produced by: Bryan Singer, Art Horan, Franois Duplat, Hans Brockmann, and Kenneth Kokin

Starring: Stephen Baldwin, Gabriel Byrne, Benicio Del Toro, Kevin Pollak, and Kevin Spacey
Released by: MGM (DVD)

15+

THE USUAL SUSPECTS

1995, 106 mins.

Plot: This is a tough one to sum up, but here goes: five criminals first meet while in a police line-up—it turns out that the line-up has been orchestrated by lawyer Kobayashi who claims to work for über-criminal and possible fable Keyser Söze. Kobayashi blackmails the group into robbing a drug-smuggling ship, but this is just a front for the real target: a man aboard the ship who is one of the only people alive who can identify Söze. The job goes awry and only the crippled "Verbal" Kint walks away alive. The film opens with him telling this story to the police.

Review: Won a much-deserved Oscar for Best Original Screenplay. A solid crime yarn, expertly and unusually told, with a terrific ensemble cast and a honking great plot twist at the end. The problem? You can only watch it once as it was meant to be seen. But once is enough.

FURTHER VIEWING: *Apt Pupil*
SEE ALSO: *Identity; House of Games; Reservoir Dogs*

CHAPTER 6
TALES OF TERROR

"BEWARE THE MOON . . ."

Comprising a niche genre with a core of dedicated fans, horror movies are almost cult by definition in that they're generally still not accepted as a legitimate cinematic form by the establishment. But the man just don't understand, because horror—apart from providing the simple scares and outlandish gore we often expect from the genre—has a particular cultural resonance by allowing us to express and cope with our everyday fears. Often funny, usually unnerving, and sometimes so bad they're good, the movies in this section cover all subgenres of horror, from the first zombie movie ever made to horror comedy, with pit stops at vampires, werewolves, witches, voodoo, and serial killers along the way.

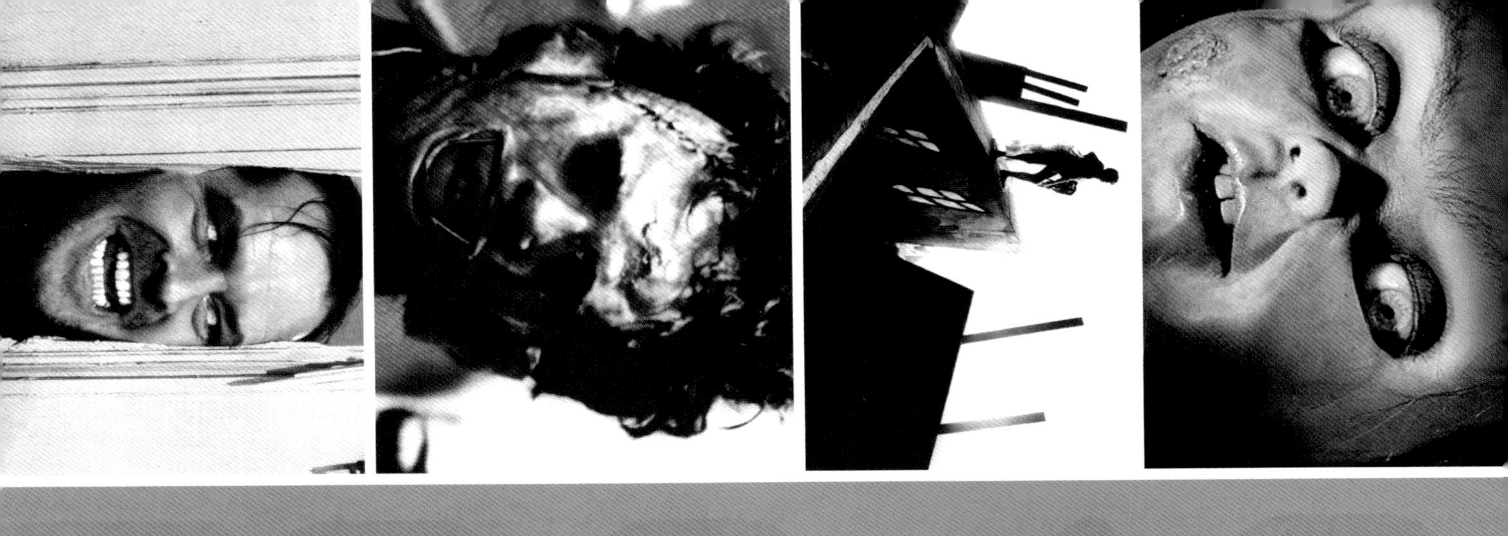

TOP 10

TALES OF TERROR...

★★★★★

Director: John Landis
Screenwriter: John Landis

Produced by: George Folsey Jr., Jon Peters, and Peter Guber

Starring: David Naughton, Griffin Dunne, and Jenny Agutter
Released by: Universal Pictures (DVD)

15+

AN AMERICAN WEREWOLF IN LONDON

1981, 97 mins.

Plot: American college students David and Jack are backpacking through Northern England when they're assaulted by a werewolf who kills Jack but only injures David. Waking up in a London hospital weeks later, David discovers the attack has left him with more than scars, and he must decide whether to continue to change and slaughter victims during every full moon, or to follow his dead friend's advice and kill himself to keep London's unwitting inhabitants safe.

Review: While most viewers would call *American Werewolf* a horror comedy, John Landis disagrees. "It still bothers me when people call this a comedy horror or horror comedy. My intention was to make a horror film . . . I wanted to make it realistic . . . and when you make a film about something fantastic, you have to create suspension of disbelief. I was trying to figure out how to create that with something like David talking to his dead friend. You know that can't be real. So that's why it's so funny."

Regardless, this is often considered the greatest horror comedy ever made; Landis' decision to use humor to ground the film proves highly effective as he walks the line between frightening and funny with enviable skill, never allowing the audience to get too accustomed to either, eliciting deeper laughs and louder screams. This is also the first werewolf film to show a full and uncomfortably graphic transformation from man to wolf, created by legendary makeup artist Rick Baker. The remastered, Blu-ray DVD is now available; you might think even Baker's Oscar-winning makeup would suffer from a sharper, more defined picture (the film is thirty years old, after all), but the exact opposite is true. Frankly, the film's physical effects are better, more visceral, and more admirable than any current pixilated CGI creation. Simply put, *American Werewolf* represents horror filmmaking at its most accomplished.

FURTHER VIEWING: *An American Werewolf in Paris; Thriller (music video/short); Innocent Blood; Beware the Moon: Remembering An American Werewolf in London*
SEE ALSO: *The Howling; Wolfen*

★★★★★

Director: Sam Raimi
Screenwriter: Sam Raimi
Produced by: Robert G. Tapert

Starring: Bruce Campbell, Ellen Sandweiss, Richard DeManincor, and Betsy Baker

Released by: Anchor Bay Entertainment (DVD)

8+

THE EVIL DEAD

1981, 85 mins.

Plot: Five college students spend the weekend at a deserted mountain cabin. In the basement they find and play recordings of mystical incantations, which raises an angry band of hell demons intent on devouring their souls. One by one the hapless students are possessed by the demons; Ash discovers that burning the *Naturan Demanto*—the book the incantations came from—causes the demons to retreat to hell, but the film ends with an unseen evil flying through the forest and descending on Ash.

Review: This is the film that launched Sam Raimi's career as a director, put Bruce Campbell on the path to cult-film icon status, and spawned two sequels—the first, *Evil Dead 2*, being more or less the same film with a higher budget (it was in this sequel that the *Naturan Demanto* book was famously renamed the *Necronomicon*). Made for a paltry $350,000, give or take—most of the money came from family, friends, and private investors—*Evil Dead* failed to find U.S. distribution at first, but once it became a hit in Europe the film was picked up Stateside and found lasting fame as an innovative entry in the horror genre. Any fan of Raimi's work will find the genesis of his directing style here; unique shots he created to work within the limited budget have appeared in most of his films since, particularly those of the horror persuasion.

Evil Dead is also mind-bendingly gross; even beyond the infamous "tree rape" scene, the sheer amount of physical abuse Campbell takes as the lead is both cringeworthy and hilarious. As one of the classic cult films of the horror genre, *Evil Dead* is a must-see.

FURTHER VIEWING: *Evil Dead 2: Dead by Dawn; Army of Darkness; Drag Me to Hell*
SEE ALSO: *Night of the Creeps; Night of the Demons; Dead Alive*

★★★★★

Director: Robert Wise
Screenwriter: Nelson Gidding

Produced by: Robert Wise and Denis Johnson

Starring: Julie Harris, Claire Bloom, Richard Johnson, and Russ Tamblyn
Released by: Warner Home Video (DVD)

12+

THE HAUNTING

1963, 112 mins.

Plot: A group of paranormal investigators—including an anthropologist, an ESP expert, the heir to Hill House, and mentally unstable Eleanor who's still reeling from the death of her dominating mother—spend the night in reputedly haunted Hill House in an attempt to gain indisputable evidence of the supernatural. They get exactly what they ask for and more as Eleanor is drawn deeper into the evil that dwells in the house, and her companions risk their lives, and their sanity, in an attempt to save her.

Review: Not to be confused with the subpar 1999 remake, *The Haunting* is entirely bloodless and accomplishes its considerable scares using sound, camera angles, and lighting alone, a rarity in a genre known for its over-the-top gore. It's as expertly handled as any Hitchcock film; the psychological tension is palpable and the frightening scenes are genuine, tapping into deep fears present in the universal human condition, rather than relying on cheap "Boo!" moments so common in modern horror. Because of this, *The Haunting* has only become more famous, more revered since its release over forty years ago, and it's often considered the most successful haunted house story of all time.

Based on the Shirley Jackson novel *The Haunting of Hill House*, this film has become incredibly influential in the modern age and a favorite of genre royalty including Sam Raimi, who makes a direct homage to the film's hallway knocking scene in *Drag Me to Hell*. *The Haunting* is one of those rare horror films that get under your skin and stays with you well after the credits finish rolling; as a cornerstone of the genre for almost half a century, it is essential viewing for horror lovers and horror haters (or those who think they hate horror) alike.

FURTHER VIEWING: *The Haunting (1999 remake); The Day the Earth Stood Still; The Curse of the Cat People*
SEE ALSO: *The Changeling; Lady in White; The Shining; The Innocents*

★★★★★

Director: Jacques Tourneur
Screenwriter: Charles Bennett and Hal E. Chester
Produced by: Hal E. Chester
Starring: Dana Andrews, Peggy Cummins, and Niall MacGinnis
Released by: Sony Pictures (DVD)

2+

NIGHT OF THE DEMON (CURSE OF THE DEMON)

1957, 95 mins.

Plot: Dr. John Holden is an American psychologist who travels to England to attend a convention, where Professor Harrington is to expose a satanic cult run by Dr. Julian Karswell. Harrington dies under mysterious circumstances, and Holden's colleagues consider the possibility of supernatural forces at work, but Holden remains skeptical. When Holden discovers he's the recipient of the same cursed parchment that seems to have killed Harrington, he finds himself at the center of more inexplicable occurrences; finally becoming a believer, he and Harrington's niece, Joanna, attempt to break the curse before it's too late.

Review: Adaptated from the M. R. James short story "Casting the Runes," *Night of the Demon* takes quite a few liberties with the original: instead of the unassuming English academic we have a dashing American skeptic in the lead; Holden is aided by Harrington's brother, Henry, in "Casting the Runes," whereas here it's Harrington's niece and Holden's love interest; Karswell was a writer on the occult, rather than a cult leader; and there is no corporeal monster in the original. There wouldn't have been one in this film, either, if it weren't for producer Hester's insistence on needing something tangible to be afraid of; but the plan backfired, and the monster has been singled out as the film's sole weakness.

Despite these changes—many of which seem to be pandering to Hollywood—*Night of the Demon* still manages to be a cracking good ghost story, one that pays dutiful homage to its source (it should be mentioned, here, that M. R. James is often considered the finest ghost story writer in the English language). Called *Curse of the Demon* in the U.S., the original British version has fewer cuts and is generally a more satisfying experience, so watch this version first.

FURTHER VIEWING: *Cat People; I Walked with a Zombie*
SEE ALSO: *The Wicker Man; The Black Cat; The Devil Rides Out*

★★★★★

Director: George A. Romero
Screenwriters: George A. Romero and John A. Russo

Produced by: Karl Hardman and Russell Streiner

Starring: Duane Jones, Judith O'Dea, and Karl Hardman
Released by: Weinstein Company (DVD)

18+

NIGHT OF THE LIVING DEAD

1968, 96 mins.

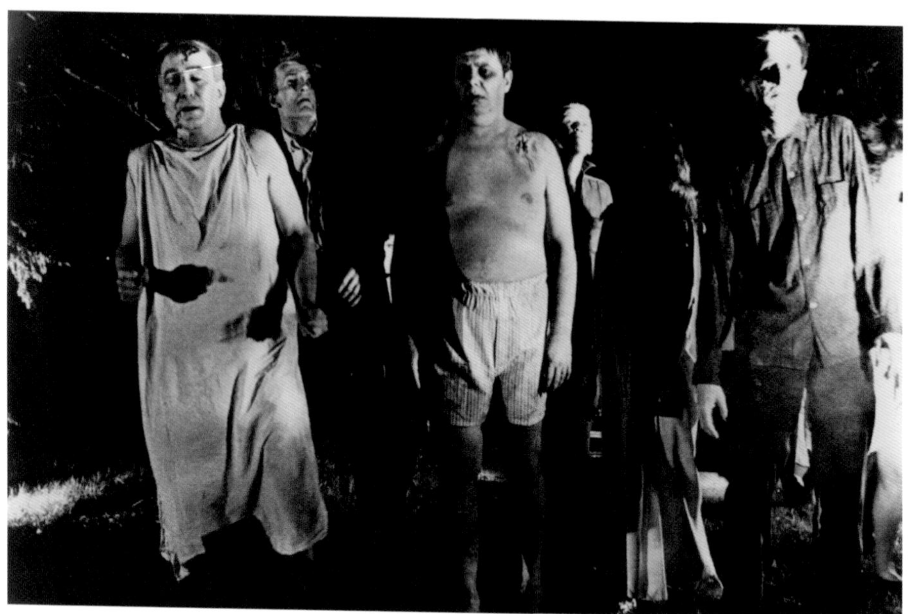

Plot: Some good old-fashioned Cold War radiation manages to bring the dead back to rotting life, and a group of Pennsylvanians hole up in a house to fight off the ravenous corpses. Infighting ensues in this microcosm of American society, and those who aren't eaten by zombies during the night are killed by humans, leaving only one man alive. But when the local posse comes in the morning to clear the area, they shoot first and don't bother with questions.

Review: Before this film, which is Romero's directorial debut, movie zombies were relegated to voodoo rituals in the Caribbean (see both *White Zombie* and *I Walked with a Zombie*), at a very safe distance from American suburbia. But *Night of the Living Dead* redefined the term "zombie" in popular culture, as well bringing the horrible beings into American backyards where they could snack on children and family pets with abandon.

Suddenly, the voodoo zombie—which was never conceived as the truly dead come back to life—got replaced by the rotting, walking, flesh-eating corpse. More importantly, they were corpses that would eat anything and kill anyone, regardless of whether their prey went to church every Sunday or led bad lives behind closed doors. Romero's apocalyptic vision is terrifyingly nihilistic and completely irrational; it's also gory and, though the effects may look cheap now, disgustingly visceral. But beyond the extreme gore—which has now become common in the horror genre, thanks in part to this film—*Night of the Living Dead* provides us with unsettling social commentary during a time when the Vietnam War and the Civil Rights movement loomed large in the background (for instance, a black leading man in a cast of whites was seen as highly controversial in 1968, though the film's female characters are still laughably one-dimensional). This is a now-classic and recognizably subversive horror film, whose influence can be detected far and wide in the horror genre even today.

FURTHER VIEWING: ***Dawn of the Dead; Day of the Dead; Land of the Dead***
SEE ALSO: ***Night of the Comet; Zombie; Nightmare City***

★★★★★

Director: Hideo Nakata
Screenwriter: Hiroshi Takahashi

Produced by: Takashige Ichise, Shinya Kawai, and Takenori Sento

Starring: Nanako Matsushima, Hiroyuki Sanada, and Rikiya Otaka
Released by: Dreamworks Video (DVD)

5+

RINGU (RING)

1998, 96 mins.

Plot: *Ringu* begins with a teenage urban legend set-up: a rumor goes around that anyone who views a certain videotape will receive a phone call immediately after, and then die in a week's time. When Imako watches the film and dies in a car accident a week later, her aunt Reiko, a TV journalist, decides to investigate. Reiko discovers that several of Imako's friends, who allegedly viewed the video together, died at the same time as Imako under strange circumstances; she tracks the videotape to a mountain cabin, views it, and receives the tell-tale phone call. Attempting to thwart the curse—which is also affecting her son—Reiko shows the tape to her ex-husband and they uncover the body of the tape's creator, the murdered child of a legendary psychic, and seem to escape the curse unharmed. But when her ex-husband dies of fright, Reiko realizes she must pass the curse on to protect herself and her son.

Review: This is the picture that kick-started America's fascination with J-horror and for good reason: relying on disturbing visuals and psychological trickery, rather than gore and violence, *Ringu* taps into an older tradition of horror. A smash hit on its release in Japan, *Ringu* duplicated its critical success in America, and Hollywood began mining Japanese horror for both theatrical releases and remake material. *Ringu* was remade as *The Ring* in 2002, beautifully directed by Gore Verbinski, but the original film's unique imagery filtered throughout the genre in both Japan and America. The long black tangled hair; the pixilated, shuddering ghosts; and the unnatural angles in which the ghosts move, all cracking bones and twisted necks, can find their origins right here. Perhaps the most brilliant feat of this film is that all this groundbreaking imagery surrounds a relatively simple and straightforward premise—in this case, it's not so much the story but how it's told that makes *Ringu* such a successful addition to the horror genre.

FURTHER VIEWING: *The Ring (2002 remake); Ringu 2*
SEE ALSO: *Ju-on (The Grudge); Pulse; Memento Mori*

★★★★★

Director: Stanley Kubrick
Screenwriters: Stanley Kubrick and Diane Johnson

Produced by: Stanley Kubrick, Jan Harlan, and Martin Richards

Starring: Jack Nicholson, Shelley Duvall, Danny Lloyd, and Scatman Crothers
Released by: Warner Home Video (DVD)

18+

THE SHINING

1980, 146 mins.

Plot: Jack Torrance is looking to get away from it all. He's a recovering alcoholic with aspirations of writing a novel, so he packs up his wife and son and takes them to the isolated Overlook Hotel, where Jack will act as caretaker during the hotel's winter closure. Of course he doesn't heed the hotel manager's warning that the previous caretaker succumbed to cabin fever and ended up killing himself and his family, but he should have. The hotel's old ghosts prey on Jack's many weaknesses, as well as his son's psychic abilities (or "shining"), and it all ends in buckets of tears and elevators of blood.

Review: "Heeeeeeere's Johnny!" Based on Stephen King's novel of the same name, *The Shining* was Kubrick's follow-up to the historical epic *Barry Lyndon*, and his first (and only) foray into genre horror. Critical reviews on its release were mixed; King in particular, having been shut out by Kubrick from the scripting and production process, found the adaptation to be disappointing at best. But, as with most of Kubrick's films, time has been kind, and *The Shining* is now considered one of the scariest and most artistically satisfying psychological horror films ever made, particularly in the post-seventies era.

Production was not without its problems: the script was being constantly rewritten during the shoot so that actors often only had minutes to memorize their lines, and Kubrick and Duvall reputedly fought like cats during the entire process. But none of this shows in the finished product, which is self-assured with a masterful build-up of tension and plenty of now-iconic imagery. As a result, *The Shining* has been highly influential in not just horror but also general pop-culture for the past thirty years, and it is an absolute must-see.

FURTHER VIEWING: ***Full Metal Jacket***
SEE ALSO: ***Carrie; Don't Look Now; The Stepfather; The Haunting***

★★★★★

Director: John Carpenter
Screenwriter: Bill Lancaster

Produced by: David Foster and Lawrence Turman

Starring: Kurt Russell, Wilford Brimley, and Keith David
Released by: Universal Pictures (DVD)

8+

THE THING

1982, 109 mins.

Plot: Evoking a sense of isolation is key in any good horror film, and what's more remote than Antarctica? A team of American researchers are treated to a bizarre scene: Norwegians from a nearby station are using everything from rifles to explosives to try to kill a lone dog. The Norwegians and their helicopter are blown up by a carelessly set charge; the Americans don't speak the language and never find out what all the fuss was about. With the best of intentions they take the dog into their own kennel, but they soon discover just why the Norwegian team was trying to destroy it: turns out the dog's a murderous alien in wolf's clothing.

Review: Remakes are generally worse than originals, but *The Thing* is not your average remake. While 1951's *The Thing from Another World* was the first film to tackle this story, *The Thing* is less a recycling of that film and more a fresh look at the original source material, the novella *Who Goes There?* by John W. Campbell Jr.

The Thing bombed at the box office on first release, and in retrospect most critics blame the opening of the far more family friendly *E.T. the Extra-Terrestrial* two weeks earlier. But reviews at the time pointed heavily to Carpenter's use of Rob Bottin's realistic and disgusting special effects as a particular turn-off—scenes such as the amalgamation of the dogs in the kennel into a single/multiple hell beast are relentlessly and stomach-churningly graphic in their portrayal. They are also brilliantly executed and well ahead of their time in terms of quality and realism, which is just one reason why *The Thing* had garnered such an intense cult following over the years. Another reason could be the empathetic, but not melodramatic, performances from frequent Carpenter collaborator (and former teen idol) Kurt Russell and Wilford Brimley (yes, that would be the old guy from *Cocoon* and the oatmeal commercials).

FURTHER VIEWING: *The Thing from Another World*
SEE ALSO: *Alien; The Andromeda Strain*

★★★★★

Director: Robert Aldrich
Screenwriter: Lukas Heller
Produced by: Robert Aldrich

Starring: Bette Davis, Joan Crawford, and Victor Buono
Released by: Warner Home Video (DVD)

18+

WHAT EVER HAPPENED TO BABY JANE?

1962, 134 mins.

Plot: "Baby Jane" was a star on the vaudeville circuit as a child, but when she grew up it became clear that her appeal rested more on cuteness than actual acting talent. Having been sidelined for years as her sister received all the attention, Blanche grew into her own and became a respected film actress just as Jane's star began to fade. In the 1930s a car accident crippled Blanche, cutting her career short; the accident was blamed on drunken, jealous Jane. Now, in 1962, the two sisters are living together in mutual animosity—Jane torments Blanche while trying to orchestrate a comeback, and Blanche attempts to get away from Jane but has no resources. Years of guilt, jealousy, and hatred come to a head as we find out what really happened the night of the accident.

Review: Oh, the days when Hollywood had meaty roles for older women, the kind that could lead to Academy Award nominations and revitalize an aging actress' career . . . If you're feeling wistful for just such a film, or you're simply hankering for a grand, old-fashioned but skillfully constructed psychological horror flick, look no further than *What Ever Happened to Baby Jane?* The first of Robert Aldrich's female horror trilogy (see also *Hush . . . Hush, Sweet Charlotte* and *What Ever Happened to Aunt Alice?*), *Baby Jane* plumbs the deepest depths of insanity, jealousy, revenge, guilt, and comeuppance, all from a highly female perspective.

Made to look intentionally grotesque in her baby-doll makeup, Bette Davis gives one of the finest performances of her career as Jane, the long-faded star who refuses to let go of her youth; she delicately walks the line of pathetic and pitiful, never allowing the viewer to get too comfortable despising her or feeling sorry for her, which leads brilliantly into the twist ending. After a decade of financial and critical failures, Davis earned Oscar, BAFTA, and Golden Globe nominations for her role; Joan Crawford, also in her fifties and in need of a career boost, was nominated for a BAFTA.

FURTHER VIEWING: ***Hush . . . Hush, Sweet Charlotte; What Ever Happened to Aunt Alice?***
SEE ALSO: ***The Dark Mirror; Sisters***

★★★★★

Director: Robin Hardy
Screenwriter: Anthony Shaffer
Produced by: Peter Snell

Starring: Edward Woodward, Christopher Lee, and Diane Cilento
Released by: Starz/Anchor Bay (DVD)

8+

THE WICKER MAN

1973, 88 mins.

Plot: Police Sergeant Howie receives a letter suggesting that a young girl has disappeared from Summerisle, an island in the Scottish Hebrides; he immediately flies to the island to investigate. But something odd is going on in Summerisle—not only do the inhabitants claim they've never heard of the missing girl, they all seem to be practicing pagans, living an earthy, sexually liberated lifestyle. For Howie, a devout Christian who doesn't believe in sex before marriage, the experience is disturbing, to say the least. After many allusions to the upcoming Mayday ceremony—including a ritual to appease the old gods—Howie deduces the girl must be alive and is being held for sacrifice, and he races to find her before the ritual begins.

Review: For a horror film, *The Wicker Man* isn't particularly scary, and it never really tries to be—but it is unendingly creepy, intelligent in its themes, and effective in its execution. It's also uniquely British in its treatment of the clash between Celtic paganism and Christianity, a war between the old gods and the new played out in the fields of men.

Christopher Lee is of course well known to horror fans through his work with Hammer, but he takes on a different role here as the calm, content, and human aristocratic leader of a pagan cult. Lee has a long-standing interest in the occult (which he credits to a brief meeting with M. R. James when he was young), and he was a driving force in getting the film made during a financial crisis in the British film industry.

The Wicker Man didn't impress critics or audiences to any great degree on its initial release, but a forward-thinking *Cinemafantastique* magazine dubbed it "the *Citizen Kane* of horror movies" well before the film built up its healthy cult following. Eschewing the vogue for shocking gore and serial-killing stalkers that came to prominence in the 1970s, *The Wicker Man* continues to force viewers out of their comfort zones with its sympathetic view of paganism and shocking twist ending. A parting word of warning: avoid the 2006 Neil LaBute remake at all costs—it lacks any and all of the original's intelligence and purpose.

FURTHER VIEWING: *The Wicker Tree*
SEE ALSO: *Angel Heart; The Changeling*

289
500

★★★★

Director: Danny Boyle
Screenwriter: Alex Garland
Produced by: Andrew Macdonald

Starring: Cillian Murphy, Naomi Harris, and Noah Huntley

Released by: Twentieth Century Fox (DVD)

15+

28 DAYS LATER

2002, 113 mins.

Plot: The accidental release of a so-called "rage virus" in Britain infects most of the island's residents, changing them into fast-running, flesh-eating, blood-vomiting fiends. In the virus' post-apocalyptic aftermath, *28 Days Later* follows four survivors who escape from London to less-populated and presumably safer northern climes.

Review: Ostensibly a zombie movie, *28 Days Later* has moved on from the supernatural abominations of *White Zombie* and Romero's more straightforward reanimated dead. Crucially, this film's infected are still alive, and while the science doesn't always seem to add up (a live person puking buckets of blood wouldn't survive three hours, let alone three weeks), it allows for a much faster-paced and immediate threat than the film's more traditional zombie forebears.

FURTHER VIEWING: ***28 Weeks Later; Sunshine; Shallow Grave***
SEE ALSO: ***Doomsday; Night of the Living Dead; The Omega Man***

290
500

★★★★

Director: Lewis Teague
Screenwriters: John Sayles and Frank Ray Perilli

Produced by: Brandon Chase
Starring: Robert Forster and Robin Riker
Released by: Lionsgate (DVD)

15+

ALLIGATOR

1980, 89 mins.

Plot: After being flushed down the toilet as a baby, an alligator is mutated to giant size by experimental growth hormones flushed into the sewers by a nefarious professor. When the alligator erupts from the sewer and begins a killing spree, a cop haunted by his past finds himself its unwitting hunter.

Review: Despite borrowing heavily from *Jaws* (but then what creature feature doesn't?) this is superior fare due to an excellent, ironic script from John Sayles, focusing far more on Robert Forster's cop, with his tortured past that the alligator forces him to confront, and his budding romance with a gorgeous but lonely herpetologist. Peppered with some great lines, it's sweet and touching—and let's not forget the fun you can have with a giant alligator.

FURTHER VIEWING: ***Cujo; Cat's Eye; Jewel on the Nile; Navy Seals; Matawan; Lone Star; Jackie Brown***
SEE ALSO: ***Black Water; The Host; Jaws; Jaws II; Lake Placid; Piranha***

291

★★★★★

Director: Sam Raimi
Screenwriter: Sam Raimi and Ivan Raimi
Produced by: Robert G. Tapert
Starring: Bruce Campbell and Embeth Davidtz
Released by: Universal Studios (DVD)

15+

ARMY OF DARKNESS

1993, 81 mins.

Plot: After getting sucked into a vortex in *Evil Dead 2*, Ash falls out of the sky to land in Medieval England, which is being overrun by bloodthirsty "Deadites." Ash's only hope to return home rests on his finding the *Necronomicon* and using it to concoct a magical potion. If you've seen the previous films in the *Evil Dead* trilogy, you can guess how well that turns out.

Review: As the most ambitious in the *Evil Dead* trilogy, *Army of Darkness* is bigger, louder, grosser, and funnier than any of Raimi's previous films. Bruce Campbell solidifies his position as the B-Movie King by remaining incongruously sexy and charming while spouting chauvinist dialog and suffering cartoonish abuse in (sometimes overlong) slapstick sequences. The best version is the 96-minute director's cut with the less happy but more appropriate "Ash is screwed" ending.

FURTHER VIEWING: *The Evil Dead; Evil Dead 2; The Quick and the Dead*
SEE ALSO: *The Mummy; Bad Taste; Cemetery Man*

292

★★★

Director: Ted Post
Screenwriter: Abe Polsky
Producer: Abe Polsky
Starring: Anjanette Comer, Ruth Roman, and Marianna Hill
Released by: Geneon/Pioneer (DVD)

18+

THE BABY

1973, 85 mins.

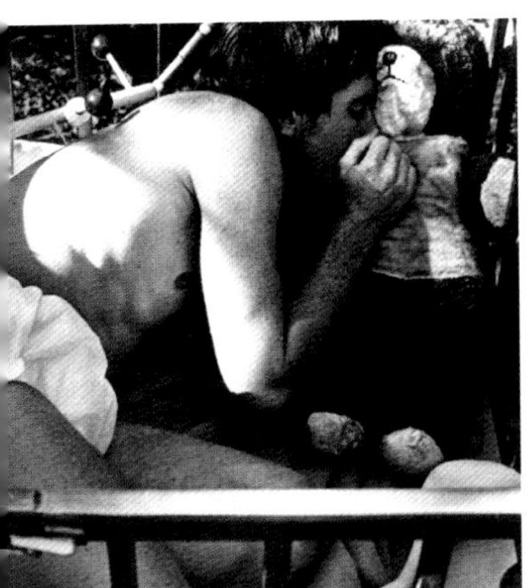

Plot: A middle-aged housewife, Mrs Wadsworth, lives in suburbia with her two beautiful daughters and her son, known as Baby. And that's what he is—a fully grown man who spends his day in a crib, having his nappies changed and breast feeding on the babysitter! When a social worker discovers Baby, she makes it her personal mission to take him away from his disturbed family, whatever the cost.

Review: Profoundly twisted, *The Baby* is baffling to watch. Coming across as blend of John Waters' crackpot cinema and the sort of thing you'd only be able to see on freaky websites, a film like this could never be made today and break out to a mass audience. The conclusion will knock you for six—it's got to be seen to be believed.

FURTHER VIEWING: *Night Kill; Hang 'Em High*
SEE ALSO: *The Manitou; It's Alive!*

293/500

★★★

Director: Peter Jackson
Screenwriters: Peter Jackson, Tony Hiles, and Ken Hammon
Produced by: Peter Jackson

Starring: Peter Jackson, Terry Potter, Peter O'Hearne, Craig Smith, and Mike Minett
Released by: Starz/Anchor Bay (DVD)

18+

BAD TASTE

1987, 91 mins.

Plot: A four-man special government force is dispatched to a small New Zealand town to investigate strange weather patterns and lights in the sky. It turns out the town has been invaded by aliens intent on harvesting humans to use as the "special meat" for their intergalactic fast-food franchise, and the team must defeat them before they take their slaughter pen global.

Review: Completely nonsensical and loads of fun, *Bad Taste* lives up to its name by reveling in madcap grossness. Of special note is Peter Jackson's hilarious turn as Derek, the geeky anti-hero who's accidentally blasted into space and determined to destroy the alien race with only a chainsaw and his insanity for weapons.

FURTHER VIEWING: ***Meet the Feebles; The Frighteners; Braindead; Dead Alive***
SEE ALSO: ***Killer Klowns from Outer Space; The Toxic Avenger***

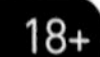

294/500

★★★

Director: Frank Henenlotter
Screenwriter: Frank Henenlotter
Produced by: Edgar Ievins

Starring: Kevin Van Hentenryck, Terri Susan Smith, and Beverly Bonner
Released by: Image Entertainment (DVD)

18+

BASKET CASE

1982, 91 mins.

Plot: A young man settles into a sleazy New York motel. He's hauling a wicker basket that contains not the laundry but his horrifically deformed, insatiably hungry, and very angry twin (non-identical). They're in town to inflict bloody vengeance on the doctors that separated them and tried to kill the abominable brother. Carnage ensues.

Review: A comedy of terrors done with next to no money but rich in good intentions, this is also a tale of brotherly love. The special effects border on the hilariously bad—as does some of the acting—but the movie does prove blood is thicker than water, especially as it contains so much of the former.

FURTHER VIEWING: ***Basket Case 2; Basket Case 3: The Progeny; Bad Biology***
SEE ALSO: ***Bad Taste; Brain Damage; Driller Killer; Re-Animator***

95

★★★★

Director: Kinji Fukasaku
Screenwriter: Kenta Fukasaku
Producer: Kenta Fukasaku, Kimio Kataoka, Chie Kobayashi, and Toshio Nabeshima
Starring: Takeshi Kitano, Tatsuya Fujiwara, Aki Maeda, and Tarô Yamamoto
Released by: Toei (DVD)

8+

BATORU ROWAIARU (BATTLE ROYALE)

2000, 122 mins.

Plot: In an alternate but modern-day Japan, unemployment is rife and rebellious students refuse to attend school. In response, the government passes the "Battle Royale Act" that selects a school class by lottery to fight to the death on an undisclosed island. Initially the students are afraid and some refuse to cooperate, but when the more ambitious classmates begin to take the game seriously, those with integrity are forced to play too—merely to survive.

Review: Takeshi Kitano stars as the callous teacher who seems to take inane pleasure in seeing his ex-students slaughtered in a variety of inventive—and extremely bloody—ways. Asking a bold question, "Could you kill your best friend?," this haunting film will stay with you long after it's ended.

FURTHER VIEWING: ***Battle Royale II: Requiem; Kuotokage (Black Lizard)***
SEE ALSO: ***Suicide Club; Visitor Q***

96

★★★★★

Director: Jonathan King
Screenwriter: Jonathan King
Produced by: Phillipa Campbell
Starring: Peter Feeney and Nathan Meister
Released by: The Weinstein Company (DVD)

15+

BLACK SHEEP

2007, 87 mins.

Plot: Henry Oldfield has a pathological fear of sheep, a product of having a bad experience while growing up on a New Zealand sheep farm. Returning to the farm after a long absence to settle his father's estate, Henry finds his brother has been conducting bizarre genetic experiments that mutate the herd from docile to deadly.

Review: Eschewing subpar CGI on a low budget, *Black Sheep* features some of the most stunning physical gore effects of the new millennium. Like fellow New Zealander Peter Jackson's early work, gross and funny are the key notes, and this film hits both with aplomb. One of the best horror comedies since *An American Werewolf in London.*

FURTHER VIEWING: ***Under the Mountain***
SEE ALSO: ***Bad Taste; Dead Alive; Night of the Lepus; Prophecy***

★★★

Director: Daniel Myrick and Eduardo Sánchez
Screenwriters: Daniel Myrick and Eduardo Sánchez

Produced by: Bob Eick, Gregg Hale, and Kevin J. Foxe
Starring: Heather Donahue, Joshua Leonard, and Michael C. Williams

Released by: Lionsgate (DVD)

15+

THE BLAIR WITCH PROJECT

1999, 86 mins.

Plot: Three student filmmakers investigate the legend of the Blair Witch in the woods around Burkittsville, Maryland, and are never to be seen again. Their film footage is later found and shows that not only is the Blair Witch real, she caused their demise in horrifying fashions.

Review: Made on a shoestring budget, *The Blair Witch Project* exploded into mainstream cinemas thanks to a savvy "true story" marketing campaign and its improvised, guerrilla-style shooting.

Though the narrative sometimes suffers from the improvised dialog (for example, the cast never offers a credible reason for throwing away the map other than plot advancement), this is the original rough and ready "found footage" horror film much copied in recent years

FURTHER VIEWING: *Book of Shadows: Blair Witch 2; Curse of the Blair Witch; The Massacre of the Burkittsville Seven*
SEE ALSO: *Cloverfield; [Rec]; The Last Broadcast*

98

★★★★

Directors: Irvin S. Yeaworth Jr. and Russell S. Doughten Jr.
Screenwriters: Irvine Millgate, Kay Linaker, and Theodore Simonson
Produced by: Russell S. Doughten Jr. and Jack H. Harris
Starring: Steve McQueen and Aneta Corsaut
Released by: Criterion (DVD)

5+

THE BLOB

1958, 82 mins.

Plot: A meteor crashes to Earth in Downingtown, PA. Bad-boy teen Steve and his girl Jane are the only people in town to witness the pink gooey substance within emerge and start eating people. Predictably, the authorities don't believe their story (but, really, who would?), so, having seen the Blob engulf several people at this point, they set off the town's air-raid alarms. The townspeople gather and demand an explanation, but Steve is let off the hook when the Blob attacks the crowd, leading to a showdown in a diner: man versus goo.

Review: *The Blob* was a huge drive-in theater hit in its day and despite the silliness of pink gelatinous snot playing the villain, it's solid sci-fi horror and Steve McQueen's first starring role.

FURTHER VIEWING: *Beware! The Blob; The Blob (1988 remake); 4D Man*
SEE ALSO: *It Came from Beneath the Sea; Creepshow 2; Tremors*

99

★★★

Director: Herschell Gordon Lewis
Screenwriter: Allison Louise Downe
Producer: David F. Friedman
Starring: William Kerwin, Mal Arnold, and Connie Mason
Released by: Image Entertainment (DVD)

8+

BLOOD FEAST

1963, 67 mins.

Plot: A serial killer is doing the rounds in a small community, first killing and then butchering the bodies. The victims are all attractive young women, and the police have no clues to go on. The stolen body parts are cooked in meals and offered up to the Egyptian goddess Ishtar, of which the killer has a giant statue at the back of his exotic food shop. This ancient "feast" is available to anyone who asks . . . for a price.

Review: Painfully acted and with a ghastly script, the sheer balls-out badness of *Blood Feast* makes it so enjoyable. Extremely gory even by today's standards, it's an EC comic visualized with murder, cannibalism, and buckets of blood on the menu. The good-looking ladies make up the dessert.

FURTHER VIEWING: *The Wizard of Gore; Two Thousand Maniacs!*
SEE ALSO: *Deranged; The Texas Chain Saw Massacre*

300/500

★★★★

Director: David Cronenberg
Screenwriter: David Cronenberg
Producer: Claude Héroux

Starring: Oliver Reed, Samantha Eggar, and Art Hindle
Released by: MGM (DVD)

18+

THE BROOD

1979, 93 mins.

Plot: A psychotherapist (Oliver Reed), who practices a rather unusual form of treatment called "Psycho-Plasmics," has been looking after the deeply troubled Nola (Samantha Eggar), much to the chagrin of her husband Frank (Art Hindle). The therapy produces an adverse physical effect on the patient, where their anxieties manifest on their bodies. In the case of Nola, it's a brood of disturbed and violent child-like beings, who act upon her negativity with horrific results.

Review: Featuring an absolutely chilling scene where two of the titular brood attack a school teacher, beating her to death with wooden hammers while a classroom of school children look on, Cronenberg's 1979 classic is another example from his "body horror" oeuvre, whereby the transformation from human to something grotesque provides the dramatic twist.

FURTHER VIEWING: ***Rabid; Shivers***
SEE ALSO: ***Don't Look Now; The Village of the Damned***

301/500

★★★★

Director: Roger Corman
Screenwriter: Charles B. Griffith
Produced by: Roger Corman

Starring: Dick Miller, Ed Nelson, and Bert Convy
Released by: MGM (DVD)

15+

A BUCKET OF BLOOD

1959, 66 mins.

Plot: Drippy Walter Paisley is a waiter in a hip beat café, and he just doesn't belong to the in-crowd. The stark contrast between his geeky self and the popular, smooth-talking beatniks sparks his jealousy, but he never dreamed that accidently killing his landlady's cat would be his entrée into their world. He tries to hide his misdeed by encasing the cat in clay—all of a sudden his "sculpture" is the talk of the town. To keep up with demand, Walter starts killing animals of the human variety.

Review: Probably Corman's finest horror comedy, despite its extremely low budget (even for a Corman film). Dick Miller is fantastic as the hapless Walter Paisley, so much so that the character has become a cult figure in his own right—Miller has played characters named Walter Paisley in at least five other films. Simply excellent, and an inspiration to low-budget filmmakers.

FURTHER VIEWING: ***A Bucket of Blood (1995 remake); Little Shop of Horrors***
SEE ALSO: ***Blood Car; The Woman Eater; Terror from Within***

Director: Robert Wiene
Screenwriters: Carl Mayer and Hans Janowitz

Produced by: Erich Pommer and Rudolph Meinert

Starring: Werner Krauss and Conrad Veidt
Released by: Kino Video (DVD)

THE CABINET OF DR. CALIGARI

1920, 67 mins.

Plot: "A tale of the modern re-appearance of an 11th Century Myth involving the strange and mysterious influence of a mountebank monk over a somnambulist." So declares the first title card of *The Cabinet of Dr. Caligari*. Dr. Caligari is a traveling hypnotist whose somnambulist, Cesare, is never far behind. During Caligari's visit to a small German town, a series of murders occur; when local man Francis' best friend is killed, he suspects Caligari but receives no help from the police, and Francis is forced to investigate the murders on his own.

Review: An incredibly influential German Expressionist film from the silent era. All sharp angles and shadows presiding over fantastical, abstract set pieces, *Dr. Caligari* is nothing less than a moving work of art, and echoes of its proto-noir atmosphere can be seen in the Hollywood crime films of the thirties and forties.

FURTHER VIEWING: *Genuine: The Tragedy of a Strange House; The Hands of Orlac*
SEE ALSO: *Nosferatu; Dr. Mabuse; M*

303
500

★★

Director: Umberto Lenzi
Screenwriter: Umberto Lenzi
Producer: Mino Loy

Starring: Giovanni Lombardo Radice, Lorraine De Selle, and Danilo Mattei
Released by: Aquarius Releasing (DVD)

18+ CANNIBAL FEROX

1981, 93 mins.

Plot: A Ph.D. student from New York heads to the Amazon to debunk an article on the existence of cannibalism. Naturally, things take a turn for the worst and she and her best friend and brother become targets for a village of cannibals who have been victimized by two other outsiders—a drug-dealing womanizer called Mike and his doped-up friend Joe. The murder of some of the villagers only seems to incense them more . . .

Review: Sensational in its day for allegedly being banned in most countries, it should have become notorious for the distinctly unlikable characters that populate the film. The gore scenes have dated somewhat, but the documentarian approach keeps things interesting. Some may find the animal cruelty grim.

FURTHER VIEWING: ***Deep River Savages; City of the Walking Dead***
SEE ALSO: ***Cannibal Holocaust; Eaten Alive!***

304
500

★★★

Director: Herk Harvey
Screenwriters: Herk Harvey and John Clifford
Produced by: Herk Harvey

Starring: Candace Hilligoss and Frances Feist
Released by: Criterion (DVD)

15+ CARNIVAL OF SOULS

1962, 78 mins.

Plot: Mary Henry is a talented musician just driving around with two friends when a group of boys challenge them to a drag race. The girls' car drives over the side of a bridge into the water below; all the passengers die apart from Mary, who mysteriously survives with no recollection of her ordeal. Mary tries to leave the tragedy behind by moving to Utah to take up a position as a church organist, but she begins to experience otherworldly visions and is inexplicably drawn to an abandoned carnival site.

Review: For a low-budget B-movie, *Carnival of Souls* is a genuinely creepy supernatural tale that explores the blurred line between life and death. Its twist ending may seem fairly standard and predictable now, but this film features one of the conceit's earlier appearances and is well worth viewing.

FURTHER VIEWING: ***Carnival of Souls (1998 remake)***
SEE ALSO: ***Jacob's Ladder; An Occurrence at Owl Creek Bridge; The Sixth Sense***

Director: Tom Holland
Screenwriters: Tom Holland, Don Mancini, and John Lafia

Produced by: Barrie M. Osborne, David Kirschner, Elliot Geisinger, and Laura Moskowitz

Starring: Catherine Hicks, Chris Sarandon, and Alex Vincent
Released by: MGM (DVD)

8+

CHILD'S PLAY

1988, 87 mins.

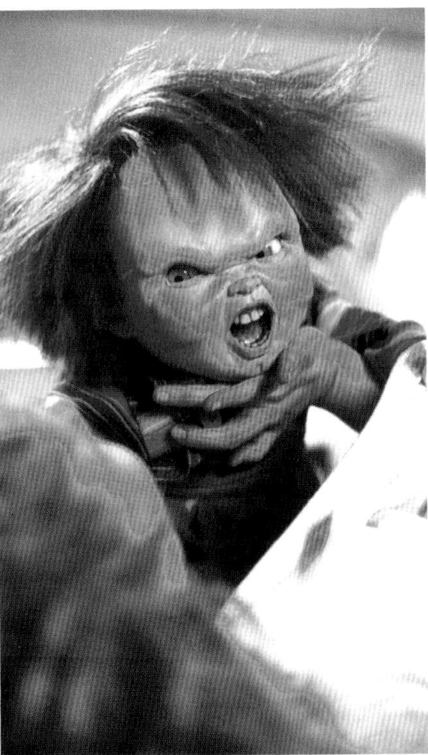

Plot: Serial killer Charles Lee Ray finds the perfect alibi: just before dying in a police shootout, he uses a voodoo spell to transfer his soul into a "Good Guy" doll. When little Andy Barclay's wish for a Good Guy comes true, he soon realizes that his new best friend Chucky isn't nearly as good as the advertising suggests. Chucky continues his murder spree in doll form but, restricted by his height and anatomical incorrectness, plans to transfer his soul to Andy's body.

Review: For viewers who always thought those glassy-eyed porcelain dolls were creepy, Chucky the Carrot-Topped Murder Puppet will provide nightmare material for a lifetime.

FURTHER VIEWING: *Child's Play 2: Chucky's Back; Child's Play 3: Look Who's Stalking; Bride of Chucky; Seed of Chucky; Fright Night*
SEE ALSO: *Puppet Master and its many sequels*

★★★★★

Director: Stanley Kubrick
Screenwriter: Stanley Kubrick
Produced by: Stanley Kubrick

Starring: Malcolm McDowell, Patrick Magee, and Michael Bates
Released by: Warner Home Video (DVD)

18+

A CLOCKWORK ORANGE

1971, 136 mins.

Plot: Adapted from Anthony Burgess' 1962 novel of the same name, *A Clockwork Orange* follows Alex DeLarge's ultraviolent exploits in London with his gang of "droogs." After a string of rapes and burglaries, Alex commits the ultimate crime, murder, and is arrested. In prison, he volunteers to be a subject for the experimental "Ludovico" technique, a reconditioning therapy designed to induce physical aversion to violence. Declared cured, Alex rejoins a very different society than he left two years before and becomes the object of others' need for ultraviolence.

Review: Kubrick is no stranger to social commentary, and this is perhaps his most unsubtle psychological and sociological treatise. It's a fascinating and artistically satisfying exploration of the methods and morality of behavioral modification treatment, as well as its ultimate unreliability. To continue the fruit metaphor, Kubrick (and Burgess) demonstrate that shining the skin of a rotten apple won't change the state of its core; the decay beneath will eventually seep through.

FURTHER VIEWING: ***Eyes Wide Shut; Full Metal Jacket; The Shining***
SEE ALSO: ***If . . . ; Trainspotting; Man Bites Dog; Naked***

37

Director: Peter Sasdy
Screenwriter: Jeremy Paul
Produced by: Alexander Paal
Starring: Ingrid Pitt and Nigel Green
Released by: MGM (DVD, with *The Vampire Lovers*)

8+

COUNTESS DRACULA

1971, 93 mins.

Plot: Based on the legend of Hungarian Countess Elizabeth Bathóry, also known as the "Blood Countess" because she allegedly slaughtered and bathed in the blood of young girls to temporarily restore her beauty (and sexual appetite). In *Countess Dracula*, youth proves addictive, and the Countess takes her daughter's identity to allay suspicion, but when her real daughter returns she finds herself in a bit of a blood-soaked pickle.

Review: "The more she drinks, the prettier she gets." This is standard Hammer fare, except that the legend gets a slightly more authentic treatment due to the fact that all the key behind-the-scenes talent are Hungarian. Of course, "authentic" is a far cry from historically accurate, but who cares? Grab your rubber ducky and jump on in.

FURTHER VIEWING: *Pretty much anything produced by Hammer*
SEE ALSO: *Stay Alive; Carmilla; Daughters of Darkness; Razor Blade Smile*

38

Director: Guillermo del Toro
Screenwriter: Guillermo del Toro
Produced by: Alejandro Springall, Arthur Gorson, Bernard L. Nussbaumer, Bertha Navarro, and Jorge Sánchez
Starring: Frederico Luppi, Ron Perlman, Claudio Brook, and Margarita Isabel
Released by: Lionsgate (DVD)

CRONOS

1993, 94 mins.

Plot: In this Spanish film, aging antiques dealer Jesus Gris discovers a 450-year-old mechanical device and is injected with the venom of a scarab-like insect that still lives inside. He regains his vitality and virility at the price of a strong craving for blood. The device needs to be used regularly to prolong life, and Jesus soon learns that a dying millionaire wants it for himself. Caught between his own need and his worry that the millionaire wants it for nefarious purposes, Jesus endangers his granddaughter in his quest to keep it.

Review: In a superb reimagining of the vampire myth, del Toro gives us a non-demonic, fangless old man as an anti-heroic bloodsucker, one who is sympathetic even as he succumbs to his blood cravings. The film focuses on how the prospect of immortality affects both good and bad men, inviting the viewer into an argument that is as philosophical as it is engrossing.

FURTHER VIEWING: *Blade 2; The Devil's Backbone; Hellboy; Hellboy 2: The Golden Army*
SEE ALSO: *The Hunger; The Orphanage*

309 / 500

★★★★

Director: Vincenzo Natali
Screenwriters: Vincenzo Natali, André Bijelic, and Graeme Manson

Produced by Betty Orr, Colin Brunton, and Mehra Meh

Starring: Nicole de Boer, Nicky Guadagni, David Hewlett, and Andrew Miller
Released by: Lionsgate (DVD)

15+

CUBE

1997, 90 mins.

Plot: Seven strangers wake up in a vast labyrinthine Cube with no notion of how they got there or why. With only the assumption that they're in the grips of some bizarre experiment for no known purpose, they attempt to escape and find the Cube is rigged with deadly traps throughout.

Review: *Cube* goes a long way to prove Sartre's assertion that hell is other people; it serves as more of a sociological study of fear when faced with a complete unknown than a blood-soaked horror fest. Possibly the film's most compelling aspect is that the audience knows just as much (or as little) as the characters, which invites viewers to join in with their speculations and recriminations.

FURTHER VIEWING: ***Nothing; Elevated (short)***
SEE ALSO: ***Primer; Saw; Alive***

---

310 / 500

★★★★

Director: George A. Romero
Screenwriter: George A. Romero

Produced by: Alfredo Cuomo, Claudio Argento, Donna Siegel, and Richard P. Rubinstein

Starring: David Emge, Ken Foree, and Scott H. Reiniger
Released by: Starz/Anchor Bay (DVD)

18+

DAWN OF THE DEAD

1979, 126 mins.

Plot: Taking place just a few months after the events of *Night of the Living Dead, Dawn of the Dead* follows a group of survivors—some military, some civilian—who hole up in an abandoned shopping mall to escape the world teeming with zombies outside. Their hideout seems perfect, but when a roaming gang of bikers turns up, the group find they have to fight the living as well as the dead to survive.

Review: Part horror romp, part commentary on the stultifying nature of consumerist culture, *Dawn of the Dead* is one of those rare sequels that match the excellence of the first film in the series. Tom Savini's gore effects are, as always, graphic and nauseating, and stretches of unmolested social interaction mean the characters are unusually well defined for a horror film. Essential viewing for zombie fans.

FURTHER VIEWING: ***Dawn of the Dead (2004 remake); Night of the Living Dead; Day of the Dead***
SEE ALSO: ***Night of the Comet; The Return of the Living Dead; Zombie***

311

★★★★★

Directors: Alberto Cavalcanti, Basil Deardon, Charles Crichton, and Robert Hamer

Screenwriters: John Baines and Angus MacPhail

Produced by: Michael Balcon

Starring: Mervyn Johns, Roland Culver, and Mary Merrall

Released by: Optimum Home Entertainment (DVD, region 2 only)

12+

DEAD OF NIGHT

1945, 99 mins.

Plot: Five eerie stories are framed by a tale of the tellers: a group of strangers meet at a spooky, isolated house, but not one of them knows why he or she is there. They talk to pass the time, and relate stories of frightening events from their pasts, including meeting a driver with room for another in his hearse, a haunted mirror with a hunger for souls, and a Christmas ghost story.

Review: *Dead of Night* is often considered the most creatively successful anthology horror film ever made, and it comes together as a coherent whole despite its four different directors. Using classic British ghost stories, it has been highly influential on the genre, and shades of this film can be seen in all horror anthologies—with varying success—made after its release in 1945. Essential viewing for horror fans, or those who prefer written ghost stories.

FURTHER VIEWING: *The Man Who Haunted Himself; The Mind Benders; The Scapegoat*

SEE ALSO: *Creepshow; Tales from the Darkside: The Movie; Tales of Terror; Tales from the Crypt; The Vault of Horror*

312

★★★★

Director: Michele Soavi

Screenwriters: Gianni Romoli and Tiziano Sclavi

Produced by: Heinz Bibo, Tilde Corsi, Gianni Romoli, and Michele Soavi

Starring: Rupert Everett, François Hadji-Lazaro, and Anna Falchi

Released by: Starz/Anchor Bay (DVD)

8+

DELLAMORTE DELLAMORE (CEMETERY MAN)

1996, 105 mins.

Plot: Dellamorte, guardian of the cemetery in Buffalora, Italy, is tasked with more than just landscaping and burials. For some reason the dead in Buffalora cemetery have a nasty habit of rising, and Dellamorte spends most of his tenure killing the dead a second time before they roam beyond the cemetery walls. Losing both his loves and his mind to death, he slips into an obsessive depression and finds that there may be nothing beyond this repetitive cycle of dead and undead after all.

Review: Based on the *Dylan Dog* comics, *Dellamorte Dellamore* ("of death/ of love") explores the boundary between love and death, finding it blurred and crossable. This film's strengths are in its wry and often surprising humor, and Everett's sympathetic turn as the laconic but desperate Dellamorte.

FURTHER VIEWING: *The Church; Deliria*

SEE ALSO: *I Bury the Living; Suspiria; The Frighteners*

★★★★★

Director: Neil Marshall
Screenwriter: Neil Marshall

Produced by: Christopher Figg, Tom Reeve, and David E. Allen

Starring: Sean Pertwee, Kevin McKidd, and Liam Cunningham
Released by: First Look Pictures (DVD)

15+

DOG SOLDIERS

2002, 105 mins.

Plot: An elite unit of British soldiers is flown into the remote Scottish Highlands to complete a training exercise. They soon discover the area is inhabited by a family of werewolves, and are forced into an all-out war for survival.

Review: Tense, exciting, and hilarious—this is horror/comedy in the vein of *An American Werewolf in London*, as it seamlessly interweaves the jokes and the scares to create a film that transcends genre stereotypes.

Marshall's werewolves are unusual in that they retain their human intelligence even in animal form, which makes them a more formidable foe than the usual wolf-based horror offerings. While the ensemble cast is uniformly brilliant, the battle-hardened yet soft-hearted company sergeant played by Sean Pertwee still manages to steal the show.

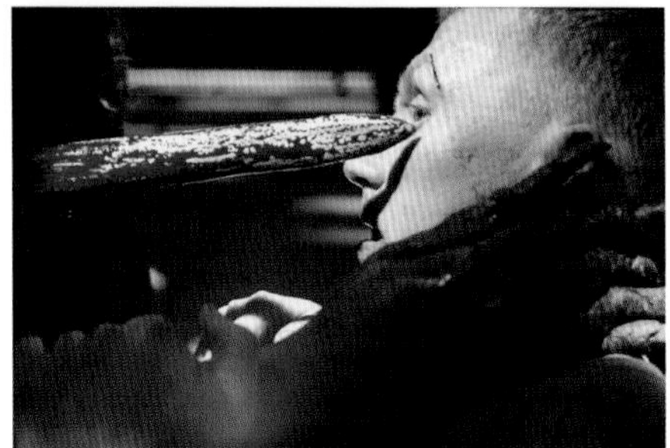

FURTHER VIEWING: ***The Descent; The Descent 2; Doomsday***
SEE ALSO: ***An American Werewolf in London; The Howling; Bad Moon***

14

★★

Director: Abel Ferrara
Screenwriter: Nicholas St. John
Produced by: Rochelle Weisberg
Starring: Abel Ferrara, Carolyn Marz, and Baybi Day
Released by: Cult Epics (DVD)

8+

DRILLER KILLER

1976, 96 mins.

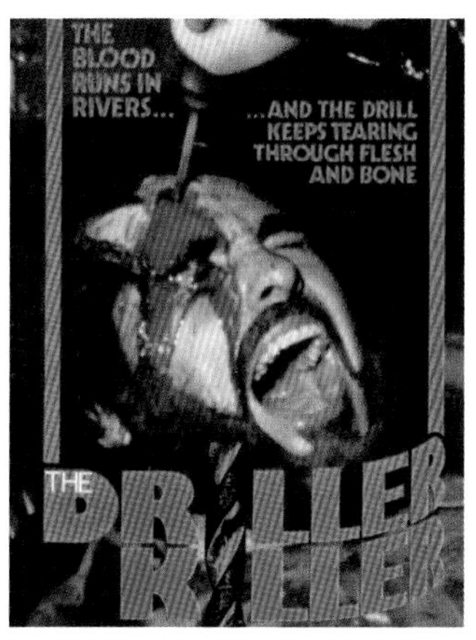

Plot: Reno Miller is a struggling young artist with overwhelming responsibilities. After an unpleasant meeting with his homeless, alcoholic father and one overdue utility bill too many, he snaps and begins killing bums with a portable drill. At first he keeps his murderous extracurricular activities separate from his home life, but following a few personal disappointments he starts killing those closest to him.

Review: Abel Ferrara's directorial debut was also one of the first "video nasties" in the UK; it was banned in Germany as well for excessive violence. *Driller Killer* isn't a particularly good film, but it did secure enough notoriety to elevate it to cult status.

FURTHER VIEWING: *Ms. 45; Bad Lieutenant; The Addiction*
SEE ALSO: *Maniac!; Nail Gun Massacre; Henry: Portrait of a Serial Killer; Last House on the Left*

15

★★

Director: John Alan Schwartz
Screenwriter: John Alan Schwartz
Producer: Rosilyn T. Scott
Starring: Michael Carr
Released by: Gorgon Video (DVD)

8+

FACES OF DEATH

1978, 105 mins.

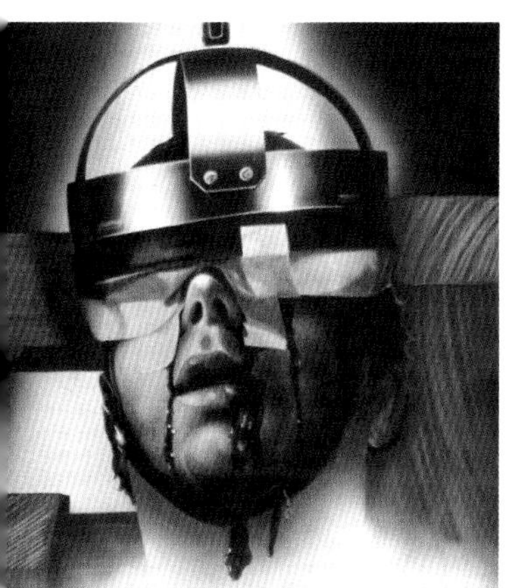

Plot: The notorious seventies documentary that became an underground phenomenon is made up of real and fake footage of death of both humans and animals. Narrated by Dr. Francis B. Gross, footage includes open-heart surgery, pit-bull fighting, seal clubbing, electric-chair electrocution, dining on fresh monkey brains, an alligator attack, and much more.

Review: *The* mondo documentary for many high school kids, *Faces of Death* still has the power to shock when you spend most of the time trying to work out what's real and what's not. Its cult status was secured by a sensationalist marketing ploy of it being banned in forty countries as well as our fascination with seeing what we're not supposed to. A field of recently bludgeoned seals is not easy Saturday night viewing.

FURTHER VIEWING: *Faces of Death 2; Faces of Death 3*
SEE ALSO: *Mondo Cane; Shocking Asia*

★
★

Director: Arthur Crabtree
Screenwriter: Herbert J. Leder
Produced by: John Croydon

Starring: Marshall Thompson, Terry Kilburn, and Michael Balfour
Released by: Criterion (DVD)

12+

FIEND WITHOUT A FACE

1958, 77 mins.

Plot: When four murders take place near an isolated American nuclear base, the major investigating the killings discovers the victims have had their brains removed. The trail leads to a British scientist working on telekinesis who has inadvertently created a species of nuclear-mutated superbrains that suck knowledge from their victims. Out of control and with the death toll rising, they must be stopped!

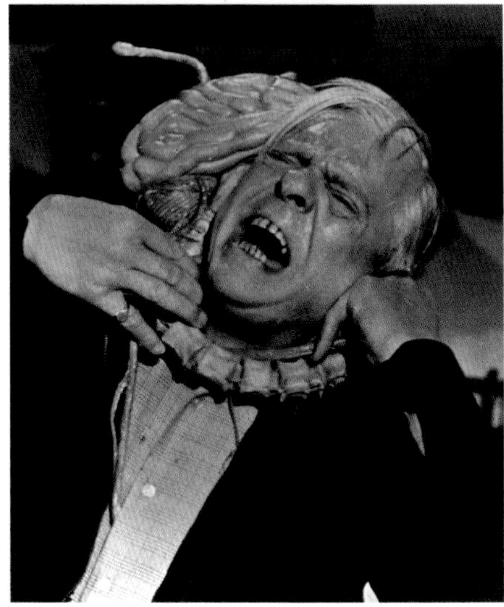

Review: Another "terrifying" warning of what nuclear mutations are capable of, this is, naturally, great fifties drive-in fare masquerading as social commentary. The acting, screenplay, and special effects are of their time and sometimes unintentionally hilarious, but even so, giant brains as mental vampires makes for a unique addition to the Golden Age of trash sci-fi!

FURTHER VIEWING: *Morning Call; Death over My Shoulder; Horrors of the Black Museum*
SEE ALSO: *The Blob; Godzilla; Night of the Lepus; Them; The Thing From Another World*

317

★ ★ ★

Director: Tod Browning
Screenwriter: Tod Robbins
Produced by: Tod Browning

Starring: Wallace Ford, Leila Hyams, and Olga Baclanova
Released by: Warner Home Video (DVD)

15+

FREAKS

1932, 64 mins.

Plot: Circus midget Harry falls desperately in love with beautiful, regular-sized trapeze artist Cleopatra. Cleopatra has already pledged herself to the strongman, but she finds out that Harry is set to inherit a fortune, marries him, and plots to murder him for his money. But things go horribly, heinously wrong when she discovers that slighting one freak means slighting them all—and they're not the kind of people to exact a standard revenge.

Review: Being an ex-carny himself—he specialized in a "buried alive" trick—Tod Browning used real circus "freaks" as actors, but the film suffers from their lack of acting talent. However, the freaks and the disturbing revenge scenario made this one of the most reviled films ever on its release—the studio, MGM, spent decades pretending it didn't exist. Darker and more twisted than Burton, nastier than any "video nasty," *Freaks* is unique, unpleasant, and fascinating.

FURTHER VIEWING: ***The Unknown; The Unholy Three***
SEE ALSO: ***Even Dwarfs Started Small; The Red Dwarf; Ratboy; Sideshow: Alive on the Inside***

318

★ ★ ★

Director: Robert Rodriguez and Sarah Kelly
Screenwriters: Quentin Tarantino and Robert Kurtzman

Produced by: Elizabeth Avellan, Doug McCallie, Gianni Nunnari, and John Esposito

Starring: George Clooney, Harvey Keitel, and Quentin Tarantino
Released by: Dimension (DVD)

18+

FROM DUSK TILL DAWN

1996, 108 mins.

Plot: Bankrobbing brothers Seth and Richie are fugitives fleeing to Mexico to escape the law. On the way they kidnap a faithless pastor and his young family to help them get over the border, but the border police turn out to be the least of their worries. Soon after arriving at a strip club in the middle of the Mexican desert, the place turns out to be staffed entirely by vampires; the brothers and their hostages must fight until dawn to survive.

Review: Quite apart from the story, acting, and characterizations—which are all perfectly entertaining—it's Salma Hayek's sequence as a snake-stroking, erotic-dancing stripper/vampire that's worth more than the price of admission alone. Even outstanding actors such as Harvey Keitel and George Clooney are no match for Hayek's gyrational talents.

FURTHER VIEWING: ***Planet Terror; From Dusk Till Dawn 2: Texas Blood Money; El Mariachi***
SEE ALSO: ***Innocent Blood; Tales from the Crypt Presents Bordello of Blood; Vampires; Near Dark***

319/500

★★★★

Director: Brian De Palma
Screenwriter: John Farris
Produced by: Frank Yablans, Jack B. Bernstein, and Ron Preissman
Starring: Kirk Douglas, John Cassavetes, Carrie Snodgress, and Amy Irving
Released by: Twentieth Century Fox (DVD)

18+ THE FURY

1978, 120 mins.

Plot: Robin Sandza is a young psychic boy who's been kidnapped. Robin's father Peter hires another psychic, Gillian, to find his son, and Gillian learns that Robin has been taken to the Paragon Clinic, a secret government facility that performs dangerous experiments on people with psychic abilities in the course of attempting to harness those powers as weapons. Gillian spent some time in the clinic herself when she was younger; she and Peter race to rescue Robin before he's used up and eliminated.

Review: Brian De Palma followed up his ultra-successful *Carrie* with another examination of psychokinesis in the form of *The Fury*, a combination horror/thriller; the two films feature similarly grim endings by supernatural means. *The Fury's* story does suffer from over-complication, so the narrative ride isn't very smooth, but John Williams' haunting and beautiful score does take the edge off a bit.

FURTHER VIEWING: ***Carrie; The Fury (2000 remake); Sisters***
SEE ALSO: ***The Dead Zone; Firestarter; Eyes of Laura Mars***

320/500

★★★★

Director: John Fawcett
Screenwriters: Karen Walton and John Fawcett
Produced by: Karen Lee Hall and Steven Hoban
Starring: Emily Perkins and Katharine Isabelle
Released by: First Look Pictures (DVD)

15+ GINGER SNAPS

2000, 108 mins.

Plot: Joined-at-the-hip sisters Ginger and Brigitte are outcasts in their small town, and not only because of their fascination with death; they also take an "us against them" stance toward all outsiders. But when older sister Ginger is attacked by an animal one night and begins to exhibit bizarre behavior—including biting, scratching, irrational lust, and hair growth—Brigitte vows to do anything to bring her sister back to her even as they grow farther apart.

Review: Much like Angela Carter's fiction, *Ginger Snaps* uses bestial allegory to parallel the natural development of a girl growing up. That Ginger is a werewolf is incidental; that her physical and emotional changes, much akin to a pubescent girl's, are coming between her and her younger, non-menstruating sister form the crux of this tale. Getting left behind is almost harder than growing up, and that harsh truth is unabashedly displayed here.

FURTHER VIEWING: ***Ginger Snaps 2: Unleashed; Ginger Snaps Back: The Beginning***
SEE ALSO: ***The Company of Wolves; The Craft***

321

★★

Director: Ken Russell
Screenwriter: Stephen Volk

Produced by: Al Clark, Robert Devereux, Penny Corke, and Robert Fox

Starring: Gabriel Byrne, Julian Sands, and Natasha Richardson
Released by: Synergy Entertainment (DVD)

18+

GOTHIC

1986, 88 mins.

Plot: Geneva, 1816: Mary Shelley, Percy Bysshe Shelley, and Lord Byron spend a rainy summer indoors telling each other stories in front of the fire. *Gothic* is a fictional account of this time that would result in both Shelley's seminal horror novel *Frankenstein* and the skeleton of Polidori's *The Vampyre*.

Review: Fraught and hallucinatory, *Gothic* shouldn't be taken as a realistic account of those Genevan summer days—it's more of a fever dream one could imagine would materialize from such delicate creative sensibilities, which was then adapted to the screen by Russell. Sometimes beautiful, sometimes ridiculous, and always nonsensical, with a bit of unintentional comic relief provided by Julian Sands' notoriously bad acting and Gabriel Byrne's Byronic hunchback.

FURTHER VIEWING: *Women in Love; Lisztomania; Valentino; Salome's Last Dance*
SEE ALSO: *Haunted Summer; Frankenstein; Rowing with the Wind*

322

★★★★★

Director: Robert Harmon
Screenwriter: Eric Red

Produced by: Charles R. Meeker, David Bombyk, Edward S. Feldman, Kip Ohman, and Paul Lewis

Starring: Rutger Hauer, C. Thomas Howell, and Jennifer Jason Leigh
Released by: HBO Home Video (DVD)

18+

THE HITCHER

1986, 97 mins.

Plot: Jim Halsey is making a few bucks by driving a car from Chicago to its delivery point in San Diego. Along the way he gives a ride to a hitchhiker; what follows is the ultimate cautionary tale against picking up random strangers on deserted highways.

Review: The finger-in-the-fries scene and the bit where Jennifer Jason Leigh gets torn apart by two eighteen-wheelers are justifiably famous for their callous and unrelenting violence, but the true horror of this film is the hitcher himself, known only as Ryder. Rutger Hauer, not known for his cuddly on-screen personas, delivers a chilling performance as the calmly murderous maniac. Moreover, Ryder's reason for stalking, torturing, and killing his victims is never revealed, never even hinted at, a tactic that is as refreshing as it is terrifying.

FURTHER VIEWING: *The Hitcher (2007 remake); The Hitcher 2: I've Been Waiting*
SEE ALSO: *Duel; Creepshow 2; The Hitch-Hiker; Road Games*

323/500

★★★★

Director: Tony Scott
Screenwriters: James Costigan, Ivan Davis, and Michael Thomas
Produced by: Richard Shepherd
Starring: Catherine Deneuve, David Bowie, and Susan Sarandon
Released by: Warner Home Video (DVD)

18+

THE HUNGER

1983, 97 mins.

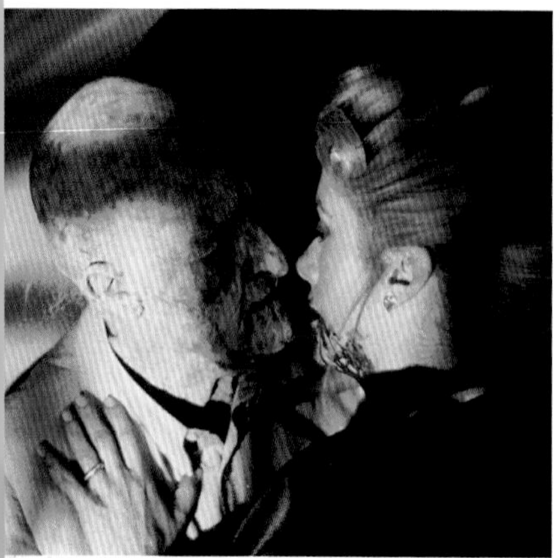

Plot: Anti-aging specialist Sarah Roberts gets a visit from an unusual man who is worried about aging too quickly, but looks to be in his twenties. She keeps him waiting for hours, and by the time he leaves her office he looks decades older. Intrigued, Sarah investigates the matter and finds that the man is the consort of a centuries-old vampire named Miriam who can give the gift of seemingly eternal youth—until, of course, the spell wears off.

Review: Tony Scott is much better known for his straightforward and intensely eighties action films, but *The Hunger* is a highly stylized foray into mysticism and otherworldly sensuality. While it can be overly avant-garde at times—coming back full-circle to artifice and banality—the film poses some interesting questions concerning the negative side of immortality (or the promise of it).

FURTHER VIEWING: ***The Hunger (TV series)***
SEE ALSO: ***Daughters of Darkness; Near Dark; Nadja; Cronos***

324/500

★★★

Director: Albert Band
Screenwriter: Louis Garfinkle
Producer: Albert Band
Starring: Richard Boone, Theodore Bikel, and Peggy Maurer
Released by: United Artists (DVD)

12+

I BURY THE LIVING

1958, 80 mins.

Plot: Richard Boone stars as cemetery owner Robert Craft in this wonderfully hokey black and white horror, where he believes he has the power of life over death. Robert carefully marks out the owners of the plots using black and white pins—white for the plot has been reserved, black for when there's a body buried there. When he accidentally puts the wrong pins into the board and he finds the occupants-to-be have died prematurely, his moral dilemma almost drives him to madness.

Review: Like a feature-length episode of *The Twilight Zone*, this low-budget proto-zombie flick is limited to only a few sets, but is excellent at cranking up Boone's anxiety as the bodies keep piling up. While it's good for business, it's bad for his heart.

FURTHER VIEWING: ***Face of Fire; The Young Guns***
SEE ALSO: ***Night of the Living Dead; I Walked with a Zombie; Cemetery Man***

25

★★

Director: Antonio Margheriti
Screenwriter: Antonio Margheriti
Produced by: Felice Testa Gay

Starring: Barbara Steele, George Ardisson, and Halina Zalewska
Released by: Not Available

5+

I LUNGHI CAPELLI DELLA MORTE

(THE LONG HAIR OF DEATH)

1964, 100 mins.

Plot: A woman falsely accused of murder and witchcraft is burned alive in medieval Italy. Before her oldest daughter can take revenge on the lord and his son who framed her mother, she too is killed. The youngest sister is then married off to the lord's vile son. Soon, the homicidal ghost of the oldest daughter—with her long hair—returns to avenge her mother.

Review: Laden with sinister castles, bleak landscapes, and debauched lords, this piece has shades of *Hamlet* and *Macbeth* with its hauntings, murder most foul, and supernatural vengeance. The true star is Barbara Steele, playing both dead and living daughters, and bringing real glamour to the proceedings.

FURTHER VIEWING: *Danza macabra (Castle of Blood); I criminali della galassia (The Galaxy Criminals); Flesh for Frankenstein; Killer Fish*
SEE ALSO: *The Advocate; Black Sunday; House of Usher; Masque of the Red Death; The Raven; Witchfinder General*

26

★★★★★

Director: Jacques Tourneur
Screenwriters: Curt Siodmak and Ardel Wray

Produced by: Val Lewton
Starring: Frances Dee, Tom Conway, and James Ellison

Released by: Turner Home Entertainment (DVD)

2+

I WALKED WITH A ZOMBIE

1943, 69 mins.

Plot: In a new interpretation of *Jane Eyre*, Canadian nurse Betsy Connell is sent to the Caribbean island of Saint Sebastian to care for the wife of dashing but morose plantation owner Paul Holland. Holland's wife is a beautiful but empty shell, what the island people who practice voodoo would call a zombie; as Holland denies his growing feelings for Betsy, Betsy decides the best way to quench her own forbidden passion is to restore Holland's wife. When medicine fails, Betsy turns to voodoo, raising more questions than cures.

Review: Jacques Tourneur has an indisputable talent for atmospheric horror, and *I Walked with a Zombie* is one of his most visually evocative films. Occasionally creepy and full of quiet desperation, this is probably closer to melodrama than horror on the spectrum, but that's more a result of the director's high-brow aspirations, which he meets and exceeds.

FURTHER VIEWING: *Night of the Demon; Cat People*
SEE ALSO: *Wide Sargasso Sea; White Zombie; The Serpent and the Rainbow*

327/500

★★★

Director: Ray Dennis Steckler
Screenwriter: Gene Pollock
Producer: Ray Dennis Steckler

Starring: Ray Dennis Steckler, Carolyn Brandt, and Brett O'Hara
Released by: Guilty Pleasures (DVD)

15+

INCREDIBLY STRANGE CREATURES WHO STOPPED LIVING AND BECAME MIXED-UP ZOMBIES!!?

1964, 82 mins.

Plot: Jerry (played by the director), Harold, and Angela head out to an amusement park. There they meet a mystic who warns of bad tidings, but the group laugh it off. Jerry catches sight of a beautiful but alcoholic stripper, Carmelita, at one of her performances and instantly falls in love. Unluckily for him she is related to the mystic, and Jerry is turned into a blood-crazed zombie.

Review: Less of a horror film and more a kitsch nightmare, Steckler's directorial ineptitude permeates nearly every shot of this weird B-movie. Any attempt to digest the plot rationally is not recommended—instead, prepare yourself for the rollercoaster ride of one of cinema's first monster musicals.

FURTHER VIEWING: ***Sinthia, the Devil's Doll; The Thrill Killers***
SEE ALSO: ***The Happiness of the Katakuris; Monster a-Go Go***

328/500

★★★★★

Director: Steven Spielberg
Screenwriters: Peter Benchley and Carl Gottlieb

Produced by: David Brown and Richard D. Zanuck

Starring: Roy Scheider, Richard Dreyfuss, and Robert Shaw
Released by: Universal Pictures (DVD)

12+

JAWS

1975, 119 mins.

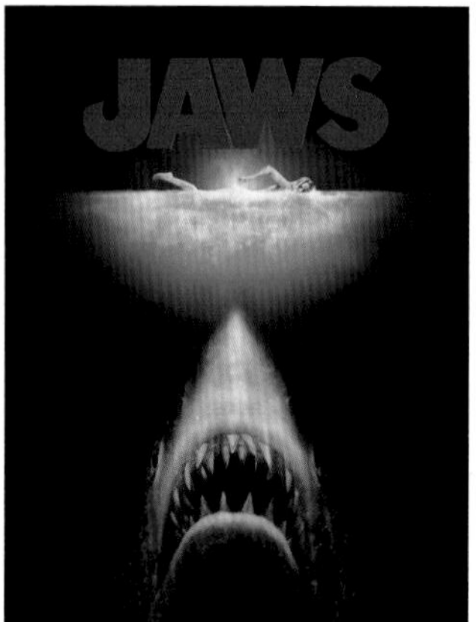

Plot: A great white shark begins killing bathers off the beaches of Amity, a town whose survival depends on summer tourists. As the death toll mounts, Amity's timorous Police Chief Brody, veteran shark hunter Quint, and heroically naïve marine biologist Hopper head out to sea to face this twenty-five-foot, three-ton force of nature.

Review: Regarded as the film that gave us the "summer event movie," filming was plagued by problems with the model shark. However, this turned into a boon for the actors and director, who transformed what might have been a high-budget B-movie into a masterpiece of suspense. There can now be few people who don't hear John Williams' terrifying theme when they go in the sea.

FURTHER VIEWING: ***Jaws 2; Jurassic Park; Duel; Sugarland Express; Schindler's List; Saving Private Ryan***
SEE ALSO: ***Deep Blue Sea; Lake Placid; Tremors***

29

★★★★

Director: Takashi Shimizu
Screenwriter: Takashi Shimizu

Produced by: Hiroki Numata and Takashige Ichise

Starring: Megumi Okina, Misaki Ito, and Misa Uehara
Released by: Lionsgate (DVD)

5+

JU-ON (THE GRUDGE)

2003, 92 mins.

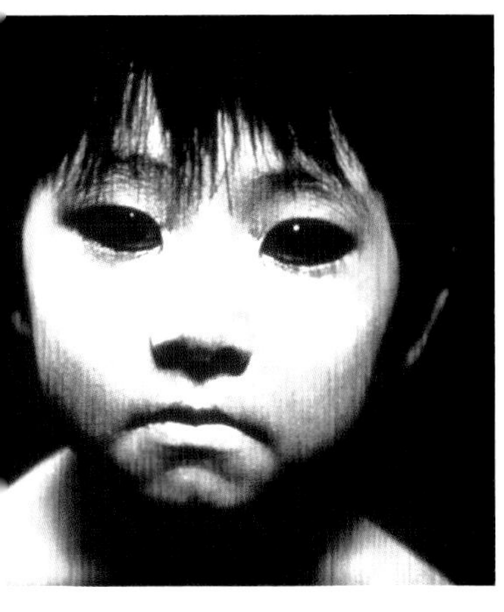

Plot: A Ju-on, or grudge, is a curse the angry dead inflict on the living. *Ju-on* follows one such curse as it affects five different people who all had contact with a house, or the people living in it, in which a horrible murder occurred. They begin to see and hear the dead, but these are no ethereal apparitions—they are up close, physical, intent on killing, and always successful.

Review: Long silky hair has never been so terrifying. Originally made for Japanese television, *Ju-on* became an international hit and one of the top J-horror films ever made. There is nothing funny or lighthearted about this film; the director offers no comic relief from the disconcerting visions. The spider-like movements of the unquiet dead as they stalk their victims—bones twisting and crunching—is a particularly creepy and often-copied concept. As far as straight psychological horror goes, this is one of the best.

FURTHER VIEWING: *The Grudge (2004 remake); Ju-on 2 (extended version)*
SEE ALSO: *Ringu; Dark Water; Whispering Corridors; Wishing Stairs*

30

★★★

Director: Michael Mann
Screenwriter: Michael Mann

Produced by: Gene Kirkwood and Howard W. Koch Jr.

Starring: Scott Glenn, Gabriel Byrne, and Ian McKellen
Released by: Not Available

5+

THE KEEP

1983, 96 mins.

Plot: Romania, 1943: the Nazis have occupied an ancient citadel with a bad reputation in the Carpathian Alps, and the soldiers notice that the interior is ringed with crosses embedded into the walls. As the crosses appear to be silver, two of the braver (or dumber) soldiers decide to pry one loose, and in doing so unleash a hell-being that powers up by draining the men's life-forces. Meanwhile, a mysterious stranger with a fancy sword arrives from out of town—he knows the true nature of the beast and is intent on killing it before it escapes the citadel.

Review: A far cry from Mann's better-known crime/noir films—including *Heat, Collateral,* and *Miami Vice*—*The Keep* serves mainly as a playground for experimental imagery. With its hypnotic soundtrack composed by Tangerine Dream, the film's narrative is second string to Mann's desire to create a visual abstraction akin to a tangible dream world. Truly mesmerizing.

FURTHER VIEWING: *Manhunter; The Last of the Mohicans*
SEE ALSO: *The Bunker; Deathwatch; The Supernaturals*

331
500

★★★

Director: Stephen Chiodo
Screenwriters: Stephen Chiodo, Charles Chiodo, and Edward Chiodo

Produced by: Charles Chiodo, Christopher Roth, Edward Chiodo, and Helen Szabo

Starring: Grant Cramer, Suzanne Snyder, John Allen Nelson, John Vernon, and Michael Siegel
Released by: MGM (DVD)

18+

KILLER KLOWNS FROM OUTER SPACE

1988, 88 mins.

Plot: Debbie and Mike witness a meteor falling to Earth while making out on lovers lane, and when they investigate they find a circus tent. But this isn't your average Barnum & Bailey's; the alien Klowns are grotesque and creepy, and they're here to suck human blood for food. Their arsenal of weapons includes balloon-animal attack dogs, cotton-candy cocoons, and popcorn guns.

Review: This film isn't about production values, or acting talent, or even a coherent narrative—it's about *clowns from outer space who kill people with circus toys*. Essentially a spoof, *Killer Klowns* is sick, hilarious, and totally worth your time.

FURTHER VIEWING: ***Callalilly; Critters; Team America: World Police***
SEE ALSO: ***The Toxic Avenger; Attack of the Killer Tomatoes; The Funhouse***

332
500

★★★★

Director: Wes Craven
Screenwriters: Wes Craven and Ulla Isaksson

Produced by: Katherine D'Amato, Sean S. Cunningham, Steve Dwork, and Steve Miner

Starring: Sandra Peabody, Lucy Grantham, David Hess, Fred J. Lincoln, and Jeramie Rain
Released by: MGM (DVD)

18+

THE LAST HOUSE ON THE LEFT

1972, 84mins.

Plot: Mari and her friend Phyllis are having a night on the town to celebrate Mari's seventeenth birthday when they have a run-in with a group of junkies recently escaped from prison. The cons kidnap and rape the girls, then, within spitting distance of Mari's home, murder them both; afterward the group seek shelter with Mari's parents but betray themselves as Mari and Phyllis' killers. Mari's parents take revenge in some of the foulest ways imaginable.

Review: This is Wes Craven's first feature, and it's a hell of a calling card for the genre. Heavily censored in many countries for violence and sadism, *The Last House on the Left* became a video nasty in the eighties. Like many "torture porn" horror films, it is unrelenting in its depiction of violence. An incredibly difficult film to watch, but its lasting influence makes it an essential.

FURTHER VIEWING: ***The Hills Have Eyes; The Last House on the Left (2009 remake); Night Train Murders***
SEE ALSO: ***Funny Games; I Spit on Your Grave; Ms. 45; The Virgin Spring; Straw Dogs***

Director: Joel Schumacher
Screenwriters: Janice Fisher, James Jeremias, and Jeffrey Boam

Produced by: Harvey Bernhard and Richard Donner

Starring: Jason Patric, Corey Haim, and Kiefer Sutherland
Released by: Warner Home Video (DVD)

THE LOST BOYS

1987, 93 mins.

Plot: Michael, Sam, and their mother Lucy move to Santa Carla, California, to live with their nutty grandfather following Lucy's messy divorce. It turns out that Santa Carla is crawling with vampires, and after Michael is infected, he and Sam, with the help of the irascible Frog brothers, must find and kill the head vampire before Michael turns to the dark side for good.

Review: *The Lost Boys* is an absolute pleasure to watch. Despite its dated eighties look, it is just an excellently crafted teen horror comedy that holds up not only to repeated viewings but also to almost twenty-five years of age (which is more like 125 years in celluloid time). This film never tries to be anything more than fun and contains what might be the greatest final line of dialog in any horror comedy.

FURTHER VIEWING: *Lost Boys: The Tribe; Flatliners; The Number 23*
SEE ALSO: *Martin; Fright Night; Salem's Lot*

334
500

★★

Director: William Lustig
Screenwriter: Larry Cohen
Produced by: Larry Cohen

Starring: Bruce Campbell, Robert Z'Dar, Tom Atkins, and Laurene Landon
Released by: Synapse Films (DVD)

18+

MANIAC COP

1988, 87 mins.

Plot: A serial killer is on the loose in New York City, and the twist is that he's murdering in full police uniform. Most cops are convinced that the guy is just a maniac in a rented monkey suit, but lead investigator Detective Frank McCrae suspects the killer is actually a cop. Officer Jack Forrest is locked up for the crimes, but McCrae is murdered while he's in jail, and Forrest takes over the investigation in an attempt to fully clear his name.

Review: Let's get this out of the way: this is not a good film, and Bruce Campbell, at least at this point, is not a good actor. But that doesn't matter: most cult horror film fans would happily watch Campbell pick the fluff out of his belly button, and *Maniac Cop* is just bad enough to be funny.

FURTHER VIEWING: ***Maniac Cop 2; Maniac Cop 3: Badge of Silence; Relentless***
SEE ALSO: ***The Ambulance; Unlawful Entry; Dangerous Game***

335
500

★★★★

Director: Kathryn Bigelow
Screenwriters: Eric Red and Kathryn Bigelow

Produced by: Charles R. Meeker, Diane Nabatoff, Edward S. Feldman, Eric Red, and Mark Allen

Starring: Adrian Pasdar, Jenny Wright, Lance Henriksen, and Bill Paxton
Released by: Lionsgate (DVD)

18+

NEAR DARK

1987, 95 mins.

Plot: Young Caleb spends a night with drifter Mae, who leaves him with two punctures in his neck as a parting gift. Predictably, Caleb develops photosensitivity and an insatiable thirst. Mae returns with a gang of white-trash vampires and takes Caleb away from his family, but when the gang kidnaps Caleb's sister as well, Caleb's father throws down on the fang gang to save his family.

Review: *Near Dark* is a classic reimagining of the vampire myth; instead of brooding eighteenth-century European romantics, these vampires are trailer-park rejects tooling around the dust bowl of Oklahoma killing time until the next massacre. But they still feel a human need for companionship, just not in functional terms. With such a brilliant set-up, it's hard not to feel let down with the ending, which is simplistic to the point of being lackluster.

FURTHER VIEWING: ***The Loveless; Strange Days***
SEE ALSO: ***The Forsaken; Martin; The Hunger***

Director: F. W. Murnau
Screenwriter: Henrick Galeen
Produced by: Enrico Dieckmann and Albin Grau
Starring: Max Schreck, Gustav von Wangenheim, and Greta Schröder
Released by: Image Entertainment (DVD)

2+ NOSFERATU

1922, 94 mins.

Plot: *Nosferatu* is a direct (though uncredited at the time) adaptation of Bram Stoker's *Dracula*. Wisborg real-estate agent Thomas Hutter meets with mysterious Count Orlock at his castle to finalize a deal and discovers the Count sleeps in a coffin. He escapes, but the Count soon moves in to his new house in Wisborg, where the villagers begin dying from a strange plague that leaves them bloodless and with holes in their necks.

Review: Despite Murnau being sued by Stoker's wife for this "borrowing" of *Dracula*'s plot and characters, this film has become horror legend—it even inspired a fictionalized film, *Shadow of the Vampire*, about its making. The gothic aesthetic and slow pace can seem more quaint than scary, but Nosferatu's makeup is truly repulsive and a far cry from the new romantic vampire look so popular now. An antique, to be sure, but one of blinding inspiration.

FURTHER VIEWING: *Shadow of the Vampire; Faust; Nosferatu the Vampyre (1979 remake)*
SEE ALSO: *The Cabinet of Dr. Caligari; The Fall of the House of Usher*

Director: Mario Bava
Screenwriter: Romano Migliorini
Producer: Luciano Catenacci
Starring: Giacomo Rossi-Stuart, Erika Blanc, and Fabienne Dali
Released by: VCI Video (DVD)

5+ OPERAZIONE PAURA (KILL, BABY, KILL)

1966, 84 mins.

Plot: A series of murders in a quant Italian village draws a perfectly coiffed coroner to investigate. His arrival does nothing to loosen the tongues of the terrified locals, who believe something supernatural is at work. The gold coins found near the hearts of the victims can't be explained by the enthusiastic sleuth until he finds the village has been cursed for the murder of a baroness' daughter many years before.

Review: An early example of the Giallo genre, *Kill, Baby, Kill*'s main draw is its beautiful cinematography—eerie gothic buildings form the majority of the sets, and the fine costumes add to the authenticity of the period. The disturbing laughter of the giggling ghost child is an effective (and cheap) tool for chills.

FURTHER VIEWING: *Black Sabbath; Danger: Diabolik*
SEE ALSO: *Susperia; Black Sunday*

★★★★

Director: Michael Powell
Screenwriter: Leo Marks
Produced by: Nat Cohen
Starring: Karlheinz Böhm, Moira Shearer, and Anna Massey
Released by: Criterion (DVD)

18+

PEEPING TOM

1960, 101 mins.

Plot: Mark Lewis had an unusual childhood—his psychologist father kept him under constant photographic surveillance in order to record his reactions to various fear-based stimuli, including his mother's death. When older, Mark partly follows in his father's footsteps, but takes the experiment even further by killing women and filming their deaths while showing them their own fear with a well-placed mirror. Meanwhile, the police are getting closer . . .

Review: *Peeping Tom* is an incredibly controversial film, so much so that it ruined eminent filmmaker Michael Powell's career at the time. But time has treated it well, and critical reactions are more favorable now, viewing it as masterpiece of psychological examination and horror.

FURTHER VIEWING: *Black Narcissus*
SEE ALSO: *Psycho; Rear Window; Henry: Portrait of a Serial Killer; White of the Eye*

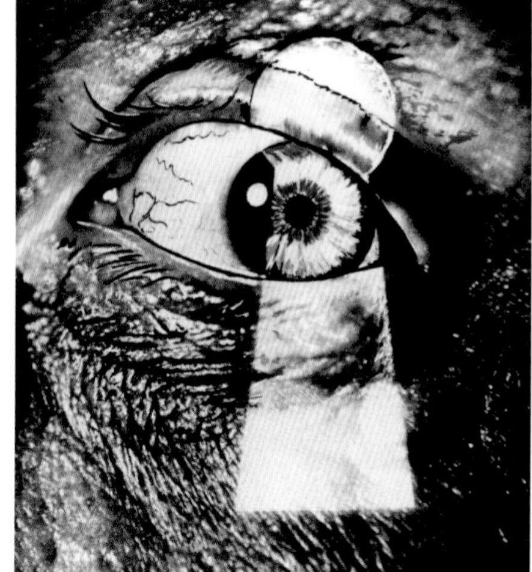

39

★★★

Director: Brian De Palma
Screenwriter: Brian De Palma
Producer: Edward R. Pressman
Starring: Paul Williams and William Finley
Released by: Twentieth Century Fox (DVD)

2+

PHANTOM OF THE PARADISE

1974, 88 mins.

Plot: Talented musician Winslow Leach writes a beautiful cantata, which a megalomaniacal record producer, Swan, hears and steals so his most popular band, The Juicy Fruits, can perform it live. Easily manipulated into giving up his music, Winslow is unable to get access to Swan. Disfigured by a record press, he takes to the rafters of the Paradise Theater dressed in a face mask and cloak to bring Swan's show to its knees.

Review: Marilyn Manson stole much of Leach's disfigured phantom appearance for his own glam rock act twenty years after this film came out. Brian De Palma's direction is second-to-none, proving he can direct a musical as well as a satirical horror at the same time. In short: Ziggy Stardust of the Opera.

FURTHER VIEWING: *Carrie; Body Double*
SEE ALSO: *The Rocky Horror Picture Show; The Abominable Dr. Phibes*

40

★★★

Director: Joe Dante
Screenwriter: John Sayles
Produced by: Jon Davidson and Chako van Leeuwen
Starring: Bradford Dillman, Heather Menzies, and Kevin McCarthy
Released by: New Concorde (DVD)

8+

PIRANHA

1978, 94 mins.

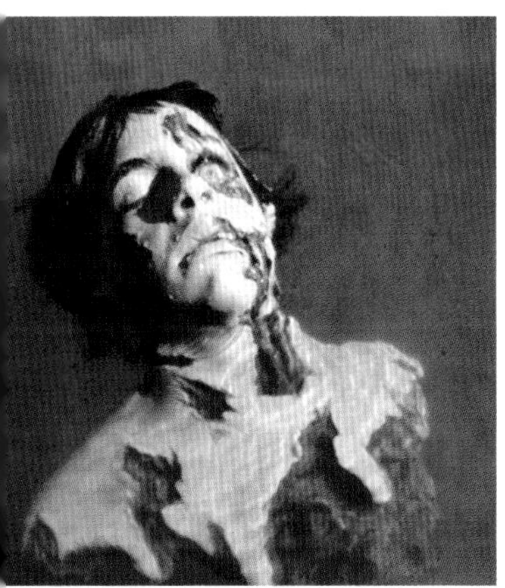

Plot: A spoof of 1975's megahit *Jaws, Piranha* takes place in a resort town on the banks of Lost River Lake. Two teenagers go missing, and Maggie, an insurance investigator, is sent to Lost River by her company to find them. She hires a local drunk to guide her, and the two stumble upon a military camp inhabited by Dr. Hoak, who headed a project to breed killer piranhas for use in the Vietnam War and kept the experiment alive even after the project was shut down. The piranhas escape the compound and begin to rip apart the tourists.

Review: *Piranha* has some of the most hilarious death scenes ever filmed on underwater cameras. And if you thought Mayor Vaughn was awful, wait till you get a load of resort-owner Buck Gardner. It's so refreshing to watch B-movie horror that, for a change, is actually meant to be funny.

FURTHER VIEWING: *Piranha 2: The Spawning; Piranha (1995 remake); Gremlins*
SEE ALSO: *Jaws; Killer Fish; Alligator*

341/500

Director: Don Sharp
Screenwriters: Arnaud d'Usseau and Julian Zimet
Produced by: Andrew Donally

Starring: Nicky Henson, Mary Larkin, and Ann Michelle
Released by: Image Entertainment (DVD)

12+

PSYCHOMANIA

1971, 95 mins.

Plot: A notorious motorcycle gang called The Living Dead terrorizes the British countryside but their leader wants more. Aided by his occult-loving mother and her sinister butler, he makes a pact with the Devil to live forever. After killing himself, he does indeed return from the dead and, after persuading his gang to follow in his footsteps, they go on the rampage.

Review: Typically, eccentrically British. While American Hells Angels were knifing each other, taking drugs, and having lots of sex, The Living Dead are ignoring road signs and upsetting the Home County locals—truly terror on two wheels. Done with little gore and sex, it's still a totally groovy slice of seventies horror kitsch and ludicrously great fun!

FURTHER VIEWING: ***The Adventures of Hal 5; The Kiss of the Vampire; The Devil-Ship Pirates; Curse of the Fly; The 39 Steps; Bear Island***
SEE ALSO: ***The Devil Rides Out; Dracula A.D.1972; Ghostrider***

342/500

★★★

Director: Larry Cohen
Screenwriter: Larry Cohen
Producer: Larry Cohen

Starring: Michael Moriarty, David Carradine, and Richard Roundtree
Released by: Blue Underground (DVD)

15+

Q THE WINGED SERPENT

1982, 93 mins.

Plot: Quetzacoatl, a giant winged serpent, has been summoned by an Aztec cult in New York City and goes on a rampage that would put King Kong to shame. As blood and guts rain down on the poor pedestrians, the cops are stumped as to how so many bodies are turning up. Incredulous at first, they can't deny the existence of Q when a petty crook (played brilliantly by Michael Moriarty) offers them the beast's nest for $1,000,000 in cash, tax-free.

Review: Legendary B-movie director Larry Cohen struck gold again with this cool creature feature set in Manhattan. Part homage to the classic stop-motion monster flicks of yore and part crime yarn, the amount of gore on display would put an abattoir to shame.

FURTHER VIEWING: ***It's Alive; The Stuff***
SEE ALSO: ***Piranha; Alligator***

43

Director: Val Guest
Screenwriters: Richard Landau and Val Guest
Produced by: Anthony Hinds
Starring: Brian Donlevy, Jack Warner, Richard Wordsworth, and Margia Dean
Released by: Simply Media (DVD, region 2 only)

2+

THE QUATERMASS XPERIMENT

(THE CREEPING UNKNOWN)

1955, 82 mins.

Plot: American scientist Bernard Quatermass designs a rocket that launches three astronauts into space. But when the rocket crashes in England, only one astronaut is on board, and he's in a catatonic state. A camera in the rocket shows that the astronauts were attacked by an energy form; the survivivor, meanwhile, has escaped and discovers he has the power to absorb living things. Quatermass must find and kill him before he endangers all of humanity.

Review: Based on the British TV show, this was Hammer's first experiment in horror, having already made sci-fi films. It was so successful financially that Hammer turned soley to horror and has since had a profound effect on the genre. *Quatermass* itself is quite good fun, if a bit grim at times.

FURTHER VIEWING: ***Quatermass 2; Quatermass; Quatermass and the Pit***
SEE ALSO: ***The Day of the Triffids; X The Unknown***

44

Director: Russell Mulcahy
Screenwriter: Everett De Roche
Produced by: Hal McElroy
Starring: Gregory Harrison, Arkie Whiteley, and Bill Kerr
Released by: Starz Home Entertainment (DVD, region 2 only)

RAZORBACK

1984, 95 mins.

Plot: Jake Cullen's grandson was killed by the same wild boar (razorback) that destroyed his house; to pile insult on to injury, no one believed him, and Jake was accused of murder. Two years later investigative journalist Beth is also killed by a razorback in Jake's town, and when Beth's distraught husband travels to Australia looking for answers, he teams up with Jake to hunt the pig they believe killed their loved ones.

Review: "Razorbacks . . . God and the Devil couldn't have created a more despicable species." Before Russell Mulcahy directed *Highlander*, he made this tongue-in-cheek film about a giant killer pig. Ridiculous though it sounds, *Razorback* is a well-made, suspenseful horror film with enough wry humor to keep the audience interested in the down time.

FURTHER VIEWING: ***Highlander; Tale of the Mummy; Resurrection***
SEE ALSO: ***Murders in the Zoo; Python***

345/500

★★★★★

Director: Stuart Gordon
Screenwriters: Stuart Gordon, William Norris, and Dennis Paoli
Produced by: Brian Yuzna
Starring: Jeffrey Combs, Bruce Abbott, and Barbara Crampton
Released by: Starz/Anchor Bay (DVD)

18+

RE-ANIMATOR

1985, 86 mins.

Plot: Herbert West is a genius and a medical student at Miskatonic University, which we know can't be a good combination. He develops a neon-green serum that can reanimate dead flesh, whether an entire body or just parts of it. But there are complications, and the revived corpses are either unnaturally violent—and must be immediately dispatched—or disappointingly zombie-like. When West's unscrupulous supervisor discovers his secret, he attempts to blackmail West, but, now no stranger to death, West kills Hill and reanimates him. Even worse dead than he was alive, Hill steals the serum and creates an undead army that only West can stop.

Review: An adaptation of H. P. Lovecraft's story "Herbert West: Re-Animator," *Re-Animator* is fast-paced, sly, and very funny, but never crosses the line into camp territory, mainly due to Jeffrey Combs' quietly intense performance. A must-see B-movie.

FURTHER VIEWING: ***Bride of Re-Animator; Beyond Re-Animator***
SEE ALSO: ***Dead Alive; Cemetery Man; The Resurrected***

346/500

★★★★★

Director: Roman Polanski
Screenwriter: Roman Polanski
Produced by: William Castle
Starring: Mia Farrow, John Cassavetes, and Ruth Gordon
Released by: Paramount (DVD)

18+

ROSEMARY'S BABY

1968, 138 mins.

Plot: Rosemary Woodhouse appears to have everything: a handsome actor husband who adores her, a sunny disposition, and a brand new apartment in a lovely building. But her husband's career isn't going that well, and her building has an unsavory history. When Rosemary gets pregnant after a night with her husband she can't remember, the pregnancy is problematic, and everyone starts acting a bit funny in a Satanic kind of way.

Review: Not a film for expectant mothers. At first, Rosemary comes across as the sort of wet-blanket character you'd love to hate, but Mia Farrow's performance is just so sweet and innocent and honest that she becomes the anchor of the film, staying grounded as Polanski deftly weaves the outlandish narrative around her. An extremely well-crafted horror/thriller.

FURTHER VIEWING: ***The Tenant; Repulsion; The Ninth Gate; Look What's Happened to Rosemary's Baby***
SEE ALSO: ***Audrey Rose; Don't Look Now; Night of the Eagle***

47

★★

Director: James Wan
Screenwriter: Leigh Whannell
Producer: Mark Burg

Starring: Lee Whannell, Cary Elwes, and Danny Glover
Released by: Lionsgate (DVD)

8+ SAW

2004, 103 mins.

Plot: Two men come to in a dimly lit and locked bathroom, not knowing how they got there or who the other is. They are chained to pipes, and in their possession are rusty saws, which while not sharp enough to cut through any metal, may be good enough to hack through ankles instead. They have been imprisoned by the Jigsaw Killer, who wishes to show them the value of their lives—through death.

Review: Expanded from a nine-minute short film, *Saw* has become a staple Halloween movie at multiplexes as it heads towards six sequels. The cat-and-mouse plot and shock twist ending more than justify the gratuitous torture on offer—plus Billy the Puppet is cinema's most vile dummy since *Devil Doll*.

FURTHER VIEWING: *Saw 2; Saw 3*
SEE ALSO: *Hostel; Turistas (Paradise Lost)*

48

★★★★

Director: David Cronenberg
Screenwriter: David Cronenberg
Produced by: Claude Héroux

Starring: Jennifer O'Neill, Stephen Lack, Patrick McGoohan, and Michael Ironside
Released by: MGM (DVD)

8+ SCANNERS

1981, 103 mins.

Plot: A group of women were given an experimental drug called Ephemerol while pregnant and subsequently gave birth to "scanners," children with telepathic and telekinetic powers. The children, now adults, are scattered around the world; most are incapable of living in society, but some have accepted their abilities and formed a support network. Renegade scanner Darryl Revok is neither—he's intent on forming an army of scanners to rule the world and kills anyone who isn't willing to join him. His outcast brother is the only scanner capable of stopping him.

Review: Though not as well received as Cronenberg's other films, *Scanners* still features the abstract thinking and bizarre special effects that the director is known for. Viewers who find the likes of *The Brood* and *Videodrome* too incomprehensible will find this more accessible.

FURTHER VIEWING: *Scanners 2: The New Order; Scanners 3: The Takeover; The Dead Zone*
SEE ALSO: *Firestarter; The Fury; The Gift; Patrick*

349
500

★★★

Director: Wes Craven
Screenwriters: Adam Rodman and Richard Maxwell

Produced by: David Ladd, Doug Claybourne, Keith Barish, and Rob Cohen

Starring: Bill Pullman, Cathy Tyson, and Zakes Mokae
Released by: Universal Studios (DVD)

18+ THE SERPENT AND THE RAINBOW

1988, 98 mins.

Plot: Ethnobotanist Dennis Alan is approached by a large and well-funded pharmaceutical company to investigate a drug used in Voodoo rituals in Haiti. The drug, an untested anesthetic/paralytic, is rumored to assist in the creation of zombies. During his research in Haiti, Alan is drawn into the Voodoo religion and experiences firsthand its effect on the human psyche.

Review: Very loosely based on ethnobotanist Wade Davis' autobiographical book of the same name, detailing his own experiences in Haiti; Davis subsequently denounced the film. This isn't one of Craven's best, but it is an interesting, if only pseudo-scientific, take on the roles magic and medicine play in Haitian Voodoo.

FURTHER VIEWING: ***A Nightmare on Elm Street; Chiller***
SEE ALSO: ***White Zombie; I Walked with a Zombie; The Skeleton Key; The Believers***

350
500

★★★★

Director: David Cronenberg
Screenwriter: David Cronenberg
Producer: Ivan Reitman

Starring: Paul Hampton, Joe Silver, and Lynn Lowry
Released by: Image Entertainment (DVD)

18+ SHIVERS

1975, 87 mins.

Plot: A futuristic housing complex armed with every modern convenience becomes infested with a manmade parasite that causes the infected to go on sex-crazed rampages. The building's doctor, Roger St. Luc, attempts to quell the outbreak, but the persistence of the new lifeform sees the inhabitants falling under its influence at a terrifying speed that threatens to escape into the outside world.

Review: Cronenberg's first feature was also his first experiment in body horror deliberately designed to get under your skin, and with a low budget and little time to film, he produced his first masterpiece. The apocalyptic ending throws up two possible conclusions—either we are too prudish, or it's the ultimate expansion of a free society. Either way, nobody wins

FURTHER VIEWING: ***Scanners; Videodrome***
SEE ALSO: ***Dawn of the Dead; Outbreak***

51

★ ★ ★

Director: Ken Wiederhorn
Screenwriter: John Kent Harrison
Producer: Reuben Trane
Starring: Peter Cushing and Brooke Adams
Released by: Blue Underground (DVD)

5+

SHOCK WAVES

1977, 86 mins.

Plot: A group of vacationers traveling by boat are forced to head to a remote island after their ship is damaged. Once there, they speak with an ex-SS commander who admits to creating a new form of Nazi—*Der Toten Korps*—living dead soldiers who can survive underwater. Gradually, the poor travelers are picked off one by one by the members of the *nouveau-Reich*.

Review: Unlike typical zombie films of the period, Wiederhorn's relies on ominous music, drably dressed sets, and a sense of foreboding to create its terror—you won't find lots of gore here. Neither will you bear witness to much else in the plot that you've not seen before, but you probably haven't seen many underwater zombie films either. Enjoyable trash.

FURTHER VIEWING: *Eyes of a Stranger; Return of the Living Dead: Part 2*
SEE ALSO: *Dead Snow; Outpost*

352

★ ★

Director: Brian Yuzna
Screenwriter: Rick Fry and Woody Keith
Produced by: Keith Walley, Keizo Kabata, Paul White, and Terry Ogisu
Starring: Billy Warlock, Ben Slack, and Patrice Jennings
Released by: Starz/Anchor Bay (DVD)

8+

SOCIETY

1989, 99 mins.

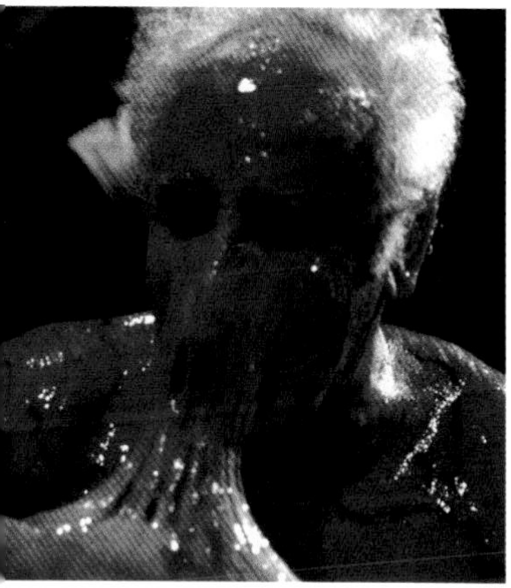

Plot: Bill Whitney is your average, everyday rich kid living it up in Beverly Hills high society. But he just never seemed to fit in with his family. A friend gives him an audio tape of what sounds like his family engaging in an orgy, so Bill starts to investigate, and finding out he's adopted turns out to be the least of his worries.

Review: *Society* has to be seen to be believed. It's a rare feat for a film to lead the audience to believe there's some nasty incest secret just waiting to be discovered, only when the secret is unearthed, it's *worse* than incest. And it shows everything in slimey, pulsating detail. This film is genius, in a way, but not for those with weak stomachs or even a smidgen of scruples.

FURTHER VIEWING: *Bride of Re-Animator; The Dentist*
SEE ALSO: *Tokyo Gore Police; They Live; Parents*

★★★

Director: Dario Argento
Screenwriter: Dario Argento
Produced by: Claudio Argento
Starring: Anthony Franciosa, Christian Borromeo, and Mirella D'Angelo
Released by: Anchor Bay (DVD)

18+

TENEBRAE

1982, 110 mins.

Plot: American mystery author Peter Neal has flown to Rome on a signing tour. However, it would seem a particularly avid fan has decided to act out the murders in his latest novel. Soon, Neal himself is under threat and, with the police struggling, he decides to use his own skills at constructing mysteries to turn the hunter into the hunted.

Review: Highly stylized serial killer flick from the master of Italian horror. Graphic, steamy, and high fashion, Argento uses snappy direction and visual inventiveness to pile on the tension. Full of red herrings and plot twists, psychosexual symbolism, and with nods to Hitchcock and Conan Doyle, this is Euro-horror at its finest.

FURTHER VIEWING: ***Suspiria; Inferno; Opera; Il fantasma dell'opera (Phantom of the Opera)***
SEE ALSO: ***Dressed to Kill; Manhunter; Psycho***

★★★★

Director: Tobe Hooper
Screenwriters: Kim Henkel and Tobe Hooper

Produced by: Tobe Hooper and Lou Peraino

Starring: Marilyn Burns, Allen Danziger, Paul A. Partain, and William Vail
Released by: Dark Sky Films (DVD)

8+ THE TEXAS CHAIN SAW MASSACRE

1973, 84 mins.

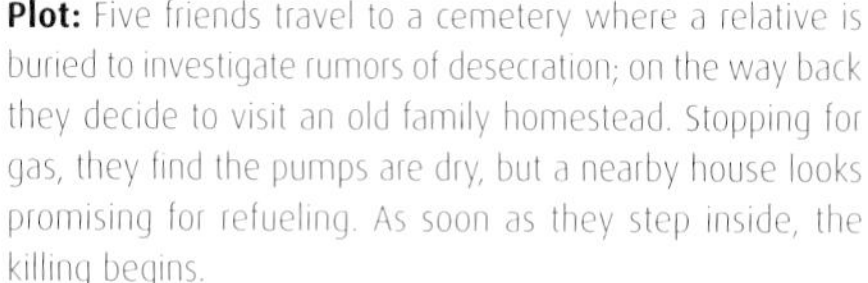

Plot: Five friends travel to a cemetery where a relative is buried to investigate rumors of desecration; on the way back they decide to visit an old family homestead. Stopping for gas, they find the pumps are dry, but a nearby house looks promising for refueling. As soon as they step inside, the killing begins.

Review: Inspired by the activities of serial killer Ed Gein (who also influenced characters Norman Bates from *Psycho* and Buffalo Bill from *Silence of the Lambs*), Leatherface is a true amalgamation of inescapable nightmares.

The quintessential seventies slasher film, *Chain Saw* has been highly influential in the horror genre; its legacy of high suspense and minimal gore can be seen in the work of Carpenter and Ridley Scott, and Rob Zombie is a fan. Often cited as one of the scariest horror films ever made.

FURTHER VIEWING: *The Chainsaw Massacre 2; The Return of the Texas Chainsaw Massacre; The Texas Chainsaw Massacre (2003 remake)*
SEE ALSO: *The Hills Have Eyes; Tourist Trap; Last House on the Left*

355
500

★★★

Director: Richard Wenk
Screenwriters: Donald P. Borchers and Richard Wenk
Produced by: Donald P. Borchers

Starring: Chris Makepeace, Sandy Baron, and Robert Rusler
Released by: Anchor Bay (DVD)

18+

VAMP

1986, 93 mins.

Plot: A.J. and Keith go looking for a stripper to round off the party they're throwing. Finding themselves in the wrong part of town, they visit a strip joint—and are blown away by the provocative, sensual act of Katrina. However, she and the rest of the club's regulars are vampires and the boys are soon up to their necks, so to speak, in trouble.

Review: With its strong monotone color palette, fluorescent sleaze, gore aplenty, and the stunningly exotic, erotically ugly/beautiful Grace Jones, you can't say that this movie is in any way understated. The characters are engaging, the gags are sharp, the effects gruesomely effective; all in all, it's a clever mix of quirky, charming, funny, and horrific.

FURTHER VIEWING: ***Dracula Bites the Big Apple; Just the Ticket; Wishcraft***
SEE ALSO: ***After Hours; Fright Night; From Dusk Till Dawn; Innocent Blood; The Lost Boys; Manhunter; Near Dark***

356
500

★★★★

Director: Victor Halperin
Screenwriter: Garnett Weston
Produced by: Edward Halperin

Starring: Bela Lugosi, Madge Bellamy, Robert Frazer, and John Harron
Released by: Alpha Video (DVD)

12+

WHITE ZOMBIE

1932, 73 mins.

Plot: Charles Beaumont invites young couple Neil and Madeleine to his Haitian plantation to be married. Charles wants Madeleine to himself, but cannot persuade her to leave Neil and the wedding goes ahead. But Charles won't let go, so he enlists the help of local witch doctor Legendre (Bela Lugosi) to turn Madeleine into a zombie subject to his will. It could have been happily ever afterlife, but Legendre wants Madeleine as well. That's what happens when you make a deal with a guy whose nickname is "Murder."

Review: Highly rated by film historians, this is the very first zombie film ever made—for that alone it should be required viewing for aficionados of the genre. But *White Zombie* is also a beautifully atmospheric piece of independent filmmaking, and just goes to show what miracles could be accomplished on a Hollywood backlot in the early days of celluloid sound.

FURTHER VIEWING: ***Supernatural; Revolt of the Zombies***
SEE ALSO: ***I Walked with a Zombie; The Plague of the Zombies; Day of the Dead; The Serpent and the Rainbow***

57

★★★★

Director: Michael Reeves
Screenwriters: Michael Reeves, Louis M. Heyward, Ronald Bassett, and Tom Baker
Produced by: Arnold L. Miller and Louis M. Heyward
Starring: Vincent Price, Ian Ogilvy, Rupert Davies, and Hilary Heath
Released by: MGM (DVD)

8+

THE WITCHFINDER GENERAL

1968, 86 mins.

Plot: Matthew Hopkins finds opportunity amidst the unrest of the English Civil War—he claims to have been appointed the "Witch-Finder General" by Parliament and proceeds to terrorize East Anglia during his profitable pursuit of witches.

Review: No matter what way you play it, Vincent Price can be terrifying, and this is his nastiest, most evil role, completely absent of his usual camp delivery. Heavily censored and reviled when first released due to its graphic depictions of torture and sexual violence, *Witchfinder General* now enjoys a more favorable place in the horror film canon, mainly for its honest consideration of power and corruption. Relentless and difficult, but rewarding.

FURTHER VIEWING: ***The Sorcerers; La sorella di Satana (The She Beast); Il castello dei morti vivi (Castle of the Living Dead)***
SEE ALSO: ***Pit and the Pendulum; The Dunwich Horror; Cry of the Banshee***

358

★★★

Director: Lucio Fulci
Screenwriter: Elisa Briganti
Producer: Fabrizio De Angelis
Starring: Tisa Farrow, Ian McCulloch, and Richard Johnson
Released by: Shriek Show (DVD)

18+

ZOMBI 2 (ZOMBIE FLESH EATERS)

1979, 91 mins.

Plot: An abandoned boat belonging to a missing scientist turns up in New York's harbor—on board is a zombie that kills a cop before being gunned down. The scientist's daughter traces him to a remote island where he has been trying to find out what has caused the dead to rise. The locals claim it's voodoo, and before long the zombie outbreak is too big to contain.

Review: Not as sophisticated as Romero's *Dawn of the Dead* (*Zombi 2* was billed as a sequel in Italy, even though it wasn't), *Zombi 2* features some gruesome effects, including a stomach churning eye-piercing on a splinter and a zombie versus tiger shark fight. The final stolen shot was probably something Romero wished he'd been able to do.

FURTHER VIEWING: ***City of the Living Dead; The New York Ripper***
SEE ALSO: ***Dawn of the Dead; Zombie Holocaust***

CHAPTER 7
CULT HUMOR

"THAT RUG REALLY TIED THE ROOM TOGETHER"

It's not enough for a cult film to just be funny, oh no. It also has to be exceptionally intelligent (or extremely stupid), and if it chronicles the kind of excruciating childhood experiences that make you squirm and giggle uncomfortably, then all the better. Stories that target small sections of society—rock stars, superheroes, high-schoolers—are encouraged, and the darker the humor, the more devoted the following. Here you'll find the blacker-than-black Ealing Studios' comedies that made grievous acts of murder elegant and hilarious; backstabbing teenage scenarios that can only be laughed at in hindsight; and, of course, the Coen brothers.

CULT HUMOR

★★★★★

Director: Joel Coen
Screenwriters: Ethan Coen and Joel Coen
Produced by: Ethan Coen

Starring: Jeff Bridges, John Goodman, and Steve Buscemi
Released by: Universal Studios (DVD)

18+

THE BIG LEBOWSKI

1998, 118 mins.

Plot: Unemployed sixties reject Jeff Lebowski (aka "The Dude") spends his days doing absolutely nothing apart from spouting stoner philosophy and bowling with a couple of other L.A. outcasts, namely unhinged Vietnam-veteran Walter and shy, naïve ex-surfer Donny. But The Dude's low-key lifestyle changes when two men kick his door in to collect a debt his wife owes. Since The Dude doesn't have a wife or a debt, it turns out they have the wrong Lebowski. It could have ended there, but the men urinated on his rug and The Dude thinks it's only just that the real Lebowski replace it, so he goes in search of the reclusive millionaire and gets caught up in possibly the most random, nonsensical series of events and people ever recorded on celluloid.

Review: This is most definitely a love-it-or-hate-it film, and those who love it are devotees to the point of fanaticism, practically memorizing the whole of the Coen brothers' quick-fire dialog. Similar to *The Rocky Horror Picture Show*'s following, fans of *The Big Lebowski* stage midnight screenings to dress up and quote lines from the script at each other; there are even festivals dedicated to celebrating the film on both sides of the pond (including The Lebowski Fest, which takes place in several cities around the U.S., and The Dude Abides in the UK).

So what's all the fuss? Well, detractors may say that The Dude is too laid back, too lazy to be a sustaining hero for a film; that the witty dialog frequently spills over into self-indulgent territory; and that the Coens' desire to showcase "ideas" rather than tell a story has resulted in a fractured narrative. As valid as those criticisms may be, *The Big Lebowski* delivers laughs just as a comedy should and introduces us to some truly incredible characters, most notably the ever-amazing John Goodman as the loud and twitchy Walter.

FURTHER VIEWING: ***Raising Arizona; Fargo***
SEE ALSO: ***Dead Men Don't Wear Plaid; Kiss Kiss Bang Bang; Crimewave***

Director: Don Coscarelli
Screenwriter: Don Coscarelli

Produced by: Don Coscarelli, Jason R. Savage, Ronnie Truss, and Mark Wooding

Starring: Bruce Campbell and Ossie Davis
Released by: MGM (DVD)

15+

BUBBA HO-TEP

2002, 92 mins.

Plot: A man who claims to be the real Elvis Presley—having switched places with an impersonator years before—lies dying of cancer of the penis in an East Texas nursing home. Though he planned to swap back with the impersonator after an extended vacation of anonymity, before he could do so the impersonator died on the toilet and the "real" Elvis' only proof of identity was destroyed in a trailer-park fire. So Elvis spends his time feeling sorry for himself and waiting to die, often philosophizing about his grand past compared to his undignified present, until another resident—a black man claiming to be John F. Kennedy—enlists his help to fight an ancient mummy that is systematically sucking the souls out of the elderly nursing-home residents.

Review: *Bubba Ho-Tep* appearing in the comedy section of this book is more for the ease of categorization than an accurate assessment of the film's genre, as it could just as easily come under drama, with its treatment of the indignity of aging, deep friendship, and self-sacrifice; horror, purely on the basis of its mummified villain; and experimental or even fantasy, as the film operates on the premise that Elvis is still alive and John F. Kennedy survived the assassination attempt, only to be "dyed black" by conspirators and abandoned in a nursing home in the middle of nowhere. But *Bubba Ho-Tep* is also extremely funny, so here we are.

As ambitious and wide-ranging as its themes may be, *Bubba* is never confused and doesn't stray from its central narrative: that the two most unlikely candidates—aging men deemed useless by society—are given a second chance to be heroes, to be more in their twilight than even thought to be in their prime. They aren't particularly sane or physically capable of the winning war they've chosen to fight, but that only makes their actions more poignant. As Elvis, this is the best performance of Bruce Campbell's career, and Ossie Davis is so into his character you can't help but suspect he might actually be Kennedy, despite the mountain of evidence belying his claim. *Bubba Ho-Tep* is an immaculate film on every level.

FURTHER VIEWING: *Phantasm; Phantasm 2*
SEE ALSO: *Cemetery Man; The Frighteners; Jack Brooks: Monster Slayer*

★★★★★

Director: Bob Clark
Screenwriters: Jean Shepherd, Leigh Brown, and Bob Clark

Produced by: Bob Clark, René Dupont, and Gary Goth

Starring: Peter Billingsley, Melinda Dillon, and Darren McGavin
Released by: Warner Home Video (DVD)

A CHRISTMAS STORY

1983, 94 mins.

Plot: Nine-year-old Ralphie Parker has only one Christmas wish, and it's not for his two front teeth. He wants an "Official Red Ryder Carbine-Action Two-Hundred-Shot Range Model Air Rifle," but the more he begs for it in the run-up to Christmas the more unlikely it seems that he'll get it. He attempts to get both a department-store Santa and his teacher to sanction his request, but adults only warn him that he'll shoot his eye out. His one-track gun obsession is variously interrupted by bullies, Ovaltine, inappropriate swearing, his father's epic battles with a furnace, the consequences of sticking your tongue to a pole on a winter's day in the Midwest, and a sexy lamp that seems destined to ruin Ralphie's parents' marriage. Just another day in the life of a kid growing up in Indiana in the forties, then.

Review: This is the dysfunctional but heartwarming antidote to watching *It's a Wonderful Life* over the Christmas season. Based on Jean Shepherd's semi-autobiographical short fiction, the film is also narrated by Shepherd (as the older "Ralphie") to hilarious and thought-provoking effect. Like his creator, Ralphie is an inveterate dreamer, and we're treated to imaginative vignettes of childish revenge throughout (after yet another night with a bar of soap in his mouth for swearing, Ralphie dreams of growing up and returning home blind—when his mother asks how this happened, he struggles to enunciate just two words: "Soap poisoning!").

A Christmas Story is essentially a coming-of-age tale, one that both children and their parents can identify and laugh with even as they cringe in knowing embarrassment.

FURTHER VIEWING: *Porky's and Porky's 2 (both funny but not family-oriented); Black Christmas (holiday horror)*
SEE ALSO: *The Santa Clause; Miracle on 34th Street; National Lampoon's Christmas Vacation*

Director: Stanley Kubrick
Screenwriters: Stanley Kubrick, Peter George, and Terry Southern

Produced by: Stanley Kubrick, Leon Minoff, and Victor Lyndon

Starring: Peter Sellers, George C. Scott, and Sterling Hayden
Released by: Sony Pictures (DVD)

2+

DR. STRANGELOVE

OR HOW I LEARNED TO STOP WORRYING AND LOVE THE BOMB

1964, 92 mins.

Plot: Brigadier General Jack D. Ripper is having some problems performing sexually. Being a military man and an ardent anti-Communist, he blames his dysfunction on the Soviets and their alleged conspiracy to sap America's virility by fluoridating its water. Seriously. Ripper's answer to this problem is to order B-52s to enter Soviet airspace and drop their nuclear payloads unprovoked, though he tells his subordinates at Burpelson Air Base that the Soviets have already attacked the U.S. The President discovers the ruse and calls the Soviets to help shoot down the B-52s, but the Soviets have already activated the Doomsday device, which will annihilate all life on Earth in the event of a nuclear strike against Russia. Eventually all the planes are either shot down or recalled, except for one . . .

Review: "If you don't get the President of the United States on that phone, you know what's gonna happen to you? You're gonna have to answer to the Coca-Cola company." It seems that the comedies with the most devoted cult followings have memorable and, more importantly, quotable lines—whether or not they make sense out of context. Predictably, *Dr. Strangelove* suffers from no shortage of great dialog, which in this case is generally uttered alongside random moments of slapstick brilliance.

One might have thought that a comedy about nuclear weapons in the hands of trigger-happy idiots released less than two years after the Cuban Missile Crisis, two months after the Kennedy assassination, and at the height of the Cold War would fall flat, but one would be underestimating Kubrick's genius as a filmmaker. Nominated for four Academy Awards—including Best Picture, Best Director, and Best Actor for Peter Sellers' three brilliant performances—*Dr. Strangelove* deftly channels the absurd as a satirical weapon, which here proves almost as devastating as the titular bomb.

FURTHER VIEWING: *Full Metal Jacket; Paths of Glory*
SEE ALSO: *M*A*S*H; Canadian Bacon*

★
★
★
★

Director: Michael Lehmann
Screenwriter: Daniel Waters
Produced by: Denise Di Novi

Starring: Winona Ryder
and Christian Slater
Released by: Anchor Bay (DVD)

18+

HEATHERS

1989, 103 mins.

Plot: Veronica Sawyer joins the most elite clique in her high school, the Heathers, which is made up of wealthy, popular girls all with the same first name. Veronica is torn between the need to be popular and her dislike of her so-called friends' cruelty and shallowness, so when rebel loner J.D. joins the school she is instantly attracted. Inevitably the Heathers turn cruel, and in a bid for revenge Veronica tries to feed a hungover Heather milk and orange juice to make her vomit, but J.D. slips in drain cleaner instead and Heather dies. The two cover it up as a suicide, and while Veronica wants to lay low, J.D. has developed a taste for killing popular kids. Veronica ultimately denounces J.D.'s murderous antics and manages to prevent him from blowing up the school, but not himself.

Review: *Heathers* is the darkest of black teen comedies—there's no Hughes-esque redemption, no "we're all the same even though I'm popular and you're not!" moral to the story. The popular kids are cruel, the unpopular kids become cruel to be popular, and the loners just want revenge on their tormentors. As such, this is probably the perfect representation of the outsider's view of the high-school experience—that is, they can't wait to leave and they wish they could blow it up before graduation.

Christian Slater's acting may be more of a subpar Jack Nicholson impression from the bargain bin than a solid performance, but Winona Ryder flexes the sweet naïveté that made her famous, and the film itself vicariously satisfies every disillusioned, abused high-school student's revenge fantasy . . . and then some. This is exactly the film you need to watch the next time you get contacted to hang balloons for another high-school reunion when you'd really just prefer to stab yourself in the eye with a hot poker.

FURTHER VIEWING: ***Meet the Applegates; Hudson Hawk; Airheads***
SEE ALSO: ***Jawbreaker; Welcome to the Dollhouse; Mean Girls; The Last Supper***

Director: Robert Hamer
Screenwriters: Robert Hamer and John Dighton

Produced by: Michael Balcon and Michael Relph

Starring: Dennis Price, Alec Guinness, and Valerie Hobson
Released by: Criterion (DVD)

2+

KIND HEARTS AND CORONETS

1949, 106 mins.

Plot: In Edwardian England we begin with an age-old aristocratic romance, wherein the young heiress elopes with an Italian opera singer, eschewing her family's wishes to pursue a love match; she is, of course, disowned by the family. *Kind Hearts* takes this fairy-tale premise and turns it on its head when our heiress' son, Louis Mazzini, enraged that his rich relatives won't bury his mother in the family crypt, decides to succeed to the dukedom by knocking off the eight family members who stand to inherit before him. Louis manages to murder six without reprise—the other two die of happy coincidence and he becomes the Duke of Chalfont. But trouble with a mistress sees Louis convicted for a murder he didn't commit, and he tells his story while awaiting execution.

Review: Considered one of the best British films of all time, *Kind Hearts and Coronets* practically wrote the book on black comedy. This is the quintessential Ealing Studios comedy, and considering this is the studio that also brought out *The Lavender Hill Mob* and *The Ladykillers*, that is high praise indeed. Along with *Dead of Night*, this is the second Ealing picture you'll find in our Top Ten lists, and it's no coincidence: Ealing has left a legacy of imaginative, relatively low-budget but very well-constructed films that prize story and character over fads and glitz—the very ingredients in the recipe for longevity. (Director Robert Hamer also contributed a segment for *Dead of Night*.)

Special mention must be made of Alec Guinness, who plays no fewer than eight—eight!—roles, appearing as all of Louis' relatives, including a hilarious turn as *Lady* Agatha. Well before he became internationally famous for his role as Obi-Wan, Guinness made a solid name for himself as a brilliant comedic actor—mostly with Ealing—whose oeuvre holds up well against even the visionary Peter Sellers. Nowhere is this better demonstrated than in *Kind Hearts*; for that reason alone this is essential viewing.

FURTHER VIEWING: *School for Scoundrels; Dead of Night*
SEE ALSO: *The Lavender Hill Mob; The Ladykillers; Murder by Death*

★★★★★

Director: Jim Sharman
Screenwriters: Richard O'Brien and Jim Sharman

Produced by: Lou Adler and Michael White
Starring: Tim Curry, Susan Sarandon, and Barry Bostwick

Released by: Twentieth Century Fox Film Corporation (DVD)

18+

THE ROCKY HORROR PICTURE SHOW

1975, 100 mins.

Plot: Young, straight, and square couple Brad Majors and Janet Weiss are newly engaged and on the road on a dark and stormy night when a tire blows. Venturing out in search of a phone, the two happen upon a suspiciously gothic castle. Igor-like butler Riff-Raff answers the door, and the couple are treated to the spectacle of the Annual Transylvanian Convention, presided over by Dr. Frank. N. Furter, a "sweet transvestite from Transsexual, Transylvania." Frank has created the golden toy-boy Rocky Horror in his lab, but when delivery boy Eddie shows up Frank kills him out of jealousy and sends Brad and Janet to bed. After a night of carnal awakenings, Frank forces Brad and Janet to perform for his pleasure, but Riff-Raff and his sister Magenta have had enough of Frank's antics, staging a mutiny with a view to returning to their home planet.

Review: Essentially a camp send-up of horror and sci-fi B-movies, *The Rocky Horror Picture Show* bombed at the box office before its incredibly successful run on the midnight movie circuit. So successful, in fact, that it has been on limited release for almost four decades straight and is considered the longest-running release in film history.

Viewers who see this film on DVD—or, heaven forefend, television—are only experiencing the shallow end of this spectacle; for the real action, *Rocky Horror* must be seen, and participated in, at one of the late-night showings that still happen regularly around the country. Theater-goers dress in outlandish costumes matching the characters on-screen, throw props, shout rehearsed lines, and often have a small cast reenacting the scenes as they're projected. Of all the films in this book, *Rocky Horror* is truly the gold-standard of cult with a devoted following spanning generations.

FURTHER VIEWING: ***Shock Treatment; Richard O'Brien's Rocky Horror Tribute Show; A Regular Frankie Fan***
SEE ALSO: ***Little Shop of Horrors; Hairspray; Cry-Baby***

★★★★★

Director: Rob Reiner
Screenwriters: Christopher Guest, Michael McKean, and Harry Shearer, and Rob Reiner

Produced by: Karen Murphy
Starring: Christopher Guest, Michael McKean, and Harry Shearer
Released by: MGM (DVD)

15+

THIS IS SPINAL TAP

1984, 82 mins.

Plot: British heavy metal band Spinal Tap hasn't had a hit in years, and they're embarking on an American tour in support of their new album *Smell the Glove*. Filmmaker Marty DiBergi documents the trials and travails of the trio during the tour, beginning with a disagreement with their label over the "sexist" artwork for the album. Further tour difficulties include repeated show cancellations, props that make midgets looks like giants, and a girlfriend who tries to take over the band.

Review: "Certainly, in the topsy-turvy world of heavy rock, having a good solid piece of wood in your hand is often useful." And when making a backstage mockumentary of heavy rock, it's equally useful to have a good solid ensemble cast with exceptional improvisational skills. *This Is Spinal Tap* is the first (and best) mockumentary from the team that later brought us *Best in Show* and *A Mighty Wind*.

As you would expect from a comedy following a band of idiots on the downward spiral, this film is incredibly funny; its largely ad-libbed dialog is both ridiculous and natural to the point of cringing believability. But, more notably, the surreal situations the band find themselves in—such as getting lost on the way to the stage *while in the building*, playing second fiddle to a puppet show, and abruptly changing musical styles on-stage when the guitarist quits in the middle of a show—have left a host of real-life rock musicians crying in their beers, incredulous at the sheer realism of the insanity surrounding, and within, the band. The music in the film, all written by the actors and Reiner, is actually pretty damn good, despite the intentionally silly lyrics that have only furthered the film's popularity. *This Is Spinal Tap* is essential comedy viewing with the caveat that if you're in a band, you might just find it depressing.

FURTHER VIEWING: *Waiting for Guffman; Best in Show; A Mighty Wind; The Return of Spinal Tap*
SEE ALSO: *The Decline of Western Civilization 2: The Metal Years; The Rutles: All You Need Is Cash; The Last Polka*

★★★★★

Director: Bruce Robinson
Screenwriter: Bruce Robinson

Produced by: Paul Heller, George Harrison, and Denis O'Brien

Starring: Paul McGann and Richard E. Grant
Released by: Criterion (DVD)

18+

WITHNAIL AND I

1986, 107 mins.

Plot: Withnail and "I" (aka Marwood) are struggling actors living the chemical dream in London in 1969. Withnail comes from money but rails at the unfairness of society for his lack of personal prosperity, while Marwood is impressionable and goes along with Withnail's schemes. Feeling burnt out and strapped for cash, the two friends decide to visit Withnail's uncle Monty at his crumbling cottage in the country. The stresses of rural living and its surly locals—along with Monty's desire for a sexual relationship with Marwood, whom Monty believes is homosexual from Withnail's insinuations—puts strain on the two friends and their relationship. Soon the pair return to London and Marwood, having got a lead theatre role, leaves Withnail to begin a new life, alone.

Review: Adapted by Bruce Robinson from his own novel, *Withnail and I* is an autobiographical retelling of Robinson's days as a young actor in London when he shared a flat with actor Vivian MacKerrell (assumed to be the basis for Withnail). The film has become one of the most quotable in cult history, with cracking surreal lines of hilarious dialog; its drunkenly incongruous situations are endlessly entertaining, and its Ralph Steadman-drawn publicity materials are some of the most recognizable, and memorable, in the industry.

But the real draw of this film is the relationship between Withnail and Marwood, and its gradual breakdown owing to Withnail's narcissism and arrogance. Withnail is a fascinating character; he has a privileged background, but he almost refuses to allow himself success, constantly ruining his work and relationships with his machinations and never admitting those failures are anything other than the fault of others. Marwood, as narrator, initially believes Withnail's tales of woe, but his hero-worship wanes as he falls victim to Withnail's selfishness. Despite this, Richard E. Grant manages to inject plenty of likeability into Withnail—small wonder, then, that this is the role that launched Grant's acting career.

FURTHER VIEWING: ***How to Get Ahead in Advertising***
SEE ALSO: ***Fear and Loathing in Las Vegas; Life Is Sweet; Going Places***

★★★★

Director: Mel Brooks
Screenwriters: Gene Wilder and Mel Brooks
Produced by: Michael Gruskoff
Starring: Gene Wilder, Peter Boyle, Marty Feldman, and Madeline Kahn
Released by: Twentieth Century Fox (DVD)

A

YOUNG FRANKENSTEIN

1974, 106 mins.

Plot: *Young Frankenstein* is very loosely based on the Mary Shelley novel. Dr. Frederick Frankenstein is an American lecturer in medicine who inherits a Transylvanian estate from his mad-scientist grandfather. Frankenstein travels to Transylvania with his uptight but rich fiancée, and discovers his grandfather's secret lab. He becomes obsessed with replicating his grandfather's corpse-reanimating experiments, and secures the body of an executed criminal. But instead of getting a brilliant scientist's brain, Frankenstein uses an "abnormal" one, and his monster turns out to be a lumbering, music-loving idiot with an irrational fear of fire. When the monster escapes, the townspeople are angered by Frankenstein's unholy experiments, and he must capture and placate the monster before the townspeople destroy him.

Review: After he took on the western with *Blazing Saddles*, Mel Brooks made this reverent parody of the classic Universal horror films from the thirties and forties—he even insisted it be shot in black and white to echo the pre-Technicolor look, and most of the lab props are from Universal's 1931 film *Frankenstein*. So this is no mockery of the horror genre, but rather a cheeky love letter to a group of films that Brooks considers both influential and entertaining.

But is it funny? Five words: "Mel Brooks and Gene Wilder." Of course it is, but it's the kind of endearing, belly-laughing funny that only comes from affectionate ribbing and a cast that is clearly having more fun than should be allowed in the workplace. Wilder is suitably weasely as the ashamed social climber Frankenstein, Peter Boyle is awkward and sympathetic as his monster, and the rest of the supporting cast—including Marty Feldman, Teri Garr, Madeline Kahn, and a blink-and-you'll-miss-him appearance by Gene Hackman—is filled with enough comic geniuses to make this one of the funniest horror-inspired comedies of all time.

FURTHER VIEWING: *Blazing Saddles; Spaceballs; Dracula: Dead and Loving It*

SEE ALSO: *Fright Night; Transylvania 6-5000; Love at First Bite*

369
500

★★★

Director: Frank Zappa
Screenwriter: Frank Zappa
Produced by: Herb Cohen

Starring: The Mothers of Invention, Ringo Star, and Keith Moon
Released by: Not Available

18+

200 MOTELS

1971, 98 mins.

Plot: Ringo Star and Keith Moon appear alongside The Mothers of Invention in Frank Zappa's loose memoir of being in a rock band on the road, and how it drives you insane.

Review: Frank Zappa's first film is impossible to characterize, having practically no plot and being mainly a series of colorful surrealist imagery, musical numbers, and bizarre animated sequences. At the time, he expected it to receive the worst reviews for any film ever made, but was confident that his fans would rush out to see it on those grounds. Its hard-to-find status now cements it as one of the key cult movies of the seventies—and on a scale of ten for demented viewing, it quite easily clocks in at eleven.

FURTHER VIEWING: ***The Dub Room Special; Baby Snakes***
SEE ALSO: ***Magical Mystery Tour; Lisztomania***

370
500

★★★

Director: Michael Winterbottom
Screenwriter: Frank Cottrell Boyce
Produced by: Andrew Eaton

Starring: Steve Coogan, John Thomson, and Nigel Pivaro
Released by: MGM (DVD)

18+

24 HOUR PARTY PEOPLE

2000, 115 mins.

Plot: British comedian Steve Coogan plays Factory Records founder Tony Wilson in an astonishing dramatization of the rise and fall of the Manchester music scene. It covers a twenty-year period beginning with the signing of iconic band Joy Division and the successes of Factory artists New Order and the Happy Mondays, to the closure of Wilson's club, the Hacienda.

Review: Covering the same period as Anton Corbijn's *Control*, Winterbottom's docudrama is not as depressing as the latter, treating his characters with reverence and never losing sight of what made this period of British music unique—the ambitions of one man who didn't take it too seriously, even in its darkest moments. Worth watching for Coogan and Danny Cunningham's Shaun Ryder alone.

FURTHER VIEWING: ***9 Songs; I Want You***
SEE ALSO: ***Control; Velvet Goldmine***

371

★★★★

Director: Stephan Elliot
Screenwriter: Stephan Elliot

Produced by: Al Clark and Michael Hamlyn

Starring: Hugo Weaving, Guy Pearce, and Terence Stamp
Released by: MGM (DVD)

15+

THE ADVENTURES OF PRISCILLA, QUEEN OF THE DESERT

1994, 104 mins.

Plot: Three drag queens—played by Terrance Stamp, Guy Pearce, and Hugo Weaving—travel from Sydney to the Middle of Nowhere, Australia, to perform at a remote hotel. During the long trip through the Outback, they encounter Aboriginal tribes, hatred and homophobia, and one queen's estranged wife, but never lose their senses of humor, close friendship, or joie de vivre.

Review: Everything about *Priscilla* is so joyous and funny it's impossible to resist. From its bright colors to its quick wit, this is one of those rare comedies that can brighten your whole day, if not your outlook on life. But beware: Terrance Stamp makes one ugly woman. You've been warned.

FURTHER VIEWING: *Frauds; Welcome to Woop Woop*
SEE ALSO: *To Wong Foo, Thanks for Everything! Julie Newmar; The Birdcage*

372

★★★★★

Director: Frank Capra
Screenwriters: Julius J. Epstein and Philip G. Epstein

Produced by: Frank Capra and Jack L. Warner

Starring: Cary Grant, Priscilla Lane, and Raymond Massey
Released by: Turner Home Entertainment (DVD)

12+

ARSENIC AND OLD LACE

1944, 118mins.

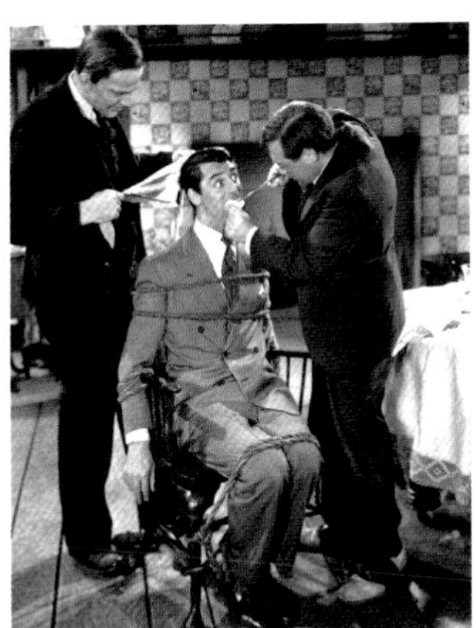

Plot: Former bachelor and drama-critic Mortimer Brewster visits his childhood home just after marrying. When Brewster finds a corpse hidden in the window seat, he immediately suspects his lunatic brother, but his two elderly aunts reveal they've been killing old bachelors for years as an act of mercy. To complicate things, Brewster's other brother, an unhinged gangster, shows up to throw his own colorful characters into the mix, and Brewster is driven to the brink in trying to conceal all from his new wife.

Review: This is a classic, fast-paced black comedy that manages to break the confines of the original stage production. Beyond the fantastic ensemble cast, Cary Grant proves himself a formidable comedic talent as the put-upon lead, and the elderly aunts will have you wishing you could invite them to tea even as they're carted off to the asylum.

FURTHER VIEWING: *Here Comes the Groom; You Can't Take It with You*
SEE ALSO: *Kind Hearts and Coronets; The Ladykillers*

373/500

★★

Director: Nathan Juran
Screenwriter: Mark Hanna
Produced by: Bernard Woolner

Starring: Allison Hayes, William Hudson, and Yvette Vickers
Released by: Warner Home Video (DVD)

A

ATTACK OF THE 50 FT. WOMAN

1958, 66 mins.

Plot: Rich socialite Nancy Archer has a close encounter of the third kind. Being a woman in the fifties, as well as a recovering alcoholic, no one believes her. Her husband finally agrees to take her out into the desert, intending to prove her wrong; instead they find a spaceship, and he leaves Nancy to the mercies of the aliens. Nancy later pops up at home unconscious, but she's having a bit of a growth spurt, and while her husband is off with his mistress she grows fifty-feet tall. When she wakes, she goes on the rampage like the proverbial scorned woman.

Review: Often parodied in modern pop culture, *Attack* is truly ridiculous. Don't try to figure out whether it's feminist or not—it's the unintentional hilarity that makes this worth a watch.

FURTHER VIEWING: ***Attack of the 50 Ft. Woman (1993 remake); The 7th Voyage of Sinbad; The Brain from Planet Arous***
SEE ALSO: ***The Incredible Shrinking Woman; The Amazing Colossal Man***

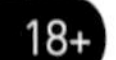

374/500

★★★

Director: Rolf de Heer
Screenwriter: Rolf de Heer
Produced by: Rolf de Heer

Starring: Nicholas Hope, Claire Benito, and Ralph Cotterill
Released by: Blue Underground (DVD)

18+

BAD BOY BUBBY

1993, 114 mins.

Plot: Thirty-five-year-old Bubby has spent his entire life living in a single room with his mother, who mentally and physically abuses him. Convinced that the outside is filled with poisonous gas and that the next life holds only pain for his sins, the arrival of his father throws his existence into turmoil when he is forced into the world to survive alone. What he discovers there is as alien to him as he is to society.

Review: De Heer's black comedy makes for uncomfortable viewing, yet Bubby's hilarious real-world encounters make for a sharp counterpoint. While experimental in places, the unusual sound and visual presentation help us to become immersed in Bubby's world, and the emotional ending will melt the iciest of hearts. Twisted brilliance.

FURTHER VIEWING: ***The Quiet Room; Dance Me to My Song***
SEE ALSO: ***Eraserhead; Lost in Translation***

★
★

Director: Woody Allen
Screenwriters: Woody Allen and Mickey Rose

Produced by: Axel Anderson, Antonio Encarnacion, Jack Grossberg, and Manolon Villamil

Starring: Woody Allen, Louise Lasser, and Carlos Montalbán
Released by: MGM/UA (DVD)

5+

BANANAS

1971, 82 mins.

Plot: Down-on-his-luck Fielding Mellish has an apparent change of fortune when he meets activist Nancy. However, when she dumps him, he takes a vacation to the turbulent South American state of San Marco—just in time for a revolution. Captured by rebels, he ends up the leader of the country, but then is tried in the U.S. as a subversive!

Review: An early shot from the canon of Woody Allen, this is a less sophisticated, more slapstick parody with Mellish as a prototype of his neurotic Jewish loser. However, it still touches on his fascinations with sex, psychology, and religion, and there are flashes of real comic genius (the court room scene in particular). Also, watch out for a bit part from a very young Sylvester Stallone.

FURTHER VIEWING: *What's Up, Tiger Lily?; Sleeper; Annie Hall; Manhattan; Zelig; Broadway Danny Rose*
SEE ALSO: *Blazing Saddles; Young Frankenstein*

★★★

Director: Richard Lester
Screenwriter: John Antrobus
Produced by: Richard Lester and Oscar Lewenstein

Starring: Rita Tushingham, Ralph Richardson, and Peter Cook

Released by: BFI Video (DVD, region 2 only)

12+

THE BED SITTING ROOM

1969, 90 mins.

Plot: A desolate, post-nuclear holocaust Britain, whose energy is supplied by one man on a bicycle dynamo, and the aristocracy fear mutating into rentable studio flats. Across the country, survivors do their best to rebuild Britain including a family forced to the blasted surface after they finish the last chocolate bar on the London Underground. Life goes on.

Review: A stellar cast of British comedic talent fire off a staccato clatter of gags clearly originating from the *Monty Python/Goon Show* school of surreal humor. With lots of Blitz spirit, social satire, and eccentric characters, this has apocalyptic shades of *Waiting for Godot*, the characters tragically comic while being very "British" and making the best it all.

FURTHER VIEWING: ***A Hard Day's Night; A Funny Thing Happened on the Way to the Forum; The Three Musketeers; Robin and Marian***
SEE ALSO: ***Dr. Strangelove Or: How I Stopped Worrying and Learned to Love the Bomb; The Charge of the Light Brigade; Oh What a Lovely War***

77

★★★★

Director: Christopher Guest
Screenwriters: Christopher Guest and Eugene Levy
Produced by: Gordon Marj and Karen Murphy
Starring: Jay Brazeau, Parker Posey, and Michael Hitchcock
Released by: Warner Home Video (DVD)

12+

BEST IN SHOW

2000, 90 mins.

Plot: A mockumentary covering five entrants in the Mayflower Kennel Club Dog Show, from arrival to the show itself and the aftereffects.

Review: This is yet another satire from Christopher Guest (of *This Is Spinal Tap* and *A Mighty Wind*), focusing on a very small section of society who treat their pets like the most valued members of their families. Unlike most largely unscripted films that come across as nonsensical and flat, some of Hollywood's best improvisational talent appear here—including Guest himself, Eugene Levy, Michael McKean, and Catherine O'Hara—so the dialog always seems fresh, natural, and cringe-worthily honest. Fred Willard stands out (as always), but the ensemble cast make this a must-see comedy.

FURTHER VIEWING: *This Is Spinal Tap; A Mighty Wind; Waiting for Guffman*
SEE ALSO: *Drop Dead Gorgeous; The History of White People in America Vols. 1–3*

78

★★★

Director: Wes Anderson
Screenwriter: Wes Anderson
Produced by: Cynthia Hargrave
Starring: Luke Wilson, Owen Wilson, and Ned Dowd
Released by: Sony Pictures (DVD)

15+

BOTTLE ROCKET

1996, 91 mins.

Plot: Dignan is a man with a dream. He wants to be revered in the underworld and impress Mr. Henry, his potential future employer. His best friend Anthony on the other hand has just left a mental institution and couldn't care less. Hooking up their friend Bob, they launch into a bungling career as small-time robbers. But Dignan's plans get interrupted when Anthony falls for motel cleaner Inez, and Bob flies the coop.

Review: Ignored by audiences but loved by critics, *Bottle Rocket* launched the careers of the Wilson brothers and was Wes Anderson's directorial debut. Like much of Anderson's other work, low-key is the order of the day and dialog is king. Subtle in its humor, it rewards on repeat viewings.

FURTHER VIEWING: *Rushmore; The Royal Tenenbaums*
SEE ALSO: *Fargo; Stranger than Paradise*

379/500

★★★★

Director: Howard Hawks
Screenwriters: Dudley Nichols and Harag Wilde

Produced by: Howard Hawks and Cliff Reid

Starring: Katharine Hepburn, Cary Grant, and Charles Ruggles
Released by: Turner Home Entertainment (DVD)

A BRINGING UP BABY

1938, 102 mins.

Plot: Paleontologist David Huxley is a bit stressed out—not only is he getting married to possibly the most disapproving woman on Earth, he must also court the favor of a wealthy museum patron. Life doesn't get any easier when he meets free-spirited Susan, who falls in love with him and decides to waylay him at her house. But things get really complicated when Susan's pet leopard, Baby, runs away.

Review: Cary Grant has fantastic comedic timing, which is showcased in this role of the exasperated Huxley caught in a series of strange circumstances. Katherine Hepburn, as always, shines as the leopard-owning Susan, and she and Grant make an engagingly ridiculous couple in the midst of this light and successful screwball comedy.

FURTHER VIEWING: ***His Girl Friday; Only Angels Have Wings***
SEE ALSO: ***Who's that Girl?; What's Up Doc?***

380/500

★★★★

Director: Hal Needham
Screenwriter: Brock Yates
Produced by: Albert S. Ruddy

Starring: Burt Reynolds, Dom DeLuise, Roger Moore, and Farrah Fawcett
Released by: HBO Home Video (DVD)

THE CANNONBALL RUN

1981, 95 mins.

Plot: Washed-up race-car driver J. J. McClure and his sidekick Victor Prinzim (aka Captain Chaos) enter a cross-country, illegal car race using a suped-up ambulance. Hilarity ensues.

Review: Hilarity really does ensue in this film based on the real-life Cannonball Baker Sea-to-Shining-Sea Memorial Trophy Dash, run four times during the seventies and organized by the screenwriter. Apart from its lovable—and possibly schizophrenic—leads Burt Reynolds and Dom DeLuise, *Cannonball Run* has one of the largest casts of impressive cameo appearances ever assembled, including Dean Martin, Sammy Davis Jr., Jackie Chan, Roger Moore, and Terry Bradshaw. A truly bizarre and funny film. After you get your head around portly DeLuise in his shiny superhero costume, absolutely do not miss the outtakes at the end.

FURTHER VIEWING: ***Cannonball Run 2; Smokey and the Bandit; Smokey and the Bandit 2***
SEE ALSO: ***Bite the Bullet; The Gumball Rally; Cannonball!***

31

Director: Mike Nichols
Screenwriter: Jules Feiffer
Produced by: Mike Nichols

Starring: Jack Nicholson, Candice Bergen, and Art Garfunkel
Released by: MGM/UA (DVD)

3+ CARNAL KNOWLEDGE

1971, 98 mins.

Plot: The sexual/romantic/relationship history of two friends, one brash and passionate, the other cautious and self-deprecating, their travels beginning as they struggle to lose their virginity at college. They mature (or not, as the case may be) from puppy love through thrilling adventures, marriage, mid-life crises, impotence, and self-destruction.

Review: Constructed almost as a series of vignettes, Nichols uses the opposite personalities of the two leads to provide counterpoints, insights, and sometimes-vicious disagreements on love and desire. Sex is treated as some sort of self-assembly pack you build in stages, each female character used to highlight the various phases; from first loves when sex was almost mythological through wild, amorous encounters, to the turgid mendacity of marriages gone wrong.

FURTHER VIEWING: *Who's Afraid of Virginia Woolf?; Catch-22; Regarding Henry; The Birdcage; Charlie Wilson's War*
SEE ALSO: *In The Company of Men; Closer*

32

Director: Val Guest, Ken Hughes, John Huston, Jospeh McGrath, and Robert Parrish

Screenwriters: Wolf Mankowitz, John Law, and Michael Sayers
Produced by: Charles K. Feldman

Starring: David Niven, Peter Sellers, and Ursula Andress
Released by: MGM (DVD)

2+ CASINO ROYALE

1967, 131 mins.

Plot: An aging James Bond comes out of retirement to bring down the secret organization SMERSH, run by the evil and very short Dr. Noah. He plans to detonate a biological weapon that will kill all men over four and half feet tall, making him the tallest man on the planet. Spoiler alert! And then everyone blows up.

Review: This spoof is very loosely based on Ian Fleming's 007 novel. With so many directors, great talents though they may be, the film can seem chaotic and unfocused. But it manages to be much more due to its incredible ensemble cast: David Niven as Bond, Peter Sellers, Ursula Andress, Orson Welles, Woody Allen, Deborah Kerr, William Holden, John Huston (who also spent some time behind the camera), Ronnie Corbett, and more. Highly recommended for those uninterested in the franchise's current direction.

FURTHER VIEWING: *Where the Spies Are; Assignment K*
SEE ALSO: *Top Secret!; Austin Powers: International Man of Mystery; Spy Hard*

383
500

★★★

Director: Kevin Smith
Screenwriter: Kevin Smith
Produced by: Scott Mosier and Kevin Smith

Starring: Brian O'Halloran, Jeff Anderson, and Marilyn Ghigliotti
Released by: Miramax (DVD)

18+

CLERKS

1994, 92 mins.

Plot: Dante Hicks is a clerk at a Quick Stop convenience store in New Jersey, where he and his best friend Randall talk about life, love, and the Death Star while the store is frequented by a collection of oddball characters.

Review: The film that launched Kevin Smith's career went at least as far to define Generation X as *Reality Bites* or any other nineties slacker movie. Though the constant cleverer-than-thou but ultimately pointless repartee between Dante and Randall can be grating, the minor characters, particularly Jay and Silent Bob (played by Smith), keep the pace going. Critically acclaimed and a true independent cult classic in every sense.

FURTHER VIEWING: ***Clerks 2; Jay and Silent Bob Strike Back; Mallrats; Dogma***
SEE ALSO: ***High Fidelity; Reality Bites; Slacker***

384
500

★★★

Director: Sam Raimi
Screenwriters: Ethan Coen, Joel Coen, and Sam Raimi

Produced by: Edward R. Pressman and Irvin Shapiro

Starring: Louise Lasser, Paul L. Smith, and Brion James
Released by: StudioCanal (DVD, region 2 only)

CRIMEWAVE

1985, 83 mins.

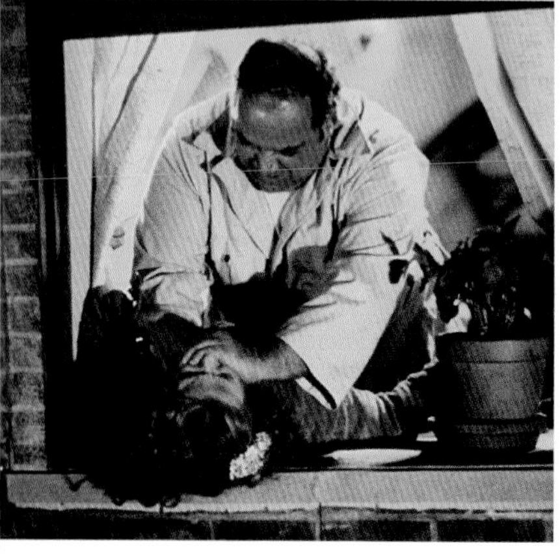

Plot: Mr. Trend, co-owner of Trend-Odegard Security, finds out that his partner is going to sell the company, so he hires a couple of exterminators to dispense with Mr. Odegard. But employee Vic finds out about the plan; while Mr. Trend distracts him, the exterminators perpetrate a series of slapstick murders that are then pinned on the hapless Vic.

Review: After the success of *Evil Dead*, Sam Raimi got back to his slapstick roots and made this crime/comedy film. Joel Coen had been an assistant editor on *Evil Dead*, and, with his brother Ethan, *Crimewave* marks their first proper collaboration with Raimi (the team would later make *The Hudsucker Proxy* together). Clearly influenced by the Three Stooges, this isn't for everyone, but if you think you might enjoy seeing kids thrown out of elevators and dead bodies stuffed into the Salvation Army donation box, it's definitely worth a view.

FURTHER VIEWING: ***The Hudsucker Proxy; Raising Arizona***
SEE ALSO: ***The Devil and Miss Jones; Johnny Dangerously***

★★★

Director: Roman Polanski
Screenwriters: Gérard Brach and Roman Polanski

Produced by: Gene Gutowski, Michael Klinger, and Tony Tenser

Starring: Donald Pleasence, Françoise Dorléac, and Lionel Stander
Released by: Not Available

5+ CUL-DE-SAC

1966, 113 mins.

Plot: While on the run though northern England, two wounded gangsters stumble across an isolated castle. Its only inhabitants are a mismatched married couple, he effete and eccentric, she amorous and willful. So begins a bizarre and blackly comic stand-off, the upper hand shifting back and forth between hostage and hostage-taker.

Review: Though the vistas are austere and ageless, it's the sharp script and witty collection of characters that give this movie its real charm. There's a gangster straight out of a Jimmy Cagney flick, an aristocratic English eccentric, and a fiery French New Wave vixen, the three making for a brisk culture clash that veers between Stockholm syndrome and outright resistance.

FURTHER VIEWING: *Repulsion; Chinatown; Tess; Bitter Moon; Death and the Maiden*
SEE ALSO: *Knife in the Water; The Ref; Splinter*

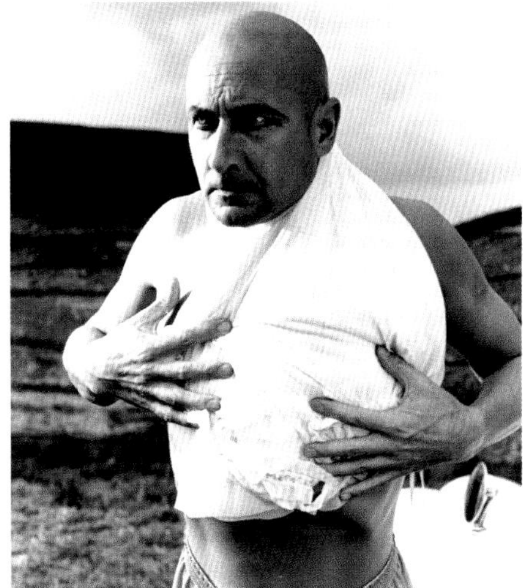

386/500

Director: John Carpenter
Screenwriters: Dan O'Bannon and John Carpenter
Produced by: John Carpenter, J. Stein Kaplan, and Jack H. Harris
Starring: Brian Narelle, Cal Kuniholm, and Dre Pahich
Released by: VCI Entertainment (DVD)

12+

DARK STAR

1974, 83 mins.

Plot: The crew of the spaceship *Dark Star* have been isolated in space for twenty years; their mission is to destroy unstable planets that may interfere with human colonization. But all those years in space have taken their toll, and the crew is close to psychosis. When one of the "smart bombs" threatens to detonate on the ship, the crew engages in a philosophical discussion with it to get it to stand down. Does it work? Yes . . . for a while.

Review: A completely absurd, low-budget sci-fi film, packed with ideas on philosophy and psychology, but the humor makes the film's high-brow ruminations both entertaining and easy to swallow.

FURTHER VIEWING: ***Memoirs of an Invisible Man; Big Trouble in Little China***
SEE ALSO: ***Spaceballs; The Hitchhiker's Guide to the Galaxy***

387/500

Director: Jim Jarmusch
Screenwriter: Jim Jarmusch
Produced by: Alan Kleinberg
Starring: Tom Waits, John Lurie, and Roberto Benigni
Released by: Criterion (DVD)

15+

DOWN BY LAW

1986, 107 mins.

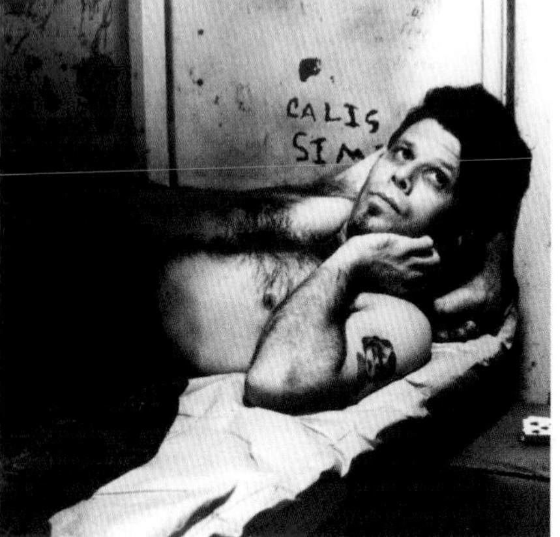

Plot: Through bad luck and corrupt cops, a lowlife DJ and a high-end pimp end up sharing a prison cell. Joined by an eccentric, ebullient Italian cardshark, they pass the time driving each other nuts and slowly beginning to at least tolerate each other. After escaping from jail, they embark on a shambling flight through the Louisiana bayous.

Review: This is essentially a film that goes nowhere, much like its characters, but that's not the point. What starts out as a long, languid insight into prison life shifts into a low-gear road movie on foot, yet there's no thrills or chases, no sentimental friendships or lasting bonds. It's more like taking a journey with three funny but annoying cousins you just can't help but like.

FURTHER VIEWING: ***Stranger than Paradise; Mystery Train; Night on Earth; Dead Man***
SEE ALSO: ***Paradise Alley; Rumble Fish; Ironweed; Short Cuts; Cool Hand Luke; The Shawshank Redemption***

188

★★★★

Director: Alexander Payne
Screenwriters: Alexander Payne and Jim Taylor

Produced by: Albert Berger, David Gale, Keith Samples, and Ron Yerxa

Starring: Matthew Broderick, Reese Witherspoon, and Chris Klein
Released by: Paramount (DVD)

15+

ELECTION

1999, 102 mins.

Plot: Set in a suburban high school, *Election* chronicles a student council election that's taken just a little too seriously by one of its alpha-female participants, Tracy Flick. Teacher Jim McAllister has obsessions of his own, and when Tracy is nominated for class president, he goes far beyond the call of moral duty to thwart her ambitions as his personal life crumbles around him.

Review: As Tracy Flick, Reese Witherspoon makes you want to punch her in the face repeatedly, but only because she plays the irritating, self-obsessed, conniving character so well. The film is an exaggerated but truthful comment on high-school politics and prejudices, and thankfully delivers enough laughs to soften the blow when the best man loses.

FURTHER VIEWING: *About Schmidt; Sideways*
SEE ALSO: *To Die For; Saved!; Rushmore*

189

★★★

Director: Burt Reynolds
Screenwriter: Jerry Belson
Produced by: Lawrence Gordon

Starring: Burt Reynolds, Dom DeLuise, and Sally Field
Released by: MGM Home Entertainment

8+

THE END

1978, 100 mins.

Plot: Wendell Lawson discovers he has a rare disease that will kill him in six months. With little to live for, he decides to speed the process up and takes an overdose, but wakes up instead in a mental institution. He befriends one of the inmates and the two invent ways Wendell can kill himself, but after one unsuccessful attempt, he decides he doesn't want to die. The inmate, however, has other ideas.

Review: There's slapstick gallows humor galore in a movie that shouldn't be funny in the slightest, considering the subject matter. Reynolds is great at both the directing and acting, but it's his regular high-jinks collaborator, Dom DeLuise, who, firing on all comedic thrusters, runs away with this film, getting all the best lines for his enthusiastic, loveable lunatic.

FURTHER VIEWING: *The Cannonball Run; Smokey and the Bandit II; Sharkey's Machine*
SEE ALSO: *Heaven Can Wait; It's a Wonderful Life; A Matter of Life and Death*

390/500

★★★

Director: Amy Heckerling
Screenwriter: Cameron Crowe

Produced by: Art Linson, C. O. Erickson, and Irving Azoff

Starring: Sean Penn, Jennifer Jason Leigh, and Judge Reinhold
Released by: Universal Studios (DVD)

18+

FAST TIMES AT RIDGEMONT HIGH

1982, 90 mins.

Plot: High school freshman Stacy Hamilton feels she's wordly enough to engage in casual sexual relationships, but soon realizes she was wrong when she gets pregnant from a one-night stand (or in this case, a one-poolhouse stand). She has an abortion, and then settles down with the shy and nerdy guy with no sexual strings attached.

Review: Critically panned on its release, *Fast Times at Ridgemont High* struck a chord with America's youth at the time and is now often praised for its honesty in dealing with sensitive and difficult teenage issues. Possibly the most memorable aspect of this film, however, is Sean Penn's performance as surfing stoner Jeff Spicoli, who stands head and shoulders above an all pre-stardom cast including Jennifer Jason Leigh, Nicholas Cage, Anthony Edwards, and Forest Whitaker.

FURTHER VIEWING: ***Almost Famous; Loser***
SEE ALSO: ***Summer School; American Graffiti; The Breakfast Club***

391/500

★★★

Director: Roman Polanski
Screenwriters: Roman Polanski and Gérard Brach
Produced by: Gene Gutowski

Starring: Jack MacGowran, Alfie Bass, Sharon Tate, and Ferdy Mayne
Released by: Warner Home Video (DVD)

THE FEARLESS VAMPIRE KILLERS

OR PARDON ME BUT YOUR TEETH ARE IN MY NECK

1967, 108 mins.

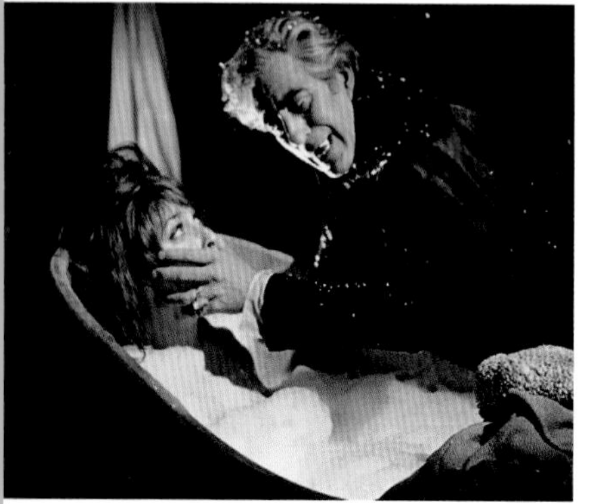

Plot: In Transylvania, Professor Abronsius and his dimwitted assistant Alfred are on the hunt for vampires. Being Transylvania, they don't have to search for long. They accept mysterious Count von Krolock's invitation to stay in his crumbling, gothic castle, and try to both kill the Count and save the damsel.

Review: "Two men on a vampire hunt. Simple? They certainly are." Before Roman Polanski proved that he could make a pitch-perfect, creepy horror film with *Rosemary's Baby*, he made this excellent horror comedy that's not above slapstick or base humor to get a laugh. A great parody.

FURTHER VIEWING: ***Rosemary's Baby; The Ninth Gate***
SEE ALSO: ***Young Frankenstein; Dracula: Dead and Loving It; Transylvania Twist***

92

★★★★★

Director: John Hughes
Screenwriter: John Hughes

Produced by: John Hughes, Jane Vickerilla, Michael Chinich, and Tom Jacobson

Starring: Matthew Broderick, Alan Ruck, and Mia Sara
Released by: Paramount (DVD)

FERRIS BUELLER'S DAY OFF

1986, 103 mins.

Plot: It's a lovely day and too-cool-for-school Ferris Bueller doesn't want to waste it learning his equations and eating cafeteria pizza. He concocts an elaborate facade of illness and half-kidnaps his girlfriend Sloane Petersen and his hypochondriac friend Cameron Frye to spend a madcap day in Chicago, all the while trying to avoid his paranoid school principal and his vindictive sister.

Review: One of the seminal eighties teen films, but with a lighter tone than John Hughes' many other contributions to the category. Matthew Broderick as Ferris is so effortlessly cool it should be annoying, but we love him just as much as the film's besotted characters. This is really nothing beyond breezy wish fulfillment for down-trodden high schoolers, but it's so entertaining it doesn't need to be more than it is.

FURTHER VIEWING: ***Weird Science; The Breakfast Club; Sixteen Candles; Pretty in Pink***
SEE ALSO: ***Better Off Dead; Real Genius***

93

★★★★

Director: Michael Ritchie
Screenwriter: Andrew Bergman

Produced by: Peter Douglas and Alan Greisman

Starring: Chevy Chase, Joe Don Baker, and Dana Wheeler-Nicholson
Released by: Universal Pictures (DVD)

FLETCH

1985, 98 mins.

Plot: Based on a series of novels by Gregory Mcdonald, Chevy Chase plays investigative journalist Irwin M. Fletcher ("Fletch") whose methods can only be described as unorthodox. Dressed as a beach bum during an investigation, Fletch is accosted by a wealthy man who asks Fletch to kill him. Fletch is understandably suspicious and probes the man's life, using a series of increasingly flamboyant personas, and discovers the Los Angeles drug traffic stems from high up in the police force.

Review: There's no need to worry: *Fletch* was made back in the "Chevy Chase is still funny" era. Both witty and introspective, Chase plays the deadpan funnyman to everyone else's straight-man characters to incongruous and captivating effect. The sequel is just as good, if not better.

FURTHER VIEWING: ***Fletch Lives***
SEE ALSO: ***Spies Like Us; Foul Play; The Man with One Red Shoe***

★★★★

Director: F. Gary Gray
Screenwriters: Ice Cube and DJ Pooh
Produced by: Not Available
Starring: Ice Cube, Chris Tucker, and Nia Long
Released by: New Line Home Video (DVD)

18+

FRIDAY

1995, 91 mins.

Plot: Craig has just lost his job and his parents are threatening to kick him out of the house, while his friend Smokey has smoked all his consignment of weed and now owes his dealer money he doesn't have. As Craig attempts to sort out his life and Smokey tries to get the money to pay his debt, the two encounter a range of oddball characters during just another Friday in L.A.

Review: *Friday* is a quiet but seriously funny little film about the trials and tribulations of living in the hood. This is comedian Chris Tucker's second film appearance, but his first starring role, and this is where he honed the high-pitched, frantic persona that would later make him one of Hollywood's highest paid stars. As you'd expect from a film with Ice Cube, the soundtrack is worth a listen even if you don't see the film (which would be a crying shame).

FURTHER VIEWING: ***Next Friday; Friday after Next***
SEE ALSO: ***Clerks; Car Wash; House Party; Half Baked***

95

★★★★

Director: Tom Holland
Screenwriter: Tom Holland
Produced by: Herb Jaffe and Jerry A. Baerwitz
Starring: Chris Sarandon, William Ragsdale, Amanda Bearse, and Roddy McDowall
Released by: Sony Pictures (DVD)

5+

FRIGHT NIGHT

1985, 106 mins.

Plot: Teen Charlie Webster loves horror films but finds himself unprepared when he suspects a vampire, Jerry Dandridge, has moved next door to the suburban house he shares with his single mother. Neither his best friend nor his girlfriend believe him, so he recruits a late-night horror show host to help fight his fanged neighbor. After a chance encounter with a mirror reveals Dandridge casts no reflection, Dandridge sets out to exterminate all the witnesses, and Charlie must save his friends, his mom, and himself from certain undeath.

Review: Tom Holland terrified a generation with a creepy doll in *Child's Play*, but first he filmed a comedy love letter to the horror genre in the form of *Fright Night*. Like its vampiric offspring *The Lost Boys*, this is one of those pitch-perfect eighties horror comedies that simply astounds with its watchability and entertainment value.

FURTHER VIEWING: *Fright Night 2; Child's Play*
SEE ALSO: *The Lost Boys; The Monster Squad*

196

★★★★

Director: Ralph Bakshi
Screenwriter: Ralph Bakshi
Produced by: Steve Krantz
Starring: Skip Hinnant and Rosetta LeNoire
Released by: MGM (DVD)

8+

FRITZ THE CAT

1972, 78 mins.

Plot: Fritz is a hippie cat out for whatever he can get in this psychedelic sex comedy, be it loose women, weed, cash . . . you name it. Coming into frequent conflict with the pigs (the establishment) and the crows (the African-American community), he stumbles blindly into situations that are all too often not his to control. Finally, he decides to call for revolution.

Review: Based on the Robert Crumb comic strip of the same name, Bakshi's first film's distinctive look is down to the shaky hand inking, lending it a rough and appealing aesthetic. Considerably less abrasive than its (rather sexual) source material, its condemnation of racial stereotypes and backlash against the "positivity" of the sixties was ahead of its time.

FURTHER VIEWING: *Coonskin; Heavy Traffic*
SEE ALSO: *Crumb; The Nine Lives of Fritz the Cat*

397/500

★★

Director: Jack Nicholson
Screenwriters: John Herman Shaner, Al Ramrus, Charles Shyer, and Alan Mandel
Produced by: Harry Gittes and Harold Schneider
Starring: Jack Nicholson, Mary Steenburgen, and Christopher Lloyd
Released by: Paramount (DVD)

GOIN' SOUTH

1978, 105 mins.

Plot: "The only reason I turned to crime is there wasn't no jobs!" Ex-confederate soldier Henry Lloyd Moon is a small-time Old West criminal set to hang. But there's a loophole in the law; if a woman agrees to marry a condemned man and set him on the path to good behavior, he'll be spared the gallows. Julia Tate offers to marry Moon at the last moment and the relationship of convenience evolves into mutual love.

Review: This is Jack Nicholson's third directing effort (but only his second solo outing), and it must be said that it's not a particularly good film, despite a few very funny moments. However, it's a marvel to see so much comedic talent—including Christopher Lloyd, John Belushi (in his first film role), Danny DeVito, and Ed Begley Jr.—exercise their celluloid muscles at early stages in their careers.

FURTHER VIEWING: ***Head; The Terror; Drive, He Said***
SEE ALSO: ***Cat Ballou; City Slickers; Maverick***

398/500

★★★★

Director: Todd Solondz
Screenwriter: Todd Solondz
Produced by: Ted Hope
Starring: Jane Adams, Lara Flynn Boyle, and Philip Seymour Hoffman
Released by: Lionsgate (DVD)

HAPPINESS

1998, 134 mins.

Plot: Three sisters, their families, and their neighbors make up the characters in Solondz's controversial social satire about regular people looking for life's elusive happiness. Multiple stories weave together to form a caustic whole, including a pedophile doctor who takes interest in his son's friend, a loner who makes obscene phone calls to his neighbor, and a songwriter who just wants to be loved.

Review: In this blackest of ensemble pieces featuring Philip Seymour Hoffman and Lara Flynn Boyle, the loneliness and isolation of suburban America is put under the microscope, revealing a repugnant, unfathomable mess. While pessimistic, the underlying hopes of the characters do come to fruition, if briefly. Be prepared to be shocked into uncomfortable laughter.

FURTHER VIEWING: ***Welcome to the Dollhouse; Life During Wartime***
SEE ALSO: ***Short Cuts; Your Friends and Neighbors***

★★★★

Director: Martin McDonagh
Screenwriter: Martin McDonagh

Produced by: Graham Broadbent and Peter Czernin

Starring: Colin Farrell, Brendan Gleeson, and Ralph Fiennes
Released by: Universal Studios (DVD)

8+

IN BRUGES

2008, 107 mins.

Plot: After a murder gone horribly wrong, hitmen Ray and Ken are ordered by their boss to leave London and keep a low profile in Bruges. But for a couple of killers for hire, a hotel room in the middle of Belgium proves to be too boring, and while out getting to know the lay of the land, Ray and Ken miss their boss' phone calls. Their boss gets twitchy (more so than he already is) and travels to Bruges himself to dispose of his wayward employees.

Review: This is playwright Martin McDonagh's first feature-length film (his previous short, *Six Shooter*, won an Oscar for Best Short Film, Live Action), and it's a fine calling card. Darkly comic and sprinkled with witty dialog as exciting as the action scenes, *In Bruges* is an unusual but hilarious comedy well worth seeing.

FURTHER VIEWING: *Six Shooter (short)*
SEE ALSO: *Midnight Run; The Merry Gentleman*

400/500

★★★★

Director: Bigas Luna
Screenwriters: Cuca Canals and Bigas Luna
Produced by: Andrés Vicente Gómez
Starring: Penélope Cruz, Javier Bardem, and Anna Galiena
Released by: Umbrella (DVD)

18+

JAMÓN JAMÓN

1992, 95 mins.

Plot: Sylvia is pregnant by the son of her boss, the matriarchal owner of an underwear factory. The two are eager to marry—a prospect that appalls the mother, who smells a gold digger. She hires amateur matador Raul to seduce Sylvia, but the plan backfires horribly when Raul falls for Sylvia and vice versa, and the mother falls for Raul.

Review: Hot and steamy, this is a Freudian's dream movie, complete with oral fixation and laden with symbolism—for example, Cruz protecting herself from a storm with the broken-off scrotum of a giant model bull. This is also something of a culinary *Romeo and Juliet*, although considering the serious bed hopping that goes on, it's hard to imagine which pairing could end up the star-crossed lovers.

FURTHER VIEWING: ***Huevos de oro (Golden Balls); La teta I la lluna (The Tit & the Moon); Yo soy la Juani (My Name Is Juani)***
SEE ALSO: ***Sense and Sensibility; Volver; No Country for Old Men; Vicky Cristina Barcelona***

401/500

★★★★★

Director: Jason Reitman
Screenwriter: Diablo Cody

Produced by: John Malkovich, Brad Van Arragon, Daniel Dubiecki, Jim Miller, and Joseph Drake
Starring: Ellen Page, Michael Cera, Jennifer Garner, and Jason Bateman
Released by: Twentieth Century Fox (DVD)

12+

JUNO

2007, 96 mins.

Plot: Fast-talking, wise-cracking teen Juno falls pregnant the first time she has sex with her longtime friend Paulie. After considering an abortion, she instead decides to follow through with the pregnancy, and she finds a seemingly suitable young couple to adopt the baby. During the pregnancy she becomes a bit too friendly with the baby's adoptive father, who is trying to recapture his rock 'n' roll youth, and remains ambivalent about its biological father.

Review: Don't let the hype put you off—*Juno* is quieter, funnier, and more thought-provoking than you might expect. Ellen Page, as the feisty, self-confident, and vulnerable Juno, deserves every inch of her Oscar nomination, but J. K. Simmons and Allison Janney, who play Juno's father and stepmother, steal every scene they're in.

FURTHER VIEWING: ***Consent; Thank You for Smoking***
SEE ALSO: ***Knocked Up; Saved!; Rushmore***

12

★★★★★

2+

Director: Alexander Mackendrick
Screenwriters: Jimmy O'Connor and William Rose

Produced by: Michael Balcon and Seth Holt

Starring: Alec Guinness, Cecil Parker, Herbert Lom, and Peter Sellers
Released by: Starz/Anchor Bay (DVD)

THE LADYKILLERS

1955, 91 mins.

Plot: "Professor" Marcus' only claim to his title comes from his education in crime. He rents a room in King's Cross from sweet old widow Mrs. Wilberforce with the intention to use it as his gang's heist HQ. The robbery comes off without a hitch, but Mrs. Wilberforce discovers the money by accident and tells Marcus she will call the police. Of course she must be eliminated, but none of gang wants to kill the old lady; luckily infighting and accidents take care of the problem.

Review: An incomparable dark comedy. Nominated for an Oscar for Best Original Screenplay, *The Ladykillers'* intelligent humor and grim irony provides just the kind of role that versatile Alec Guinness excels in. In this age of gross-out and slapstick comedies, this proves that a film can be wildly funny without a single fart joke. Essential viewing.

FURTHER VIEWING: *The Ladykillers (remake); Whisky Galore!*
SEE ALSO: *Kind Hearts and Coronets; Arsenic and Old Lace*

403/500

★★★

Director: Roger Corman
Screenwriter: Charles W. Griffiths
Produced by: Roger Corman

Starring: Jonathan Haze, Jackie Joseph, and Mel Welles
Released by: Legend Films (DVD)

12+

LITTLE SHOP OF HORRORS

1960, 72 mins.

Plot: Clumsy, useless Seymour works in Mr. Mushkin's skid-row flower shop. He's just about to be fired for incompetence when he reveals his new creation: "Audrey Jr.," a cross between a venus flytrap and a butterwort (probably not the smartest combination). Audrey Jr. soon proves to prefer the taste of human flesh, and Seymour's killer plant gets a little too hungry to handle.

Review: From the size of his name on DVD boxes, you wouldn't realize Jack Nicholson only has a very small role. But no matter—though most people are only aware of Frank Oz's brilliant musical remake in the eighties, this film version has a subtler and wittier, but no less effective, brand of humor.

FURTHER VIEWING: ***Little Shop of Horrors (remake)***
SEE ALSO: ***Please Don't Eat My Mother; The Rocky Horror Picture Show***

404/500

★★

Director: Tony Richardson
Writer: Christopher Isherwood and Terry Southern

Produced by: John Calley and Haskell Wexler

Starring: Robert Morse, Jonathan Winters, and Anjanette Comer
Released by: Warner Home Video (DVD)

15+

THE LOVED ONE

1965, 122 mins.

Plot: Dennis Barlow arrives from England in time for his uncle's suicide. He is persuaded to bury him in a prestigious funeral parlor, where he meets ambitious but naïve cosmetician, Aimee. However, he has a rival for her affections—her boss, Dr. Joyboy—and the two are soon jockeying for her increasingly disillusioned attentions, with tragic consequences.

Review: This satirical swipe at the commercialization of death is unveiled through a delightful selection of morbid, camp, and occasionally OTT characters. Aided by a blackly comic, razor-sharp script and a host of cameos and bit parts (Liberace, a very young James Coburn), the film also has a quite a lot to say about the movie business, morbid obesity, and mother-fixations.

FURTHER VIEWING: ***Look Back in Anger; A Taste of Honey; The Loneliness of the Long Distance Runner; Tom Jones; The Hotel New Hampshire***
SEE ALSO: ***Carry on Screaming; Six Feet Under***

05

★★★

Director: Peter Jackson
Screenwriters: Danny Mulheron, Peter Jackson, Fran Walsh, and Stephen Sinclair

Produced by: Peter Jackson and Jim Booth

Starring: Donna Akersten, Brian Sergent, and Stuart Devenie
Released by: Jef Films (DVD)

8+

MEET THE FEEBLES

1989, 94 mins.

Plot: The Feebles are a Muppet-like team of puppets that are about to put on their first televised variety show when everything you can (and can't possibly) think of goes horribly wrong.

Review: Forget *Team America—Meet the Feebles* is the first purveyor of raunchy puppet sex on celluloid. And puppets taking drugs. And puppet amputees. And puppet warfare. The list goes on, as this is quite possibly the most insane film outside of the seventies when everyone was high as a kite anyway. While it doesn't quite beat the *Muppet* movies and show for psychedelic weirdness, it one-ups them in the grossness and explicit adult content categories. Includes a parody of the famous "Russian Roulette"scene from *The Deer Hunter*, but with frogs.

FURTHER VIEWING: *Bad Taste; The Frighteners*
SEE ALSO: *Killer Klowns from Outer Space; Fritz the Cat*

06

★★★★★

Director: Fred Dekker
Screenwriters: Fred Dekker and Shane Black

Produced by: Jonathan A. Zimbert, Keith Barish, Neil A. Machlis, Peter Hyams, and Rob Cohen

Starring: Andre Gower, Robby Kiger, and Stephen Macht
Released by: Lionsgate (DVD)

A

THE MONSTER SQUAD

1987, 82 mins.

Plot: Preteen friends Sean, Patrick, Brent, Eugene, and Rudy make up the Monster Squad—a club for kids obsessed with classic horror monsters. When those monsters all descend on the Squad's sleepy Midwestern town (the details of how are unimportant), they must use Van Helsing's lost journal, as well as the help of their neighbor "Scary German Guy," to defeat the ancient evils before the town is destroyed.

Review: Though aimed at children, *The Monster Squad* never speaks down to its audience, which is why it is just as entertaining for adults. With a host of quotable one-liners ("Wolfman's got nards!"), there are also some touching moments amidst all the ridiculousness. A timeless kid's classic, this, but don't use age as an excuse to deny yourself the viewing pleasure.

FURTHER VIEWING: *Night of the Creeps*
SEE ALSO: *The Goonies; The Lost Boys; Fright Night*

407
500

Director: Kinka Usher
Screenwriter: Neil Cuthbert

Produced by: Lawrence Gordon, Lloyd Levin, and Mike Richardson

Starring: Ben Stiller, Hank Azaria, Janeane Garofalo, and William H. Macy
Released by: Universal Studios (DVD)

12+

MYSTERY MEN

1999, 121 mins.

Plot: A group of wannabe superheroes attempt to battle Casanova Frankenstein, Champion City's resident villain, after he kidnaps the city's real superhero. But they have a lot of training to do, as the Mystery Men are made up of the likes of Mr. Furious, who gets angry a lot; The Shoveler, who has a shovel but is generally afraid to use it; and the Invisible Boy, who can only turn invisible if no one's looking.

Review: Though the film proved as useless at the box office as the Mystery Men are at fighting crime, this is a surprisingly funny and engaging spoof of the superhero comics genre and its conventions. Of special note are Tom Waits' brilliant turn as the genius inventor Dr. Heller, and Geoffrey Rush's performance as the ridiculously OTT Frankenstein.

FURTHER VIEWING: ***Not available***
SEE ALSO: ***Ghostbusters; Men in Black; The Adventures of Buckaroo Banzai Across the 8th Dimension***

408
500

★★

Director: Thom Eberhardt
Screenwriter: Thom Eberhardt

Produced by: Andrew Lane and Wayne Crawford

Starring: Robert Beltran, Catherine Mary Stewart, and Kelli Maroney
Released by: MGM (DVD)

15+

NIGHT OF THE COMET

1984, 95 mins.

Plot: The Earth passes through the tail of a comet, and the next day everyone on the planet has been fried into little piles of dust. Everyone, that is, except a handful of teenagers who spent the night in various metal containers. But lo! The metal-protected soon find other life in the form of ultra-pale zombies, and the teens must fight against zombies and tainted military scientists to survive.

Review: Whether *Night of the Comet* is a good movie or a bad one is missing the point; this is standard eighties teen wish fulfillment. It's about a world where there are no authority figures, curfews, or rules—one where all the mall security guards have crumbled to dust. This is utopia for a disaffected youth, period.

FURTHER VIEWING: ***Sole Survivor; The Night Before***
SEE ALSO: ***I Am Legend; The Last Woman on Earth; The Quiet Earth***

09

★★★

Director: Tom Schiller
Screenwriter: Tom Schiller
Produced by: Lorne Michaels

Starring: Zach Galligan, Apollonia van Ravenstein, and Lauren Tom
Released by: Not Available

2+ NOTHING LASTS FOREVER

1984, 82 mins.

Plot: A young man (Zach Galligan) returns to New York City with hopes of becoming a great artist, but upon his arrival finds the city has been taken over by the Port Authority. All jobs are assigned, and after failing the test to become an artist, Adam's journey takes him to the moon on a lunar bus in search of the woman he loves.

Review: With a cast of familiar faces from *Saturday Night Live* including Dan Ackroyd and Bill Murray, this baffling feature culls vintage footage to create an anarchic alternate future where the thirties and the eighties coexist. Unavailable in any form, it remains an influential work for those who've had the good fortune to see it.

FURTHER VIEWING: *Not available*
SEE ALSO: *Brazil; Gremlins*

10

★★★★

Director: Mike Judge
Screenwriter: Mike Judge

Produced by: Daniel Rappaport and Michael Rotenberg

Starring: Ron Livingston, Jennifer Aniston, and David Herman
Released by: Twentieth Century Fox (DVD)

5+ OFFICE SPACE

1999, 89 mins.

Plot: Peter Gibbons is a bored code monkey who reprograms bank software. He attends an "occupational hypnotherapy" session that proves too effective; ignoring his girlfriend and his job, he dedicates himself to doing nothing and being happy with it. This puts him in just the right mindset to take revenge against his company when his coworkers are fired, and they unleash a virus that diverts small amounts of money into a private account. Unfortunately, the virus glitches and a very noticeable sum disappears.

Review: *Office Space* is almost the very definition of cult: though it performed badly at the box office to mixed reviews, its life on DVD and cable has outperformed all expectations. And small wonder: in the current corporate culture where employees are expected to be overqualified but will only ever get undervalued, what better totem than this?

FURTHER VIEWING: *Idiocracy; Beavis and Butthead Do America*
SEE ALSO: *Nine to Five; Take this Job and Shove It; Clockwatchers*

411
500

★★★

Director: John Waters
Screenwriter: John Waters
Produced by: John Waters

Starring: Divine, David Lochary, and Mary Vivian Pearce
Released by: New Line Home Entertainment (DVD)

18+ PINK FLAMINGOS

1972, 93 mins.

Plot: The notorious criminal and self-proclaimed "filthiest person alive," Divine has escaped to the suburbs away from the prying eyes of the media. Connie and Raymond Marble, two pretenders to the throne, run a black market adoption service for lesbian couples as well as dealing heroin to school children. Annoyed at Divine's mere existence, they embark on a campaign to see who truly is the filthiest person alive.

Review: Vulgar—yes. Trashy—check. John Waters' first feature is a master-class in both of these and more besides; it's also extremely funny. Outrageous for a sex scene involving a live chicken and a woman being injected with a butler's sperm, its most notorious scene is its last. Those who don't appreciate coprophagia may wish to avert their eyes.

FURTHER VIEWING: ***Mondo Trasho; Multiple Maniacs***
SEE ALSO: ***Faster, Pussycat! Kill! . . . Kill!; Meet the Feebles***

412
500

★★★★

Director: John Waters
Screenwriter: John Waters
Produced by: John Waters

Starring: Divine, Tab Hunter, and Edith Massey
Released by: New Line Home Entertainment (DVD)

18+ POLYESTER

1981, 86 mins.

Plot: Baltimore housewife Francine Fishpaw wants the American Dream, but her family is made up of obnoxious hellraisers who care only for themselves. Her husband runs a porno theater and is having an affair, her daughter Lu-Lu gets pregnant by bad boy Bobo, and son Dexter is a serial-foot stamper who's been expelled. Enter Todd Tomorrow, who claims he can make all of Francine's dreams come true . . .

Review: Cleverly parodying TV's earliest home-based sitcoms, but with Waters' trashy twists, *Polyester* is the best of the pre-*Hairspray* flicks for sheer laughs. The original screenings of *Polyester* had an audience participation element—a scratch 'n' sniff card that allowed them to indulge in smells of roses, gas, and rotten eggs after one character breaks wind.

FURTHER VIEWING: ***Desperate Living; Hairspray***
SEE ALSO: ***Sitcom; Happiness***

Director: Mel Brooks
Screenwriter: Mel Brooks
Produced by: Sidney Glazier

Starring: Zero Mostel, Gene Wilder, and Dick Shawn
Released by: MGM (DVD)

2+

THE PRODUCERS

1968, 88 mins.

Plot: Broke Broadway producer Max Bialystock is only making the barest of livings by seducing money from lonely old women. Neurotic accountant Leo Bloom discovers a fraudulent error on Max's books and Max convinces him to cover it up, then Leo has a brilliant idea: oversell a show so tastelessly terrible that no one would ever audit it, leaving Leo and Max free to divide the profit. Unfortunately for them, *Springtime for Hitler*'s comedic value makes it a big hit on Broadway.

Review: Mel Brooks' directorial debut, for which he also won a Best Original Screenplay Oscar. This is classic Brooks comedy, and one of Gene Wilder's funniest roles. Ironically, the film was denounced by many critics on its release for being in bad taste, but it is now considered one of the best comedies ever made. Life truly does imitate art.

FURTHER VIEWING: *The Producers (2005 remake); Blazing Saddles; Silent Movie*
SEE ALSO: *To Be or Not to Be; A Funny Thing Happened on the Way to the Forum*

414
500

★★★★

Directors: Howard Franklin and Bill Murray
Screenwriter: Howard Franklin

Produced by: Bill Murray and Robert Greenhut

Starring: Bill Murray, Geena Davis, and Randy Quaid
Released by: Warner Home Video (DVD)

15+

QUICK CHANGE

1990, 89 mins.

Plot: For Grimm, robbing a bank dressed as a clown with just his best friend and girlfriend as backup went as smooth as could be hoped. But he didn't count on the trials and tribulations of just another day in New York City causing all kinds of headaches as the team try to make their way to the airport.

Review: *Quick Change* is Bill Murray's only directorial credit. It's difficult to see why the film never gained the rabid popularity of *Groundhog Day* considering it contains a similar morbid humor, as well as Murray acting the fed up, put-upon straight man in an untenable position. The addition of Randy Quaid's fine character acting is just the icing on this slightly insane but thoroughly enjoyable cake.

FURTHER VIEWING: ***Groundhog Day***
SEE ALSO: ***Disorganized Crime; A Fish Called Wanda; The Out-of-Towners***

415
500

★★★★

Director: Bobcat Goldthwait
Screenwriter: Bobcat Goldthwait

Produced by: Paul Colichman and Ann Luly-Goldthwait

Starring: Bobcat Goldthwait and Julie Brown
Released by: Columbia Tristar Home Video (DVD)

18+

SHAKES THE CLOWN

1992, 87 mins.

Plot: When not performing at children's parties, Shakes wallows in depression and alcohol. In a community that thrives on status and pecking order, he's pretty low down and getting lower. However, he has to stop clowning around when his boss is killed and he is framed for the murder.

Review: Played without one knowing wink to the audience, this is one of those films that takes the delightful and imbues it with the darkest, most vitriolic humor. The hate the various clown cults have for each other provides biting, ironic laughs and not everybody may like or get it, but there's a subtle genius to this movie—not the sad melancholic tears of a clown but ones spurted out with rage and pathos.

FURTHER VIEWING: ***World's Greatest Dad***
SEE ALSO: ***The Jerk; Quick Change***

16

★★★★★

Director: Edgar Wright
Screenwriters: Edgar Wright and Simon Pegg

Produced by: Tim Bevan, Eric Fellner, and Nira Park

Starring: Simon Pegg, Kate Ashfield, and Nick Frost
Released by: Universal Studios (DVD)

5+

SHAUN OF THE DEAD

2004, 99 mins.

Plot: Deadbeat Shaun gets dumped by his girlfriend and spends the night drowning his sorrows. So it really isn't far-fetched that when he wakes up the next morning with a brutal hangover, he realizes he's missed a worldwide zombie outbreak. Finally he has the chance to prove he's good at something, and he attempts to save his mother, stepfather, ex-girlfriend, and best friend from the biting fiends that surround them.

Review: From the team who brought us the British sitcom about nothing is a hit British film about zombies. In fact, *Shaun of the Dead* is based on an episode of *Spaced*, and just goes to show that a seemingly overdone horror subgenre (zombies) can still be fresh and entertaining if looked at from a different angle. Bill Nighy is especially good as the wicked stepfather with a heart of gold.

FURTHER VIEWING: ***Hot Fuzz; Spaced (TV series)***
SEE ALSO: ***Dead Alive; Planet Terror; An American Werewolf in London***

17

★★★★★

Directors: Gene Kelly and Stanley Donen
Screenwriters: Betty Comden and Adolph Green
Produced by: Arthur Freed

Starring: Gene Kelly, Donald O'Connor, and Debbie Reynolds
Released by: Warner Home Video (DVD)

A

SINGIN' IN THE RAIN

1952, 103 mins.

Plot: Set in Hollywood at the time of the release of the first talking picture, *The Jazz Singer*, *Singin' in the Rain* follows superstar Don Lockwood's attempt to transition from silent film to sound.

Review: There were two major films that came out in the fifties about the transition from silent to sound in Hollywood: one was 1950's *Sunset Boulevard*, and the other was *Singin' in the Rain*. They've both enraptured audiences for more than half a century, but for very different reasons. While *Sunset* looked at the sinister, life-destroying side of actor obsolescence, *Singin' in the Rain* finds much humor and originality in the changing times, yet is no less poignant. Gene Kelly is, of course, genuine star material and can light up any picture with just the twinkle in his eye, but Donald O'Connor deserves just as much accolade for his endearing high-octane performance.

FURTHER VIEWING: ***Seven Brides for Seven Brothers; Funny Face; Damn Yankees!***
SEE ALSO: ***Sunset Boulevard; Silent Movie***

★
★
★
★

Director: George Roy Hill
Screenwriter: Nancy Dowd

Produced by: Stephen J. Friedman and Robert J. Wunsch

Starring: Paul Newman, Strother Martin, and Michael Ontkean
Released by: Universal Studios (DVD)

18+

SLAP SHOT

1977, 123 mins

Plot: In a fading industrial town, Reggie Dunlop—an aging, once-stellar ice hockey player/coach—is watching his team vaporize and attendances collapse. Its owners decide enough is enough and figure on selling the team. The only way Dunlop can save them to is reverse their fortunes, using every trick in the game—no matter how underhand.

Review: A classic "underdogs-make-good" movie, this is a lean, mean script full of cracking one liners and plenty of rowdy laughs, especially out on the rink, with its Neanderthal brutality. Newman's fading superstar and his bunch of roughhouse losers are loveable rogues, particularly the scene-stealing, myopic, and savage Hanson brothers: three of the unlikeliest sporting stars in cinema history!

FURTHER VIEWING: ***Butch Cassidy and the Sundance Kid; Slaughterhouse-Five; The Sting; The Great Waldo Pepper; The World According to Garp***
SEE ALSO: ***Bull Durham; Dodgeball; Major League; The Mighty Ducks***

419/500

★★★

Director: Jonathan Demme
Screenwriter: E. Max Frye
Produced by: Jonathan Demme and Kenneth Utt
Starring: Jeff Daniels, Melanie Griffith, and Ray Liotta
Released by: MGM/UA (DVD)

15+

SOMETHING WILD

1986, 113 mins.

Plot: It's the old story: mild-mannered closet rebel businessman meets insatiable free-spirited beautiful wildcat; she steals him for high school reunion, they hit the road and fall foul of her psychotic ex-con ex-husband. Sex, crimes, and rock 'n' roll follow.

Review: An aspirational movie for every guy who hates wearing a suit to work, Daniels is their unlikely god, perfect as the overawed everyman derailed from his staid existence by the beautiful harpy Griffith. But what starts out as a charming road-trip romance descends into the weekend from Hell when edgy, explosive Ray Liotta roars onto the screen. Still, if nothing else you can play "spot the cameo" and enjoy the eighties fashion show.

FURTHER VIEWING: ***Married to the Mob; The Silence of the Lambs; Philadelphia; Dumb & Dumber; Working Girl***
SEE ALSO: ***Before Sunrise; Grosse Point Blank; Wild at Heart***

420/500

★★★

Director: David O. Russell
Screenwriter: David O. Russell
Produced by: Dean Silvers
Starring: Jeremy Davies, Alberta Watson, and Benjamin Hendrickson
Released by: Image Entertainment (DVD)

18+

SPANKING THE MONKEY

1994, 100 mins.

Plot: Medical student Raymond (Jeremy Davies) is forced to cancel an important summer internship by his controlling father so he can look after his mother, who's bedridden with a broken leg. Frustrated by his situation and his inability to have time to himself, he and his mother develop an incestuous relationship that is to be his ultimate downfall.

Review: Oedipus for Gen X is the quickest way to sum up Russell's darkly comic tale of teen angst in suburban America. All of the characters' selfish needs fuel Raymond's guilt, which stops him from forming regular relationships with other people, yet his own inability to step out from his dominating family proves to be his greatest failure. Tragicomic rather than laugh-out-loud.

FURTHER VIEWING: ***Flirting with Disaster; I Heart Huckabees***
SEE ALSO: ***Storytelling; The House of Yes***

★ **Director:** Woody Allen
★ **Screenwriter:** Woody Allen
★ **Produced by:** Robert Greenhutt

Starring: Woody Allen, Charlotte Rampling, and Jessica Harper
Released by: MGM (DVD)

15+

STARDUST MEMORIES

1980, 89 mins.

Plot: Renowned for his lightweight comedies and troubled by the state of the world, director Sandy Bates wants to make more serious movies. While guest of honor at a retrospective on his earlier oeuvre, he has time to ponder life, relationships, and romance—especially when he meets the beautiful Dorrie.

Review: Allen engages in some introspective navel gazing as he ponders his art and what it means to his fans and critics; not all of them are treated that well as Allen works out his issues with the likes of fans who want their breasts signed. In places melancholic and nostalgic, this is of course Woody Allen at his best, so there are moments of comic genius—sci-fi conventions beware!

FURTHER VIEWING: ***Annie Hall; Bananas; Sleeper; Everything You Ever Wanted to Know about Sex but Were Too Afraid to Ask; Manhattan***
SEE ALSO: ***8 1/2; La dolce vita***

★★★

Director: Ivan Reitman
Screenwriters: Harold Ramis, Daniel Goldberg, and Len Blum
Produced by: Ivan Reitman, Daniel Goldberg, and Joe Medjuck
Starring: Bill Murray, Harold Ramis, and Warren Oates
Released by: Sony Pictures (DVD)

5+

STRIPES

1981, 106 mins.

Plot: Cab driver John Winger has the worst day of his life and decides to join the army (doesn't it always happen like that?). He convinces his best friend Russell, a disgruntled teacher, to come along, and they have just the kind of slapstick Basic Training experience you would expect. After graduation, they engage in some Cold War antics because . . . well, it's the eighties.

Review: Before *Ghostbusters* there was *Stripes*, which was Ramis' first acting gig. This early Murray/Ramis team-up proved prescient, though, and many up-and-coming comedians got their first big Hollywood breaks here, including John Larroquette, Judge Reinhold, John Candy, and Dave Thomas. The film does drag a bit once the boys leave training, but with this kind of bulletproof star power, story issues just fade into irrelevance.

FURTHER VIEWING: *Meatballs; Ghostbusters; Dave*
SEE ALSO: *Private Benjamin; M*A*S*H; Biloxi Blues*

423/500

★★★★

Director: Preston Sturges
Screenwriters: Preston Sturges and Ernst Laemmle

Produced by: Paul Jones, Buddy DeSylva, and Preston Sturges

Starring: Joel McCrea, Veronica Lake, and Robert Warwick
Released by: Criterion (DVD)

12+

SULLIVAN'S TRAVELS

1941, 90 mins.

Plot: John Sullivan is a rich and spoiled Hollywood film director who decides to take a page from George Orwell's book and live the life of the down and out for a while. He wants to make socially important dramas instead of the brainless, high-grossing comedy action pictures for which he's known, and needs the research. He eventually meets a failed actress (Veronica Lake) who becomes his traveling companion. When Sullivan loses his memory and becomes a real bum, he realizes that comedy films really are the best balm for the downtrodden sections of society.

Review: Though *Sullivan's Travels* is highly regarded by critics today and often considered Preston Sturges' greatest film, it wasn't nearly so well received at the time. But whatever the critics say, it's still a mighty funny indictment of Hollywood politics

FURTHER VIEWING: ***The Great McGinty; The Lady Eve***
SEE ALSO: ***O Brother, Where Art Thou?; Mr. Deeds Goes to Town***

424/500

★★★

Director: Lukas Moodysson
Screenwriter: Lukas Moodysson
Produced by: Lars Jönsson

Starring: Lisa Lindgren, Michael Nyqvist, and Emma Samuelsson
Released by: MGM (DVD)

15+

TILLSAMMANS (TOGETHER)

2000, 106 mins.

Plot: Set in Sweden in the mid-1970s, *Together* is the name of a commune for like-minded hippies run by the kind-natured Goran, whose aim to please everyone doesn't always work out how he'd like it to. When his middle-class sister and her two children move in to take refuge from her abusive husband, things begin to change as domestic middle-class values come into conflict with the commune's ideals.

Review: Moodysson's film is both a celebration of the seventies and a condemnation of the hippie ideals that so many wanted to be a part of; free love is as destructive as the bomb, for instance. More than a hippie comedy, the gentle set-up and complex storylines produce a heart-warming whole.

FURTHER VIEWING: ***Fucking Åmål; Container***
SEE ALSO: ***The Idiots; High Hopes***

25/33

★★

Directors: Lloyd Kaufman and Michael Herz

Screenwriters: Lloyd Kaufman, Michael Partington Terry, Joe Ritter, and Stuart Strutin

Produced by: Lloyd Kaufman and Michael Herz

Starring: Andree Maranda, Mitch Cohen, and Jennifer Prichard

Released by: Troma Entertainment (DVD)

8+

THE TOXIC AVENGER

1986, 87 mins.

Plot: "He was 98lbs. of solid nerd until he became . . . The Toxic Avenger, the first super-hero from New Jersey!" Melvin Ferd is a scrawny janitor at a gym in Tromaville, constantly tormented by muscleheads until he falls into a barrel of toxic waste (this *is* Jersey, after all) and gains superhuman powers. Not only does Toxie take revenge on his tormenters, he begins to fight crime almost inadvertently and gains the affections of the citizens of Tromaville, despite his hideous appearance.

Review: Troma is known for producing fly-by-night, low-budget B-movies; *The Toxic Avenger* is its most famous and most cult to date. And deservedly so—apart from being a send-up of the usually hokey superhero genre, it's also very funny with a hero you can't help but identify with and cheer for.

FURTHER VIEWING: *The Toxic Avenger Part 2; The Toxic Avenger Part 3: The Last Temptation of Toxie*

SEE ALSO: *Tromeo and Juliet; Cornman: American Vegetable Hero; Surf Nazis Must Die*

26/33

★★★★

Director: Mel Brooks

Screenwriter: Mel Brooks

Produced by: Michael Hertzberg

Starring: Frank Langella, Dom DeLuise, and Ron Moody

Released by: Twentieth Century Fox (DVD)

A

THE TWELVE CHAIRS

1970, 93 mins.

Plot: Impoverished Russian nobleman Vorobyaninov is called to his mother-in-law's deathbed—along with the obligatory priest—and is told that a fortune in jewels has been hidden in one of twelve chairs from a dining set once owned by the family. The chairs had been confiscated by the government and sold separately years before; in searching for them, Vorobyaninov joins forces with lower-class conman Bender and the two race to find the jewels ahead of the priest, who has left the church to seek his fortune in the chairs.

Review: A much-loved and very funny comedy to follow Mel Brooks' highly controversial first film *The Producers*. Dom DeLuise's frantic performance as the money-crazed priest is a joy to watch.

FURTHER VIEWING: *It's in the Bag!; The Producers; Life Stinks*

SEE ALSO: *Rat Race; Scavenger Hunt; Million Dollar Mystery*

427
500

★★

Director: Russ Meyer
Screenwriters: Roger Ebert and Russ Meyer
Produced by: Russ Meyer
Starring: Edward Schaaf, Robert McLane, and Elaine Collins
Released by: Russ Meyer (DVD)

18+

UP!

1976, 80m mins.

Plot: In a backwater logging town, German-speaking Hitler clone Adolph Schwatrz is found murdered in his bath after an S&M session. Cause of death: piranhas. Meanwhile, buxom Margo Winchester arrives in town, sparking a furor among the men and beginning a cascade of rape and murder.

Review: This is not exactly *Twin Peaks*. Or *The Boys from Brazil*. While there are violent rednecks, voluptuous country girls, and Nazi conspiracies a-go-go, it's more about the exuberant sexuality, nonsensical plot, flowery dialog, and fast pacing. And if it all gets too confusing, Meyer thoughtfully lays on a Greek Chorus to help with any sticky plot points. It can get pretty brutal, but generally the movie errs on the side of warped, energetic insanity.

FURTHER VIEWING: ***Beyond the Valley of the Dolls; Faster, Pussycat! Kill! . . . Kill!; Beneath the Valley of the UltraVixens***
SEE ALSO: ***Dead Men Don't Wear Plaid; The Producers***

428
500

★★★

Director: Lou Adler
Screenwriters: Tommy Chong and Cheech Marin
Produced by: Lou Adler and Lou Lombardo
Starring: Cheech Marin, Tommy Chong, and Strother Martin
Released by: Paramount (DVD)

18+

UP IN SMOKE

1978, 86 mins.

Plot: Plot? It's about a couple of stoners ending up in strange situations while trying to get stoned. And something about a battle of the bands at the end.

Review: *Up in Smoke* is a parent's worst nightmare, which is exactly why it became one of the highest grossing films of 1978, mostly due to word-of-mouth and an innovative street marketing campaign. It also spawned a host of sequels, none quite matching the popularity of the first. Whether you're a devotee of the reefer or not, Cheech and Chong are just so irresistibly loveable and clueless that it's impossible not to be swept up in (or drawn into their smoky cloud of) madcap adventures

FURTHER VIEWING: ***Cheech and Chong's Next Movie; Still Smokin'; Cheech and Chong's The Corsican Brothers***
SEE ALSO: ***Half Baked; Friday; Jay and Silent Bob Strike Back***

29

★★★

Director: Todd Solondz
Screenwriter: Todd Solondz
Produced by: Todd Solondz

Starring: Heather Matarazzo, Victoria Davis, and Christina Brucato
Released by: Columbia Tristar Home Video (DVD)

5+

WELCOME TO THE DOLLHOUSE

1995, 90 mins.

Plot: Neither attractive nor popular, life is tough for seventh grader Dawn Weiner. Ridiculed and bullied by the other kids, she is also the butt of her family's jokes, who hold her in is as much disregard as her schoolmates. To make matters even worse, her younger, cuter, and incredibly irritating sister is apparently kidnapped because of Dawn's inaction.

Review: While the subject matter may not be the most original—"ugly" nerdling suffering through school hell—it's the way it's portrayed that makes this such a stand-out movie. Heather Matarazzo gives a brilliant tragic-comic performance as Dawn, her life studied in meticulous near-documentary and sometimes blisteringly funny detail. There's no saccharine "Hollywood" ending, but it remains an award-winning triumphal revenge for nerds, geeks, and freaks everywhere.

FURTHER VIEWING: ***Fear, Anxiety and Depression; Happiness; Storytelling***
SEE ALSO: ***Elephant; Heathers; Napoleon Dynamite***

30

★★★

Director: Pedro Almodóvar
Screenwriter: Pedro Almodóvar
Produced by: Pedro Almodóvar

Starring: Carmen Maura, Antonio Banderas, and Julieta Serrano
Released by: Warner Home Video (DVD)

WOMEN ON THE VERGE OF A NERVOUS BREAKDOWN

1988, 90 mins.

Plot: After her older boyfriend leaves her, actress Pepa discovers she's pregnant and contemplates extreme measures to keep him. However, a friend in trouble with terrorists disrupts her plans, along with curious cops, outraged ex-wives, drugged fiancés, and airport shoot-outs, leaving Pepa to somehow talk her way out of the mess.

Review: A thoroughbred in Almodóvar's stable, this, like its lead actress, is mature and complicated; a darkly comedic sitting-room farce that grows more histrionic—and funny—as the story goes into meltdown. It's all the more satisfying for the work the director puts into dovetailing all the story strands, and proving twenty-four hours is a long time in an Almodóvar movie.

FURTHER VIEWING: ***Entre tinieblas (Dark Habits); Matador; Tie Me up! Tie Me Down!; Kika; Volver***
SEE ALSO: ***Jamón Jamón***

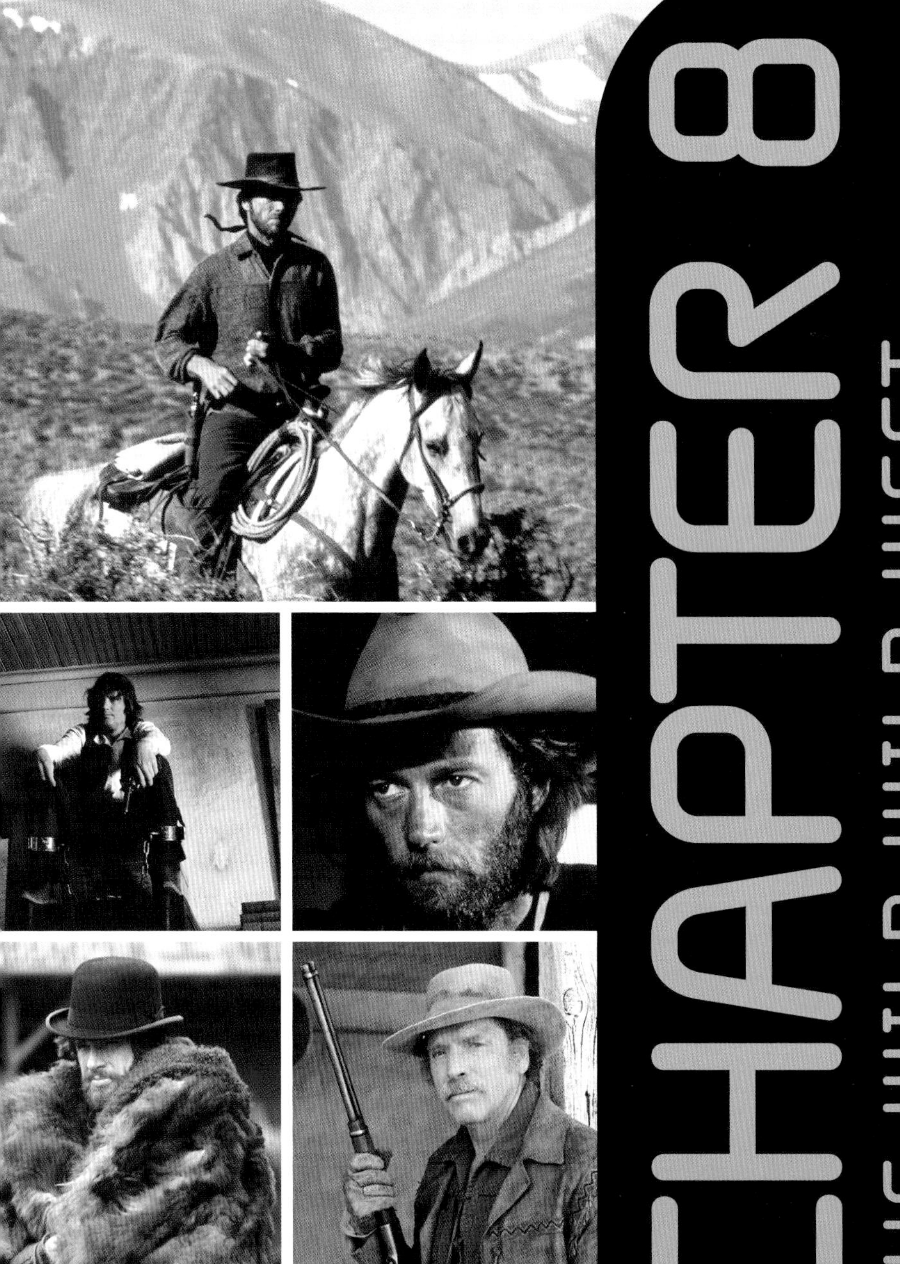

CHAPTER 8

THE WILD WILD WEST

"THERE ARE TWO KINDS OF PEOPLE IN THE WORLD, MY FRIEND: THOSE WITH A ROPE AROUND THE NECK, AND THE PEOPLE WHO HAVE THE JOB OF DOING THE CUTTING"

If this category had to be summed up in just two words, those words would probably be "Clint Eastwood." Which isn't to say that he's the only worthwhile aspect of the genre (in fact, far from it), but that he is a major influence as well as a defining characteristic of the more cult section of westerns—which you'll be able to tell from the number of times he crops up in the following movies both as actor and director. But he's not the only draw here; for example, alongside Eastwood's loner anti-hero comes Sergio Leone's epic treatment of the genre, reverent and genre-busting at the same time. With blood-stained dirt and desolate tumbleweed, these westerns explore our conflicts with ourselves and the world at large, and they get to do it with guns.

THE WILD WEST

Director: Elliot Silverstein
Screenwriter: Walter Newman
Producer: Harold Hecht

Starring: Jane Fonda, Lee Marvin, and Michael Callan
Released by: Sony Pictures (DVD)

12+

CAT BALLOU

1965, 97 mins.

Plot: A straight-laced young lady, Catherine Ballou (Jane Fonda), is returning to her father's ranch by train after completing her education. She meets drunken con-man Jed dressed as a preacher and his nephew Boone, a horse-rustler. When the sheriff arrives to arrest Boone, Jed and Catherine help him evade capture. Arriving in Wolf City, Wyoming (Catherine's home town), she finds that her father has been threatened by Silvernose (Lee Marvin) for refusing to give up his property to a land developer. Silvernose kills Catherine's father, and so the grief-filled girl forms her own posse including Jed, Boone, a local Indian known as Jackson Two-Bears, and a legendary outlaw called Kid Shelleen (also played by Lee Marvin) to have her revenge.

Unfortunately, Shelleen spends most of his days in a state of constant inebriation, and in the film's highlight moment, is unable to shoot a target on the side of a barn until he's downed half of a bottle of whiskey. With her new gang in tow, revenge is only a bullet away . . . if they don't hang her first.

Review: Lee Marvin won the Best Actor Oscar for his dual role as the devious Silvernose and his brother Kid Shelleen, flipping between po-faced outlaw and comedic stumblebum in this career-best role. Fonda is playful and assertive, lighting up the screen with her presence and making an ideal foil for Marvin's drunk. The film is framed by a traveling Greek chorus who sing of Cat's imminent hanging—richly performed by Stubby Kaye and Nat "King" Cole (Cole was to die shortly before the film screened). This isn't just a musical—*Cat Ballou* is very funny, not relying on slapstick to garner the laughs, but on a witty script by Walter Newman. The film's warmth earns repeat viewings.

FURTHER VIEWING: ***A Man Called Horse; The Car***
SEE ALSO: ***Paint Your Wagon***

Director: Jim Jarmusch
Screenwriter: Jim Jarmusch
Produced by: Demetra J. MacBride

Starring: Johnny Depp, Gary Farmer, Crispin Glover, and Lance Henriksen

Released by: Miramax Home Entertainment (DVD)

18+

DEAD MAN

1995, 116 mins.

Plot: Arriving in the town of Machine, prim accountant William Blake finds he's too late to take a position at the town's metal works. He seeks solace with a local beauty, but after a fatal encounter with her lover, Blake finds himself mortally wounded, on the run, and with a bounty on his head. Aided by Nobody, an eccentric Indian who believes Blake to be the English poet and artist, the two wander the frontier, leaving a trail of corpses in their wake while Blake himself moves closer to death.

Review: Jim Jarmusch turns his innovative eye on the western—with great success. From Crispin Glover's off-kilter, egocentric cameo, you know this is about as existential as postmodern westerns get. Depp handles his transition to philosophical pistolero with ease, but the cornerstone of the movie is his charmingly offbeat relationship with Gary Farmer's Nobody. An Indian Virgil leading Blake on his quest to that most final of destinations, his philosophical waxings are both funny and perplexing. And death itself, given cavalier treatment in most westerns, is handled far more uncomfortably, the shot stumbling, going down as they lose functional control—the sad stanzas for Blake's new poetry.

The cinematography is beautiful: the wilderness in glorious clarity full of wonderful shapes and textures, adding to the transcendental spirit of the movie. Various cameos simply add character to the vistas, many as bleak and twisted as the landscape: Mitchum's gruff industrialist, Iggy Pop's hilarious transvestite trapper, and so many more. And laid over the film is Neil Young's guitar, adding a haunting score to a mystical, brutal, and truly unique take on the western.

FURTHER VIEWING: *Stranger than Paradise; Coffee and Cigarettes; Down by Law; Mystery Train; Ghost Dog: The Way of the Samurai*
SEE ALSO: *The Assassination of Jesse James by the Coward Robert Ford; A Man Called Horse; The Searchers; Unforgiven*

★
★
★
★
★

Director: Sergio Leone
Screenwriters: Age and Scarpelli, Sergio Leone, and Luciano Vincenzoni
Produced by: Alberto Grimaldi
Starring: Clint Eastwood, Lee Van Cleef, and Eli Wallach
Released by: MGM (DVD)

15+

IL BUONO, IL BRUTTO AND IL CATTIVO

(THE GOOD, THE BAD AND THE UGLY)

1966, 161 mins.

Plot: During the American Civil War, "The Bad" bounty-hunter Angel Eyes—so-named for his dark beauty and aptly played by Lee Van Cleef—is hired to find Bill Carson, who knows where a stash of Confederate gold is hidden. Meanwhile, "The Good" (loner gunman Blondie—Eastwood) and "The Ugly" (Wallach, as bandit Tuco) are running a town-by-town scam wherein Blondie poses as a bounty hunter, turns Tuco in, collects the reward money, and then returns later to break Tuco out of jail. Blondie abandons Tuco after a disagreement; Tuco exacts his revenge by marching Blondie across the unforgiving desert. Blondie's on the verge of collapse when a runaway carriage crosses their path—inside is a fatally wounded Bill Carson, who reveals to Tuco that the Confederate gold is buried in Sad Hill cemetery, but he only tells Blondie which grave it's in. Tuco and Blondie team up to find the gold but run in with Angel Eyes—the three form an uneasy partnership and make it to the cemetery, where their backstabbing natures culminate in one of the most famous Mexican standoffs in cinematic history.

Review: This is the last, and often considered the best, in Sergio Leone's "Dollars" trilogy of spaghetti westerns spanning the period of 1964 to 1966. "Epic" doesn't even begin to describe the film, as the original Italian cut was three hours long before being edited to a paltry two and a half hours for international release. But the length is justified by the film's scope—the story is almost as vast as the landscape in which it takes place. With Spain subbing for the American southwest, the film is beautifully photographed in what was then brand-new Techniscope, emphasizing the enormity of the terrain and the desolation it engendered.

While the term "spaghetti western" was most often used derogatively in the genre's heyday, *The Good, the Bad and the Ugly* is now considered not only the best in its genre, but a cinematic classic. The film uses its setting to comment on the wastefulness and mindless destruction of war, as well as to turn western hero clichés on their heads—Blondie, though known as "The Good," is just as mean and murderous as his counterparts, and one suspects he was given the title just because he's so damn handsome. Such character, genre, and landscape studies allow the film to transcend the seeming "Cowboys and Indians" simplicity and become a truly epic exploration of a unique era in American history.

FURTHER VIEWING: ***A Fistful of Dollars; For a Few Dollars More; Once Upon a Time in the West***
SEE ALSO: ***The Outlaw Josey Wales; A Professional Gun; The Dirty Dozen***

★★★★

Director: Sergio Corbucci
Screenwriter: Mario Amendola
Producer: Marcello Papaleo

Starring: Jean-Louis Trintignant, Klaus Kinski, and Frank Wolff
Released by: Fantoma (DVD)

5+

IL GRANDE SILENZIO

(THE GREAT SILENCE)

1968, 105 mins.

Plot: In the snowy mountain area of Snowhill, the great blizzard of 1899 has left families trapped without food and supplies, making them resort to theft and petty crime to survive. They do their best to keep out of sight of the bounty hunters who have invaded the region, including one particular group led by the "law abiding" Loco (Klaus Kinski) who will kill as many as it takes to claim a reward. A man known as Silence is feared among these bounty hunters—his unscrupulous method of killing is based on a loophole of instigation that stops him being imprisoned. One group of people who are being hunted hire Silence to take out Loco and his henchmen, leading to a bleak and unforgettable showdown between the two opposed killers.

Review: The "great silence" of the title refers to a number of things: the mute lead character, Silence, whose reputation is of a killer who shoots after his enemies draw their pistols first; the snowy plains of Silence's harsh frontier world, which are symbolic as a landscape of frozen unmarked headstones and guilt-free murder; and a state of being in which the desperate scavenge for whatever they can find to stay alive with the knowledge that death is stalking them. A moving score by Ennio Morricone haunts the film every step of the way just as it does in Leone's westerns, and is predominantly used at key dramatic moments such as the final face-off between Silence and Loco—Corbucci lingers on their eyes as they wait for each other to pull their pistols. Jean-Louis Trintignant's staggering performance as Silence puts the "cold" into cold-blooded killer—it is rumored that he refused to learn the Italian dialog in the first place. The film's surprising and desperately depressing ending is not typical of the genre and explains why western fans consider this one of the best spaghetti westerns made.

FURTHER VIEWING: *Django; I crudeli (The Hellbenders)*
SEE ALSO: *The Good, the Bad and the Ugly; Gunfighters Die Harder*

★
★
★
★
★

Director: Clint Eastwood
Screenwriter: Ernest Tidyman
Producer: Robert Daley

Starring: Clint Eastwood, Verna Bloom, and Marianna Hill
Released by: Universal Studios (DVD)

18+

HIGH PLAINS DRIFTER

1973, 105 mins.

Plot: Eastwood plays it cool as the Stranger, who arrives in Lago only wanting peace and quiet for an hour to enjoy a beer and a bottle in their saloon. Three of the locals immediately take a dislike to him and surround him in the barber shop where he's trying to get a shave and a bath. Unable to intimidate him, he guns them down and leaves them for dead in the street. A dwarf hands him a cigar and says, "What did you say your name was, again?" The stranger replies, "I didn't." From here, he is bumped into by the attractive but sluttish Callie who lures him into a violent sexual encounter. His duties performed, he holes up in the hotel. The townsfolk, still terrified by his quiet, looming figure, beg him to remain to defend them from a group of crooks who are due to be released from jail shortly. The stranger is not interested until they offer him "anything," from which point he trains them how to defend themselves from attack. The town is painted red and renamed "Hell," and the stranger leaves. His return only signals further violence, and the question of his identity once again rears its ugly head.

Review: Eastwood's first directed western—and his best—presents him as a ghostly intruder whose presence in the town only attracts death and destruction. Similar to the lead character in *Yojimbo*, the fearful townspeople are drawn to his enigmatic personality and his ability to control and survive. Gently paced, the windswept town of Lago is as much a ghost as the stranger, with moments of silence broken only by the sounds of spurs on the ground. Eastwood produced a passionate ode to the films of Leone, as well as establishing his name as one of the finest American directors to have ever lived.

FURTHER VIEWING: ***The Outlaw Josey Wales; Unforgiven***
SEE ALSO: ***A Fistful of Dollars; For a Few Dollars More***

★ **Director:** Nicholas Ray
★ **Screenwriter:** Philip Yordan
★ **Produced by:** Herbert J. Yates

Starring: Joan Crawford, Sterling Hayden, and Mercedes McCambridge
Released by: Universal Pictures UK (DVD)

12+

JOHNNY GUITAR

1954, 110 mins.

Plot: Tough, lovely Vienna runs a saloon in a small Arizona town and hopes that the arrival of the railway will change her fortunes. However, her views, unpopular with local cattle ranchers, and her involvement with a local outlaw, the Dancin' Kid, have made life difficult. But when her ex-lover, gunslinger Johnny Guitar, arrives in town, she feels safe enough—until the Dancin' Kid robs the town's bank.

Review: By no means your average western, this film ducks the usual themes to focus on the romantic rivalries between two female leads: Joan Crawford's Vienna and her nemesis, Emma McIvers, played with venom-dripping relish by Mercedes McCambridge.

And it's not just the story that makes the film so interesting. Visually, it's lit more like a musical. The colors are bold, even garish, in total contrast to the muted, naturalistic tones of more "classic" westerns. But then this movie doesn't set out to follow in the giant footsteps of Ford and Wayne. Instead, it flies in the face of convention. The ironic twist on the traditional gender roles in westerns is exemplified by Johnny himself, played with deftness and amused detachment by the much underrated Sterling Hayden. He actually seems like something of a bystander to all the mayhem. His spectacular arrival in town merely seems to light the touch paper for all the passion and fury that follows; he even says to the Dancin' Kid that he's a stranger himself in town—in the context of the movie, both metaphorically and literally.

Instead, the real hero is Vienna; pragmatic but wistful, she wears her lipstick and neck tie in bright red, so no real surprise that her bitter rival should she her as something of a scarlet woman. Meanwhile, the repressed, enraged Emma is dressed, along with her all-male minions, in puritanical black and white. However, you get the feeling that had the Dancin' Kid just given Emma what she wanted, and needed, this whole mess could have been avoided. But then we'd have missed out on such a fascinating and thrilling western.

SEE ALSO: *In a Lonely Place; Flying Leathernecks; Rebel without a Cause; The Savage Innocents; 55 Days in Peking*
FURTHER VIEWING: *Calamity Jane; Silverado*

★★★★★

Director: Marlon Brando
Screenwriter: Guy Trosper
Producer: Frank P. Rosenberg

Starring: Marlon Brando, Karl Malden, and Katy Jurado
Released by: Westlake Entertainment (DVD)

12+

ONE-EYED JACKS

1961, 141 mins.

Plot: Three bandits make their living by raiding banks in Mexico until one is killed in a botched robbery. Rio (Marlon Brando) and his other partner Dad (Karl Malden) escape on horseback into the hilly horizon pursued by the authorities. With one of their horses shot, they bet on who should take the able horse to bring another back. Dad wins the bet, but doesn't return—as a result, Rio ends up in jail for five years for the gold robbery. Upon his release, he seeks out Dad once again and they reach a resolution that no harm will befall Dad now he's become a respected sheriff and family man. But Rio is still burning with a desire to exact revenge, and with the aid of two new accomplices plans another daring bank job, with the death of the double-crossing ("one-eyed jack") Dad as the sweetener.

Review: *One-Eyed Jacks* was originally to be a Stanley Kubrick project but was passed over to Brando after it ran over budget, and the famed director ran out of patience for the subject matter. Sam Peckinpah was also involved in the early stages of production, writing the first draft of the script, but claimed later he was fired by Brando for portraying Rio as a killer (despite him being loosely based on real-life outlaw Billy the Kid). Despite the troubled birth and the lengthy running time, *One-Eyed Jacks* put a new spin on the antihero, never allowing you to see into Rio's mind for long enough to be able to understand his true motivations or moral ambivalence. For western revisionists, it's this that makes the film so compelling; for Brando, its box-office failure spelled the end of his career as a director and remains his only feature.

FURTHER VIEWING: *Not available*
SEE ALSO: *The Appaloosa; The Searchers*

★★★★

Director: Clint Eastwood
Screenwriters: Sonia Chemus and Philip Kaufman
Produced by: Robert Daley
Starring: Clint Eastwood, Chief Dan George, and Sondra Locke
Released by: Warner Home Video (DVD)

8+

THE OUTLAW JOSEY WALES

1976, 135 mins.

Plot: A peaceful farmer becomes a vengeance-driven Rebel guerrilla fighter after his family is massacred during the American Civil War. But when the Confederates are defeated, Wales refuses to surrender and becomes a much-hunted outlaw trying to find sanctuary and peace.

Review: Clearly a labor of love for Eastwood, the eponymous antihero stands as one of his greatest roles: laconic, deadpan, melancholic, he's a man who can't escape his past. The movie was something of a gamble for Eastwood, made when the western was considered a genre past its sell-by date. Perhaps what enabled him to fly in the face of fashion was to make a film that you didn't have to be a fan of westerns to enjoy; the themes are more timeless and generic: tragedy, revenge, the search for sanctuary. He could be a jaded, modern-day bounty hunter or Vietnam veteran. Everything else is just window dressing. But he also took a few more, pretty bold steps, with a more off-hand approach to the Civil War. The savage guerrilla war between the various militias had rarely made it to celluloid; the usual portrayal was the huge set pieces between armies of gray and blue, so this again was an interesting variation on a theme, not least in exposing the charnel excesses of men using their supposed values as a cover for murder and pillage.

The film also boasts a wonderful collection of supporting characters, especially Chief Dan George's laconic, long-in-the-tooth Indian, who gets some great (and comical) moments, especially when he's needling or being needled by Wales. Worth mentioning is Wales' one-time comrade, now reluctant-pursuer Fletcher. Played with aplomb by John Vernon, he actually reveals more about Wales than the character himself, and is in many ways the film's narrator. And it's through Fletcher that the movie's poignant climax is played out; not the gun battle you're expecting but something more subtle and far more powerful, defying expectations and proving just what a brilliant film this is.

FURTHER VIEWING: *A Fistful of Dollars; The Good, the Bad and the Ugly; High Plains Drifter; Pale Rider; Unforgiven*
SEE ALSO: *The Long Riders; Ride with the Devil; Seraphim Falls; Silverado*

★★★★★

Director: John Ford
Screenwriter: Frank S. Nugent
Produced by: Merian C. Cooper
Starring: John Wayne, Jeffrey Hunter, and Vera Miles
Released by: Warner Home Video (DVD)

THE SEARCHERS

1956, 119 mins.

Plot: Returning home after the Civil War, fighter Ethan Edwards' hopes of settling down are destroyed when a Comanche raiding party attack his family homestead, killing everyone but his niece. Ethan sets off in an unremitting and increasingly obsessive pursuit of the girl and her Indian kidnappers, his motives becoming more dark and uncertain.

Review: While *True Grit* netted John Wayne his Oscar, this is arguably his finer performance as the driven war veteran consumed by hatred. His performance fills the screen, Wayne as rugged and wind-blasted as one of the huge buttes of Monument Valley that Ford captures so perfectly.

But Ethan is more like the wind, restless and unsettled, and as the pursuit unfolds it becomes clear Ethan's hunt is not just for his missing niece Debbie but something missing from inside himself. He's searching for an inner peace across a mental landscape as tortured and damaged as any badlands he traverses and, unable to find it, he's left angry and bitter. His rage is such that even though Jeffrey Hunter's young, headstrong Martin is just a fraction Indian, it's more than enough for Ethan's sense of misplaced righteous fury to damn him, even when he proves himself just as dedicated to the hunt despite the search beginning to defy logic and become obsessive.

The savage twist of irony is that Ethan's hunt is no longer benign. Believing Debbie to be buck-soiled and no longer fit to live among good Christian folk, he wrestles with the notion that to save her he has to kill her—the source of violent conflict with Martin and setting up the makings of a thrilling climax.

But Ford's masterstroke is that even after a successful conclusion to the hunt, Ethan still cannot return to the bosom of his family and walks off into the dust alone, in perhaps one of the greatest and saddest final shots in cinema history.

FURTHER VIEWING: ***Stagecoach; My Darling Clementine; Fort Apache; She Wore a Yellow Ribbon; Rio Grande***
SEE ALSO: ***True Grit; Rio Bravo; Unforgiven***

★★★★

Director: Sam Peckinpah
Screenwriters: Walon Green and Sam Peckinpah

Produced by: Phil Feldman
Starring: William Holden, Ernest Borgnine, and Robert Ryan

Released by: Warner Home Video (DVD)

18+

THE WILD BUNCH

1969, 145 mins.

Plot: After a bank heist turns into a bloody fiasco, Pike Bishop flees with his band of aging outlaws into Mexico, where they are hired by a local generalissimo to seize an arms shipment. But when one of their number falls foul of the general, the gang must choose between taking the money or taking their comrade back . . . by force.

Review: The opening shot of children torturing scorpions in an ants' nest is the perfect allegory for Peckinpah's bunch of aging desperados; the "bunch" is not so much wild as just a group of hard men usually outnumbered but rarely outgunned—and they never go down without a fight. These are complicated, reflective warriors out of time as the modern age catches up with the Old West (it's curious seeing cars in a western). Robert Ryan's Deke Thornton and William Holden's Pike Bishop are the heart of the movie; old friends looking toward the end of long, tough careers. You can feel this history between them, especially in Holden, consumed with misplaced senses of loyalty and honor as the two men become hunter and hunted. But Ryan plays it with equal strength of character, resigned to bringing his friend to justice but for all the wrong reasons. The irony is that while the relationship between the outlaws is underpinned with strong bonds, the forces of law and order are greedy, brutal trash only interested in collecting the bounty on the Bishop's head.

Of course there's a superb cadre of wonderful character actors giving considerable support to the two leads: Warren Oates, Ernest Borgnine, Strother Martin, etc. They add real acting weight to the awesomely bloody, magnificently choreographed action scenes that the film is best known for, especially the charnel-house climax. Taken as whole, and although made nine years after it, *The Wild Bunch* is *The Magnificent Seven*'s older, more world-weary and brutalized, yet brooding and thoughtful brother.

FURTHER VIEWING: *Major Dundee; Straw Dogs; The Getaway; Pat Garrett and Billy the Kid; Bring Me the Head of Alfredo Garcia; Cross of Iron*
SEE ALSO: *The Magnificent Seven; The Good, the Bad and the Ugly; Once Upon a Time in the West; The Long Riders*

441/500

★★★

Director: Damiano Damiani
Screenwriter: Salvatore Laurani
Produced by: Bianco Manini
Starring: Gian Maria Volonté, Klaus Kinski, and Martine Beswick
Released by: Anchor Bay (DVD)

15+

EL CHUNCHO, QUIEN SABE?

(A BULLET FOR THE GENERAL)

1966, 135 mins.

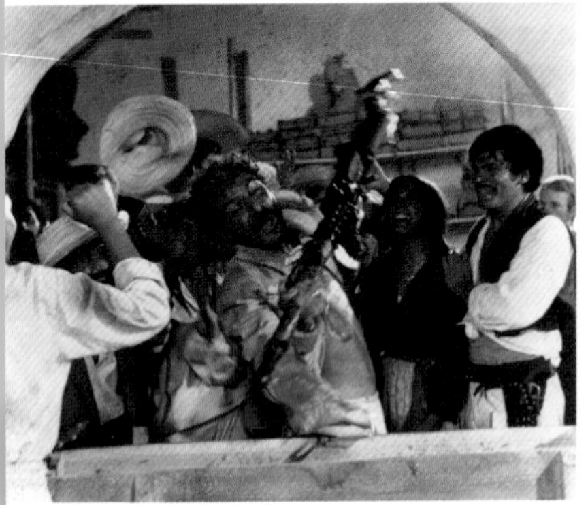

Plot: A group of Mexican banditos steal arms to sell to revolutionaries, joined by a young American, Bill Tate. He and the banditos' leader, El Chuncho, become friends, but as the Mexican becomes more involved with the revolution, the friendship is at odds as Tate is an assassin for the U.S. government.

Review: While politics are on the agenda, this movie still has everything you want in a spaghetti western: train robberies, shoot-outs, corrupt land-owners, and beautifully desolate landscapes. However, it's the inevitably tragic friendship at its heart that makes this movie so interesting.

FURTHER VIEWING: *Il sicario; La noia (The Empty Canvas); La strega in amore (The Witch); Il sorriso del grande tentatore (The Tempter/The Devil is a Woman); Lenin: The Train*
SEE ALSO: *Django; A Fistful of Dynamite; The Magnificent Seven; Once Upon a Time in the West; The Wild Bunch; Viva Zapata!*

442/500

★★★

Director: Wayne Coe
Screenwriter: Wayne Coe
Producer: Richard Hahn
Starring: James Earl Jones, Brad Dourif, and Will Hare
Released by: Academy Home Entertainment (VHS only)

GRIM PRAIRIE TALES

1990, 86 mins.

Plot: James Earl Jones and Brad Dourif star in an anthology movie that takes place around the flickering flames of a prairie camp fire. Farley Deeds is an upright man trying to reach his wife by traveling on foot across the country; Morrison is a bounty hunter who's lugging a corpse on his horse for reward money. They each tell two stories to each other, trying to out-do one another with the most grotesque.

Review: Coe's only feature film work was this western horror, and it's a shame it hasn't seen a wider release considering the two stars who were at the helm. The story about the woman who sucks up men into her belly during sex is a stroke of demented genius.

FURTHER VIEWING: *Not available*
SEE ALSO: *Campfire Tales; Creepshow*

143

★★★★

Director: Peter Fonda
Screenwriter: Alan Sharp
Producer: William Hayward

Starring: Peter Fonda, Warren Oates, and Verna Bloom

Released by: Sundance Channel Home Entertainment (DVD)

12+

THE HIRED HAND

1971, 90 mins.

Plot: After one of a trio of drifters is killed after being caught with another man's wife, the others exact their revenge on the murderer by stealing his horses and leaving him crippled. Collings then returns home to his estranged wife, who after a seven-year absence will only take him back as a hired hand. When his friend Harris is captured by the men they smote, Collings must choose between loyalty to his wife or to his friend.

Review: The sad death of Griffen in the first act sets a somber tone, and, coupled with Bruce Langhorne's haunting soundtrack, you'll find Fonda's directorial debut lingers in your memory long after the final reel. Warren Oates co-stars as loyal friend Harris.

FURTHER VIEWING: *Idaho Transfer; Wanda Nevada*
SEE ALSO: *High Noon; The Man Who Shot Liberty Valance*

144

★★★

Director: Walter Hill
Screenwriter: Bill Bryden
Producer: Tim Zinnemann

Starring: David Carradine, Keith Carradine, Robert Carradine, and James Keach

Released by: MGM (DVD)

18+

THE LONG RIDERS

1980, 99 mins.

Plot: A gang of crooks led by Jesse James become the most wanted men on the frontier after a series of daring raids on banks and trains. They're pursued by the Pinkerton agency as well as law enforcement who want them dead or alive. The gang temporarily breaks up, before coming back together to perform one last heist.

Review: Walter Hill turned in this ultraviolent western the year after his acclaimed gang warfare film *The Warriors*. The selling point is in the casting of four clans of real-life acting brothers: the Carradines, the Quaids, the Keaches, and the Guests. We're also given the rare opportunity to see outlaws as the men they are, rather than glorified and unjustified. Ry Cooder provides the stunning soundtrack.

FURTHER VIEWING: *The Warriors; Wild Bill*
SEE ALSO: *Last Stand at Saber Riber; Macho Callahan*

445
500

★★★★

Director: Robert Altman
Screenwriter: Robert Altman
Producer: Michell Brower

Starring: Warren Beatty, Julie Christie, and Rene Auberjonois
Released by: Warner Bros. Pictures (DVD)

15+

MCCABE AND MRS. MILLER

1971, 120 mins.

Plot: Gambler John McCabe (played brilliantly by Warren Beatty) establishes a whorehouse in a new frontier town in Washington State. With only three ladies on offer and barely able to control them, he forms a partnership with an opium addicted madam (Julie Christie) to take care of business. After McCabe refuses to sell his land to a violent businessman, bounty hunters arrive in the town to kill him.

Review: Capturing the beauty of America's wild frontier, Altman's snow-covered film is tinged with sadness, in part due to the morose Leonard Cohen score. Beatty's hapless entrepreneur never seems in control of his dealings—his frosty end is to be expected from the first time he opens his mouth. An atmospheric and beautifully composed film.

FURTHER VIEWING: ***M*A*S*H; The Long Goodbye***
SEE ALSO: ***The Outlaw Josey Wales***

446
500

★★

Director: Arthur Penn
Screenwriter: Thomas McGuane

Produced by: Elliott Kastner and Robert M. Sherman

Starring: Marlon Brando, Jack Nicholson, and Randy Quaid
Released by: MGM/UA (DVD)

15+

THE MISSOURI BREAKS

1976, 125 mins.

Plot: While looking for a suitable base of operations out in the badlands of Montana, a gang of care-free horse thieves incur the wrath of a reactionary, brutal rancher. After his own harsh efforts fail to stop the stealing, he hires a cold-blooded—and eccentric—bounty hunter to rid himself of the thieves once and for all.

Review: Featuring two great actors—Nicholson and Brando—at the height of their powers, it's really Brando's show. With a performance apparently as eccentric off screen as it was on, his cross-dressing, bird-loving, dandified killer is a film stealer. But that shouldn't overshadow what is still an offbeat, gritty, raucous, and often funny western with a great cast of superb character actors.

FURTHER VIEWING: ***The Train; Bonnie and Clyde; Little Big Man; Night Moves; The Dead of Winter***
SEE ALSO: ***Butch Cassidy and the Sundance Kid; The Long Riders; Tombstone; Tom Horn***

Director: Sam Peckinpah
Screenwriter: Rudy Wurlitzer
Producer: Gordon Carroll

Starring: James Coburn, Kris Kristofferson, and Richard Jaeckel
Released by: Warner Home Video (DVD)

8+

PAT GARRETT AND BILLY THE KID

1973, 122 mins. (director's cut)

Plot: Peckinpah's final western is an emotive study of the relationship between famed outlaw Billy the Kid (Kris Kristofferson) and the ruthless sheriff who's hunting him, Pat Garrett (James Coburn). At the start of the movie, the Kid is jailed and sentenced to hang. He escapes by blasting his way to freedom and heads across the country, pursued by the lawman who wants him dead, not alive.

Review: The film's chaotic production was in no doubt due to Peckinpah's propensity for drink—studio relations crumbled as he soared over budget and was late delivering a final cut. It was released in an abridged and critically panned version; however, the extended cut is more violent and restores much of the director's original ideas. The circular narrative ensures no one gets away unscathed.

FURTHER VIEWING: *The Wild Bunch; Ride the High Country*
SEE ALSO: *The Left Handed Gun; Chisum*

448
500

★★

Director: Carlo Lizzani
Screenwriters: Lucio Battistrada, Andrew Baxter, Adriano Bolzoni, and Armando Crispino

Produced by: Carlo Lizzani and Ernst R. von Theumer

Starring: Lou Castel, Mark Damon, and Pier Paolo Pasolini
Released by: Not Available

15+

REQUIESCANT (KILL AND PRAY)

1967, 110 mins.

Plot: A band of Mexican revolutionaries are massacred by Southern troops, the slaughter led by land-hungry fop George Ferguson. The only survivor is the son of the banditos' leader; he is found and raised by a Quaker family. When the family's daughter is lured away into big city prostitution, the boy pursues her only to discover the brothel where she works belongs to Ferguson. The scene is set for thrilling vengeance.

Review: This curious little spaghetti western is more focused, and has a lot more social commentary, than some of the more operatic members of the genre. There are moments of unintentional humor—the impromptu musical number in particular—but the script is not your usual good and evil narrative, and the climatic duel is surely unique in the annals of the western.

FURTHER VIEWING: ***Siluri umani (Human Torpedoes); Il gobbo (The Hunchback of Rome); The Dirty Game; Torino nera (Black Turin); Cattiva (The Wicked)***
SEE ALSO: ***Django; A Fistful of Dollars; For a Few Dollars More***

449
500

★★★

Director: Samuel Fuller
Screenwriter: Samuel Fuller
Producer: Samuel Fuller

Starring: Rod Steiger, Sara Montiel, and Brian Keith
Released by: Fox (DVD)

RUN OF THE ARROW

1957, 85 mins.

Plot: Touching on the moral conflict of those left standing at the end of the Civil War, Rod Steiger plays Private O'Meara, an Irishman who chose the wrong side. Disillusioned with fighting, he heads west and attempts to integrate with the Sioux Indians by taking a native wife. When the war arrives on his doorstep once again, he must make a choice between joining his new allies or those who will liberate the country.

Review: *Run of the Arrow* is notable for being the first movie to utilize blood squibs. In one scene, a man who is being gutted by a Sioux Indian is shot by his accomplice to stop his prolonged torture—a short burst of bloody violence that would be at home in any Peckinpah film.

FURTHER VIEWING: ***I Shot Jesse James; Forty Guns***
SEE ALSO: ***Major Dundee; Escape from Fort Bravo***

50

★★★★

Director: Ralph Nelson
Screenwriter: John Gay

Produced by: Gabriel Katzka and Harold Loeb

Starring: Candice Bergen, Peter Strauss, and Donald Pleasence
Released by: Lionsgate (DVD)

18+ SOLDIER BLUE

1970, 112 mins.

Plot: The slaughter of a U.S. cavalry column by the Cheyenne leaves just two survivors: a young, naive trooper and a foul-mouthed, brazen white woman once held captive by the Cheyenne chief. The two strike up a tender, tempestuous friendship and a confused romance as they trek across the badlands seeking safety.

Review: Full of bawdy humor and grimly realistic violence, this was one of a slew of veritas westerns that attempted to redress the cinematic historical record and show Native Americans in a far more sympathetic light. In the shocking climax, Levine recreates one of the worst excesses by "white" forces, the Sand Creek Massacre, raising the question of just who exactly were the savages.

FURTHER VIEWING: *Lilies of the Field; Father Goose; Duel at Diablo; Counterpoint; Charly*
SEE ALSO: *Carnal Knowledge; Dances with Wolves; Little Big Man; A Man Called Horse; The Searchers*

51

★★★

Director: Robert Aldrich
Screenwriter: Alan Sharp
Producer: Carter DeHaven

Starring: Burt Lancaster, Bruce Davison, and Jorge Luke
Released by: Warner Home Video (DVD)

18+ ULZANA'S RAID

1971, 120 mins.

Plot: An Apache scout and his men start a campaign of terror against the new American settlers, committing acts of robbery and murders whenever they please. A fresh-faced lieutenant (Bruce Davison) and grizzled scout (Burt Lancaster) follow their trail until they engage the Indians in a long and treacherous fire fight in a valley gorge.

Review: The thinly veiled Vietnam allegory aside, Aldrich serves up a violent slice of the Old West, complete with rapes, suicides, and spectacular gunfights. Addressing the barbarism of man during war, no side is left untarnished: despite Major Cartwright asking those in his command how any man created by God could commit such barbaric acts, he still has Ulzana and his men killed.

FURTHER VIEWING: *Apache; The Frisco Kid*
SEE ALSO: *Valdez Is Coming; Lawman*

CHAPTER 9

FILM LAB

"THE ONLY PERFORMANCE THAT MAKES IT, THAT MAKES IT ALL THE WAY, IS THE ONE THAT ACHIEVES MADNESS"

Film Lab is probably the most diverse section in the book, as it covers movies of all genres—the common denominator is an element of the art house, an experimentalism, a sense of pushing boundaries. Where else are you likely to find Disney, Roger Corman, Mick Jagger, Stanley Kubrick, and The Monkees lumped together in the same category? This section is full of surprises—some pleasant, some less so—but there's no need to tread carefully: all of these movies are rewarding in some sense, and prizing style over substance is no crime here. Now is not the time for caution, so cannonball into the deep end and prepare to be amazed, appalled, and enlightened.

FILM LAB

★★★★

Director: Werner Herzog
Screenwriter: Werner Herzog

Produced by: Werrner Herzog and Hans Prescher

Starring: Klaus Kinski, Helena Rojo, and Del Negro
Released by: Anchor Bay (DVD)

12+

AGUIRRE: DER ZORN GOTTES

(AGUIRRE: THE WRATH OF GOD)

1972, 93 mins.

Plot: Driven by greed and religious fervor, a column of Conquistadors push deep into the jungle in search of the illusory city of gold—El Dorado. Cracking the whip is the megalomaniac Aguirre, whose insanity darkens as they travel into the rainforest, abandoning all pretences of civilization.

Review: The making of this movie has generated a mythology all of its own. It's hardly surprising; wearing armor while negotiating jungle rapids can't have been much fun for anybody concerned. But such ordeals just add a veneer of torment to this Conquistador "heart of darkness," shot like a survival travelogue with superior cinematography. It's very easy to imagine that, as the Spanish drive the unfortunate locals manhandling their cannons through thick mud, Herzog didn't even bother to yell, "Action!"—he just simply set up the camera and left the cast to it.

Mother Nature is one of the film's central characters, the jungle and the river battling their human adversaries at every turn. Both are also analogous with Aguirre's mounting obsession and insanity, widening and deepening the further he pushes into them; the same could be true of the rafts the Conquistadors travel on, growing more unstable and derelict the longer the journey drags on.

Klaus Kinski is ideal as the reptilian villain—a veritable Iago at the start; a truly mad Hamlet by the end, insidiously supplanting the expedition's more cautious leaders, then using sheer force of will to drive his disintegrating crew onward to destruction. Clearly he bears as much responsibility for their deaths as the spears and arrows of the natives whose homes Aguirre is invading, if indeed that is the right word. Beset by illness and violence from within and without, it's more like the Conquistadors are being sucked down to their inevitable demise, leaving Aguirre like another mad king trying to hold back the inevitable, insane and alone before the encroaching tide of the jungle.

FURTHER VIEWING: ***Fitzcarraldo; Nosferatu; Cobra Verde; Grizzly Man; Rescue Dawn***
SEE ALSO: ***Apocalypse Now; The New World***

★★★★

Director: Stanley Kubrick
Screenwriter: Stanley Kubrick
Produced by: Stanley Kubrick

Starring: Ryan O'Neal, Marisa Berenson, and Patrick Magee
Released by: Warner Home Video (DVD)

2+

BARRY LYNDON

1975, 184 mins

Plot: The film is divided into two parts: the first, "By What Means Redmond Barry Acquired the Style and Title of Barry Lyndon," follows the early life of Redmond Barry, beginning with the death of his father. A young Barry falls in love with his cousin but is thrown over for a man with a fortune; poor and without prospects, Barry (apparently) kills his rival in a duel and joins the British Army to escape prosecution. Barry quickly deserts, but is then blackmailed into joining the Prussian Army. He soon falls in with gambler and suspected spy Chevalier de Balibari, and after many adventures Barry decides to imitate his past and gain his fortune by marrying well. Enter the Countess of Lyndon, whom Barry seduces.

The second part, "Containing an Account of the Misfortunes and Disasters which Befell Barry Lyndon," sees Barry marry the countess, fight with his stepson, lose his influential friends, and witness the death of his own son. Barry begins drinking heavily, and after the countess attempts suicide, his stepson challenges him to duel. He's wounded in the leg; it is later amputated. Barry is now penniless and physically broken; his stepson bribes him to leave the countess, which Barry accepts.

Review: Based on the Thackeray novel *The Luck of Barry Lyndon*, this film did not at first achieve the commercial or critical successes of Kubrick's previous efforts; a relatively obscure and slow-paced costume drama seemed an odd follow-up. Clocking in at three hours, *Barry Lyndon* is probably most like *Eyes Wide Shut*—there is such an attention to beauty and the beauty of detail in both, that it almost eclipses the narratives. Also, the characters seem emotionally straitjacketed, so that it's hard to identify with them or warm to them. As such, Barry Lyndon is long, heavy, and, mostly, unpleasant, but the sheer artistry in all aspects makes it more than worth the time. Having won Oscars for Cinematography, Art Direction, Costumes, and Adapted Score (plus nominations for Best Picture and Best Director) despite its failure at the box office, *Barry Lyndon* has found a sizable audience over time and proved to be an artistic masterpiece.

FURTHER VIEWING: *Eyes Wide Shut; 2001: A Space Odyssey*
SEE ALSO: *Far from the Madding Crowd; The Duellists; Moll Flanders; Marie Antoinette*

★★★★

Director: Penelope Spheeris
Screenwriter: Penelope Spheeris
Produced by: Jeff Prettyman
Starring: Black Flag, Circle Jerks, Fear, etc.
Released by: Not Available

15+

THE DECLINE OF WESTERN CIVILIZATION

1981, 100 mins.

Plot: Rough-looking 16mm documentary charting the rise (and fall?) of the L.A. punk scene in the late seventies. Featuring many of the key acts that remain influential to music nuts, geeks, and freaks, such as the powerful politicized Black Flag (pre-Rollins); the shambolic and self-destructive Germs; and lesser-knowns the Circle Jerks, Catholic Discipline, Fear, The Bags, and X. Mingling live footage from over-the-top shows, vox-pop interviews, and "at home" conversations between the director and the bands, viewers are treated to an unexpurgated view of punk as it lives and breathes from the people who created it.

Review: "There are no rock stars now," says one skinhead kid interviewed at the start of the film. That's what punk was all about—anyone could get on stage, regardless of their talent, and play loud, fast, and mobilize a crowd with their music. It's a sharp contrast with the pre-packaged reality talent shows that are so popular today, or the Beatles, Stones, or Floyd that punk was rebelling against. Packed with insightful interviews on and off the stage, you can work out quite easily who are the poseurs and who just love making music. The Germs' manager said working for the band was akin to being the mother of four three-year-olds whom she wanted to beat senseless. On the other hand, Black Flag vocalist Ron Reyes paid $16-a-month rent to live in a closet. Spheeris tries to dig deeper into what creates the aggression at punk shows, with one interviewee claiming it's down to his dirty environment; another admits to just liking beating people up. The hypocrisy of being afraid of individuality and the scene's underlying violence is brought to the fore. Ultimately, it's a time capsule of a marginalized section of society and their artistic response that smeared an indelible marker over the closing decades of the twentieth century.

FURTHER VIEWING: ***Dudes; The Decline of Western Civilization Part II: The Metal Years***
SEE ALSO: ***Dig!; Sid and Nancy***

★
★
★
★
★

Director: Richard Kelly
Screenwriter: Richard Kelly

Produced by: Adam Fields, Nancy Juvonen, and Sean McKittrick

Starring: Jake Gyllenhaal, Jena Malone, Mary McDonnell, and Maggie Gyllenhaal
Released by: Twentieth Century Fox (DVD)

15+

DONNIE DARKO

2001, 113 mins.

Plot: Donnie Darko is a brilliant, challenging, and troubled teenager who has stopped taking his medication and started hallucinating visitations from a man named Frank, who appears in what is possibly the creepiest bunny costume ever. Frank tells Donnie that the world will end in just under a month, and at the same time a jet engine of unknown origin crashes into the bed Donnie left only minutes before.

Frank urges Donnie to commit pranks at home and at school, but also tells him about the possibilities of time travel. As Donnie falls in love with the new girl at school, he is increasingly aware of the approaching end of the world, and becomes the only person who can reverse the catastrophes that have followed his surviving the jet-engine crash.

Review: Comparisons to Henry Koster's brilliant film *Harvey* (1950) are almost inevitable given that both feature rabbit-shaped hallucinations, but the two also make compelling statements on the nature of mental illness (including how easily people will use mental illness to explain things they simply don't understand). Like *Harvey*, *Donnie Darko* tells a heart-wrenching story while chipping steadily away at the audience's disbelief in the fantastic, making us realize, then accept, that the most rational explanations for odd events aren't always the most truthful.

But in a narrative teeming with fantasy and science fiction, told by an (for all intents and purposes) unreliable narrator, it's Donnie—and Jake Gyllenhaal's performance—who provides a central anchor point that keeps the fantasy grounded. That Gyllenhaal as the possibly paranoid schizophrenic off his medication can convince us that he's not only the stable center of the picture but the most reliable narrator of them all only speaks to his enormous talent as an actor. A truly excellent, if totally bizarre, story.

FURTHER VIEWING: *Southland Tales*
SEE ALSO: *Harvey; Nowhere*

★★★★★

Director: David Lynch
Screenwriter: David Lynch
Producer: David Lynch

Starring: Jack Nance, Charlotte Stewart, Allen Joseph, and Jeanne Bates
Released by: Absurda/Ryko (DVD)

18+

ERASERHEAD

1977, 89 mins.

Plot: Henry works as a printer and lives alone in a small apartment, listening to records and avoiding awkward exchanges with his attractive but strangely alluring neighbor. One night, he's called to dinner at his girlfriend Mary's home, meeting her extremely odd family for the first time. After an embarrassing dining incident where he is asked to carve the meat, Henry is informed that he has become the father to a grotesque aberration—a child that is neither man nor beast, wrapped in a swaddle and spending its time vomiting and crying. As Henry tries to deal with his newfound fatherhood, he experiences terrible and frightening visions that are a portent of his deepest desires.

Review: David Lynch's first full-length feature is a nightmare made flesh, set in a dimly lit, rusty pipe-laden world bereft of birdsong or pleasure. At first irrational, once *Eraserhead* has taken hold, you quickly embrace its stream of surreal juxtaposed imagery, the overwhelming sonic assaults and skewed view of a relationship transformed by the miracle of birth. While dark and absurdist, it cemented Lynch's career as the go-to guy for weird, and by comparison makes *Blue Velvet* seem mundane. It's both a homage to the fifties movies of his youth as well as a radical re-evaluation of the nuclear family household—despite the crucifix on the wall and the conservative attitude toward sex, Mary's mother makes obscene tongue gestures, comes on to Henry, and is generally vile. The anxiety of one man dealing with an unwanted child and a faltering relationship is dealt with in a surprising fashion, culminating in the shocking final images of his creature-child split open like a piñata. Jack Nance's suitably odd performance (complete with shock Bride of Frankenstein hairdo) guaranteed him roles in all of Lynch's films to follow.

FURTHER VIEWING: ***The Elephant Man; Lost Highway***
SEE ALSO: ***Un Chien Andalou; Freaks***

★★★★★

Directors: Samuel Armstrong, James Algar, Ford Beebe, Norman Ferguson, Jim Handley, T. Hee, Wilfred Jackson, Hamilton Luske, Bill Roberts, Paul Satterfield, and Ben Sharpsteen
Screenwriters: Joe Grant and Dick Huemer
Produced by: Walt Disney
Starring: Leopold Stokowski, Deems Taylor, and Mickey Mouse
Released by: Walt Disney Video (DVD)

A

FANTASIA

1940, 125 mins.

Plot: *Fantasia* consists of seven interlinked short films set to music: "Toccata and Fugue in D Minor" begins with live-action musicians, then segues into abstract animation; "Nutcracker Suite" shows the changing of seasons with dancing fairies, flowers, and fish, among other personified aspects of nature; "The Sorcerer's Apprentice," easily the most famous of the pieces, demonstrates the danger of overstepping one's bounds and is based on Goethe's poem; "The Rite of Spring" takes us through the history of the universe; "The Pastoral Symphony" shows an ancient Greek celebration of Bacchus; "Dance of the Hours" features hippos and alligators in tutus; and, finally, "Night on Bald Mountain" is the deep and dark story of the demon Chernabog.

Review: There's something odd about classic Disney films: they seem educational and innocent while scaring the hell out of children, and *Fantasia* is no exception. A cross between a silent film and a musical—there's no dialog apart from voiced introductions, and all the action is set to classical music—*Fantasia* is probably the pinnacle in the marriage of animation and music. It's hard to believe such a timeless piece of experimental filmmaking was first released in 1940; nothing like it existed before that time, and, frankly, nothing has matched it since. It is truly a masterpiece, with the added bonus of Mickey Mouse.

Fantasia proved to be too far ahead of its time, however; it didn't do very well on its first release, partly as it was over two hours long. Subsequently edited down, it's now on DVD at nearly its original length. *Fantasia* is truly a generation-busting film, a picture that children and adults alike can enjoy and marvel at (and possibly shiver a little at the sinister mops in "The Sorcerer's Apprentice"—after all, it wouldn't be classic Disney without the casual creepiness!).

FURTHER VIEWING: *Fantasia 2000; Pinocchio; Dumbo*
SEE ALSO: *Peter and the Wolf; Peter Pan; Melody Time; Make Mine Music*

★★★★★

Directors: Donald Cammell and Nicolas Roeg

Screenwriters: Donald Cammell and Anita Pallenberg
Produced by: Sanford Lieberson

Starring: James Fox and Mick Jagger
Released by: Warner Home Video (DVD)

PERFORMANCE

1970, 105 mins.

Plot: Chas is having a bit of a problem—it's swinging 1960s London, he's an enforcer for an East End gang, and he broke the rules. Now he's being pursued by his employers and they're out for blood (literally), so Chas finds the perfect hiding place: the basement apartment of has-been rock star Turner, who lives with two women and hasn't written a song in years. What begins purely as a business relationship—Turner needs Chas' money and Chas needs Turner's anonymity—becomes something deeper as Chas begins sexual relationships with Turner's companions, and Turner challenges Chas' homophobia and misogyny. Turner gives Chas mushrooms, which marks the turning point in his exploration of his own identity, and when he is seemingly welcomed back by his old gang, it's not necessarily Chas who leaves the apartment.

Review: Despite the film's obvious appeal to children of the sixties and seventies, featuring The Rolling Stones' Mick Jagger in the lead role as rock-star Turner, this is not purely a star vehicle. *Performance* delves deep into questions of the nature of identity and the roles we play, or performances we give, based on outward expectations, and audiences of the seventies simply weren't ready for its graphic depictions of violence, sex, and drug use.

With the almost Svengali-like influence of Keith Richards' partner Anita Pallenberg (who plays Turner's sexual companion Pherber), *Performance* morphed from Cammell's original idea of a light-hearted romp into one of the darkest and frankest explorations into the sixties ethos of sexual freedom and mind expansion through mind-altering substances; it's a pity no one told the studio they weren't getting the Stones' equivalent of a Beatles' film. The studio were reluctant to release the film, and it gained infamy for its lack of the expected theatrical release. Although the unsavory images of the film might seem almost tame now, its emotional frankness remains unsettling; forty years on, *Performance* has just as much value as the story of a personal odyssey of growth and acceptance as a cultural artifact.

FURTHER VIEWING: ***Eureka; Bad Timing; Demon Seed***
SEE ALSO: ***Blow-Up; Get Carter; Persona***

★★★★★

Director: Alex Cox
Screenwriter: Alex Cox

Produced by: Peter McCarthy, Michael Nesmith, Gerald T. Olson, and Jonathan Wacks

Starring: Emilio Estevez, Fox Harris, and Harry Dean Stanton
Released by: Universal Studios (DVD)

5+

REPO MAN

1984, 92 mins.

Plot: Otto is a Clash-style punk rocker in L.A., aimless, raging at the world, and living with his parents. When he finds his girlfriend having sex with his so-called best friend at a house party, and learns that his hippie parents have donated his school money to a television preacher, he takes up with hardened, cynical repo-man Bud (played by Harry Dean Stanton). Though repossessing cars from poor unfortunates who can't pay their loans clashes with Otto's punk ethos at first, he soon realizes that, despite the healthy remuneration package, he enjoys the intensity of the job as well as the danger and drugs it entails. He leaves the now-boring punk lifestyle and becomes completely immersed in ripping cars; when rumor goes around of a $25,000 reward for a Chevy Malibu he puts his hat in the ring. Unbeknownst to Otto—and his rival repo men—the car contains a mysterious and deadly glowing package in the trunk, and Otto ends up racing against the FBI to find the car and collect the reward first.

Review: Ever wondered where the concept for that mysterious glowing suitcase in *Pulp Fiction* came from? Look no further than *Repo Man*. This is Alex Cox's first film, often considered his best, and it clearly set the punk-rock tone that his next outing, the Sid Vicious biopic *Sid and Nancy*, would embrace wholeheartedly.

This has all the hallmarks of a Cox film: seemingly nonsensical details, like watches without hands and a running sight gag with air fresheners; an absolutely fantastic punk soundtrack (featuring a live performance by the Circle Jerks); the ambiguous driving-into-the-sky ending; and a defiance of categorization. Is it a music vehicle? Fantasy? Science fiction? A coming-of-age film? Comedy? Well, the answer to all those questions is, simply, "yes." It all makes perfect sense if you don't think about it, so why bother trying to dissect such a vastly entertaining film? Featuring probably the best performance of Emilio Estevez's career, and one of the best by Harry Dean Stanton, *Repo Man*'s goofy mystery is one of its main strengths, elevating it to cult status and giving it a much-deserved place on this list.

FURTHER VIEWING: *Sid and Nancy; Straight to Hell*
SEE ALSO: *The Decline of Western Civilization; Dudes*

★
★
★
★

Director: Roger Corman
Screenwriter: Jack Nicholson
Produced by: Roger Corman

Starring: Peter Fonda, Dennis Hopper, and Susan Strasberg

Released by: MGM (DVD, part of the *Roger Corman Collection*)

18+

THE TRIP

1967, 85 mins.

Plot: Groves is a television commercial director whose personal life has hit the skids. His stunning wife has had an affair, and Groves is ambivalent about the pending divorce. As a typical sixties coping mechanism, he decides to take an LSD trip with the help of a guru, but soon finds himself alone on the street and completely off his head. Groves' trip takes him to the Sunset Strip, where he flits in and out of clubs and bars at random—and sometimes into strangers' homes, but it's the sixties and everyone's on drugs anyway so that's fine—and meets a beautiful young woman who's fascinated by LSD. The two sleep together as Groves' trip culminates, and Groves ends his adventure feeling a new man with a better perspective on life.

Review: Before *Easy Rider*, there was *The Trip*. Legendary low-budget director and producer Roger Corman encouraged Jack Nicholson's "out there" approach to screenwriting (see The Monkees' vehicle *Head* for more information), and what came of it was this homage to the mind-expanding properties of LSD. Previously as straight as a drug-free arrow, by his own admission, Corman and his production team decided that in order to make a veracious film about LSD, they'd have to experience the drug for themselves. Being filmmakers, they put together a production-like schedule for the users and the handlers so that all involved would have a personal reference with the drug to draw from, and the result is this visually warped representation of a trip on film, almost as if we're truly seeing the world through the eyes of a man on LSD.

While pretty much every film by Corman could be considered "cult," *The Trip* holds a special place in the hearts of viewers for its veracity, its truthful and non-judgmental representation of drug-taking. And as a precursor to that other cult masterpiece, *Easy Rider*, *The Trip* is a valuable commentary on LSD and its vaunted place in sixties counterculture.

FURTHER VIEWING: ***Head; One Flew over the Cuckoo's Nest***
SEE ALSO: ***Easy Rider; Naked Lunch***

★
★
★
★
★

Director: Monte Hellman
Screenwriter: Rudy Wurlitzer
Producer: Michael Laughlin

Starring: James Taylor, Dennis Wilson, Warren Oates, and Laurie Bird
Released by: Criterion (DVD)

15+

TWO-LANE BLACKTOP

1971, 102 mins.

Plot: The road movie to end all road movies, *Two-Lane Blacktop* is about a couple of unnamed guys known in the movie as The Driver and The Mechanic (played by musicians James Taylor and Dennis Wilson) who seem to live permanently in their suped-up 1955 Chevy. They survive on the road by challenging others to races for cash, knowing their car will leave their opponents in the dust. Warren Oates plays their foil, GTO, who becomes obsessed with beating them after they repeatedly pass each other across three states. He challenges them to a cross-state race to Washington, D.C.; the bet being they take the other's car if they lose. From there, their difficult journeys take them to new places and breakneck speeds until the film literally burns up during its final scene on a lonely stretch of highway.

Review: Carefully crafted through multiple script rewrites, both *Rolling Stone* and *GQ* called it the greatest road movie ever made a year before its release. When it hit theaters in 1971, it was with a whimper and not a bang. Time, however, has been kind, and its influence can be seen in Tarantino's love letter to seventies road movies, *Death Proof*. Hellman keeps the camera firmly fixed on the revving engines and the yellow lines on the road that speed by; the highway is as much an important character as those behind the wheel. Despite being untrained actors, and not having much dialog, Taylor and Wilson make for good grungy leads. Oates is also impeccable as their road-weary opponent, whose different stories for how he ended up in the GTO are sometimes funny and clearly all lies; the man has no history out on the road. The only thing one could criticize about this movie is not knowing who won the race, but you'll enjoy the ride getting there through every minute of it.

FURTHER VIEWING: *Back Door to Hell; The Shooting*
SEE ALSO: *Vanishing Point; Easy Rider*

★
★
★

Director: Nagisa Ôshima
Screenwriter: Nagisa Ôshima
Producer: Anatole Dauman

Starring: Tatsuya Fuji, Eiko Matsuda, and Aoi Nakajima
Released by: Criterion (DVD)

18+

AI NO CORRIDA (IN THE REALM OF THE SENSES)

1976, 108 mins.

Plot: Based on a real-life crime that shocked Japan in the 1930s, Eiko Matsuda plays former prostitute Sada Abe who now works as a hotel maid. The other workers treat her with contempt despite having to sexually satisfy the hotel owner Ishida (Tatsuya Fuji) on a daily basis. He soon makes his move on the new girl, and they begin a passionate affair. But the relationship takes a sado-masochistic turn the more jealous Abe becomes despite Ishida's affirmations that he will never leave her, even in death.

Review: A chilling look at the lengths people will go for pleasure, as well as a criticism of Japanese politics at the time, Ôshima's drama pushed the boundaries by incorporating real coitus between the actors into the story.

FURTHER VIEWING: ***Merry Christmas, Mr. Lawrence; Ai no borei (In the Realm of Passion/Empire of Passion)***
SEE ALSO: ***Double Suicide; Last Tango in Paris***

★
★
★
★

Director: Andrew Jarecki
Screenwriter: None
Produced by: Andrew Jarecki and Marc Smerling

Starring: Arnold Friedman, Elaine Friedman, David Friedman, Seth Friedman, and Jesse Friedman

Released by: Warner Home Video/ HBO (DVD)

15+

CAPTURING THE FRIEDMANS

2003, 107 mins.

Plot: An award-winning teacher and his son go from pillars of the community to pedophiliac monsters following accusations of child molestation. Under microscopic scrutiny by the media and the police, and with public hysteria mounting, the family begins freefalling out of control.

Review: Aided by the Friedmans' compulsion to film everything, this haunting documentary takes news footage and stands it in sharp relief to some shockingly honest home movies. As the family battles to come to terms with the horrific charges leveled against them, it's left to the viewer to decide just how guilty the men were, but then watching a drama is one thing; watching a family shatter for real is something else entirely.

FURTHER VIEWING: ***Just a Clown; All Good Things***
SEE ALSO: ***Happiness; The Woodsman***

Director: Rémy Belvaux
Screenwriter: Rémy Belvaux
Producer: André Bonzel

Starring: Benoît Poelvoorde, Jacqueline Poelvoorde-Pappaert, Nelly Pappaert, and Hector Pappaert

Released by: Criterion (DVD)

18+

C'EST ARRIVÉ PRÈS DE CHEZ VOUS
(MAN BITES DOG)

1993, 95 mins.

Plot: Ben is a charming man, good son to his mother, hard worker, and able to speak on any subject at length. He is also a serial killer. A three-man film crew follow him around as he explains the art of murder and how to dispose of bodies without getting caught. It's not long before the crew become participants in Ben's lunacy, despite their deepest reservations.

Review: Despite being shot in black and white and the grim subject matter, *Man Bites Dog* is bizarrely comic—like *Clerks*, but with a murderer as the star. Benoît Poelvoorde is brilliant at being able to switch between affable and psychotic at the drop of a hat. Grim stuff—those who enjoy art-house will appreciate the irony of the set up.

FURTHER VIEWING: *Not available*
SEE ALSO: *The Blair Witch Project; Blue Velvet*

Director: Uli Edel
Screenwriters: Uli Edel, Herman Weigel, Horst Rieck, and Kai Hermann

Produced by: Bernd Eichinger, Bertram Vetter, and Hans Kaden

Starring: Natja Brunckhorst, Thomas Haustein, and David Bowie
Released by: Image Entertainment (DVD, out of print)

18+

CHRISTIANE F.

1981, 138 mins.

Plot: In the 1970s, young teenager Christiane is bored and restless, so when she hears of the opening of Sound, a new nightclub in the center of Berlin, she dresses up to look older and blags her way in. There she meets Detlev, an older man who experiments with drugs, and soon Christiane progresses from recreational pills to full-on heroin addiction, turning to prostitution to support her habit.

Review: Based on the autobiography of Christiane Felscherinow, *Christiane F.* is an entirely unglamorous look at the degradation of drug addiction against a solid backdrop of David Bowie songs. This is not Sunday afternoon viewing; the film is darker than dark, depressing, and graphic, but it is a remarkably evenhanded (if not at all shy) depiction of what it was like being a teenaged junkie in seventies Berlin.

FURTHER VIEWING: *Last Exit to Brooklyn; Body of Evidence*
SEE ALSO: *Streetwise; Kids; Panic in Needle Park; The Man with the Golden Arm*

466/500

★★★

Director: Peter Greenaway
Screenwriter: Peter Greenaway

Produced by: Daniel Toscan du Plantier, Denis Wigman, Kees Kasander, and Pascale Dauman

Starring: Richard Bohringer, Michael Gambon, and Helen Mirren
Released by: Starz/Anchor Bay (DVD, out of print)

18+

THE COOK, THE THIEF, HIS WIFE, AND HER LOVER

1989, 124 mins.

Plot: Albert Spica is a gangster with an appetite who buys the classy French La Hollandais restaurant and uses it as his nightly dinner table. His behavior is appalling to everyone, including his genteel wife Georgina, who begins an affair with regular patron and bookshop owner Michael. But once Spica discovers the affair, he force-feeds Michael pages from books until he dies; Georgina then takes her revenge by forcing Spica to eat something far worse.

Review: This is the definition of an Art Film: unpalatable to many, but to some the rarest and most sought-after delicacy imaginable. It's littered with violence and nudity (as well as a bit of scatological excess) and can be difficult to stomach, but it's a chance to marvel at Jean-Paul Gaultier's costumes.

FURTHER VIEWING: ***Prospero's Books; The Belly of an Architect; Drowning by Numbers***
SEE ALSO: ***Orlando; Edward II; Titus***

467/500

★★★★

Director: Terry Zwigoff
Screenwriter: None

Produced by: Terry Zwigoff, Albert Berger, David Lynch, Lawrence Wilkinson, and Lianne Halfon

Starring: Robert Crumb, Aline Kominsky, Charles Crumb, Maxon Crumb, and Robert Hughes
Released by: Sony Pictures (DVD)

18+

CRUMB

1995, 119 mins.

Plot: A documentary about groundbreaking and controversial underground comics creator Robert Crumb, who's most well known for his neurotic and sexually explicit comics including *Fritz the Cat* and *Mr. Natural*. Through a series of interviews with Crumb's friends and family, we're given a glimpse into the origins of his sexually obsessed and often disturbing creations.

Review: This is not an easy film to watch, and the fact that it's a documentary makes it all the more difficult. Compared to his psychopathic siblings and domineering mother, Crumb appears positively well adjusted, though his honesty when talking about his work—"If I don't draw for a while I get really crazy, I start getting really depressed and suicidal . . . but then while I'm drawing I feel suicidal too"—belies this notion. A sometimes endearing, sometimes upsetting look at underground comics' most influential creator.

FURTHER VIEWING: ***Fritz the Cat; Ghost World***
SEE ALSO: ***American Spendor; Comic Book Confidential; Pretty as a Picture: The Art of David Lynch***

68

★★★

Director: Richard Linklater
Screenwriter: Richard Linklater

Produced by: Richard Linklater, Anne Walker-McBay, James Jacks, and Sean Daniel

Starring: Matthew McConaughey, Jason London, and Rory Cochrane
Released by: Universal Studios (DVD)

15+

DAZED AND CONFUSED

1993, 102 mins.

Plot: It's 1976, the grooviest year of the century, on the last day of school for the students of Lee High School. *Dazed and Confused* follows a disparate group of unfocused seniors as they get caught up in freshman hazing, pot smoking, and keg parties to welcome summer and the beginning of the rest of their lives.

Review: Like *Fast Times at Ridgemont High*, *Dazed and Confused* features a slew of pre-stardom actors in its ensemble cast, including Matthew McConaughey, Ben Affleck, Milla Jovovich, and Queen of the Indies Parker Posey. But while this is a coming of age tale, it's more a nostalgic look back at the fun and fancy-free lives of kids in the seventies than a hard-hitting dissection of the perils of growing up. And that's probably why this film has become so popular—there's no didacticism to be found, just entertainment.

FURTHER VIEWING: ***Slacker; School of Rock***
SEE ALSO: ***Fast Times at Ridgemont High***

69

★★★

Director: Jean-Jacques Beineix
Screenwriter: Jean-Jacques Beineix
Producer: Serge Silberman

Starring: Wilhelmenia Fernandez, Frédéric Andréi, and Richard Bohringer
Released by: Lionsgate (DVD)

15+

DIVA

1981, 123 mins.

Plot: A Parisian postman secretly bootlegs an opera performance by a singer who has never released a recording. When another tape falls into his possession that incriminates the chief of police in a prostitution racket, Jules goes underground by hiding out in a bohemian's loft. The lure of singer Cynthia Hawkins draws him out, and with a price on his head, it will take more than love to stay alive.

Review: Arguably a style-over-substance affair, *Diva* is a reaction to depressing seventies French cinema, replacing washed out grays with cool blues, and mixing up opera with rock 'n' roll on the soundtrack. The thrilling Métro scene, with Jules making his getaway from the police on his sputtering moped, shows just how chase sequences should be done.

FURTHER VIEWING: ***La lune dans le caniveau (The Moon in the Gutter); Roselyne et les lions (Roselyne and the Lions)***
SEE ALSO: ***Subway; Peril***

470
500

★★★

Director: Stacy Peralta
Screenwriters: Stacy Peralta and Craig Stecyk
Produced by: Agi Orsi

Starring: Sean Penn (narrator), Jay Adams, Tony Alva, and Jeff Ament
Released by: Sony Pictures (DVD)

DOGTOWN AND THE Z BOYS

2001, 91 mins.

© glen E. friedman

Plot: In the inner-city beach slums of L.A., a pack of anti-mainstream surfers stake out a territory on the beachfront and make surfing an art form. However, their evolution takes them back on land as they turn a bunch of skateboarders into unwitting pop culture stars: the Zephyr Team, better known as The Z-Boys.

Plot: An emo princess' wet dream, this insightful, beautiful documentary deconstructs how inner-city punks became a kinetic art installation, revolutionizing urban culture with their skill, intensity, and mesmerizing balletic style. With such beauty and grace it's easy to forget they're on black asphalt and not blue waves, and you realize why skaterboyz were so cool long before anyone had heard of Tony Hawk—or Avril Lavigne.

SEE ALSO: ***Riding Giants; Made in America***
FURTHER VIEWING: ***Big Wednesday; BMX Bandits***

471
500

★★★★

Director: Peter Greenaway
Screenwriter: Peter Greenaway
Produced by: David Payne

Starring: Anthony Higgins, Janet Suzman, Anne-Louise Lambert, and Hugh Fraser

Released by: Fox Lorber (DVD)

THE DRAUGHTSMAN'S CONTRACT

1982, 103 mins.

Plot: In Restoration England, the beautiful, estranged wife of a rich landowner hires a young, handsome, egotistical artist to draw a series of pictures of her husband's estate. Their relationship soon moves beyond the formal and when the husband is found dead, the significance of the artist and the pictures becomes far deeper and darker.

Review: A real visual and cerebral feast, this film's multilayered narrative and symbolic nuances provide substance to turn a Restoration murder mystery into a subtle discussion on the burgeoning sexual and social politics of the time. Erotic, lush, and funny, it's shot almost as a series of gorgeous paintings; it's also fascinating to watch the power play between the lovers unfold until you realize it's the women who really hold the whip.

FURTHER VIEWING: ***The Belly of the Architect; The Cook, the Thief, His Wife, and Her Lover; Drowning by Numbers; Prospero's Books; The Pillow Book; A Zed and Two Noughts***
SEE ALSO: ***Barry Lyndon; Restoration***

★ **Director:** James William Guercio
★ **Screenwriter:** Robert Boris
★ **Producer:** James William Guercio

Starring: Robert Blake, Billy Green Bush, and Mitch Ryan
Released by: MGM (DVD)

18+ ELECTRA GLIDE IN BLUE

1973, 113 mins.

Plot: Highway patrol officer John Wintergreen wants nothing more than to be a member of the homicide division, but his applications keep getting rejected. After determining an apparent suicide is actually a murder, he is finally promoted and made Harve Poole's personal driver. His hard-line way of dealing with suspects makes things difficult for Wintergreen, and soon he's back on the road on his Electra Glide bike to get to the bottom of this wicked crime.

Review: Guercio's only movie is a hard-boiled modern western, wonderfully photographed, and utilizing the majesty of Arizona's Monument Valley as a backdrop. Robert Blake gives an understated performance as Wintergreen, whose honesty (and height) doesn't do him any favors among the bitter and corrupt Arizona law enforcement officers.

FURTHER VIEWING: *Not available*
SEE ALSO: *Magnum Force; Easy Rider*

473/500

★★★

Director: Gus Van Sant
Screenwriter: Gus Van Sant
Producer: Dany Wolf

Starring: Alex Frost, Eric Deulen, and John Robinson
Released by: HBO Home Video (DVD)

ELEPHANT

2003, 81 mins.

Plot: Loosely based on the Columbine School Massacre in 1999, two bullied high school kids take destiny into their own hands by organizing a full-on assault of their school, where the jocks, teachers, and pupils who made their lives so unbearable will say their prayers to the barrel of a gun.

Review: Van Sant's film is different from his others in that it's comprised mainly of long, unbroken tracking shots of the characters as they go about their day-to-day lives. At first, this allows us to understand the complexities of the modern high school and introduce us to the principal players; later it becomes a technique that captures the uncertainty of life and death as the two killers stalk the hallways of the school.

FURTHER VIEWING: ***To Die For; Last Days***
SEE ALSO: ***Zero Day; Heart of America***

474/500

★★★★★

Director: Thomas Vinterbeg
Screenwriters: Mogens Rukov and Thomas Vinterberg

Produced by: Birgitte Hald and Morten Kaufmann

Starring: Ulrich Thomsen, Henning Moritzen, and Thomas Bo Larsen
Released by: Polygram USA Video (DVD)

FESTEN (THE CELEBRATION)

1998, 105 mins

Plot: Celebrating his sixtieth birthday, a family patriarch hosts a dinner for his friends and family, including his two sons and daughter. However, one of the sons, Christian, is distraught at the recent suicide of his twin sister. Giving a speech at the dinner, Christian accuses his father of molesting her and Linda as children, forcing the family to face up to its dark past.

Review: The first of the Danish Dogme '95 movies, it's a hell of a way to start. Shot almost as a high-end home movie, it certainly captures, with complete realism, the moment a family is caught like a deer in headlights, its darkest secrets thrown open for public scrutiny. By turns darkly funny (the family chef is a total scene stealer), gripping, and agonizingly painful, this is genuine, innovatively genius filmmaking of the highest caliber.

FURTHER VIEWING: ***Dogville; Idioterne (The Idiots); The Third Lie; It's All About Love; Dear Wendy***
SEE ALSO: ***Happiness; Hope Floats***

75

★ ★ ★

Director: Paul Morrissey
Screenwriter: Paul Morrissey
Producer: Andy Warhol

Starring: Joe Dallesandro, Geraldine Smith, and Patti D'Arbanville
Released by: Image Entertainment (DVD)

8+

FLESH

1968, 86 mins.

Plot: Young hustler Joe needs to make cash, and he needs it now. His lesbian wife is pregnant and needs an abortion, and it's going to take $200 to make it happen. A good guy, though uneducated and naïve, Joe spends his day encountering various characters willing to help him—and his only commodity is his naked flesh.

Review: Pop culture tzar Andy Warhol's first collaboration with filmmaker Paul Morrissey produced this curious gem, harshly edited in Burroughs' cut-up style that renders most of the dialog useless but gives us an idea of the day-to-day life of a young guy hustling to survive. Its primary goal is to sexualize and iconize Joe with his frequent nudity and lingering close-ups; his ennui of his own desirability is its most interesting facet.

FURTHER VIEWING: *Trash; Heat*
SEE ALSO: *Bad; Gift*

76

★ ★

Director: Andrew Bujalski
Screenwriter: Andrew Bujalski
Produced by: Ethan Vogt

Starring: Kate Dollenmayer, Mark Herlehy, and Christian Rudder
Released by: Fox Lorber (DVD)

15+

FUNNY HA HA

2002, 85 mins.

Plot: Marnie is just out of college and wondering what to do with herself. Careerless, loveless, apathetic, she meets people, goes to parties, struggles with an unrequited crush, and does . . . stuff.

Review: This doesn't feel like a movie; it's more like watching a fly-on-the-wall documentary following the everyday existence of the central character. Kate Dollenmayer's Marnie is great: endearingly confused and a picture of slacker melancholy. It's also one of those films where you'll end up arguing about which character you're most like or which situation you most relate to: drunken confessions, confused relationships, all the classic twenty-something angst moments.

FURTHER VIEWING: *Mutual Appreciation; Beeswax*
SEE ALSO: *Slacker; Reality Bites; Trees Lounge; Clerks*

477/500

★★★★

Director: Albert Maysles, David Maysles, Ellen Hovde, and Muffie Meyer
Screenwriter: None

Produced by: Albert Maysles, David Maysles, and Susan Froemke

Starring: Edith "Little Edie" Bouvier Beale and Edith "Big Edie" Ewing Bouvier Beale
Released by: Criterion (DVD)

GREY GARDENS

1976, 100 mins.

Plot: *Grey Gardens* is a documentary that follows Big Edie (in her seventies) and Little Edie (in her fifties), the "eccentric" aunt and first cousin of Jacqueline Kennedy Onassis. After their twenty-eight room estate, Grey Gardens, in East Hampton was designated uninhabitable by the health board, Onassis gave them the money to fix it up. Filmmakers Albert and David Maysles made several visits to speak to the women after the renovations.

Review: We all have skeletons in our closets too horrible to name, which is why we like to gawk when the skeletons of others make their escape—*Grey Gardens* lets us do just that. Big Edie and Little Edie are odd ducks in that Miss Havisham way that comes from having a prominent family, lots of money, and a refusal to let time march on. The women tell their own fascinating and nostalgic stories, which are filled with old romances, better times, dreams of escape, and even a lost singing career.

FURTHER VIEWING: ***A Visit with Truman Capote; Meet Marlon Brando***
SEE ALSO: ***Brother's Keeper; Vernon, Florida; Tarnation***

478/500

★★★

Director: Bob Rafelson
Screenwriters: Bob Rafelson and Jack Nicholson

Produced by: Bob Rafelson and Jack Nicholson

Starring: Peter Tork, Michael Nesmith, Davy Jones, and Micky Dolenz
Released by: Rhino Theatrical (DVD)

HEAD

1968, 86 mins.

Plot: Starring the manufactured pop sensation The Monkees, *Head* has no plot. Instead, it's structured more as a series of acid flashbacks with its seemingly incongruous collection of scenes including sight gags, parodies, and musical numbers.

Review: Despite the popularity of The Monkees, *Head* made absolutely no money when it was first released, but has since become a classic example of sixties psychedelia. The film seems to function primarily as a self-reflexive satire on The Monkees' status as a manufactured pop band and was their way of trying to break out of the mold (which probably didn't help the film's popularity). Fun and fantastical, *Head* features some pretty major sixties cameos by Victor Mature, Annette Funicello, Sonny Liston, and Frank Zappa.

FURTHER VIEWING: ***Elephant Parts; The Monkees (TV series); Five Easy Pieces***
SEE ALSO: ***And Now for Something Completely Different; The Beatles: Magical Mystery Tour; Rock 'n' Roll High School***

479

★★★★

Director: Lars von Trier
Screenwriter: Lars von Trier
Produced by: Vibeke Windeløv
Starring: Bodil Jørgensen, Jens Albinus, and Anne Louise Hassing
Released by: Zentropa (DVD)

18+

IDIOTERNE (THE IDIOTS)

1998, 117 mins.

Plot: A group of normal, healthy people seek to fly in the face of society's unimaginative social strictures. To do this, they release their "inner idiots," acting in public as though mentally impaired. This frees them to push the boundaries of acceptable behavior, provoke outrage, and highlight societal fears and hypocrisy toward those actually disabled.

Review: Unstructured, random, badly shot in places, and highly controversial, this was the second of the Dogme '95 "movies" and captures the essence of the project, doing everything it can to catch the viewer off guard. There's no structured narrative to speak off, just documentary-style cause and effect, enhanced by entirely plausible, entirely natural characterization and some offensively hilarious moments. This isn't guerrilla filmmaking; it's an armored assault on movie conventions.

FURTHER VIEWING: *The Kingdom; Breaking the Waves; Dancer in the Dark; Dogville; Antichrist*
SEE ALSO: *My Name Is Sam; Rain Man; Tropic Thunder*

480

★★★

Director: John Byrum
Screenwriter: John Byrum
Producer: Davina Belling
Starring: Richard Dreyfuss, Jessica Harper, and Bob Hoskins
Released by: MGM (DVD)

INSERTS

1974, 117 mins.

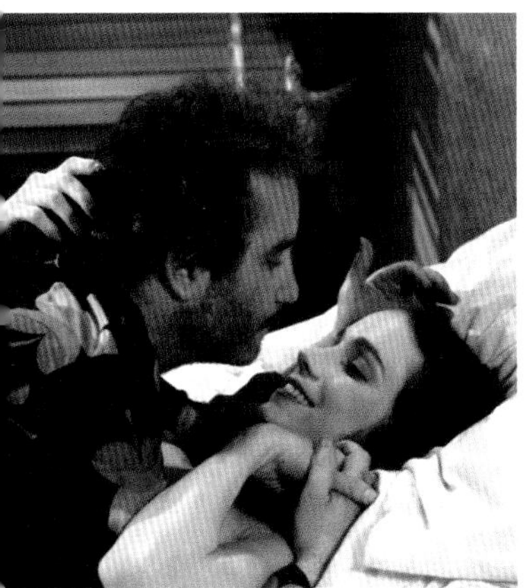

Plot: Set in the earliest days of Tinseltown, a once-great director of silent films now lives a hermit-like existence in the Hollywood Hills after his failure to adapt to the newfound and popular "talkies." At a loss and having turned to the bottle, he decides to make pornos instead using Rex the Wonder Horse as his star and a local hood's girl as his prime actress under the auspices of them being the greatest things committed to celluloid.

Review: Originally billed as a "degenerate film, with dignity," Byrum's work gives us no obvious reasons as to why Boy Wonder was ruined by Hollywood—do we blame his drinking, his womanizing, or perhaps just his ineptitude? Off-beat and dramatic, it's possible to view *Inserts* as comedic as well as a damning portrayal of those spat out by the machine.

FURTHER VIEWING: *Heartbeat; The Razor's Edge*
SEE ALSO: *Boogie Nights; The Day of the Locust; Sunset Boulevard*

481/500

★★★★

Director: Gaspar Noé
Screenwriter: Gaspar Noé

Produced by: Brahim Chioua and Vincent Cassel

Starring: Monica Bellucci and Vincent Cassel
Released by: Lionsgate (DVD)

18+

IRRÉVERSIBLE

2002, 97 mins.

Plot: Told in reverse order, Marcus and Pierre—ex-lovers—trawl grim, tawdry streets in search of the man who brutally raped Marcus' lover, Alex. When they find the supposed attacker, their vengeance is savage and bloody.

Review: A reverse evolution from appalling violence and degradation to idyllic romantic bliss, this is a remarkable and explicitly horrifying feat of moviemaking. Technically brilliant, with extended, single shots (including the nine-minute rape scene) and some incredible camera work that leaves you reeling, the backward-running narrative makes for painful viewing: the brutalized Bellucci unfolds to blissfully ignorant beauty, and you know what awaits her. With its grimly resigned commentary on the nature of revenge and sexual conquest, this is grueling but essential viewing.

FURTHER VIEWING: *Tintarella de luna; Sodomites; Seul contre tous (I Stand Alone); Enter the Void; Eastern Promises; Les rivières pourpres (Crimson Rivers)*
SEE ALSO: *A Clockwork Orange; Memento; Requiem for a Dream*

482/500

★★★

Director: Chris Marker
Screenwriter: Chris Marker
Producer: Anatole Dauman

Starring: Jean Négroni (narrator), Hélène Chatelain, and Davos Hanich
Released by: Criterion (DVD)

LA JETÉE (THE PIER)

1962, 28 mins.

Plot: Following the destruction of Paris during World War III, the remaining inhabitants have perfected time-travel that will allow those who are strong willed to go into the past and future in search of anything that can save them. One man takes up the challenge, visiting the past and meeting a woman from his memories who irreparably ties him to his childhood and his own ultimately devastating fate.

Review: The primary inspiration for Terry Gilliam's fantastic 1995 film *Twelve Monkeys*, Chris Marker's original French film is a strange beast, shot in black-and-white still photographs and featuring a voice-over narrative rather than actors' dialog. Its static appearance contradicts the figurative movements on-screen.

FURTHER VIEWING: *Sans Soleil (Sunless); Le joli mai*
SEE ALSO: *Twelve Monkeys; Solaris*

83

★★★

Director: Dennis Hopper
Screenwriter: Stewart Stern
Producer: Paul Lewis

Starring: Dennis Hopper, Stella Garcia, and Julie Adams

Released by: United American Video (VHS only)

8+

THE LAST MOVIE

1971, 108 mins.

Plot: A movie shoot in Peru goes off the rails after the death of a stuntman, causing another actor, Kansas (played by a delirious Dennis Hopper), to quit filmmaking completely. Instead of returning to the U.S., he shacks up with a local whore. When the locals start making their own mock western that results in actual deaths, Kansas is forced to step in to stop a bloodbath.

Review: Dennis Hopper's notorious "follow up" to the hugely successful *Easy Rider* was a bust commercially, but artistically way ahead of its time, making use of several behind-the-scenes filmmaking techniques that confounded audiences. Over forty hours of footage was edited down to less than two hours to create a narrative—no mean feat!

FURTHER VIEWING: *Out of the Blue; Colors*
SEE ALSO: *Lost in La Mancha; 8½*

★★★★

Director: Martin Scorcese
Screenwriter: None
Producer: Robbie Robertson

Starring: Robbie Robertson, Rick Danko, Richard Manuel, Levon Helm, and Garth Hudson

Released by: MGM (DVD)

A

THE LAST WALTZ

1978, 117 mins.

Plot: Martin Scorsese's documentary/concert film celebrates sixteen years of Canadian rock group The Band as they play their farewell concert at the Winterland Ballroom in San Francisco on Thanksgiving, 1976. Additional musicians included Bob Dylan, Ringo Starr, Muddy Waters, Van Morrison, Neil Young, and Joni Mitchell.

Review: Scorsese's film is widely hailed as one of the best concert films of all time (and is certainly better than his back-slapping Rolling Stones film *Shine a Light*), utilizing some of the best names in cinematography, and putting The Band's career in context with insightful interviews from all its members from their Malibu studio. Purist fans will love it, but casual viewers can enjoy the magic on stage and the classical sets.

FURTHER VIEWING: ***Shine a Light***
SEE ALSO: ***I Am Trying to Break Your Heart; DiG!***

★★★

Directors: Kathryn Bigelow and Monty Montgomery
Screenwriters: Kathryn Bigelow and Monty Montgomery
Producer: A. Kitman Ho
Starring: Willem Dafoe, Robert Gordon, and Marin Kanter
Released by: Blue Underground (DVD)

8+

THE LOVELESS

1982, 85 mins.

Plot: Willem Defoe makes his acting debut in a colorful study of leather-clad bikers on their way to a bike event in Florida. Stopping off in Georgia at a small-town diner, Vance chats with the locals, drinks innumerable cups of coffee, and waits for other greasers to arrive. He soon hooks up with the beautiful and wild Telena, whose mother killed herself. When her father finds out about their relationship, all hell breaks loose.

Review: Bigelow and Montgomery's collaboration (as both co-writers and directors) not only introduced an unsuspecting world to Defoe, but led to the cult smash *Near Dark* in 1987. Period-perfect locations on an abandoned U.S. highway add to the authenticity.

FURTHER VIEWING: *Near Dark; The Hurt Locker*
SEE ALSO: *The Wild One; Wild at Heart*

486
500

★★★★★

Director: James Marsh
Screenwriter: None
Produced by: Simon Chinn

Starring: Philippe Petit
Released by: Magnolia Home Entertainment (DVD)

12+

MAN ON WIRE

2008, 94 mins.

Plot: In 1974, while America is gripped by Watergate, a lone man fulfills what for him is a dream but to most people would be unmitigated lunacy: to walk across a tightrope strung a quarter of a mile up between the twin towers of the World Trade Center!

Review: Beautifully splicing a collage of dramatized recollections, newsreel, and interviews, this remarkable documentary charts the amazing, audacious career of guerrilla wire-walker Philippe Petit. With all the highs and lows of the intricate preparations, the result has all the trappings of a great heist story, but is something anarchic, insane, exhilarating, breathtaking, and, most of all, magical.

FURTHER VIEWING: ***Red Riding: 1980; The King***
SEE ALSO: ***Touching the Void***

487
500

★★★★

Director: Joe Berlinger and Bruce Sinofsky
Screenwriter: None

Produced by: Joe Berlinger and Bruce Sinofsky

Starring: James Hetfield, Lars Ulrich, Kirk Hammett, and Robert Trujillo
Released by: Paramount (DVD)

15+

METALLICA SOME KIND OF MONSTER

2003, 141 mins.

Plot: After more than twenty years of making heavy metal music, Metallica decide to go into therapy to mend rifts between the band members, and they take their fans with them. Their therapy sessions are cut with studio footage of the making of *St. Anger*, their first studio album in five years.

Review: For those of us who remember the global uproar when Metallica cut their hair short in the mid-nineties, this documentary needs no further justification. Many believed that was the moment they lost their Samson-esque powers of rock, but the fact is they remain the one of the world's most successful metal bands. This is documentary filmmaking at its most personal and voyeuristic—chronicling struggles with drugs, the creative process, and each other—and it's essential viewing for Metallica fans.

FURTHER VIEWING: ***Paradise Lost; Brother's Keeper***
SEE ALSO: ***The Decline of Western Civilization 2: The Metal Years***

488

★ **Director:** Paul Schrader
★ **Screenwriter:** Paul Schrader
★ **Producer:** Tom Luddy

Starring: Ken Ogata
Released by: Criterion (DVD)

15+ MISHIMA A LIFE IN FOUR CHAPTERS

1985, 120 mins.

Plot: A highly dramatized retelling of the life of acclaimed Japanese novelist Yukio Mishima that's broken up into four distinct chapters: each with a retelling of one of Mishima's stories, black-and-white segments that fill in details about his past, as well as a reconstruction of his final day alive. The film culminates in his death by seppuku (a Japanese suicide ritual of death by disembowelment).

Review: A medley of styles and storylines populate Schrader's beautifully structured film that deconstructs the myth of the great man's life that many in Japan are still unable to understand. Mishima's primary struggle was in confronting the nature of existence, for which he offers up no explanations. The film puts his life and work into an easily digestible context, with a voiceover by Roy Scheider.

FURTHER VIEWING: *Patty Hearst; American Gigolo*
SEE ALSO: *Hitokiri (Tenchu!); Kurotokage (Black Lizard)*

489

★ **Director:** Shane Carruth
★ **Screenwriter:** Shame Carruth
★ **Produced by:** Shane Carruth

Starring: Shane Carruth and David Sullivan
Released by: New Line Home Video (DVD)

PRIMER

2004, 77 mins.

Plot: While trying to improve on one of their inventions, two engineers stumble across an incredible phenomenon that has earth-shattering consequences. Realizing they can make themselves very rich, they begin playing with causality and time, but the vast complexities of their game have unpredictable and devastating consequences.

Review: As riveting as it is mind-bendingly dense, this is a "time travel" movie in the loosest possible sense. As it toys with causality and quantum mechanics, there is palpable tension building as the plot unfolds, all of it done without the need for any CGI lightshows. This is an entirely cerebral affair that only serves to make this feat of low-budget indie filmmaking all the greater.

FURTHER VIEWING: *Not available*
SEE ALSO: *The Time Machine; Back to the Future; Donnie Darko*

490
500

★
★
★

Director: Peter Greenaway
Screenwriter: Peter Greenaway

Produced by: Masato Hara, Kees Kasander, Katsufumi Nakamura, Yoshinobu Namano, Denis Wigman, and Roland Wigman

Starring: John Gielgud, Michael Clark, and Michel Blanc
Released by: Not Available

15+

PROSPERO'S BOOKS

1991, 129 mins.

Plot: Once Duke of Milan, Prospero is now an exiled magician, cast away on a forgotten island with his daughter Miranda and his books. When his enemies are shipwrecked on the island, Prospero has an opportunity to at last exact revenge, only for Miranda to fall in love with the son of his foe.

Review: Not so much a film as a moving medieval illuminated manuscript or giant Renaissance artwork flick book, the real star of Greenaway's sumptuous movie is the production design, particularly the eponymous books. Visually stunning, this innovative retelling of Shakespeare's *The Tempest* combines art, poetry, dance, calligraphy, and music, and maximizes to the fullest extent what is visually possible on-screen—without the use of any computer trickery.

FURTHER VIEWING: ***The Cook, the Thief, His Wife, and Her Lover; The Draughtsman's Contract; A Zed and Two Noughts***
SEE ALSO: ***Caravaggio; Baz Lurhman's Romeo and Juliet***

491
500

★
★
★
★

Director: Darren Aronofsky
Screenwriters: Darren Aronofsky and Hubert Selby Jr.

Produced by: Eric Watson and Palmer West

Starring: Jared Leto, Jennifer Connelly, Ellen Burstyn, and Marlon Wayans
Released by: Artisan (DVD)

18+

REQUIEM FOR A DREAM

2000, 102 mins.

Plot: Three New York City junkies—friends Harry and Tyrone, and Harry's girlfriend Marion who's estranged from her wealthy family—try to score a pound of heroin to sell for profit and turn their lives around, but they become even more mired in their addictions. Harry alternately uses and neglects his lonely widowed mother Sara, who becomes dependent on amphetamines, and the three friends spiral deeper into unchecked degradation.

Review: Even if you haven't seen the film you've most likely heard the soundtrack—former Pop Will Eat Itself frontman Clint Mansell's stunning "Lux Aeterna" theme song has since been used in myriad film trailers, including *The Lord of the Rings: The Two Towers*. On the foundation of its mournful soundtrack and with Aronofsky's fanciful but intense directing style, *Requiem for a Dream* takes a brutally honest look at the perils and pitfalls of addiction.

FURTHER VIEWING: ***Pi; The Fountain; The Wrestler***
SEE ALSO: ***Trainspotting; Drugstore Cowboy; The Panic in Needle Park***

32

★★★

Director: Francis Ford Coppola
Screenwriters: Francis Ford Coppola and S. E. Hinton

Produced by: Doug Claybourne and Fred Roos

Starring: Matt Dillon, Mickey Rourke, and Diane Lane
Released by: Universal (DVD)

8+ RUMBLE FISH

1983, 94 mins.

Plot: Rusty James is a reckless, self-destructive, and dull street punk trying to escape the shadow of Motorcycle Boy—his revered brother. But when his older sibling returns home, tormented by family secrets and unwanted hero worship, life begins to fall apart around them.

Review: An homage to earlier motorcycle movies, this is a monochrome, arthouse *West Side Story* (without the songs, of course). Dillon's Rusty James is all style over substance, lacking the intellect of his troubled street-Caesar brother, played with effortless cool by Rourke. Stark cinematography and a complex soundscape capture the inner city noir perfectly, making it easy to understand why they would want to escape such a desolate, dead-end world.

FURTHER VIEWING: *The Rain People; The Godfather; The Outsiders; Gardens of Stone*
SEE ALSO: *Diner; Drugstore Cowboy; Rebel without a Cause; The Wild One*

33

★

Director: Pier Paolo Pasolini
Screenwriter: Sergio Citti

Produced by: Alberto de Stefanis, Antonio Girasante, and Alberto Grimaldi

Starring: Paolo Bonacelli, Giorgio Cataldi, and Umberto Paolo Quintavalle
Released by: Criterion (DVD)

8+ SALÒ O LE 120 GIORNATE DI SODOMA

(SALO, OR THE 120 DAYS OF SODOM)

1975, 116 mins.

Plot: In the dying days of Fascist Italy, a cohort of its leaders prepares to exercise absolute power over a group of teenagers. Free of morality or ethics, they begin a regime of torture, subjugation, and abject humiliation.

Review: Loosely based on writings of the Marquis de Sade but exchanging Revolutionary France for Mussolini's Italy, this is a treatise on political and sexual totalitarianism, and how the two seem synonymous. Never stinting in its portrayal of sadism and abuse, it was reviled on its release and it remains very uncomfortable viewing even in these more desensitized times.

FURTHER VIEWING: *Accattone; Il vangelo secondo Matteo (The Gospel According to St. Matthew); Uccellacci e uccellini (The Hawks and the Sparrows); Il Decameron (The Decameron); Il fiore delle mille e una notte (Arabian Nights)*
SEE ALSO: *The Night Porter; Caligula; Hostel*

494
500

★★★★

Director: Steven Soderbergh
Screenwriter: Steven Soderbergh
Produced by: John Hardy and Robert Newmyer

Starring: Andie MacDowell, James Spader, Peter Gallagher, and Laura San Giacomo
Released by: Sony Pictures (DVD)

18+

SEX, LIES, AND VIDEOTAPE

1989, 100 mins.

Plot: Ann (MacDowell) is anxious and with good reason: her lawyer husband John (Gallagher) is carrying on an affair with her sister Cynthia (San Giacomo). The arrival of John's college friend, the unusual Graham (Spader), disrupts their relationships and all four characters are forced to reconsider their lives—especially their sexual relationships.

Review: Critically lauded (and very profitable), Soderbergh's small-scale breakthrough picture set the scene for the indie hits of the 1990s. It's a calm, intriguing study of character development and sexual politics, beautifully acted throughout—and Graham's erotic video habit makes for some memorable scenes. With the passing of time, Soderbergh's commentary on the mediation of sex by the camera and the screen has only become more relevant: a brilliant debut.

FURTHER VIEWING: ***Full Frontal; Bubble; Traffic***
SEE ALSO: ***The Ice Storm; The Big Chill***

495
500

★★★

Director: Irving Klaw
Screenwriter: None
Producer: Irving Klaw

Starring: Bettie Page, Tempest Storm, and Cherry Knight
Released by: Image Entertainment (DVD)

15+

TEASERAMA

1955, 80 mins.

Plot: Irving Klaw's cult classic burlesque movie features Tempest Storm and Bettie Page in a variety of amusing situations, as well as short bits from other dancers, transvestites, and comedy acts. There's no plot to speak of beyond that.

Review: Despite the short running time, *Teaserama* is not an easy film to sit through from start to finish—however, it's a great snapshot of the American underground adult entertainment scene from the fifties. Page struts and smiles seductively, and Storm pouts and waves her 40D chest around like it's a battering ram. A vintage curiosity that's dated, but now has added camp appeal. As a piece of Americana, you'll remember Bettie Page more than anything else from this silly piece.

FURTHER VIEWING: ***Varietease; Buxom Beautease***
SEE ALSO: ***The Notorious Bettie Page; Striporama***

★★★★

Director: Kevin Macdonald
Screenwriter: None
Produced by: John Smithson
Starring: Brendan Mackey, Nicholas Aaron, and Richard Hawking
Released by: MGM (DVD)

15+

TOUCHING THE VOID

2003, 106 mins.

Plot: In 1985, two recklessly bold young climbers head for the remote mountains of Peru. Their intention is to scale an as-yet unclimbed mountain face. After successfully completing the ascent, they start back down, but a terrible accident teaches them the true meaning of survival.

Review: Just looking at the breathtaking cinematography in the reconstructed scenes makes you wonder what goes through the mind of these men. The mountains have a staggering beauty that is also totally terrifying to the layman. Interviews with the climbers reveal their passion and help you understand why they do it, but what follows is unlikely to make any converts to mountaineering. However, it will teach you an awful lot about human endurance, resilience, and courage.

FURTHER VIEWING: *One Day in September; The Last King of Scotland; State of Play*
SEE ALSO: *Cliffhanger; K2; Alive*

497
500

★
★
★
★

Director: Orson Welles
Screenwriter: Orson Welles
Producer: Dominique Antoine

Starring: Orson Welles, Oja Kodar, and Joseph Cotten
Released by: Criterion (DVD)

A

VÉRITÉS ET MENSONGES (F FOR FAKE)

1973, 85 mins.

Plot: Orson Welles made this peculiar documentary in the early seventies (possibly using material from other filmmakers) about two of the world's greatest forgery artists—Elmyr de Hory and Clifford Irving. De Hory became notorious for producing paintings that he claimed were by masters. Irving wrote, and was later exposed for, a fake Howard Hughes autobiography. The film tells both of their stories in a free-form vox-pop fashion.

Review: Marie-Sophie Dubus and Dominique Engerer's quick-cut style of editing is now everywhere on primetime television and in film, and *F for Fake* is the first example of it being used to distort the narrative for great effect. Welles takes center stage, eulogizing about fakery in his own dramatic voice in the last completed film of his career

FURTHER VIEWING: ***Citizen Kane; Le procès (The Trial)***
SEE ALSO: ***The American Dreamer; American Movie***

498
500

★
★
★

Director: Jean-Luc Godard
Screenwriter: Jena-Luc Godard
Produced by: Not available

Starring: Mireille Darc and Jean Yanne
Released by: New Yorker Video (DVD)

15+

WEEK END

1967, 105 mins.

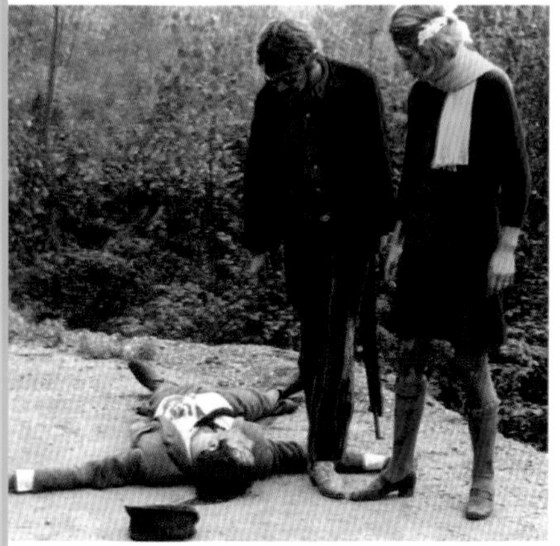

Plot: An unhappy, vile couple, both adulterous, both murderous, set out on a road trip to see the husband's father, hoping to secure an inheritance—by any means necessary. However the journey turns into an extended nightmare of wrecks, shootings, violence, hijackings, and finally cannibalism.

Review: Made when revolution was fomenting across France, this is a searing polemic on out-of-control consumerism and the empty virtues of capitalism (as seen in 1967). The shallow greed of the central couple, the violent anarchy of a society explosively decompressing, the traffic jam as allegory of a self-centered society going nowhere, this is thought-provoking stuff. But it doesn't overlook the fact that this is unconventionally brilliant moviemaking—and not without a few dark laughs along for the ride.

FURTHER VIEWING: ***Alphaville; Breathless; Pierrot le fou; Amore e rabbia (Love and Anger); Passion; Masculin, feminine; King Lear***
SEE ALSO: ***The Cars that Ate Paris***

★★

Directors: Woody Allen and Senkichi Taniguchi
Screenwriters: Woody Allen, Julie Bennett, Frank Buxton, Louise Lasser, Len Maxwell, Mickey Rose, and Bryan Wilson
Produced by: Charles Joffe
Starring: Tatsuya Mihashi, Akiko Wakabayashi, and Mie Hama
Released by: Image Entertainment (DVD)

WHAT'S UP, TIGER LILY?

1966, 80 mins.

Plot: Not so much a plot as a reworked ADR of a Japanese detective movie, topped and tailed by Allen's straight-to-audience sequences. The story, however, involves Japanese secret agent "Phil Moskowitz" on the hunt for the world's greatest egg salad recipe.

Review: This is a curious one. Allen takes a passably decent Asian spy flick, removes the dialog and replaces it with his own. While some of the gags may now be regarded as stereotypical and un-PC, and some of the jokes are a bit hit and miss, the juxtaposition of Jewish psychobabble wit and chop-sockey action segues hilariously well on occasion. The result is a *Mystery Science Theater 3000* for the observational comedy set.

FURTHER VIEWING: *Bananas; Sleeper; Annie Hall; Manhattan; Zelig; Broadway Danny Rose*
SEE ALSO: *Casino Royale; Our Man Flint; Austin Powers: International Man of Mystery*

★★★★★

Director: Leon Gast
Screenwriter: None
Producer: Leon Gast
Starring: Mohammad Ali and George Foreman
Released by: Universal Studios (DVD)

WHEN WE WERE KINGS

1996, 89 mins.

Plot: In 1974, Mohammad Ali and George Foreman were to face off in what's now known as the "Rumble in the Jungle." Using archive press footage as well as new interviews with writer Norman Mailer, filmmaker Spike Lee, and journalist George Ames Plimpton, Gast reconstructs the build-up to one of the biggest boxing matches of the last century, its impact on black culture in Africa and America, and the ensuing aftermath.

Review: Tightly edited, presenting balanced viewpoints from both sides of the ring, and deeply fascinating even for the non-sports fan, *When We Were Kings* rightfully won the Oscar for Best Documentary in 1996—both Ali and Foreman were present to help collect the award. A knock out.

FURTHER VIEWING: *Hells Angels Forever; 1 Love*
SEE ALSO: *Fallen Champ; Hoop Dreams*

LAKERS
99

REFERENCE

INDEXES AND CREDITS

INDEX BY TITLE

INDEX BY DIRECTOR

PICTURE CREDITS

GENERAL INTRODUCTION

Ladykillers, The: The Kobal Collection/Ealing/Rank/Evans, Arthur
Nightmare Before Christmas, The: The Kobal Collection/Touchstone Burton/Di Novi

CHAPTER 1

37°2 Degres Le Matin (Betty Blue): The Kobal Collection/Constellation-Cargo/Alive
Addiction, The: The Kobal Collection/Fast Films
All About Eve: The Kobal Collection/20th Century Fox
Almost Famous: The Kobal Collection/Dreamworks Llc/Preston, Neal
Amores Perros: The Kobal Collection/Alta Vista
Beguiled, The: The Kobal Collection/Universal
Best of Everything, The: The Kobal Collection/20th Century Fox
Big Wednesday: The Kobal Collection/Warner Bros
Black Narcissus: ITV/Rex Features
Blackboard Jungle: The Kobal Collection/MGM
Boys in the Band, The: The Kobal Collection/Cinema Center/Leo
Breakin': The Kobal Collection/Cannon
Brief Encounter: ITV/Rex Features
Bring Me The Head Of Alfredo Garcia: The Kobal Collection/United Artists
Bronenosets Potyomkin (Battleship Potemkin): The Kobal Collection/Goskino
Carny: The Kobal Collection/United Artists
Cisco Pike: The Kobal Collection/Columbia
Cockfighter: The Kobal Collection/Rio Pinto/New World/Artists Ent.
Das Experiment: The Kobal Collection/Senator Film
Dawn Patrol, The: The Kobal Collection/Warner Bros
Days of Heaven: The Kobal Collection/Paramount
Devils, The: The Kobal Collection/Warner Bros
Don't Look Now: The Kobal Collection/Casey Prods-Eldorado Films
Duellists, The: The Kobal Collection/Scott Free/Enigma/Paramount
Easy Rider: The Kobal Collection/Columbia
Far From Heaven: The Kobal Collection/Killer Films
Five Easy Pieces: The Kobal Collection/Columbia
Funny Games: The Kobal Collection/Wega Film
Ghost and Mrs Muir, The: The Kobal Collection/20th Century Fox
Ghost World: The Kobal Collection/Capitol/Granada/Jersey/UA/Bennett, Tracy
Ghosts...of the Civil Dead: The Kobal Collection/Correctional Services
Girl on a Motorcycle, The: The Kobal Collection/Mid-Atlantic/Ares/Claridge
Glen or Glenda?: The Kobal Collection/Screen Classics
Harold and Maude: The Kobal Collection/Paramount
House of Games: The Kobal Collection/Orion
Hush...Hush, Sweet Charlotte: The Kobal Collection/20th Century Fox
Idi I Smotri (Come and See): The Kobal Collection/Mosfilm
In the Company of Men: The Kobal Collection/Fair And Square Productions/Atlantis
Kids: The Kobal Collection/Shining Excalibur/Independent Pictures
Killing of Sister George, The: The Kobal Collection/Palomar
Lady Eve, The: The Kobal Collection/Paramount
Le Mépris (Contempt): The Kobal Collection/Rome-Paris-Films
Lenny: The Kobal Collection/United Artists
Les Valseuses (Going Places): The Kobal Collection/C.A.P.A.C/Uranus Gloria
Light Sleeper: The Kobal Collection/Carolco
Lolita: The Kobal Collection/MGM
Loneliness Of The Long Distance Runner, The: The Kobal Collection/Woodfall
Lost Weekend, The: The Kobal Collection/Paramount
Love Streams: The Kobal Collection/Golan-Globus/Shaw, Sam
Marnie: The Kobal Collection/Universal
Martin: The Kobal Collection/Laurel Entertainment
Midnight Cowboy: The Kobal Collection/United Artists
Mommie Dearest: The Kobal Collection/Paramount
Mudhoney: The Kobal Collection/Delta Films
My Own Private Idaho: The Kobal Collection/New Line
Naked Kiss, The: The Kobal Collection/Allied Artists
Naked Tango: The Kobal Collection/Sugarloaf/Gotan Productions
Ninth Configuration, The: The Kobal Collection/Lorimar
One Flew Over The Cuckoo's Nest: The Kobal Collection/United Artists/Fantasy Films
Outsiders, The: The Kobal Collection/Warner Bros
Paris Texas: The Kobal Collection/Road/Argos/Channel 4
Rebel Without a Cause: The Kobal Collection/Warner Bros
Reefer Madness: The Kobal Collection/G&H Productions
Rushmore: The Kobal Collection/Touchstone
Salvador: The Kobal Collection/Hemdale
Servant, The: The Kobal Collection/Associated British
Shawshank Redemption, The: The Kobal Collection/Castle Rock Entertainment (TL) Weinstein, Michael
Showgirls: The Kobal Collection/MGM/UA/Close, Murray
Sid and Nancy: The Kobal Collection/Zenith-Initial/Goldwyn
Sunset Boulevard: The Kobal Collection/Paramount
Sweet Smell of Success: The Kobal Collection/United Artists
Swimmer, The: The Kobal Collection/Columbia
Taxi Driver: The Kobal Collection/Columbia
To Sleep With Anger: The Kobal Collection/Svs Films
Tracks: The Kobal Collection/Trio
Trois Couleurs: Bleu; Blanc; Rouge: The Kobal Collection/MK2/CED/France 3/CAB/TOR/Canal +
Twin Peaks: Fire Walk With Me: The Kobal Collection/Lynch-Frost/Ciby 2000
Walk on the Wild Side: The Kobal Collection/Columbia
Wild One, The: The Kobal Collection/Columbia
Wise Blood: The Kobal Collection/Ithaca-Anthea/New Line
Woman Under The Influence, A: The Kobal Collection/Faces International

CHAPTER 2

84 Charlie Mopic: The Kobal Collection/Charlie Mopic Co
Ace in the Hole: The Kobal Collection/Paramount
Angel Heart: The Kobal Collection/Union-Carolco Int/Tri Star
Apartment Zero: The Kobal Collection/Summit Company
Assault on Precinct 13: The Kobal Collection/Miracle Films
At Close Range: The Kobal Collection/Orion
Bad Timing: ITV/Rex Features
Baise-Moi (Rape Me): The Kobal Collection/Le Studio Canal/Take One
Blood Simple: The Kobal Collection/River Road Prods
Blow Up: The Kobal Collection/MGM/Evans, Arthur
Boxing Helena: The Kobal Collection/Main Line
Caché (Hidden): The Kobal Collection/Sony Pictures
Cape Fear : The Kobal Collection/Universal
Conversation, The: The Kobal Collection/Paramount
Cutter and Bone: The Kobal Collection/United Artists
Das Boot: The Kobal Collection/Bavaria/Radiant
Day of the Locust, The: The Kobal Collection/Paramount
Dead Man's Shoes: The Kobal Collection/Warp Films/Big Arty Productions
Deliverance: The Kobal Collection/Warner Bros (TL) Hamilton, John
Dirty Harry: The Kobal Collection/Warner Bros
D.O.A.: The Kobal Collection/United Artists
Dressed To Kill: The Kobal Collection/Filmways
Duel: The Kobal Collection/Universal
Hell's Angels on Wheels: The Kobal Collection/Fanfare
Hill, The: The Kobal Collection/Mgm/7 Arts
Kiss Kiss Bang Bang: The Kobal Collection/Warner Bros/Bramley, John
Le Samourai (The Samurai): The Kobal Collection/Filmel-C.I.C.C./Fida Cinematografica
M: The Kobal Collection/Nero
Manchurian Candidate, The: The Kobal Collection/United Artists
Manhunter: The Kobal Collection/De Laurentiis Group
Memento: The Kobal Collection/Summit Entertainment
Mildred Pierce: The Kobal Collection/Warner Bros
Night of the Hunter, The: The Kobal Collection/United Artists
Nikita (La Femme Nikita): The Kobal Collection/Gaumont/Cecchi Gori/Tiger
Panic in the Streets: The Kobal Collection/20th Century Fox
Parallax View, The: The Kobal Collection/Paramount
Play Misty for Me: The Kobal Collection/Universal
Repulsion: The Kobal Collection/Compton-Tekli/Royal
Shock Corridor: The Kobal Collection/Allied Artists
Southern Comfort: The Kobal Collection/Phoenix/Cinema Group
Strange Love of Martha Ivers, The: The Kobal Collection/Paramount
Strategia Del Ragno (The Spider's Strategem): The Kobal Collection/Red Film/Rai
Straw Dogs: The Kobal Collection/Abc Pictures Corp/Cinerama Releasing
They Might Be Giants: The Kobal Collection/Universal
Twilight's Last Gleaming: The Kobal Collection/Lorimar/Bavaria/Geria
Un Condamné À Mort S'est Échappé Ou Le Vent Souffle Où Il Veut (A Man Escaped): The Kobal Collection/Gaumont
Vertigo: The Kobal Collection/Paramount
Viridiana: The Kobal Collection/Films 59/Alatriste/Uninci
What Ever Happened to Aunt Alice? : The Kobal Collection/Palomar Pictures
Wild at Heart: The Kobal Collection/Propaganda/Polygram/Vaughan, Stephen

CHAPTER 3

Adventures of Buckaroo Banzai Across The Eighth Dimension: The Kobal Collection/Sherwood Prods Inc
Big Trouble in Little China: The Kobal Collection/20th Century Fox
Black Sunday: The Kobal Collection/Paramount
Clash of the Titans: The Kobal Collection/MGM
Coogan's Bluff: The Kobal Collection/Universal
Danger (Diabolik): The Kobal Collection/De Laurentiis
Darkman: The Kobal Collection/Universal
Dip Huet Seung Hung (The Killer): The Kobal Collection/Film Workshop
El Mariachi: The Kobal Collection/Los Hooligans/Columbia
Death Race 2000: The Kobal Collection/New World
Escape From New York: The Kobal Collection/Avco Embassy
First Blood: The Kobal Collection/Carolco
Foxy Brown: The Kobal Collection/Aip
Gauntlet, The: The Kobal Collection/Warner Bros
The Host: The Kobal Collection/Chungeorahm Film
Knightriders: The Kobal Collection/United Artists
Long Kiss Goodnight, The: The Kobal Collection/New Line
Mad Max: The Kobal Collection/Mad Max
Man Who Would Be King, The: The Kobal Collection/Allied Artists
Mou Gaan Dou (Infernal Affairs): The Kobal Collection/Basic Pictures/ Media Asia Films Ltd
Race With The Devil: The Kobal Collection/Saber/Maslansky
Red Dawn: The Kobal Collection/Mgm/UA
Romper Stomper: The Kobal Collection/Romper Stomper/Seon Films
Shaft: The Kobal Collection/MGM
Seventh Voyage of Sinbad, The: The Kobal Collection/Columbia
Subway: The Kobal Collection/Films Du Loup/TSF/Gaumont
Taxi: The Kobal Collection/Arp/TF1 Films
Too Late The Hero: The Kobal Collection/ABC/Cinerama/Palomar
Tremors: The Kobal Collection/Universal
True Romance: The Kobal Collection/Morgan Creek/Davis Films/ (BR) Phillips, Ron
Warriors, The: The Kobal Collection/Paramount
Yojimbo: The Kobal Collection/Toho

CHAPTER 4

2001: A Space Odyssey: The Kobal Collection/MGM
Akira: The Kobal Collection/Akira
Alphaville: The Kobal Collection/Chaumiane/Film Studio/Pierre, Georges
Altered States: The Kobal Collection/Warner Bros
Andromeda Strain, The: The Kobal Collection/Universal
Barbarella: The Kobal Collection/Paramount
Blade Runner: The Kobal Collection/Ladd Company/Warner Bros
Brazil: The Kobal Collection/Universal/Embassy
Chôjin Densetsu Urotsukidôji (Urotsukidôji: Legend Of The Overfiend): Javn; West Cape
Conan The Barbarian: The Kobal Collection/De Laurentiis
Craft, The: The Kobal Collection/Columbia
Day the Earth Stood Still, The: The Kobal Collection/20th Century Fox
Delicatessen: The Kobal Collection/Constellation/UGC/Hachette Premiere
Demon Seed: The Kobal Collection/MGM
Dreamscape: The Kobal Collection/Zupnick-Curtis
Dune: The Kobal Collection/Universal
Edward Scissorhands: The Kobal Collection/20th Century Fox
El Laberinto Del Fauno(Pan's Labyrinth): The Kobal Collection/Tequila Gang/WB
Excalibur: The Kobal Collection/Orion/Warner Bros
Fahrenheit 451: The Kobal Collection/Anglo Enterprise/Vineyard
Fly, The: The Kobal Collection/20th Century Fox
Forbidden Planet: The Kobal Collection/MGM
Gojira (Godzilla): The Kobal Collection/Toho
Heavy Metal: The Kobal Collection/Columbia
Incredible Shrinking Man, The: The Kobal Collection/Universal
Interstella 5555: The Kobal Collection/Daft Life Ltd/Toei Animation Company
Invasion Of The Body Snatchers: The Kobal Collection/Allied Artists
Kôkaku Kidôtai (Ghost In The Shell): The Kobal Collection/Manga Entertainment
Kyûketsuki Hantâ D (Vampire Hunter D): The Kobal Collection/Ashi Productions
Labyrinth: The Kobal Collection/Jim Henson Productions
Liquid Sky: The Kobal Collection/Z Films
Logan's Run: The Kobal Collection/MGM
Man Who Fell to Earth, The: The Kobal Collection/EMI
Man With the X-Ray Eyes, The: The Kobal Collection/AIP
Metropolis: The Kobal Collection/UFA
Mirrormask: The Kobal Collection/Destination/Jim Henson Prods/Goldwyn
Mononoke-Hime (Princess Mononoke): The Kobal Collection/Dentsu Nippon TV
Navigator, The: The Kobal Collection/Arenafilm/Johm Maynard Productions
Nochnoy Dozor (Night Watch): The Kobal Collection/Bazelevs Production/ Channel One Russia
Nightmare Before Christmas, The: The Kobal Collection/Touchstone Burton/Di Novi
Omega Man, The: The Kobal Collection/Warner Bros
Orphée (Orpheus): The Kobal Collection/Andre Paulve/Films Du Palais Royal
Outland: The Kobal Collection/Ladd Co/Warner Bros
Pi: The Kobal Collection/Harvest/Truth & Soul/Libatique, Matthew
Plan 9 from Outer Space: The Kobal Collection/Criswell
Planet of the Apes: The Kobal Collection/20th Century Fox
Renaissance: The Kobal Collection/Pathe/Miramax Films
Rollerball: The Kobal Collection/United Artists
Santa Claus Conquers the Martians: The Kobal Collection/Embassy
Scanner Darkly, A: The Kobal Collection/Warner Independent Pictures
Screamers: The Kobal Collection/Triumph/Allegro Films
Silent Running: The Kobal Collection/Universal
Stalker: The Kobal Collection/Mosfilm
Star Trek II: The Wrath Of Khan: The Kobal Collection/Paramount
Star Wars Episode IV: A New Hope: The Kobal Collection/Lucasfilm/ 20th Century Fox
They Live: The Kobal Collection/Universal
Thing With Two Heads, The : The Kobal Collection/Saber Productions
Thx 1138: The Kobal Collection/American Zoetrope/Warner Bros
Tron: The Kobal Collection/Walt Disney Pictures
Unbreakable: The Kobal Collection/Touchstone/Masi, Frank
Videodrome: The Kobal Collection/Universal
Westworld: The Kobal Collection/MGM
Wizard Of Oz, The: The Kobal Collection/MGM

CHAPTER 5

À Bout de Souffle: The Kobal Collection/SNC
Alone in the Dark: The Kobal Collection/New Line
Anatomy of a Murder: The Kobal Collection/Columbia
Badlands: The Kobal Collection/Warner Bros
Big Combo, The: The Kobal Collection/Allied Artists
Bloody Mama: The Kobal Collection/AIP
Blue Velvet: The Kobal Collection/De Laurentiis
Bound: The Kobal Collection/Dino De Laurentiis/Summit Entertainment
Brick: The Kobal Collection/Focus Features Yedlin, Steve
Chopper: The Kobal Collection/Australian Film Finance Corp
Death Wish: The Kobal Collection/Paramount
Der Amerikanische Freund (The American Friend): The Kobal Collection/ Road Movies/Films Du Losange/Filmverlag Der Autoren
Detour: The Kobal Collection/Producers' Releasing Corporation
Dillinger: The Kobal Collection/American-International
Dog Day Afternoon: The Kobal Collection/Warner Bros
Driver, The: The Kobal Collection/20th Century Fox/EMI
Drugstore Cowboy: The Kobal Collection/Avenue
Faster, Pussycat! Kill!...Kill!: The Kobal Collection/Eve Production Inc
Goodfellas: The Kobal Collection/Warner Bros
Grifters, The: The Kobal Collection/Cineplex Odeon
Grissom Gang, The: The Kobal Collection/ABC
Hard Boiled: The Kobal Collection/Milestone
Harder They Come, The: The Kobal Collection/International Films/New World
High School Confidential: The Kobal Collection/MGM
Honeymoon Killers, The: The Kobal Collection/Roxanne Prods
Il Portiere di Notte (The Night Porter): The Kobal Collection/Italonegglio/ Lotar Film
King of New York: The Kobal Collection/Reteitalia/Scena Film
La Haine: The Kobal Collection/Lazennec/Canal +/La Sept (T) Ferrandis, Guy
Last Seduction, The: ITV/Rex Features
Le Doulos: The Kobal Collection/Rome Paris Films-Cc Champion/Pathe/ Voinquel, Raymond
Léon (The Professional): The Kobal Collection/Gaumont/Films Du Dauphin
Les Diaboliques: The Kobal Collection/Filmsonor/Mirkine
Limey, The: The Kobal Collection/Artisan Pics
Long Good Friday, The: The Kobal Collection/Calendar Prods

BP 8/10 BV 1/16
BB 6/12 BB 02/16

PICTURE CREDITS

Long Goodbye, The: The Kobal Collection/UA/Lions Gate
Mack, The: The Kobal Collection/Cinerama
Mean Streets: The Kobal Collection/Taplin-Perry-Scorsese
Narrow Margin, The: The Kobal Collection/RKO
Ne Le Dis Á Personne (Tell No One): The Kobal Collection/Les Productions Du Trésor/Europa Corp
Oldboy: The Kobal Collection/Egg Films/Show East
Phenix City Story: The Kobal Collection/Allied Artists
Point Blank: The Kobal Collection/MGM
Postman Always Rings Twice, The: The Kobal Collection/Paramount
Prowler, The: The Kobal Collection/United Artists
Reservoir Dogs: The Kobal Collection/Live Entertainment
Rope: The Kobal Collection/Warner Bros
Sonatine: The Kobal Collection/Right Vision/Bandai
Sweet Sweetback's Baadassss Song: The Kobal Collection/Yeah
Taking of Pelham 1-2-3, The: The Kobal Collection/United Artists
Tôkyô Nagaremono (Tokyo Drifter): The Kobal Collection/Nikkatsu
Touch of Evil: The Kobal Collection/Universal
Usual Suspects, The: The Kobal Collection/Polygram/Spelling (BR) Chen, Linda R.

CHAPTER 6

28 Days Later: The Kobal Collection/Dna/Figment/Fox/Mountain, Peter
Alligator: The Kobal Collection/Alligator Inc.
American Werewolf in London, An: The Kobal Collection/Polygram/Universal
Army of Darkness: The Kobal Collection/Dino De Laurentiis
Baby, The: The Kobal Collection/Quintet
Bad Taste: The Kobal Collection/Wingnut Films
Basket Case: The Kobal Collection/Basket Case Productions
Batoru Rowaiaru (Battle Royale): The Kobal Collection/Toei
Black Sheep: The Kobal Collection/Livestock Films/New Zealand Film Commission/George, Ken
Blair Witch Project, The: The Kobal Collection/Artisan Pics
Blob, The: The Kobal Collection/Allied Pictures
Blood Feast: The Kobal Collection/Friedman-Lewis
Brood, The: The Kobal Collection/New World
Bucket of Blood: The Kobal Collection/Alta Vista Productions
Cabinet of Dr. Caligari, The: The Kobal Collection/Decla-Bioscop
Cannibal Ferox: Dania Film
Carnival of Souls: The Kobal Collection/Herts Lion
Child's Play: The Kobal Collection/United Artists
Clockwork Orange, A: The Kobal Collection/Warner Bros
Countess Dracula: ITV/Rex Features
Cronos: The Kobal Collection/Iguana/Ventana/Imcine
Cube: The Kobal Collection/Feature Film Project
Dawn of the Dead: The Kobal Collection/United Film
Dead of Night: The Kobal Collection/Rank
Dellamorte Dellmore (Cemetery Man): The Kobal Collection/Audio Film/Canal+
Dog Soldiers: The Kobal Collection/Kismet Entertainment Group
Driller Killer: The Kobal Collection/Navaron
Evil Dead, The: The Kobal Collection/Renaissance Pictures
Faces of Death: The Kobal Collection/F.O.D. Productions
Fiend Without a Face: The Kobal Collection/Mlc Producers Associates
Freaks: The Kobal Collection/MGM
From Dusk Till Dawn: The Kobal Collection/Los Hooligans/A Band Apart Fury, The: The Kobal Collection/20th Century Fox
Ginger Snaps: The Kobal Collection/Lions Gate/Tmn/Telefilm Canada/Ginaud, Sophie
Gothic: The Kobal Collection/Virgin Vision
Haunting, The: The Kobal Collection/MGM
Hitcher, The: The Kobal Collection/Silver Screen/HBO/Tri Star
Hunger, The: The Kobal Collection/MGM/UA
I Bury The Living: Pictorial Press Ltd./Alamy
I Lunghi Capelli Della Morte (The Long Hair of Death): Eclectic DVD
I Walked With A Zombie: The Kobal Collection/RKO
Incredibly Strange Creatures Who Stopped Living and Became Mixed Up Zombies!!?, The: The Kobal Collection/Morgan-Steckler Productions
Jaws: The Kobal Collection/Universal
Ju-On (The Grudge): The Kobal Collection/Oz Company Ltd.
Keep, The: The Kobal Collection/Paramount
Killer Klowns from Outer Space: The Kobal Collection/Trans World Entertainment
Last House on the Left, The: The Kobal Collection/Sean S. Cunningham Films
Lost Boys, The: The Kobal Collection/Warner Bros (BR) O'neal, Jane
Maniac Cop: The Kobal Collection/Shapiro Glickenhaus
Near Dark: The Kobal Collection/F-M Entertainment/Deg
Night of the Demon (Curse of the Demon): The Kobal Collection/Columbia
Night of the Living Dead: The Kobal Collection/Image Ten
Nosferatu: The Kobal Collection/Prana-Film
Operazione Paura (Kill Baby Kill): The Kobal Collection/Ful Films
Peeping Tom: The Kobal Collection/Anglo Amalgamated
Phantom of the Paradise: The Kobal Collection/Pressman-Williams
Piranha: The Kobal Collection/Piranha Prods/New World
Psychomania: The Kobal Collection/Benmar
Q, The Winged Serpent: The Kobal Collection/Larco
Quatermass Experiment, The (The Creeping Unknown): The Kobal Collection/Hammer
Razorback: The Kobal Collection/UAA Films/Western Film Prod.
Re-Animator: The Kobal Collection/Re-Animated Productions/Empire
Ringu (Ring): The Kobal Collection/Omega/Kadokawa
Rosemary's Baby: The Kobal Collection/Paramount
Saw: The Kobal Collection/Evolution Entertainment/Saw Prods, Inc.
Scanners: The Kobal Collection/Film Plan International
Serpent and the Rainbow, The: The Kobal Collection/Universal
Shining, The: The Kobal Collection/Warner Bros
Shivers: The Kobal Collection/Cinepix/CFDC
Shock Waves: The Kobal Collection/Zopix Company
Society: The Kobal Collection/Society Prods/Wild Street
Tenebrae: The Kobal Collection/Sigma
Texas Chainsaw Massacre, The: The Kobal Collection/Vortex-Henkel-Hooper/Bryanston
Thing, The: The Kobal Collection/Universal
Vamp: The Kobal Collection/New World
What Ever Happened To Baby Jane?: The Kobal Collection/Warner Bros
White Zombie: The Kobal Collection/United Artists
Wicker Man, The: The Kobal Collection/British Lion
Witchfinder General: The Kobal Collection/Tigon
Zombi 2 (Zombie Flesh Eaters): The Kobal Collection/Variety

CHAPTER 7

24 Hour Party People: The Kobal Collection/Channel 4
200 Motels: The Kobal Collection/United Artists
Adventures of Priscilla, Queen of the Desert, The: The Kobal Collection/Polygram/Australian Film Finance/Lockwood, Elise
Arsenic and Old Lace: The Kobal Collection/Warner Bros
Attack of the Fifty Foot Woman: The Kobal Collection/Allied Artists
Bad Boy Bubby: The Kobal Collection/Fandango/Bubby PTY
Bananas: The Kobal Collection/United Artists
Bed Sitting Room, The: The Kobal Collection/United Artists
Best in Show: The Kobal Collection/Castle Rock/Warner Bros/Gregory, Doane
Big Lebowski, The: The Kobal Collection/Polygram/Working Title (T) Morton, Merrick
Bottle Rocket: The Kobal Collection/Columbia/Newcomb, Deana
Bringing Up Baby: The Kobal Collection/RKO
Bubba Ho-Tep: The Kobal Collection/Silver Sphere Corporation
Cannonball Run: The Kobal Collection/20th Century Fox/Golden Harvest
Carnal Knowledge: The Kobal Collection/Avco Embassy
Casino Royale: The Kobal Collection/Columbia/Famous Artists
Christmas Story, A: The Kobal Collection/Mgm/UA
Clerks: The Kobal Collection/View Askew
Crimewave: The Kobal Collection/Embassy/Renaissance
Cul De Sac: The Kobal Collection/Compton-Tekli
Dark Star: The Kobal Collection/Jack H. Harris Enterprises
Dr. Strangelove, or How I Learned to Stop Worrying and Love the Bomb: The Kobal Collection/Hawk Films Prod/Columbia
Down By Law: The Kobal Collection/Island Pictures
Election: The Kobal Collection/Paramount/Akester, Bob
End, The: The Kobal Collection/United Artists
Fast Times at Ridgemont High: The Kobal Collection/Universal
Fearless Vampire Killers, The: The Kobal Collection/Mgm
Ferris Bueller's Day Off: The Kobal Collection/Paramount
Fletch: The Kobal Collection/Universal
Friday: The Kobal Collection/New Line/Goode, Nicola

Fright Night: The Kobal Collection/Columbia
Fritz the Cat: The Kobal Collection/Aurica/Blackink/Steve Krantz
Goin' South: The Kobal Collection/Paramount
Happiness: The Kobal Collection/October Films
Heathers: The Kobal Collection/Cinemarque-New World
In Bruges: The Kobal Collection/Blueprint Pictures
Jamón Jamón: The Kobal Collection/Lolafilm
Juno: The Kobal Collection/Fox Searchlight/Gregory, Doane
Kind Hearts and Coronets: The Kobal Collection/Ealing
Ladykillers, The: The Kobal Collection/Ealing/Rank (BR) Evans, Arthur
Little Shop of Horrors: Everett Collection/Rex Features
Loved One, The: The Kobal Collection/MGM
Meet the Feebles: The Kobal Collection/Wingnut Films
Monster Squad, The: The Kobal Collection/Hyams/Taft/Barish
Mystery Men: The Kobal Collection/Universal/Gordon, Melinda Sue
Night of the Comet: The Kobal Collection/Film Development Fund
Nothing Lasts Forever: MGM
Office Space: The Kobal Collection/20th Century Fox/Redin, Van
Pink Flamingos: The Kobal Collection/Dreamland Productions
Polyester: The Kobal Collection/New Line
Producers, The: The Kobal Collection/Embassy Pictures
Quick Change: The Kobal Collection/Warner Bros
Shakes the Clown: IRS/Everett/Rex Features
Rocky Horror Picture Show, The: The Kobal Collection/ 20th Century Fox
Shaun of the Dead: The Kobal Collection/Big Talk/WT 2
Singin' in the Rain: The Kobal Collection/MGM
Slap Shot: The Kobal Collection/Universal
Something Wild: The Kobal Collection/Orion
Spanking the Monkey: The Kobal Collection/Buckeye/Swelter Films
Stardust Memories: The Kobal Collection/United Artists
Stripes: The Kobal Collection/Columbia
Sullivan's Travels: The Kobal Collection/Paramount
This Is Spinal Tap: The Kobal Collection/Spinal Tap Production
Tillasmmans (Together): The Kobal Collection/Memfis/SVT/ Keyfilms/Zentropa
Toxic Avenger, The: The Kobal Collection/Troma
Twelve Chairs, The: The Kobal Collection/Columbia
Up!: RM Films International, Inc.
Up In Smoke: The Kobal Collection/Paramount
Welcome To The Dollhouse: The Kobal Collection/ Suburban Pictures
Withnail and I: The Kobal Collection/Handmade Films
Women on the Verge of a Nervous Breakdown: The Kobal Collection/ El Desea-Lauren
Young Frankenstein: The Kobal Collection/20th Century Fox

CHAPTER 8

Cat Ballou: The Kobal Collection/Columbia
Dead Man: The Kobal Collection/12-Gauge Productions/Pandora
El Chuncho, Quien Sabe? (A Bullet for the General): The Kobal Collection/ MCM
Il Buono, Il Brutto and Il Cattivo (The Good, The Bad and The Ugly): The Kobal Collection/P.E.A
Il Grande Silenzio (The Great Silence): The Kobal Collection/ Les Films Corona
Grim Prairie Tales: Academy Entertainment/ East-West Film Partners
High Plains Drifter: The Kobal Collection/Universal
Hired Hand, The: The Kobal Collection/Universal
Johnny Guitar: The Kobal Collection/Republic
Long Riders, The: The Kobal Collection/United Artists
McCabe and Mrs Miller: The Kobal Collection/Warner Bros
Missouri Breaks, The: The Kobal Collection/United Artists
One-Eyed Jacks: The Kobal Collection/Paramount
Outlaw Josey Wales, The: The Kobal Collection/Warner Bros
Pat Garrett and Billy the Kid: The Kobal Collection/MGM
Requiescant (Kill and Pray): Wild East Productions, Inc.
Run of the Arrow: The Kobal Collection/Universal/RKO
Searchers, The: The Kobal Collection/Warner Bros
Soldier Blue: The Kobal Collection/Avco Embassy
Ulzana's Raid: The Kobal Collection/Universal
Wild Bunch, The: The Kobal Collection/Warner 7 Arts

CHAPTER 9

Aguirre: Der Zorn Gottes (Aguirre: The Wrath of God): The Kobal Collection/ Werner Herzog Filmproduktion
Ai No Corrida (In the Realm of the Senses): The Kobal Collection/ Argos/Oshima
Barry Lyndon: The Kobal Collection/Warner Bros
Capturing the Friedmans: The Kobal Collection/HBO Documentary/ Notorious Pictures
C'est Arrivé Près de Chez Vous (Man Bites Dog): Roxie R/Everett/ Rex Features
Christiane F: The Kobal Collection/Maran/Popular/Hans H Kaden/TCF
Cook, the Thief, His Wife and Her Lover, The: The Kobal Collection/ Allarts/Erato
Crumb: The Kobal Collection/Superior Pictures
Dazed and Confused: The Kobal Collection/Universal/Gramercy
Decline of Western Civilization, The: The Kobal Collection/ Spheeris Films Inc.
Diva: The Kobal Collection/Films Galaxie/Greenwich
Dogtown and the Z Boys: © glen E. friedman, from the book DogTown—The Legend of the Z-Boys (Burning Flags Press)
Donnie Darko: The Kobal Collection/Flower Films/Gaylord/Adam Fields Prod/Robinette, Dale
Draughtsman's Contract, The: The Kobal Collection/Bfi/United Artists
Electra Glide In Blue: The Kobal Collection/United Artists
Elephant: The Kobal Collection/HBO/Fine Line Features/Green, Scott
Eraserhead: The Kobal Collection/AFI/Libra
Fantasia: W. Disney/Everett/Rex Features
Festen (The Celebration): The Kobal Collection/Nimbus Film
Flesh: The Kobal Collection/Warhol
Funny Ha Ha: The Kobal Collection/Goodbye Cruel Releasing
Grey Gardens: The Kobal Collection/Portrait Films
Head: The Kobal Collection/Columbia
Idioterne (The Idiots): The Kobal Collection/Zentropa
Inserts: The Kobal Collection/Film & General
Irréversible: The Kobal Collection/Studio Canal+
La Jetée (The Pier): The Kobal Collection/Argos
Last Movie, The: The Kobal Collection/Universal
Last Waltz, The: The Kobal Collection/United Artists
Loveless, The: The Kobal Collection/Pioneer Films
Man on Wire: The Kobal Collection/Discovery Films/BBC
Metallica: Some Kind of Monster: The Kobal Collection/Radical Media/ Third Eye Motion Picture Co /Disanto, Annamaria
Mishima: A Life In Four Chapters: The Kobal Collection/Warner Bros
Performance: The Kobal Collection/Warner/Goodtimes
Primer: The Kobal Collection/Thinkfilm
Prospero's Books: The Kobal Collection/Allarts/Camera 1/Cinea
Repo Man: The Kobal Collection/Edge City/Universal
Requiem for a Dream: The Kobal Collection/Artisan Pictures/Baer, John
Rumble Fish: The Kobal Collection/Universal
Salò: O Le 120 Giornate Di Sodoma (Salo, or The 120 Days In Sodom): The Kobal Collection/Artistes Associes/Pea
Sex, Lies, and Videotape: ITV/Rex Features
Teaserama: Courtesy Everett Collection/Rex Features
Touching the Void: The Kobal Collection/Film Four/Pathe (BL) Sutton-Hibbert, Jeremy
Trip, The: The Kobal Collection/Allied International Pictures
Two Lane Blacktop: The Kobal Collection/Universal/GTO
Vérités et Mensonges (F for Fake): The Kobal Collection/ Films De L'astrophore
Week End: The Kobal Collection/Copernic/Comacico/Lira/Ascot
What's Up, Tiger Lily?: The Kobal Collection/Toho/Benedict
When We Were Kings: The Kobal Collection/Gramercy Pictures/ Bingham, Howard L.

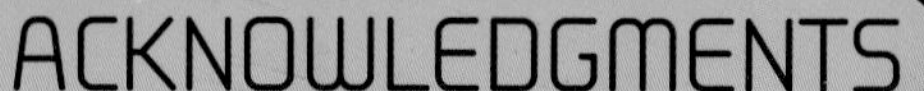

ACKNOWLEDGMENTS

First and foremost, huge thanks are due to Managing Editor Nick Jones for taking a chance on a first-time author and for being extremely patient with me. Ginny Zeal's design is excellent, clean and thoughtful, and Art Director Julie Weir's image choices show the whimsy and accuracy of a true film lover. Thanks are also due to Kobal, for supplying the images, and to Katie Greenwood for getting it done. Editor Ellie Wilson helped enormously with the project behind the scenes, and I'm grateful.

Special thanks are due to contributors Steve White and JP Rutter, whose text is insightful and often lyric. Also, thank you Roly Allen for supplying the two Soderbergh reviews.

My personal gratitude is owed to Deb Tanner, as always, for general support and all-around awesomeness. In that vein, I'd be remiss if I didn't mention Ness Evans, Miranda Harrison, Howard Watson, Charlotte Coneybeer, Dave Garwood, Therese Lyras, and Jonathan Eiss.

Picture credit: Vérités et Mensonges (F for Fake),
The Kobal Collection/Films De L'astrophore